Praise for *Julius Caesar*

W9-ASY-636

"Elegant, learned, and compulsively readable, *Julius Caesar* moves from broad sweep to brilliant detail. Freeman triumphantly tells the story of one of history's greatest and most terrible figures. He is as knowledgeable about Cleopatra's Alexandria as he is about Celtic tribes, and he writes about the Roman Senate with the assurance of an insider."

—Barry Strauss, author of *The Trojan War* and Professor of History and Classics, Cornell University

"Julius Caesar packed more into his life than most of history's great men—and Philip Freeman unpacks it all with skill and clarity. . . . The scholar will find much to admire in this book, but, better still, the newcomer to ancient Rome will turn its pages with excitement, enlightenment—and sheer narrative suspense."

—Anthony Everitt, author of *Augustus* and *Cicero*

"[Freeman's] cultural and historical knowledge bring the emperor to life and humanize him in a way no writer before him has succeeded in doing."

—*Publishers Weekly*

"Can Alexander Hamilton possibly have been right that Julius Caesar was 'the greatest man that ever lived'? Reading Philip Freeman's pacy and panoptic narrative of his life from unpromising early beginnings to the fateful Ides is one very rewarding approach to answering that perennially fascinating question."

—Paul Cartledge, Professor of Greek History, University of Cambridge

"Clear, concise, and packed with fascinating details, *Julius Caesar* skillfully captures the essence of a complex, ambitious leader. . . . Freeman understands what the newcomer to ancient Rome needs to know—and what the reader looking for a refresher course longs to rediscover."

—Jeff Sypeck, author of *Becoming Charlemagne*

"Philip Freeman has written a compact but thorough account of the life and achievements of this historical giant."

—*Booklist*

"Freeman is one of those rare writers whose enthusiasm for a subject is so irresistible, so contagious, that in their hands any subject becomes compelling. . . . Authoritative, accessible, *Julius Caesar* is a book that will be of interest not only to those studying Latin and Roman history, but to anyone fascinated by the mesmerizing power of ambition."

—Arthur T. Vanderbilt II, *The Star-Ledger* (Newark)

ALSO BY PHILIP FREEMAN

*The Philosopher and the Druids:
A Journey Among the Ancient Celts*

St. Patrick of Ireland: A Biography

*War, Women, and Druids: Eyewitness Reports
and Early Accounts of the Ancient Celts*

*The Galatian Language: A Comprehensive Survey of the Language
of the Ancient Celts in Greco-Roman Asia Minor*

Ireland and the Classical World

JULIUS CAESAR

PHILIP FREEMAN

SIMON & SCHUSTER PAPERBACKS
New York   London   Toronto   Sydney

SIMON & SCHUSTER PAPERBACKS
1230 Avenue of the Americas
New York, NY 10020

First Simon & Schuster trade paperback edition May 2009

SIMON & SCHUSTER PAPERBACKS and colophon are
registered trademarks of Simon & Schuster, Inc.
For information about special discounts for bulk purchases,
please contact Simon & Schuster Special Sales at
1-866-506-1949 or business@simonandschuster.com

Designed by Dana Sloan

Manufactured in the United States of America

9   10   8

The Library of Congress has cataloged the hardcover edition as follows:
Freeman, Philip, 1961–
Julius Caesar / Philip Freeman.
p. cm.
Includes bibliographical references and index.
1. Caesar, Julius.   2. Generals—Rome—Biography.   3. Heads of state—Rome—
Biography.   4. Rome—History—Republic, 265–30 B.C.   I. Title.
DG261.F784 2008
937.05092—dc22
[B]
2007034482

ISBN-13: 978-0-7432-8953-5
ISBN-10:   0-7432-8953-6
ISBN-13: 978-0-7432-8954-2 (pbk)
ISBN-10:   0-7432-8954-4 (pbk)

CONTENTS

JULIUS CAESAR

PREFACE

One day not long ago I was standing in front of my Latin class, lecturing on the correct formation of imperfect verbs. It was a beautiful fall day on campus, the kind that practically begs college students to toss a Frisbee around the grassy quad in front of the library. I was nearing the end of the hour and rapidly losing my audience as their eyes drifted to the idyllic scene outside the classroom windows. So I decided to postpone grammar and take a detour into Roman history.

"Okay," I asked, "who's heard of Julius Caesar?" Everyone in the class raised their hands. "All right then," I continued, "what can you tell me about him?"

A long silence followed, then one young woman offered, "He was stabbed to death wasn't he? I remember reading about it in a Shakespeare play back in high school."

"Excellent," I said, "but does anyone know when his murder occurred?"

They carefully studied their desk tops until one student looked up and said, "Wait, it was the Ides of March!"

"Good, good," I responded, always eager to encourage class participation. "He was killed by a group of Roman senators in Pompey's theater on the Ides of March, which is of course March 15. Now can anyone tell me something else about his life?"

Silence again. Then a student in back asked, "Wasn't he an epileptic? And he was born by caesarean section, right?"

"Partly right," I said. "He did have epilepsy, but the caesarean story is a myth."

I then devoted the last five minutes of class to filling them in on a few little-known facts about Julius Caesar. I told them how he was born into a poor but noble family; how he was ordered by the dictator Sulla to divorce the wife he loved, but refused, even though it meant a death sentence; how he was kidnapped by pirates as a young man; how he rose to power and became a great lawyer, politician, general, engineer, historian, and high priest of Rome; and finally, how he invented the calendar we still use today.

Class time was over and the students began heading out the door into the sunshine. I erased the board and collected my papers, then heard one of my students in the hallway say to a friend, "Man, that was amazing—I didn't know Caesar did all that stuff." It was one of those moments professors live for, when we realize a student is actually excited about learning something new. As I shuffled back to my office to grade a stack of waiting papers, I wondered how many people really know the true story of Caesar.

Julius Caesar was one of the greatest heroes of human history—or one of its most pernicious villains, depending on whom you believe. The medieval poet Dante assigned him a blessed afterlife among the most virtuous pagans while sentencing his two leading murderers, Brutus and Cassius, to the lowest level of hell. Mark Twain wrote that Caesar waged wars against barbarians not because they had done him any harm, "but because he wanted their land, and desired to confer the blessings of civilization upon their widows and orphans." Shakespeare tried to have it both ways, praising both Caesar and the conspirators who slew him. Modern scholars have been equally divided concerning Caesar's legacy. Some have seen him as a paradigm of the just ruler, but in the wake of twentieth-century dictators and devastating wars, other historians have turned a cold eye to a man who caused the death of so many and established the rule of emperors over elected magistrates. This biography, however, comes neither to praise Caesar overmuch nor to bury him among the tyrants of history. My goal is simply to tell the story of Caesar's life and times for anyone who wants to learn more about this unique man and the world in which he lived.

I am deeply indebted to those who helped me make this book a reality. To the many excellent professors at the University of Texas and Harvard, who patiently taught me about the fascinating world of ancient Rome, my eternal thanks. My home institution of Luther College tucked away among the beautiful hills of northeast Iowa was encouraging and supportive as always. Joëlle Delbourgo, Bob Bender, and Johanna Li patiently guided me through the publishing process, while Janey Lee of Hanee Designs created a beautiful Web site and allowed me to use her photographs of the Roman Forum. Many thanks as well to the libraries of Harvard University and Bowdoin College. As always, I am grateful to my long suffering wife, Alison, who put up with endless dinner-table talk on Roman politics, Vestal Virgins, and Gaulish tribal structure. But most of all I would like to thank my students who for the last fifteen years have helped me see the classical world through ever new eyes. Your enthusiasm is what makes teaching the best job in the world.

TIMELINE

B.C.

753   Traditional date for the founding of Rome

c. 500   Beginning of the Roman Republic

390   Gauls sack Rome

264–241   First Punic War

218–202   Second Punic War; Hannibal invades Italy

149–146   Third Punic War; Carthage destroyed

133   Tiberius Gracchus elected tribune

121   Gaius Gracchus killed

107   Marius first elected consul

105   Cimbri and Teutones defeat Roman armies

100   Julius Caesar born on July 13

91   Beginning of Italian War

88   Sulla marches on Rome

87   Caesar chosen as *flamen dialis*

84   Caesar marries Cornelia

81–79   Sulla dictator in Rome

80   Caesar serves in Asia, awarded the *corona civica*

75   Caesar captured by pirates

73–71   Revolt of Spartacus

69   Caesar's funeral speeches for Julia (wife of Marius) and Cornelia

4

67 Caesar marries Pompeia

63 Cicero elected consul. Conspiracy of Catiline. Caesar
    elected *pontifex maximus*

62 Scandal of Clodius. Caesar divorces Pompeia

61 Caesar governor of Further Spain

60 Beginning of the First Triumvirate

59 Caesar elected consul. Pompey marries Julia. Caesar mar-
    ries Calpurnia

58 Beginning of the Gallic War

57 Caesar fights the Belgae

56 Caesar's campaign against the Veneti

55 Caesar crosses the Rhine. First expedition to Britain

54 Second expedition to Britain. Death of Julia. Revolt of
    Ambiorix

53 Crassus killed in Parthia

52 Clodius murdered in Rome. Revolt of Vercingetorix in Gaul

51 End of Gallic War

50 Curio prevents recall of Caesar

49 Caesar crosses the Rubicon

48 Caesar defeats Pompey at Pharsalia, crosses to Egypt

47 Caesar defeats Pharnaces at Zela, lands in Africa

46 Suicide of Cato. Caesar celebrates triumph at Rome, ap-
    pointed dictator for ten years

45 Caesar defeats last of Pompeian forces in Spain, ap-
    pointed dictator for life

44 Murder of Caesar on the Ides of March

42 Brutus and Cassius defeated at Philippi

31 Octavius defeats Antony and Cleopatra at Actium

Prologue

ON THE BANKS OF THE RUBICON

Acold winter rain fell on the mountains near the sea. Only a
trickle at first, the water gathered into a tiny stream that
quickly fell down a steep and rocky valley past empty shepherd huts,
bursting at last onto the narrow coastal plain. For thousands of years,
travelers moving from the broad and fertile countryside beneath the
snow-covered Alps of northern Italy to the warm southern lands
along the Adriatic coast had crossed this small river. In summer,
when the rains were scarce, the river shrank to little more than a lazy
creek. But in winter, its waters grew swift and deep.

On this blustery January day in the year 49 B.C., Gaius Julius Caesar sat on the banks of the Rubicon River and gazed south toward
Rome. Caesar had spent the last eight years in a relentless and often
brutal campaign to bring Gaul—roughly modern France—into the
Roman world. This huge new province served not only to subdue
the troublesome Celts and keep the fierce Germans on their own side
of the Rhine, but the war booty Caesar gained made him a very
wealthy man. Enormous financial resources, popular military victories, impeccable ancestry, and one of the finest minds the ancient
world had yet produced were enough to terrify Caesar's political en-

emies. These self-proclaimed defenders of the Roman Republic had for decades used their considerable power to fight that which Rome needed most and which they most feared—reform. The conservative party, or *optimates,* led by the indomitable Cato were determined to rule the vast Roman lands stretching from Spain to Syria for the benefit of a few families according to ancient tradition, as if Rome were still a small village on the Tiber surrounded by seven hills. The power, vision, and ruthless ambition of Caesar were the biggest threats they had ever faced—and so they were determined to destroy him at any cost.

To be fair, Caesar had tried his best to prevent civil war. When his enemies proposed that he be stripped of his command in Gaul so that he could be prosecuted in Rome, Caesar had calmly outmaneuvered them. When the weak leadership of his ally, the aging general Pompey, and the quarrelsome senators allowed the city of Rome to slip into chaos and mobs to burn down the buildings of the Forum, Caesar held his hand while the Senate made Pompey a virtual dictator. When Cato and his allies demanded Caesar turn over two of his veteran legions to fight the Parthians, he complied, even though the soldiers were kept in Italy to serve Pompey. Caesar had even offered to dismiss his army at the same time as Pompey to avoid trouble, but the Senate instead rejected all his overtures of peace, assaulted his representatives, and passed an emergency decree against him, demanding that he surrender himself into the hands of his scheming enemies.

And thus as the new year began, Caesar had approached the Rubicon River, the boundary dividing his allotted province of Italian Gaul from Italy proper. He had left behind most of his vast army, bringing with him only one legion. But for a general with any troops under arms to cross the river would be treason and a clear declaration of war against Rome.

Caesar spent the day in a nearby town watching gladiators train and dining with friends. As the sun set, Caesar finished dinner and asked his guests to await his return. With just a few trusted companions, Caesar climbed into a rented cart and drove away from the Rubicon at first, only to switch direction soon and head toward the river. At the banks of the rushing stream he stopped and withdrew by himself a little distance to reflect on the magnitude of what he proposed to do. He had been troubled recently by dreams of what lay ahead for his beloved Rome if he proceeded. He seemed to his nearby friends to be deeply distressed, wavering back and forth, fiercely debating with himself about his next step. Caesar returned to his comrades still unsure and asked for their thoughts. They all agreed there would be great suffering ahead for Rome if he crossed the Rubicon, but the consequences of inaction would be his own downfall.

At last, Caesar arose with an expression of calm assurance on his face. He walked to the edge of the water and lifting his voice for all to hear, he shouted, "Let the dice fly high," and stepped swiftly into the icy stream.

IRELAND

BRITAIN

GERMANY

Rhine R.

Danube R.

Atlantic
Ocean

GAUL

Alps

CISALPINE
GAUL

Po R.

Brigantium •

Rhone R.

LIGURIA

Rubicon R.

Adriat

ETRURIA

Corfinium •

LUSITANIA

*Pyrenees
mountains*

• Ilerda

Massalia •

Rome • • ITALY

SPAIN

Balearic Islands

SARDINIA

Naples •

• Munda

• Gades

Mediterranean   Sea

Utica •

SICILY

Pillars of Hercules

NUMIDIA

Carthage •

MAURETANIA

• Thapsus

AFRICA

0 Miles   200   400

0 Kilometers   400

THE ROMAN WORLD
AT THE
TIME OF JULIUS CAESAR

SCYTHIA

CRIMEA

DACIA

Black Sea

ILLYRICUM

Danube R.

THRACE

PONTUS

• Zela

ARMENIA

MACEDONIA

BITHYNIA

Sea

• Dyrrachium

GALATIA

Brundisium •

GREECE

• Troy

Pergamum •

ASIA MINOR

Pharsalus •

Thermopylae •

Aegean Sea

Ephesus •

Tarsus

Delphi •

Miletus •

CILICIA

• Athens

Sparta •

SYRIA

CRETE

RHODES

CYPRUS

PARTHIAN
EMPIRE

Mediterranean Sea

JUDEA

Jerusalem •

• Petra

Alexandria •

ARABIA

EGYPT

Nile R.

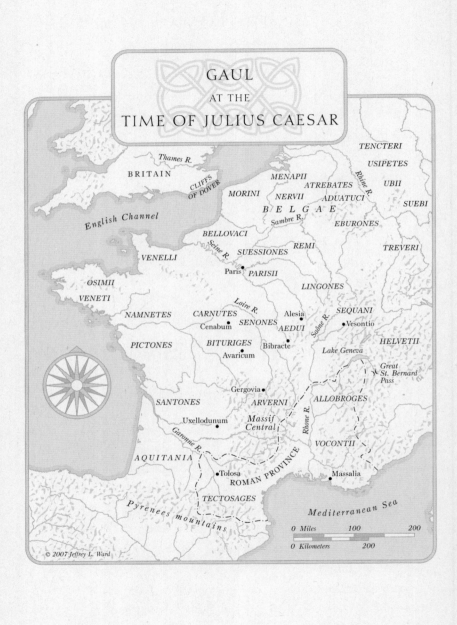

GAUL
AT THE
TIME OF JULIUS CAESAR

Thames R.

BRITAIN

CLIFFS OF DOVER

English Channel

MENAPII

MORINI

ATREBATES

NERVII

ADUATUCI

B E L G A E

Sambre R.

EBURONES

Rhine R.

TENCTERI

USIPETES

UBII

SUEBI

BELLOVACI

Seine R.

SUESSIONES

REMI

TREVERI

VENELLI

Paris • PARISII

OSIMII

VENETI

LINGONES

NAMNETES

CARNUTES

Loire R.

Cenabum • SENONES

Alesia •

AEDUI

Saône R.

SEQUANI

Vesontio •

HELVETII

PICTONES

BITURIGES

Avaricum •

Bibracte •

Lake Geneva

Great St. Bernard Pass

Gergovia •

ARVERNI

ALLOBROGES

SANTONES

Uxellodunum •

Massif Central

Rhône R.

Garonne R.

VOCONTII

AQUITANIA

• Tolosa

ROMAN PROVINCE

Massalia •

Pyrenees mountains

TECTOSAGES

Mediterranean Sea

0 Miles   100   200

0 Kilometers   200

© 2007 Jeffrey L. Ward

I

THE EARLY YEARS

> The pirates demanded twenty talents for Caesar's ransom, but he only laughed at them for not knowing his true worth. He raised the price himself to fifty.
>
> — PLUTARCH

In the early second century A.D., the Roman biographer Suetonius wrote his justly famous *Lives of the Twelve Caesars*—one of our best sources on Roman rulers from Julius Caesar and Augustus to Caligula, Claudius, and Domitian. Unfortunately, the beginning of an ancient book or a papyrus scroll was always the portion most likely to be lost to the ravages of time. Thus the first few chapters of Suetonius's *Life of Julius Caesar* disappeared forever sometime in the early Middle Ages, so our only good source on the childhood of Caesar begins: *annum agens sextum decimum* ("In his sixteenth year . . ."). As frustrating as this is for our attempt to reconstruct Caesar's life, it's not unusual to have so little reliable information about the early years of any famous figure from the past, be it Socrates, Joan of Arc, or even Abraham Lincoln. Since none of them knew they were going to be famous someday, few people paid any attention to them until they were adults.

Fortunately, we do know a great deal about the time and place in which Caesar grew up. Because the first century B.C. was such a formative period in Roman history and because so many surviving ancient authors, such as Cicero and Suetonius, wrote about the turmoil of those years, we can understand events during Caesar's youth better than many closer to our own.

The Julian family claimed descent from Julus, also known as Ascanius, the son of the Trojan warrior Aeneas, and grandson of the goddess Venus, yet they had long been on the margins of Roman power. Like financially embarrassed nobility of the Victorian era who had long ago sold the last of the family silverware, all the Julians had left by the late second century B.C. was their impeccable family name. None of Caesar's ancestors had held high office for many years. It was only with his aunt Julia's marriage to the lowborn but wealthy and ambitious general Gaius Marius that the family began to rise again. Caesar's father was then able to marry Aurelia, daughter of the former consul Cotta from a well-to-do family. Aurelia was cultured, highly intelligent, and absolutely devoted to the welfare and career of her son.

CAESAR'S FAMILY TREE

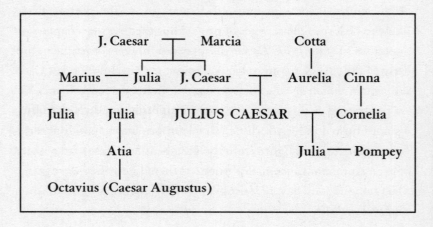

Caesar would one day be hailed as a god, but his birth in the year 100 B.C. was quite ordinary. The story that he was delivered by caesarean section is a myth that grew out of befuddled etymology. Roman folklore held that a child cut out of his mother's womb was bound for greatness. Since such an operation meant almost certain death for a pregnant woman at this time, it may have been that a mother sacrificing her own life for her child was thought to convey special powers upon him. The best argument against Caesar being born by caesarean section is that his mother, Aurelia, in fact lived for almost fifty years after his birth. There were genuine cases of caesarean delivery in the Roman era, but this usually happened when a woman had either just died in childbirth or was not expected to survive. Scipio Africanus, conqueror of Hannibal, was reportedly born by caesarean as were other famous Romans, including an ancestor of Julius Caesar. According to some ancient sources, this ancestor gave the Caesar branch of the Julian clan their name because he was *caesus* (cut) from his mother's uterus. While this is possible, the long flowing hair (*caesaries*) of one of Caesar's progenitors is another possible origin of the family name. Following Roman custom, Caesar was given the same name as his father.

We know little about Caesar's father, except that like many Roman men active in politics and the military, he was seldom at home. The demands of the Forum and army service, as well as Roman custom, meant that Caesar grew up with his father as only an occasional participant in his life. The elder Caesar was a senior magistrate in the late nineties B.C. and afterward served in the province of Asia. In 85 B.C., just as Caesar reached the age of manhood, when his father would have taken a greater role in his upbringing, the elder Caesar died at Pisa, probably during military service. Caesar had at least two sisters, both named Julia. One of these Julias had a daughter named Atia, who became the mother of Octavius, the future emperor Augustus.

Whether on a farm or in the city, the heart of Roman society was the family. This consisted of the father, mother, sons, unmarried daughters, and anyone else in the home, including slaves. The eldest male as *paterfamilias* had absolute control over his household. He could have his wife executed or sell his children into slavery if he so desired, but such extreme actions were restrained by community pressure and quite rare. Roman law considered women incompetent to manage their own affairs and so they passed seamlessly from the control of fathers to husbands as their legal guardians. But again, theory did not always match practice. At least within the walls of the home, a Roman matron ruled her household, and few husbands were foolish enough to interfere with a wife's domestic control. Divorce was easy to obtain, with a wife retaining whatever property she brought to the marriage. Infant mortality from disease was high and the abandonment of unwanted children, especially baby girls, on deserted hillsides was all too common.

Several related families formed a *gens* or clan. Every Roman bore the title of his clan as part of his name. Thus Gaius Julius Caesar had *Gaius* as his personal name, *Julius* as his clan name (being a member of the Julian *gens*), with *Caesar* as a cognomen or extra name. This final part was often a nickname in origin and frequently humorous. The cognomen also passed on from father to son, so that they had no particular relation to the individual. Among other cognomen were *Brutus* ("stupid"), *Naso* ("big nose"), and *Cicero* ("chickpea").

From earliest times, Rome was divided into haves and have-nots. The ancient families of prestige, such as the Fabian, Cornelian, and Julian clans, were know as patricians, while the mass of the common people were called plebeians or plebs. The plebeians were freeborn and often owned a small plot of land or their own business, but they could never hope to rise to the lofty heights of the patricians. Most patricians and plebeians saw this sharp division of society as the normal order of the world. A plebeian could even benefit from the system if he attached himself to a patrician as his client. The client-patron system was one of the fundamental relationships in Roman society. If a plebeian became a client of a patrician, he was bound to render political support and sometimes military service to his patron. The patron, in turn, added to his own reputation with each new client and rewarded his followers with occasional money and backing in any community disputes or legal problems. It was a mutually beneficial relationship that had no legal standing, but was deeply respected and rarely breeched. A Roman might abandon his wife or sell his vote to the highest bidder, but the client-patron relationship was sacred.

In spite of the close relationship between clients and patrons, Rome during the early days of the Republic was a hotbed of tension between patricians and plebeians. The frustration over the patrician stranglehold on power and the increasing awareness by plebeians of growing political reforms in the Greek world led the plebeians to organize themselves to fight for reform. A spate of hard economic times in the fifth century B.C. also brought the plebeians to the boiling point. Most patricians could weather the storms of crop shortages and economic woes, but many plebeians were deeply in debt and some were even forced into slavery to pay back their creditors. In a foreshadowing of tensions in following centuries, the average Roman was also called on more and more to serve longer periods in the army far from home. When Rome controlled just a small area around the city, military service was always close by and didn't significantly interfere with work on the farm. But as Rome expanded in central Italy, plebeian soldiers were forced to spend extended periods on campaign farther from home. Without men to work the fields, some smaller farms collapsed.

The plebeians devised a clever method to exact change from the patrician rulers. In 494 B.C. they marched out of town en masse and settled themselves on a nearby hill. Without the plebeians to provide labor and service, the patricians were at a loss to run the city. The

Senate sent a respected negotiator named Menenius Agrippa to the plebeian camp, who proceeded to tell them the Roman parable of the Belly and the Limbs. Once upon a time, he declared, the limbs of the body grew tired of laboring to feed the belly. They decided to starve the belly until it realized how much it needed the rest of the body. But of course as the belly grew empty the whole body weakened. It was then the limbs realized that the belly too had an important job to perform.

The plebeians were moved by the obvious parallels to their own situation and promised to return to Rome, but not before they gained official recognition of their own rights and representatives. Four more times during the next century, the plebeians withdrew from Rome when they felt the patricians were treating them badly. Each time they wrested more power from the patricians. But a strange thing happened as time went by. A few plebeians were growing wealthy as they prospered in business and trade, even as some old patrician families faded and were left with little but their ancient names to boast of. The nouveau riche among the plebeians then began to form alliances with those patrician families which still maintained their wealth and political power. From this fusion sprang a new aristocracy for Rome—a patrician-plebeian nobility that in time would become as exclusive and power-hungry as the ancient patrician families. The mass of the plebeian population was left out of true political power and continued to grumble, while impoverished old patrician families, like the Julians, dreamed of a better day.

Caesar was born and raised in the Subura neighborhood of Rome, just a short walk from the Forum. The area was an odd choice for Aurelia and her husband of the noble Julian clan. The Subura district was a lower-class neighborhood in a small valley known for tradesmen, prostitutes, and foreign residents, including many Jews. It's likely, in spite of new family connections, that Caesar's parents lacked the money needed for a home on the fashionable Palatine Hill. Since Caesar lived in his family house in the Subura for over thirty years, he must have gained a familiarity with the rough-and-tumble life of the Roman streets that few of his upper-class peers could have known. His later populist politics may in fact be due to his childhood friends and surroundings as much as political opportunism. Whatever the reasons for his family's long residence in the grimy Subura, it created in Caesar a unique individual—a patrician descendant of kings who knew intimately the lives and sorrows of common Romans.

Caesar probably grew up in a small home squeezed between the butcher shops and taverns of the Subura. Excavations from Roman towns like Pompeii provide a vivid picture of similar urban residences. Like many homes in Rome still today, an ancient Roman house faced inward, presenting only a wooden door to the street. The lower floor of a home usually had small shops on the street level, unconnected to the rest of the house, that were rented to all manner of businesses. Visitors to Caesar's childhood home would have been greeted by a slave at the front door and guided through the adjoining *vestibulum* or vestibule, where cloaks and boots would be stored. A slave would also wash the feet of any guest since Roman streets were dusty and full of animal droppings. In the center of the home an atrium opened to the sky, often with a small fish pond in the center. Around the atrium were rooms for cooking, sleeping, and storage. Bodily functions were handled by chamber pots that would be emptied by slaves into a nearby public latrine. Upper rooms of urban houses would often be leased as apartments to local residents. Everything from sausage on fresh-baked bread to exotic perfumes from Arabia would have been available just a few steps from Caesar's door. The young Caesar must have grown up surrounded by a multitude of glorious smells and sounds. Besides Latin, he would have heard Greek, Aramaic, Gaulish, Coptic, and a dozen other languages spoken by the slaves, shopkeepers, and residents of the Subura.

Religion would be an important part of Caesar's life, but worship among the ancient Romans was vastly different from most traditions of the modern western world. Like so much else in Roman life, religion was centered on the household. The Romans acknowledged the *numina* (spirits) that existed in the home and fields, but these divine forces were never fully understood. The *lares* and *penates* were spirits of the home who watched over the members of the household. They were mostly benevolent, but could cause harm if angered or ignored. Every Roman home held a small cupboard with their sacred images, and they were honored with a small portion of the family meal. Vesta was the spirit of the hearth, Janus guarded the door, Jupiter controlled rain for the fields, and Mars brought forth the plants of the earth. Unlike most modern religions, what a person *believed* about the divine forces of the Roman world was irrelevant. There were no creeds or professions of faith—it was a person's actions toward the gods that mattered. The favor of the gods could be gained by a libation of wine or the sacrifice of an animal. In return, the gods would grant a respectful Roman his due rewards. It was very businesslike and not at all based on emotion. *Do ut des,* as the Romans themselves said—"I give so that you (the god) might give back." The Romans, in fact, were suspicious of emotional religious worship, especially in those religions imported from the eastern Mediterranean.

Roman state religion grew out of household worship. The temples that were built, while borrowing their architectural form from the Etruscans and Greeks, functioned essentially as large household shrines. The city borrowed household spirits for itself and turned them into state divinities. Mars left behind his agricultural roots and became a god of war; Janus watched over the gates of the city; Jupiter became high god of the thundering sky; and a temple of Vesta was built in the Forum to house the eternal hearth fire of the city.

The different priestly offices had their origin deep in Roman history. Augurs were charged with learning the will of the gods by interpreting divine signs, both at Rome and on the battlefield. Fifteen flamens were appointed to serve particular gods, most important of which were the *flamen dialis* (Jupiter), the *flamen martialis* (Mars), and the *flamen quirinalis* (Quirinus, later identified with Romulus). Only the nobility could serve in these highest offices, though lesser posts could be held by commoners. All the flamens were forbidden to participate in politics, though the other priestly college, the *pontifices* (singular *pontifex*), could serve the state in peace or war. This small group of priests decided festival days and supervised state religious practices. The *pontifex maximus* was the leader of the religious orders, including the Vestal Virgins. His title, which means "chief bridge builder," was adopted in the Christian era by the pope. Caesar would serve as both flamen dialis and pontifex maximus in his lifetime.

The six Vestal Virgins were chosen originally from noble families to serve the goddess Vesta chastely for a period of thirty years. They were free to marry when their term was finished, but few did. Their primary tasks were to tend the sacred fire in Vesta's temple and to bake special cakes for religious festivals. Their temple contained no statue of Vesta, only a few holy objects such as—oddly enough—the image of an erect phallus. The Vestals were highly honored for their purity and service, but they were not secluded from Roman society. They could leave their temple and even attend parties, but woe to the Vestal who lost her virginity. If her guilt were proven through a discreet examination by trusted Roman matrons, the guilty Vestal would be buried alive.

With Caesar's father away from home much of the time, Aurelia was the primary influence in her son's life. It was his mother who oversaw Caesar's upbringing and education, in addition to her responsibilities managing household affairs, supervising slaves, and handling squabbles with neighbors. Life for a woman in Rome was not as restrictive as that of her counterparts in ancient Greece. In the Athens of Plato's day, women were secluded in the back of the house and rarely left, but not so in Rome. The streets were full of Roman wives bustling about shopping and visiting with friends. Women routinely attended theaters and public games, even the law courts if they wished. Poorer women labored as hard as their husbands in shops and on farms, but wealthy women were rarely pampered. They were well educated and ran the complex affairs of the home while speaking their minds freely to their husbands. The Greeks might have a *symposium* at which only males dined and conversed, but this was foreign to Roman culture where women ate and mingled freely with men.

Women normally married in their late teens to men older than themselves. The ceremony was simple but joyful. A groom arrived at his bride's house and took her right hand to speak his brief vows. A pig was sacrificed, then the guests shouted, *Feliciter!* ("Good luck!") followed by a feast. The marriage was consummated when the husband carried his new bride over the threshold of their new home to avoid the ill omen of stumbling. By the late Republic, it seems that some men were hesitant to shoulder this burden. In 131 B.C., the censor Metellus Macedonius delivered a speech to the Senate that expressed the attitude of many potential grooms:

> *Fellow Romans, if we could make do without a wife, we would all be free of such a nuisance. But nature has ordained that we can't live easily with women or without them, so we must look to our long term needs rather than our short-term happiness.*

But as the primary goal of marriage was the production of children and the continuance of the family name, most Roman men eventually chose a wife. Indeed, we have every reason to think that the majority of Roman marriages were rich in love. The tombstones of wives from Roman cemeteries, while certainly formulaic to a degree, often speak movingly of a husband's sorrow and loss. But in spite of this, divorce and remarriage for financial or political reasons were frequent among the Roman upper classes, though Caesar's parents remained together until his father's death.

When Caesar was about nine days old, a *lustratio* (purification) ceremony signaled his formal entry into the family. Roman fathers had the right to reject any child they thought unfit, but the law required they raise all healthy boys and at least the firstborn girl. Deformed or illegitimate children would be quietly left to die. These rules and customs should not, however, lead us to believe that Romans didn't love and value children. Most families longed for many offspring and often adopted unwanted boys or girls. If nothing else, the factors of high infant mortality and the lack of a social welfare system to care for the aged placed a premium on having a home full of children. Aurelia's family of only one son and two daughters was in fact unusually small.

Caesar would have been raised in a household of women both free and slave to look after him. Corporal punishment was frequent, but the life of a Roman child could be plenty of fun. Archaeology and surviving artworks show us that Roman children had many toys similar to modern boys and girls. Babies and toddlers played with bells and wooden animals full of pebbles to make them rattle. Caesar's sisters would have had cloth dolls and doll houses full of miniature furniture. Caesar himself would have played with stuffed animals, spinning tops, toy chariots, balls, hoops, board games, and joined in with neighborhood children on swings and seesaws.

Since there was no concept of public education in classical times, Roman children attended either private schools or studied at home with individual tutors. Whatever the setting, Roman education in Caesar's day followed a pattern borrowed from the Greeks. At about the age of seven, children began instruction with a *ludi magister* (schoolmaster) who taught the basics of Greek and Latin grammar, writing, and mathematics. Elementary schoolmasters were often freed slaves who set up shop in a marketplace or in the back of a store. Such schools must have been common in the Subura, but Caesar and his sisters were educated by private tutors at home. Less fortunate Roman boys and girls would march to school at sunrise to begin their lessons. Since paper would not reach the west for centuries and papyrus from Egypt was too expensive, each child would carry a small rectangular piece of wood indented in the center to hold a writing surface of wax. Students could then practice writing sentences or math problems with the point of a wooden stylus, then erase them with the blunted end. Children were expected to work very hard, while teachers maintained strict discipline with their whipping canes.

At about the age of twelve, students moved on to a *grammaticus* who continued their instruction in literature and especially poetry. The *Iliad* and the *Odyssey* of Homer were favorites, but pupils also studied early Latin poetry by masters such as Ennius and Livius Andronicus. When a boy reached adulthood at about the age of fifteen or sixteen, he could move to the third stage of Roman education with a teacher of rhetoric. The art of public speaking was vital in an age before printing, when any young man with hopes of a public career was expected to speak well before assemblies and courts. Students would study speeches from the past, then compose their own to address real or imagined situations. The art of rhetoric was subtle and intricate, emphasizing proper delivery, structure, and use of evidence—all without notes. A favorite assignment was to compose a persuasive speech in a historical situation, such as taking the role of Hannibal addressing his troops before crossing the Alps. Thorny legal cases were also common—a man has seduced two virgins in one night. One wants to marry him, but the other justly seeks his death. What do you say to the jury?

Caesar's education would have followed this same pattern even at home. We know that his parents employed a skilled tutor named Marcus Antonius Gnipho, who had been trained in Alexandria,

Egypt, and was highly proficient in both Greek and Latin rhetoric. Like other students, Caesar memorized huge amounts of literature, including the ancient Twelve Tables laying out the basis of Roman law. Records even survive of Caesar's own youthful compositions, though the writings themselves were suppressed by the emperor Augustus for unknown reasons. They include a speech praising Hercules, a tragedy based on the Oedipus story, and a collection of witty proverbs. The one surviving fragment of Caesar's poetry may also date from this period. These six lines comparing the early Roman comic playwright Terence to the famed Greek writer Menander are hardly inspiring and may well have been a simple school exercise, but they suggest an abiding interest in verse that remained with Caesar the rest of his life:

> You also, you half-Menander, are ranked among the greatest poets,
> and rightly so, you lover of pure speech.
> But how I wish your beautiful verse held force as well as form,
> that we might honor your comic lines as highly as the Greeks
> and that you might not suffer scorn because of this weakness.
> O Terence, I mourn this missing piece in your genius.

Physical education was also a key component of Caesar's training, but not in the same manner as Greek youth. Young Athenians practiced sporting events at a *gymnasion* ("naked place"), but Romans viewed this as indulgent, favoring instead a more practical training for the rigors of war. Roman students learned to fight, ride a horse, and swim in the Tiber—a skill that would one day save Caesar's life in Egypt. We know that Caesar became an expert at horsemanship in his youth, galloping bareback while holding his hands behind his back.

Caesar's boyhood years were a time of turmoil unlike anything Rome had ever known. The Italian allies of Rome who had fought

bravely and spilled their blood during the wars against Rome's enemies had finally had enough. After so many years of loyal service
with little appreciation in return, they began to organize a massive
rebellion that threatened to destroy Roman power forever. Some
statesmen saw the danger coming and tried to head it off before Italy
exploded into a full-fledged civil war. Marcus Livius Drusus, whose
father had been a leading opponent of reform, surprised everyone by
championing a campaign to grant citizenship to the Italian allies beginning in 91 B.C., when Caesar was nine years old. The leading
voices of the Senate, following their true form, staunchly opposed
any change to the status quo and soon had Drusus murdered.

To the Italians, the death of their advocate Drusus was the final
straw. The fearless Marsi tribesmen led the resistance in the central
part of the peninsula, while the Samnites rose up in the mountains of
the south. The resulting conflict was eerily similar to the American
Civil War. Like all civil wars it was particularly mean and nasty, but
the Italians of the south were blessed with brilliant generals and tens
of thousands of troops well trained in Roman-style warfare. The
Senate at first scoffed at the fighting ability of the backwoods Samnites and Marsi, but the Italians scored numerous early successes
against the Romans, such as the capture of Pompeii and other towns
around the Bay of Naples. The Senate deliberately overlooked Caesar's uncle Marius, who had famously saved Italy from German invaders a decade earlier, and instead gave control of the army to lesser
men—who promptly lost—until it finally chose Marius's former
lieutenant Sulla to take command in the southern theater. A sign of
how badly affairs were going for Rome was a bill passed in 89 B.C.
granting citizenship to all Italians who laid down their arms against
Rome—the very thing the rebels had wanted in the first place. But
the Italians quickly realized their new voting power would be nullified by Roman politics, so that in the end the proposal caused more
animosity than goodwill. At last, a Roman nobleman named Pompeius Strabo (father of Caesar's future ally and adversary Pompey)

led a fierce campaign against the rebels in central Italy and swept across the peninsula to the Adriatic like Sherman in his march to the sea. By 88 B.C., Sulla, through attrition, slaughter, and sheer dogged-ness, finally defeated the Italians. Peace was restored, the rebels were soon welcomed back into the fold, and within a few years they had gained full citizenship rights—making the Italian War one of the most wasteful and pointless conflicts in Roman history.

As difficult as Roman relations were with her Italian allies, the internal fighting at Rome during Caesar's childhood was even more violent and destructive. As soon as the Italian War was over, the Sen-ate appointed Sulla to lead a campaign against Mithridates of Pontus in Asia Minor, who had managed to create a Black Sea empire and was now threatening Roman power and fortunes in the East. Taking advantage of the chaos caused by the war in Italy, Mithridates swept through the Roman province of Asia and ordered a massacre of some 80,000 Roman and Italian residents. The residents of Asia, who had been bled dry by Roman tax collectors for years, shed no tears for the victims. Mithridates swiftly crossed to Greece and proclaimed him-self liberator and defender of the Hellenic world against the barbaric Romans. But at this time when Rome needed to stand united, a new tribune, Sulpicius Rufus, instead used his bully boys in the Forum to bash heads and forced the Senate to replace Sulla with Marius. Sulla decided he had played by the rules long enough and was not about to let his chance for advancement be seized by his former commander. Rushing to the camp of his former soldiers near Naples, he roused them to march on Rome. For the first time in Roman history, a Ro-man general seized the city. Marius was caught off guard and fled to Africa, condemned by Sulla as an outlaw. Sulla shored up his senato-rial base in Rome and regained his command, then quickly marched east against Mithridates.

But Sulla had established a dangerous precedent. After he was gone, the consul Cornelius Cinna repudiated him and led another army of discontents against Rome, this time joined by Marius. The

Senate called on Pompeius Strabo to save them, but Pompey's father
dithered and was soon dead of natural causes. In 87 B.C., Rome surrendered to Cinna and Marius, hoping for the best. Instead, they discovered the worst in Caesar's uncle. Marius led a vendetta against the
Roman aristocracy fed by decades of ill-treatment at their hands.
Leading senators were hunted down by the gangs of Marius like
criminals, murdered in cold blood, and their heads displayed on
pikes in the Forum. Rome had never seen such a vicious blood bath:
"They tossed headless bodies into the streets . . . butchered fathers in
their own homes, mutilated children, and violated their mothers."

The rage of Marius eventually drove even Cinna to despair, and
the consul ordered his own disciplined troops to cut down Marius's
thugs. Fortunately for Rome, Marius died in his bed soon afterward
at the age of seventy. It was a sorry end for a man who had done so
much for his country in years past. Cinna took over as leader in
Rome and tried to make a new beginning for the state. He passed
legislation to aid new citizens, stabilize the economy, and relieve the
crushing private debts that had built up since the Italian War. A
measure of peace descended on Rome for a few years, but everyone
knew Sulla would soon be returning with a victorious army behind
him.

During the brief years of Cinna's rule before the return of Sulla from
the East, young Julius Caesar came of age and began his public life.
One of the victims of the purge by Cinna and Marius had been Cornelius Merula, the *flamen dialis* or priest of Jupiter. This left Rome
without one of its most important priests, but few men were able or
willing to serve as *flamen dialis*. The office was still restricted to patricians and was surrounded by a host of onerous taboos with their origins lost deep in Roman history. The *flamen dialis* served for life and
could not leave the city of Rome for more than a few days. The feet
of his bed had to be covered in mud and he had to wear a pointed cap

at all times. He was exempt from oaths and was allowed to sit in the Senate, but he could not wear knots anywhere on his clothing, could never see a corpse, and was not allowed to ride a horse. He also had to be married to a patrician bride who had her own sacred responsibilities and restrictions. Unlike other Roman relationships, the marriage between the *flamen dialis* and his wife was binding as long as both lived.

Where could the Roman leaders find a qualified person willing to take on a job that effectively barred him from public life and burdened him with a hundred arcane and tiresome taboos? It was then that Cinna remembered the nephew of Marius. Caesar was a patrician of the noblest blood and, best of all, he was not old enough to object or cause any trouble. We don't know how Caesar reacted when he was told his fate, but he couldn't have been happy. Any dreams he had of military glory and a political career were now shattered. His life would be spent performing archaic rituals and burdensome priestly chores.

Caesar's family had previously arranged an excellent marriage for him to a girl named Cossutia from a wealthy family. However, since Cossutia was not a patrician, she could not be the wife of the *flamen dialis*. Instead, he became engaged to none other than Cinna's patrician daughter Cornelia. Caesar's marriage to Cornelia grew into a loving relationship, but it also tied Caesar firmly to the populist politics of his father-in-law. Caesar and his family surely realized that if Sulla returned to Rome and overthrew Cinna, the young priest's life would be in grave danger.

Before Caesar could marry or take on his religious duties, he had to enter the adult world of ancient Rome by laying aside the simple tunic of childhood and putting on the *toga virilis* ("toga of manhood"). Thus, around his sixteenth birthday, Caesar dedicated his childhood toys to the gods and took up the burden of full citizenship. It was an eventful year for young Caesar. At about the same time, his father died, leaving Caesar as the head of his household. One day

Caesar was a child studying Greek poetry at home with his tutor, then practically overnight he was a married man attending the Senate as high priest of Jupiter.

While Cinna ruled in Rome, Sulla fought against Mithridates in the East. Sulla arrived in Greece in 87 B.C. and captured Athens the next year. He then led his army north into Macedonia and across the Bosporus strait into Asia. Mithridates soon realized it was best to cut his losses and negotiated a peace treaty with Sulla near Troy. The king agreed to stay out of Roman territory, surrender his fleet, and pay a hefty indemnity. Rome then acknowledged his legitimate rule over Pontus and enrolled him as an ally. Sulla could have stormed Pontus and destroyed Mithridates, but it would have been a long, hard fight with the loss of many of his men. He knew he would need those soldiers when he returned to Italy to take on Cinna, so he cut a quick deal with Mithridates and headed west.

Cinna tried to raise a defensive army, but was killed by his own mutinous soldiers. Sulla landed unopposed at Brundisium in the heel of Italy in 83 B.C. Those senators and members of the aristocracy who had survived the purge of Marius flocked to join him there. Among these supporters was Marcus Lucinius Crassus, about thirty years old, whose father and older brother had been victims of Marius. Young Pompey, son of Pompeius Strabo, also joined Sulla, bringing with him three legions he had raised from his father's veteran soldiers in Picenum. Watching events unfold, little did seventeen-year-old Caesar know that one day these two men—Crassus and Pompey—would be his partners in ruling Rome.

Sulla marched freely into Campania and defeated one army sent against him, while the other he simply bribed away from its commander. A son of Marius rallied some of his father's old supporters against Sulla, but was blockaded inside the Latin town of Praeneste near Rome. The populist followers (the *populares*) of Marius and Cinna knew their cause was lost and so withdrew from the capital city, but not before carrying out a massacre of their enemies who had been foolish enough to stay in town. Sulla seized Rome for the second time and soon defeated the remnants of the Marian forces in Italy and Spain. Sulla was now the undisputed master of the Roman world—a king in all but name.

The bloodbath that followed made the previous political killings of Marius look mild by comparison. Sulla devised a simple system for disposing of his enemies—he posted a list of names in the Forum of all those he wanted dead. Anyone who killed them would receive a generous bounty while the state would seize the dead men's property. By these so-called proscriptions, Sulla managed to combine murder and fund-raising on a grand scale. Several thousand of Sulla's enemies died in this way, including reformist senators, but the business class that had supported Cinna and Marius was especially hard hit. Many who had little involvement in politics were placed on the proscription lists simply because they were rich. Sulla also passed a law that the son of any proscribed man was ineligible to ever hold public office. Beyond Rome, Sulla seized the Italian lands of his enemies to distribute to his loyal soldiers.

Sulla was determined to restore the preeminence of the Senate at the expense of the common people. To carry out this plan, he first had himself appointed dictator. He then increased the number of senators and passed restrictions on the plebeian magistrates. He also changed the composition of jury courts to favor the senatorial class and made northern Italy into a province so that Roman troops could be stationed there permanently, close to the capital city in case they were needed.

Among Sulla's reforms was a housecleaning of Cinna's appointees, including Caesar as *flamen dialis*. Doubtless, Caesar was relieved to be free of this burden, but he was still in danger as a nephew of Marius and son-in-law of Cinna. Sulla, however, was uncharacteristically merciful to young Caesar and merely demanded that he divorce Cinna's daughter Cornelia. Sulla had commanded several of his own followers, including Pompey, to put aside their wives because of inimical family connections, and all had promptly complied.

It was a very reasonable order given the circumstances, and everyone naturally assumed Caesar would do as he was told. But Caesar looked Sulla in the eye and refused. Sulla and his followers were stunned. Whether out of stubbornness, audacity, or simply love, Caesar was defying a man who had ordered the murder of thousands. In doing so, he lost everything he owned, and was now marked for death on the proscription lists. The tale of defiance against Sulla is one of the earliest episodes that survive about Caesar's life, but it tells us volumes about his character.

Caesar was brave, but he was not foolish enough to remain in Rome to die. He fled immediately to the mountainous Sabine country of southern Italy and went into hiding. Almost every night he moved to a new location to avoid Sulla's agents who were sweeping the countryside. The life of a fugitive was made infinitely more difficult as Caesar had contracted malaria and was suffering from anemia, fevers, and exhaustion. Finally one night, struggling to a new hiding place, Caesar was intercepted by a henchman of Sulla named Cornelius. Caesar was forced to hand over the equivalent of thousands of dollars—surely everything he had—to bribe his way to freedom. He was now a penniless, deathly ill refugee still with a price on his head, wandering the hills and valleys of Italy, but he would not give up. Fortunately for Caesar, he had friends and powerful advocates in Rome. Several of the Vestal Virgins came forward to plead with Sulla on Caesar's behalf, as did his mother's cousin Aurelius Cotta and Sulla's staunch supporter Mamercus Lepidus. They repeatedly beseeched Sulla to spare Caesar's life and allow him to return to Rome. At last Sulla gave way, perhaps with a sneaking admiration for the young man who had dared to stand up to him. But Sulla then prophetically declared:

> *Remember—this young man who you have been so desperate to save will one day destroy the aristocracy you have worked with me to preserve. For in this Caesar I see many a Marius.*

Caesar was reunited with Cornelia, but it seemed the better part of valor to quickly absent himself from Sulla's Rome. He decided to make up for lost time by beginning his military career at the age of nineteen on the staff of the propraetor of Roman Asia, Marcus Thermus. At that time Thermus was besieging the Greek town of Mytilene on the island of Lesbos, the last stubborn holdout inspired by Mithridates' rebellion against Rome. Thermus ordered Caesar to travel to the kingdom of Bithynia in northern Asia Minor to bring back ships for the siege. Bithynia was an ally of Rome and its reluctant king, Nicomedes, was obliged to offer what little assistance he could to the Roman military effort. Caesar was successful in obtaining a fleet—perhaps too successful—because rumors quickly grew that he had become the lover of Nicomedes during his visit. Caesar vociferously denied these charges, but they haunted him for the rest of his life.

Homosexuality in the classical world was viewed differently than in most modern societies. Greeks and Romans didn't really care what a man did in bed with a subordinate woman or man. The shame was not engaging in homosexual behavior, but in allowing oneself to be at the receiving end of such a partnership. Roman men might purchase male slaves for the specific purpose of serving as sexual servants, and as long as it wasn't trumpeted in the streets, people would consider it a private matter. But for a free adult male to allow himself to be used as the target of sexual actions by another man was unthinkable. Caesar could laugh off an insult better than most Romans, but he was furious when his political enemies later dragged up the charge of a youthful affair with Nicomedes. The accusation even became part of bawdy songs his soldiers sang in parade years later on their victorious return from Gaul: "Caesar conquered Gaul, but Nicomedes conquered Caesar."

His foes labeled him the "Queen of Bithynia" and called Nicomedes his *paedicator*—indicating that Caesar was his sexual subordinate. The fact that Caesar swore under oath that these charges were untrue only made people mock him more. Whatever Caesar may have done with Nicomedes behind closed doors is, of course, unknowable, but it's highly unlikely that Caesar, whatever his sexual preferences, would have deliberately risked his reputation for a fling with so prominent a figure.

Perhaps driven by this insult, Caesar threw himself into the attack on Mytilene with a vengeance. The ships that Caesar brought from Nicomedes were essential since the city rose from a small island just off the main coast of Lesbos, making it an extremely difficult operation for the legions. But through relentless determination, the Roman forces stormed the city at last with Caesar leading the way. His personal bravery in the face of imminent danger became a hallmark of his fighting style that would serve him on battlefields from Britain to Egypt. Even in later years as conqueror of Gaul and ruler of Rome, he never hesitated to join his men on the front lines. For his conspicuous service at Mytilene, Lepidus awarded Caesar the coveted *corona civica* or civic crown. This simple oak wreath in itself was not impressive to look at, but it marked Caesar as an extraordinary soldier who by his courage had saved the lives of his comrades under fire. When the wearer of a civic crown entered any Roman festival, all persons, even senators, rose to their feet in respect. It was a singular honor for young Caesar that helped to launch his political and military career.

After the fall of Mytilene, Caesar served for a short time with the proconsul Servilius Isauricus in Cilicia during one of Rome's ongoing campaigns against piracy in the eastern Mediterranean. Cilicia in southeastern Asia Minor with its countless hidden coves was a favorite haunt of pirates who hijacked unsuspecting ships and ran a lucrative kidnapping business. But in 78 B.C., news reached Asia of Sulla's death at Rome. Sulla had surprisingly laid down his dictatorship voluntarily the previous year and retired to a life of debauchery at his estate in Campania. His enemies reported that Sulla, like King Herod in the New Testament, was eaten from the inside by worms.

Whatever the cause of his death, Sulla's passing now made it safe for Caesar to return to Rome and add a reputation for civic success in the Forum to his military record. Already Roman politicians were positioning themselves to replace Sulla, including the consul Marcus Lepidus, who had pleaded for Caesar's life when he was on the run. Lepidus had abandoned Sulla's senatorial party and joined the populist movement, almost certainly in a bid for power rather than out of conviction. With other populist leaders, Lepidus was planning a new coup to seize control of Rome from Sulla's followers. Highly impressed with young Caesar, Lepidus offered him an important position in his proposed revolutionary government—but Caesar, though a fervent populist, took a careful look at Lepidus and decided neither he nor his plan inspired confidence. His political instincts were on the mark, as the plot of Lepidus quickly collapsed, leaving Caesar untouched by any hint of participation in a revolt.

The next year Caesar entered into the world of Roman law by prosecuting the ex-governor of Macedonia, Gnaeus Cornelius Dolabella, for corruption. One far-reaching consequence of Rome's expansion in the second century B.C. was the need for effective and fair government in its far-flung empire. Unfortunately, Rome was ill-equipped to manage this task. The government of Rome functioned well enough for a small city state and was barely adequate for rule of the Italian peninsula, but beyond the shores of Italy Roman rule was an orgy of exploitation.

After a man had served in Rome as a senior magistrate, it was standard procedure that he would then ship out to a province to act as governor for a year. Given the huge amount of money needed to rise in Roman government and maintain a comfortable retirement, governors came to look on their year in the provinces like children in a candy store. It was, quite simply, their opportunity to get rich quickly with a bare minimum of supervision. Of course, governors had serious duties to perform—hearing criminal cases, defending their province against invaders, squashing internal disturbances—but much of their short time was spent fleecing the provincial sheep. There were many ways to do this, such as awarding a favorable verdict in a court case to the highest bidder and soliciting "voluntary" gifts from the natives. It wasn't just governors who lined their pockets, but also wealthy Roman citizens who managed tax collection in the provinces. The government in Rome had no central taxing agency, but instead sold taxation contracts to private firms. For example, a group of citizens wishing to collect taxes in the province of Asia would bid for the job and pay a set amount to the Roman treasury up front. They would then hold the right to collect taxes from the natives of Asia to recoup their initial outlay. Of course, the goal of these *publicani* (tax collectors) was to take in as much money as possible from the provinces above and beyond what they had paid to the treasury. Local agents of these tax collectors, such as St. Matthew in the Christian gospels, became some of the most despised figures in the Roman provinces.

The provincials in Rome's empire did have a few reasons to be grateful for Roman rule. They enjoyed the benefits of the famed *Pax Romana* (Roman peace), including political stability, improved commerce, and excellent roads, but they bitterly resented being exploited by an everchanging parade of Roman governors and businessmen. Complaints and lawsuits by provincials hoping for change were rarely successful since the powerful citizens who judged such cases in Rome were the very ones who had bled the provinces dry in the past or hoped to do so in the future. And since Roman citizenship, except in rare cases, was an impossible dream for natives of the provinces, they had no hope of ever becoming full partners in Roman civilization.

Like most governors, Dolabella had harassed and extorted the natives of his province during his term in office. The Macedonians, however, decided to fight back and hired young Caesar to act as their spokesman in court. There was no such thing as a professional lawyer in ancient Rome; any educated and willing man could take on a case either as a defense attorney or prosecutor. To enter court life was a popular way for a would-be politician to make a name for himself whether he won or lost the case. The important thing was to impress the crowds who always gathered for such an event at large meeting halls in the Forum or outside in pleasant weather.

The rhetorical training Caesar had received was now put to the test as he faced two of the leading defense counsels of the day, including his cousin Gaius Aurelius Cotta. Caesar used all the techniques of elocution, persuasion, and even humor that he could muster. His speech was a tremendous success and was considered a masterpiece of oratory by none other than soon-to-be-famous Cicero, who was in the crowd that day. Cicero says that Caesar's style was perfect and his delivery vivid, like seeing a beautiful portrait painted in words.

Like Caesar's uncle Marius, who hailed from the same small town, Marcus Tullius Cicero was a *novus homo* (new man) without ancestors among the nobility. But unlike Marius, Cicero chose to make his mark on Rome in the Forum rather than the battlefield. Cicero began by prosecuting Gaius Verres for gross plunder during his term as governor of Sicily. Even though Verres doled out generous bribes, used his many powerful friends, and employed the famed advocate Hortensius, he was still not able to evade the damning evidence carefully presented by the young prosecutor. Verres retired in exile to southern Gaul (with most of his ill-gotten gains), while Cicero ensured his own oratorical fame by publishing his speeches during the trial as the *Verrine Orations*.

Of course, Caesar lost the case. It wasn't that Caesar's argument was lacking, simply that the jurors were all senators who were not about to convict so powerful a man of their own class.

Caesar's speech against Dolabella was such a success that the following year he was asked to prosecute the notorious Gaius Antonius, who had plundered Greece during the war against Mithridates. The criminal actions of Antonius were obscene even by Roman standards, so that Caesar was on the verge of a conviction when the defendant appealed to a plebeian magistrate to save him by issuing a veto. Though Caesar again lost his case, he was now firmly established as a masterful orator and an up-and-coming politician in Rome.

▣

There was soon a joyous occasion in Caesar's household when his wife Cornelia gave birth to their first child, a daughter named Julia. Caesar was a devoted father, but he was also a supremely ambitious man who knew that his rise out of the slums of the Subura depended on his reputation as an orator and his military service to the Republic. Thus it was not long after Julia's birth that Caesar again left Rome to study on the island of Rhodes with Apollonius, a Greek rhetorician who was also the teacher of Cicero. Just off the southwest coast of Asia Minor in the Aegean Sea, Rhodes was famous as a center for higher learning. A student there could attend lectures by some of the greatest names in Greek philosophy and science, including Apollonius and the Stoic philosopher Posidonius. We have no record that Caesar ever studied with or even met Posidonius, but he surely would have read the philosopher's works, such as his now-lost *History*. In this book, Posidonius described his travels among the Celts of western Europe. He detailed Gaulish politics, warriors, kings, gods, and druids—a knowledge of which would be crucial for Caesar when he invaded Gaul twenty years later.

But Caesar never reached Rhodes. In 75 B.C., just as winter was beginning, his ship was attacked by Cilician pirates somewhere off the southwestern coast of Asia Minor near Miletus. Besides the usual haul of cargo and passengers now destined for the slave markets, the pirates were thrilled to discover that they had taken a member of the Roman nobility. Piracy had been a problem in the Mediterranean since Homer wrote of it in the *Odyssey,* but no one had ever found an adequate means to bring brigandage at sea under control. A city could rid its local waters of pirates with a concerted effort, but the raiders would just move down the coast to establish another base. As long as pirates could control some hidden cove far from settled areas they could strike out at ships with impunity.

Caesar treated the pirates with a good-natured contempt that shocked and amused his captors. They were accustomed to terrified prisoners who begged for mercy, but Caesar acted more as if the pirates were a minor distraction to his busy schedule. He was insulted by their suggested ransom of twenty talents and raised the price on his head to fifty (about 300,000 silver coins). Caesar sent away several members of his traveling party to Miletus to somehow raise the money, while one companion and two slaves stayed with him. For forty days Caesar lived as a prisoner of the pirates, sharing their meals and even joining in their athletic games. He composed poetry for them and called them uncouth barbarians when they failed to appreciate his verses. He ordered them about and sent a slave to quiet them when they kept him awake at night. He also repeatedly joked that he was going to return and crucify them all once he was released. The pirates loved their bold young guest and must have been sorry to see him go when a ship bearing his ransom returned from Miletus. Laughing and waving, Caesar bade farewell to his pirate hosts.

Caesar soon reached Miletus and there commandeered some local ships and militia, setting sail almost immediately back to the pirates' base. He surprised them while they were still aboard their ships and captured most of them immediately. Caesar seized all their loot, including the fifty talents he had just paid. He then loaded the chained buccaneers onto his ships and sailed to the nearby city of Pergamum to find the Roman governor, Marcus Juncus. Discovering that the governor was in Bithynia, Caesar threw the pirates in prison and set off to seek official permission from Juncus to punish his former captors. Juncus heard Caesar's report but decided to sell the pirates into slavery and keep the profits for himself. This did not suit Caesar at all. He left Bithynia and rushed back to Pergamum before the governor's agents could arrive and take possession of his prisoners. Just as he had warned them about what he would do during his captivity, Caesar led the pirates out of their cells and immediately had them all crucified.

Crucifixion was among the cruelest punishments ever devised. It was used earlier by the Carthaginians, but the Romans employed crucifixion on a wide scale—though it was always considered poor taste to discuss it in proper society. Crucifixion was strictly a punishment for criminals and slaves, being designed as much for torture and terror as killing. A condemned man would first be flogged to humiliate and weaken him, then forced to pick up a heavy wooden beam called a *patibulum*. When he had reached the prison yard or an out-of-the-way spot on the edge of town, the prisoner was stripped naked and fastened to the beam with nails and cords. He was then hauled by ropes to the top of a sturdy pole driven deep in the ground. Sometimes there was a small seat for the tortured man to sit on, but even so the prisoner normally suffered in agony for days until finally succumbing to exhaustion and shock. Suetonius writes without irony when he says that Caesar mercifully cut the throats of the pirates before hanging each one on a cross.

Caesar again set sail for Rhodes, but it seems fate didn't intend him for a scholarly life. Mithridates soon rose in arms against Rome yet again, so Caesar quickly left his studies and sailed across to Asia Minor to offer his services. The lackluster response of the Roman provincial governor to the new threat of Mithridates drove the impatient Caesar to co-opt the local militia and take matters into his own hands. He was once more showing a characteristic disregard for playing by the rules when he believed rapid action was needed. Without any endorsement by the Senate or the governor of Asia, Caesar led a campaign against Mithridates' allies and drove them from the province. Later in the same year, Caesar was assigned to the staff of the praetor Marcus Antonius, father of Caesar's future lieutenant Mark Antony, and served in another campaign against the pirates in the coastal waters of Asia Minor.

Now twenty-seven years old, Caesar received news that he had been elected as a pontifex in Rome. Membership in this elite group was no hindrance to his military or political career as had been his previous service as *flamen dialis*. These priests, led by the pontifex maximus, were active as regulators of official religious practices and served as advisors to the state on sacred matters. A pontifex could also be elected to high political office and lead armies in the field. A position had opened in this college of priests at the death of his mother's cousin, the consul Gaius Aurelius Cotta. It may well be that Aurelia played a crucial role in the choice of her son to replace Cotta, but whatever the political maneuvering behind the scene, it was nonetheless a clear affirmation of Caesar's rising role in Roman politics.

Caesar headed back to Rome at the news of his election as a pontifex. Sailing from Asia to Greece, he then set out across the Adriatic Sea to Italy in a small boat with just two friends and ten slaves to man the oars. Pirates were still a serious problem in the Adriatic, so Caesar hoped a low-profile passage at night would help him to avoid a repeat of his earlier capture. The boat slipped through the water hour after hour until it silently approached the Italian coast. Suddenly, Caesar saw a row of masts ahead of them and quietly ordered his terrified crew to prepare for combat. There was no escape. The winner of the civic crown was determined to fight these new pirates with all his might. He stripped off his traveling clothes and strapped a dagger to his thigh, ready to take on the first seaborne bandit to step onto his small craft. But as Caesar drew nearer, he realized that the ship masts he had seen in the darkness were actually a row of trees on the Italian coast. With a hearty laugh and a greatly relieved crew, Caesar stepped onto the shore of Italy to begin the long march to Rome.

II

THE PATH TO POWER

Caesar achieved great popularity at Rome through
his skill as a speaker, while the common people loved
him because of his friendliness in dealing with them.
He was most endearing for someone so young.

— PLUTARCH

Just as Caesar was arriving in Italy, a gladiator on the other side of the
peninsula was starting a war. Spartacus was a native of Thrace who
grew up among nomadic pastoralists, who herded their flocks freely
among the mountains of the northern Balkans. He was captured and
put on the auction block, where his physique and strength caught the
eye of an Italian entrepreneur named Lentulus Batiatus, who trained
gladiators near Naples. Like most gladiators during Roman times,
Spartacus was a slave. Potential new gladiators found themselves in
schools scattered throughout Italy, though the countryside near Mount
Vesuvius was a favorite location. Given the danger posed by large
groups of slaves trained in combat, these schools were heavily guarded.

If a gladiator showed promise, he would fight in local contests for
public entertainment. Some gladiators wore light armor and used
only a trident and net, while others carried shields, swords, or scimi-
tars. Since gladiators were very expensive to purchase and maintain,

death in the arena was rare. A wounded man lying in the dust of a stadium raised a finger to ask for mercy. The crowd usually pressed the thumb and index finger together to show their appreciation for a good show, but—contrary to Hollywood movies—angry spectators encouraged a death blow by raising their thumbs upward, not down. Contests were well-advertised to draw large crowds, as in an inscription from the first century A.D.:

THE BAND OF GLADIATORS OWNED BY THE AEDILE AULUS
SUETTIUS CERTUS WILL FIGHT AT POMPEII ON MAY 31st.
THERE WILL ALSO BE A WILD BEAST FIGHT.
AWNING SHADES WILL BE PROVIDED.

But the roar of the crowd was not enough for Spartacus. In 73 B.C., along with about seventy other gladiators, he staged an escape from their training school using kitchen knives. Outside the gates they fortuitously came upon some wagons bringing weapons to the compound. They armed themselves and fled to a nearby mountain, electing three leaders, including Spartacus and his friend Crixus.

Slaves from the countryside of southern Italy flocked to Spartacus, so that soon he had an army of thousands. The Senate sent two successive armies with a few thousand soldiers to conduct what they believed would be a quick campaign against a disorganized rabble, but Spartacus and his men moved with discipline and stealth, defeating the Romans and almost capturing one commander in his bathtub. With the forces sent against them defeated, Spartacus now had the run of the Italian countryside. He was clever enough to know that although the Romans might lose battles at first, they always won the war in the end. His plan therefore was to lead his army north over the Alps so that they might return to their respective homelands of Gaul, Germany, and Thrace; but his men preferred to plunder Italy.

The Senate needed a new, decisive commander to lead the war against Spartacus, so it chose Marcus Crassus, the former ally of Sulla and one of the richest men in Rome. Many Roman noblemen joined Crassus in his campaign, including Cato the Younger—a man who would one day be Caesar's most implacable foe. Crassus brought a harsh discipline to the army by reviving an ancient punishment for men who had dropped their weapons and fled in battle. From the cowardly, he chose five hundred and divided them into fifty groups of ten each. One from each group of ten was chosen by lot to die— they were quite literally *decimated*, i.e. one out of ten (*decem*) was executed while the rest of the army watched.

Spartacus thought his men might stand a better chance if they crossed to Sicily, where there had been major slave rebellions in recent years. With potential new recruits from the Sicilian slaves, he believed they might hold out indefinitely. Retreating to the toe of Italy, he bargained with pirates to provide his army passage to Sicily, but the pirates took his money and sailed away, leaving his troops stranded on the shore. Crassus took advantage of this situation by building a wall almost forty miles long across the whole toe of Italy to trap Spartacus, nevertheless, he and most of his army were able to fight their way out. Crassus was now afraid Spartacus would march on Rome, but the former slaves split into quarreling groups, making it easier for the Romans to crush them. After several defeats, Spartacus killed his own horse to prevent any escape and led his army in a final battle against the Romans south of Naples. By the end of the day, Spartacus lay dead on the battlefield, with a few thousand of his men surviving to flee north. These were intercepted by Pompey, who killed them all and claimed credit for putting down the whole rebellion, leaving Crassus furious at Pompey for grabbing the glory for himself. Six thousand soldiers of Spartacus who had been captured earlier were finally crucified along the whole Appian Way stretching from Capua to Rome—roughly one tortured man hanging on a cross every hundred feet for over a hundred miles.

Although we don't know for certain, Caesar probably fought in the campaign against Spartacus since he had been elected by the people of Rome as a military tribune on his return to Italy. Having this office, he was now at the formal beginning of his political career.

The Roman government was a *res publica* ("state of the people") or in modern terms, a republic, with elected officials governing on behalf of all citizens. In theory, the city magistrates ruled by consent of all the people, and even the most humble farm boy could rise to the heights of Roman power. In practice, Rome was ruled by a small elite of noble families who shamelessly manipulated the political system and jealously guarded the executive offices for themselves.

Rome had several different assemblies where citizens could gather and voice their opinion on candidates for office or proposed legislation. But in order to participate in these assemblies, a man—women, of course, could not vote—had to be physically present in Rome. This was fine when Rome was a small town with all its citizens living nearby, but as the Republic grew, citizens from distant colonies or provinces were effectively excluded from voting. In addition, magistrates completely controlled what matters could be considered by an assembly during any given meeting.

The Centuriate Assembly was military in origin and so met on the Field of Mars just outside the city walls. This was necessary because military affairs had to be conducted outside the *pomerium* (sacred boundary of the city). The Centuriate Assembly was responsible for the election of chief magistrates, but the voting power was heavily weighted in favor of the wealthiest citizens. This assembly also held the power to declare war and to hear capital cases on appeal, but was not involved in legislation. The Tribal Assembly, however, could pass laws and was more egalitarian. Romans were divided into thirty-five tribes from both the urban and rural areas with each tribe having an equal vote. But as there were only four urban tribes, citizens from rural areas could dominate legislation if they could afford to be away from their farms. In practical terms, poor farmers from distant regions attended the Tribal Assembly only on rare occasions. This assembly elected the lower magistrates of the Republic and could hear noncapital cases on appeal. Finally, the Plebeian Assembly was composed solely of plebeians and, after 287 B.C., was empowered to pass legislation binding on the whole state.

But the most powerful of the political bodies in the Roman Republic was the Senate. This elite group began as a council of patrician advisors to kings, but by the time of the early Republic had become an independent gathering of the most powerful men in Rome. Three hundred wealthy patricians and plebeians formed the Senate, which prepared legislation for consideration by the people, managed foreign affairs, and issued decrees. Although these decrees had no legally binding force on the state, they were, by tradition, honored. Senior magistrates of the Republic became members of the Senate for life, unless they fell into poverty or were removed for unseemly behavior.

There were a number of magistrates within the Roman state who exercised power over different areas of the army and civil government. Many ambitious men like Julius Caesar hoped, planned, and schemed to rise through the ranks from army service to the highest executive power of the Republic. For those with this goal there was a fixed course of advancement to follow, known as the *cursus honorum* or Path of Honors.

THE PATH OF HONORS

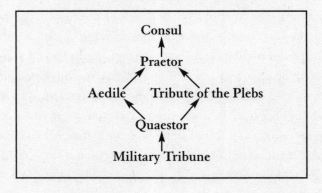

Around his seventeenth birthday, a young man would enter the army and serve for ten years in increasingly important military roles. Toward the end of his military service, a worthy soldier could be elected one of several military tribunes serving a legion. This was the first rung on the Path of Honors which Caesar now held.

In his late twenties, a man with political aspirations would seek election as one of the quaestors that served the Republic at home and abroad. Quaestors handled the mundane tasks of government work such as managing the treasury and organizing the food supply of Rome. Like all the magistrates, a quaestor was unpaid. This had the deliberate effect of limiting entry into the government service to those who had independent means of income. Magistrates served for only one year, with the result that no one ever had time to become an expert in any particular job. High Roman officials were essentially amateurs heavily dependent on the advice and consent of their superiors, especially the power brokers of the Senate.

After service as a quaestor, a rising star might be elected as an aedile for a year to oversee public buildings, temples, water supply, or police functions, among other tasks, including the public games. The state allotted some money for these games, but particularly ambitious aediles would often add to this fund from their own resources to curry public favor in their hoped-for rise up the Path of Honors. Those lacking in sufficient funds could always borrow from money lenders who saw promise in a future leader. But an aedile who spent unwisely or failed to advance after falling into debt could be financially ruined or hounded by creditors for years to come.

An ambitious plebeian could also campaign for election by the Plebeian Assembly as one of ten tribunes. In this office a tribune, whose person was sacrosanct, was charged with protecting the rights of all plebeians. In one of the most powerful actions of Roman government, a tribune could overrule any magistrate or assembly by uttering a single word—*veto* ("I forbid"). With this statement, laws, Senate decrees, and elections were invalidated. The potential for abuse of this tribunal power was enormous, though tradition and pressure from colleagues minimized the temptation, at least until the late second century B.C.

The penultimate step on the Path of Honors was service as a praetor. In this office, a magistrate might perform military service, serve the state abroad, or exercise judicial functions. A praetor also possessed *imperium,* the power of command. With this power he was vested with supreme administrative authority, including the right to impose the death penalty. Those magistrates with imperium were escorted everywhere by guards known as *lictors,* who bore a bundle of rods bound around an ax. These *fasces* were a praetor's visible symbol of the right to use force (hence our term *fascism*).

At the pinnacle of the Path of Honors were the two elected consuls, who also held imperium. The Centuriate Assembly annually chose these men to bear the highest civil and military responsibility for the Republic. The chief task of the consuls was to lead the Roman armies, but they could also carry out judicial proceedings and propose legislation to the assemblies. If a consul was abroad fighting at the end of his term, the Senate could, if it wished, extend his authority as a military leader by granting him proconsular power. Throughout most of the Republic the two consuls worked together amicably, but there was always the potential for a pair of consuls at loggerheads to grind state business to a halt.

Most men who had served as consuls settled back in their chairs at the Senate house and lived out their days as respected elder statesmen. Ex-consuls often served as governors in the conquered provinces, but there were also two other offices that a few distinguished former consuls might attain. The first was the position of censor, two of which were chosen every five years to serve a term of eighteen months. A censor was charged with conducting a census of all citizens and purging the Senate of unfit members.

The final magistrate of the Roman Republic, the dictator, served only in the most dire circumstances. When the state faced the gravest of dangers, the Senate could recommend a dictator to serve for up to six months. The dictator held supreme civil and military power, was not subject to any appeal, and could not be held accountable for his actions after his term of service. The dictator appointed a master of the horse to assist him, but all magistrates remained in office subject to his command. The legendary paradigm of a Roman dictator was the patrician Cincinnatus, who according to tradition was summoned from his fields to serve as dictator during a desperate war in 458 B.C. He reluctantly agreed, led the army to victory, then lay down his dictatorship after sixteen days to return to his plough.

We don't know exactly what Caesar did during his time as a military tribune, but we may reasonably guess that he served under Crassus against Spartacus and gained valuable experience in fighting a clever enemy. The supposition that he worked for Crassus is especially tempting since Caesar was soon to become a key supporter of Rome's richest politician.

The period after the defeat of Spartacus in 71 B.C. saw a contest for power between Crassus and Pompey—a rivalry of giants that came perilously close to a full-scale civil war. Pompey had returned from his campaigns in Spain angry at the Senate for its lack of support. He found it convenient not to dismiss his army once back in Italy, citing the continued threat from the slave revolt. He made camp with his battle-hardened forces not far from Rome, then asked the Senate if it wouldn't terribly mind allowing him to run for consul the next year, even though at thirty-five he had never held any offices on the Path of Honors. Pompey also made it clear he would overturn many of the privileges the Senate had enjoyed since Sulla's reign. With Pompey's army breathing down their necks, the senators in desperation turned to Crassus, who also still had his veteran forces on Italian soil. It was an ideal situation for Crassus. If he defeated Pompey, which was quite possible, he could enter Rome as a hero and the optimates of the Senate would hail him as savior of the Republic. But Crassus was a clever businessman who weighed the risk and took a most unexpected path—he joined Pompey. The Senate was left without a defender and watched helplessly as Pompey and Crassus were elected consuls together in 70 B.C..

The two new Roman magistrates acted with surprising cooperation and jointly dismissed both their armies. Their first task was to strip the Senate of its exclusive power to serve on juries deciding corruption cases. The senators were now forced to share their votes on such cases with wealthy businessmen of the second class known as *equites* (knights). This did little to make the Roman court system more just to abused provincials, but it did earn the consuls political capital from rich Romans outside the Senate. Even more important to the common people of Rome was the successful measure introduced by Pompey and Crassus to restore power to the tribunes of the plebs that had been stripped from them a decade earlier by Sulla. The tribunes could once again, for noble or ignoble reasons, impose their veto on any action by the Roman government. Finally, Pompey and Crassus maneuvered two censors to expel over sixty "unworthy" members of the Senate who just happened to be their political adversaries.

Caesar was active at the same time as a great supporter of Pompey and Crassus. This was to be expected as Caesar had positioned himself clearly in the populist rather than optimate camp. He stood firmly behind the consuls in their move to restore power to the plebeian tribunes. Caesar also spoke out in favor of a bill to grant amnesty to all who had previously supported the failed revolution of Lepidus in 78 B.C. This was a matter of political expediency as well as family honor since the exiles included his brother-in-law Lucius Cinna, but it also points to a characteristic that would later distinguish Caesar from his contemporaries—the quality of mercy that the Romans called *clementia,* so evident in future years during his dealings with bitter rivals.

In 69 B.C., Caesar took the second step on the Path of Honors when he was elected as a quaestor. In this role Caesar might have been assigned a tedious job in Rome overseeing the water supply or managing the importation of grain to feed the city, but instead he maneuvered a more advantageous foreign assignment with the propraetor of Further Spain. The election as quaestor also at last gave Caesar a voting membership in the Senate. However, before he could leave for Spain he was struck with grief by the death of the family matriarch, Julia, his beloved aunt and widow of Marius. It was customary to honor an elderly and respected woman like Julia with a suitable funeral oration; since her husband and son were both dead, the duty fell to Caesar. But as Marius was still vilified by the ruling aristocracy, a discreet funeral would have been the prudent course for a rising young senator. Instead, Caesar did something totally unexpected and extremely daring. On the morning of the funeral, Caesar proceeded to the speaker's platform in the Forum accompanied by a procession bearing the images of Marius himself. These were kept in the atrium of a Roman home and customarily borne in funeral marches to celebrate the glorious relatives and ancestors of the deceased. Sulla's laws had strictly forbidden such public displays of Marius's image as was befitting a *persona non grata*. Some in the crowd were outraged at Caesar's actions, but he had shrewdly calculated the effect of the images some fifteen years after the death of Marius. Although the late general and seven-time consul was still considered a murderous tyrant and destroyer of senatorial values by the optimates, the common people held a warm place in their hearts for the man who had saved Rome from the northern barbarians. Old veterans Marius had raised out of the gutters of Rome to serve proudly in the legions wept and cheered as his images passed by. It was as if the departed Marius himself had risen from the dead and was marching once again through the Forum. If there had ever been any doubt as to Caesar's populist allegiance, it was now dispelled in one bold stroke.

Caesar climbed to the top of the rostra and faced the huge crowd gathered below him. In a rousing oration for his aunt Julia bursting with family pride, he reminded senators and commoners alike just who he was:

> *The family of my aunt Julia is descended from kings on her mother's side and, through her father, from the gods themselves. For the Marcii Reges, her mother's family, are heirs of Ancus Marcius, fourth king of Rome, while the Julians, of which our clan is a member, descend from the goddess Venus herself. My family therefore holds the sanctity of kings who rule among men and of gods who rule over kings.*

Far from being put off by this audacious speech, the people of Rome loved Caesar for it. Here was a man who had grown up among them in the slums of the Subura, who was a nephew of their hero Marius, announcing to all the world that he, a descendant of kings and the gods themselves, was on their side. It was obvious to everyone that Caesar was a man of tremendous gifts who could rise high in the government if he could overcome the entrenched optimates. If he could, the common people of Rome knew that they would have a powerful advocate.

Tragedy struck Caesar again soon after his aunt Julia was laid to rest. His young wife Cornelia now suddenly died. He had been married to Cornelia since he was chosen to be the teenage *flamen dialis* by her father and Marius. He had loved her so much he risked his life by defying Sulla so that they might remain together. And from Cornelia was born his only child, his daughter, Julia, who was now about seven years old. Caesar was devastated, but he knew his career depended on leaving Rome to serve as quaestor in Spain. He probably put young Julia in the charge of his own mother, Aurelia, who had already been an important presence in her granddaughter's life and would raise her in his absence as a proper young woman of Rome. But there was one last honor he could perform for Cornelia before he lit the funeral pyre and laid her ashes in the family tomb. Although it was unheard of to do such a thing, Caesar once again mounted the rostra in the Forum to deliver a eulogy. This time there were no images or elaborate ceremony, just a brokenhearted man in mourning who spoke of his childhood bride and his love for her. Eulogies for men and older women were common, but no one had ever delivered a public funeral speech for a young woman. Caesar's words do not survive, but their effect on those gathered in the Forum that morning was profound. Perhaps they were like the moving epitaph later written by a Roman man in Egypt for his departed wife:

> I COMPETED WITH YOU, MY DEAR, IN DEVOTION, VIRTUE,
> FRUGALITY, AND LOVE—BUT I ALWAYS LOST.
> I WISH EVERYONE THE SAME FATE.

Those who heard his speech for his aunt Julia had been struck by his confidence and pride, but the softer words spoken for his wife revealed a man of gentleness and depth of feeling.

Caesar set off at last for the Roman province of Further Spain on the Atlantic coast to serve as quaestor under the governor Antistius Vetus. In this unsettled land bound by the sea on the west and mountains on the east, Caesar was charged with the difficult task of traveling among the native communities to rule on cases and settle disputes. When Caesar arrived in a town, litigants would come to him seeking justice on tax payments, property disputes, and a thousand other problems. Though the job was tedious, it gave Caesar the opportunity to make himself known among the provincials as a man who dealt with them fairly in their disputes with Rome. Even on the edge of the civilized world, it was useful for a Roman politician to establish friendly relations with the natives. The time and effort he invested in Spain would serve him well in the future.

One day when Caesar was hearing cases in the ancient Phoenician city of Gades (modern Cádiz) on the southwestern Spanish coast, he crossed to the nearby island of Cotinussa to visit the temple of Hercules. There Caesar looked out across the vast Atlantic stretching forever to the west. To the Romans, as to the Greeks, Carthaginians, and Phoenicians before them, this was truly the end of the earth. But Caesar—like all educated people in the classical world—knew that the earth was a sphere and that if he could sail far enough west he would come eventually to the fabled land of the Seres or Chinese. As Caesar entered the temple of Hercules, he saw a statue of Alexander the Great, who had died more than two centuries earlier while still in his early thirties. Caesar was now about the same age and lamented that he himself had done nothing noteworthy at an age when Alexander had already conquered all the lands from Greece to India. He left the temple in despair and was troubled even more deeply the following evening when he dreamed that he, like Oedipus, had engaged in sex with his own mother. Not normally a superstitious man, Caesar sought out a local soothsayer who interpreted his disturbing dream in a most favorable light. His mother, said the seer, was in fact the earth itself, so that his dream foretold he would one day rule the world—as Alexander the Great had.

It may have been this restless ambition that led Caesar to leave Spain before his term as quaestor was over and travel back to Rome by way of northern Italy. Here among the rich lands of the Po River valley settled by Celts four hundred years earlier were a number of Roman colonies. All the towns and lands south of the Po had been granted Roman citizenship twenty years earlier, but except for two colonies north of the river, most of the hardworking inhabitants of Cisalpine Gaul (i.e., Gaul "this side of the Alps") north of the Po were not considered fully Roman. It was a situation rife with resentment and potential for armed insurrection, as during the Italian War of the previous generation. Caesar knew this, of course, and decided to further his career as a populist by backing the disgruntled Italians north of the Po. Caesar traveled throughout the area making friends and lending a sympathetic ear to the unhappy townsmen and farmers. In Verona, he probably met the poet Gaius Valerius Catullus who was then a teenager. If Caesar traveled to nearby Mantua, as is likely, he could have met a family riding into town from their nearby farm with a toddler named Publius Vergilius Maro, who would one day be known as Virgil, the greatest of Roman poets. In spite of all the contacts he made, it is unlikely that Caesar truly wanted to foment a violent uprising. Such a revolt would only bring the legions down on the settlers and would not serve his own long-term goals, but he did succeed in establishing himself as a patron of the Celts and Romans of northernmost Italy. This move would again pay enormous dividends in the following decade when he recruited thousands of soldiers from this region for his war in Gaul and his subsequent revolution.

Caesar returned to Rome in 67 B.C. and marked the year by throwing himself wholeheartedly into the social and political life of the capital. It was unusual for a man of Caesar's status to remain single, so he took as a new wife a young woman named Pompeia. She was a remarkable choice for Caesar given that she was a granddaughter of none other than Sulla and a woman whose family on both sides were intimately tied to the optimate cause. It may be that Caesar was hedging his bets by marrying into a family of the political opposition, though he remained a dedicated populist. It could also be that Caesar simply loved Pompeia and that he saw a wonderful irony in marrying the granddaughter of the man who had tried to kill him and whose legacy he was working so hard to destroy.

In the same year Caesar also volunteered for the position of curator of the Appian Way. This most famous and important of Roman roads ran over two hundred miles south from Rome to Capua near Naples, then east across Italy to the port town of Brundisium on the Adriatic. It was a crucial connection between Rome and the rich lands of Campania, but also the main route to the lands of the East. Whenever an army departed for or arrived from Greece, Asia, or Egypt, it almost always went through Brundisium. Like all Roman roads, the Appian Way (*Via Appia*) was a marvel of both engineering and propaganda. Construction began on the roads by digging deeply into the soil to lay a foundation of rock, covering this in turn with gravel for drainage, and finally paving with virtually indestructible flagstones over which commerce rolled and armies marched. Unlike the earlier muddy tracks around much of the Mediterranean, Roman roads were meant to endure and rarely yielded to the vagaries of topography. Unless prevented by impassable mountains or impregnable swamps, the Romans built their roads straight as an arrow across the landscape. They were in fact a sermon in stone to the world—*Romans do not yield*. Two thousand years later, the Appian Way and other Roman roads still survive throughout the former Roman Empire, from Scotland to Syria. Caesar's tenure as curator of this most important Roman road gave him valuable experience in engineering and construction, but it also afforded him the opportunity to work closely with, and develop ties to, many important communities throughout southern Italy. He in fact spent vast amounts of his own borrowed money to ensure that transportation needs of the towns on the road were well served.

Supervising the Appian Way during this year did not keep Caesar from participating in politics at Rome. The numerous failures of the Romans to control the pirate menace in the Mediterranean had finally led to widespread food shortages, rampant kidnapping, and a stifling of trade at sea. The people of Rome were incensed that the Senate had been unable to eliminate piracy, so one of the tribunes of the plebs put forward a bill that would grant an extraordinary commission to a single man to destroy the pirates once and for all. The powers in this proposal were stunning—complete dominion of the entire Mediterranean Sea and inland up to fifty miles along all coasts. In addition, the man chosen would be allowed to select fifteen men from the Senate to help him carry out his plan, requisition two hundred of the best ships available, and draw unlimited funds from the treasury. Although the bill did not mention anyone by name, it was clear to everyone that Pompey was behind the whole affair and expected to be chosen as leader of the war against the pirates. The people of Rome were thrilled at the proposal, but the Senate was understandably horrified. To grant an individual the kind of sweeping power proposed in the bill was to make him a virtual king of Rome's vast domain. It would be a short step for an ambitious man to move from ruler of the seas and coasts to ruler of the entire realm. Even staunch populists in the Senate balked at the idea of Pompey being handed such power. The sole exception was Caesar. Alone among the senators, Caesar rose to speak for the proposal. Perhaps the fact that he had been kidnapped by pirates moved him to speak out, but it was primarily a political calculation. Caesar knew that the bill would fail and that as a minor member of the Senate his voice would carry little weight, but by standing up alone for the bill, he was assured that Pompey and the Roman people would remember him favorably in the future.

The rest of the senators spoke out strongly against the bill, warning Pompey that if he wanted to act like Romulus he would end up sharing the same violent fate as Rome's founder. The Senate soundly rejected the commission, but the bill was then taken directly to the people in assembly. One of the tribunes then issued a veto against the proposal, but withdrew it after the people shouted against the opposition so loudly that, according to legend, a raven flying over the Forum was knocked out of the sky. Pompey gained his commission with even more than he had asked for—he received five hundred ships, twenty-four senators as assistants, and over one hundred thou-

sand soldiers. Pompey was a poor political leader but was in his element in war. He divided the Mediterranean into thirteen districts
and swept the sea from end to end. In forty days, he had methodi-
cally cleared the Mediterranean of piracy. Pompey returned to a
Rome now overflowing with trade goods and was welcomed by the
people as a true hero. The Senate, which had for decades been unable
to act decisively and eliminate the pirates, was of course furious.

Pompey's success against the pirates prompted him to seek even
greater glory. In 66 B.C., a tribune of the plebs, undoubtedly acting
under orders, introduced a bill giving Pompey an almost unlimited
command to settle affairs in the eastern Mediterranean. Rome had
long paid scant attention to the problems posed by threatening or unstable regimes in Asia Minor and Syria, aside from ensuring that the
Senate and knights could squeeze the maximum profit from the region. But now with Mithridates once again stirring up trouble in
Asia Minor and the states of the Near East engaged in endless bickering, Romans were finally ready to force a permanent peace in the
eastern lands.

The optimates of the Senate were firmly opposed to this grand
new commission for Pompey, but they were overwhelmed by the
will of the people, especially the knights who knew that stability in
the East was good for business. Caesar once again spoke out in favor
of the bill, as did Cicero. Pompey easily won the day and took over
the command of the former consul Lucullus, who had been largely
successful against Mithridates, but was unable to bring affairs in Asia
Minor to a satisfactory conclusion. Pompey's ambition, however,
went far beyond merely cleaning up the mess Lucullus had left behind. Pompey led his troops against Mithridates and surrounded the
wily old king near the Armenian border, destroying his entire army.
Mithridates escaped with a few men and fled to the Crimea where he
was reportedly gathering a huge force to march on Italy, but his

grandiose plans were cut short when his son Pharnaces led a rebellion against him. Trapped in a fortress overlooking the Black Sea, the last great enemy of Rome in Asia took his own life.

Pompey, meanwhile, had crossed into Armenia and the Caucasus, conquering mountain tribes and perhaps hoping to open new trade routes to the Far East. He then turned south to the remnants of the Seleucid empire in Syria and to the Nabataean Arabs, a rich kingdom with their capital at rose-red Petra controlling the lucrative spice routes to Yemen and southern Arabia. But before Pompey reached Petra, he was distracted by the feuding Maccabees of Judea and turned aside to Jerusalem. Rome had long supported Judean independence as a counterweight to Syrian power in the region, but a quarrel between two brothers, Hyrcanus and Aristobulus, had plunged the Jewish state into civil war. Both brothers appealed to Pompey, who decided in favor of the weaker and more easily controlled Hyrcanus. Aristobulus reluctantly yielded, but Jewish partisans who resented Rome meddling in their affairs took over the Temple Mount and for three months resisted the legions sent against them. Pompey finally stormed the sacred mountain on the Jewish Sabbath and slaughtered the defiant priests at their altars. The Roman general entered the temple and strode boldly into the forbidden Holy of Holies at its center, though he left the treasures of the Jews untouched.

Over the course of three years, Pompey had conquered new lands and rearranged the whole political geography of the Near East—without the tedious and often futile process of seeking Senate approval. The king of Armenia, Tigranes, was left in charge of his kingdom as a buffer against the mighty Parthian empire of Mesopotamia. The old Seleucid state was broken up and Syria established as a Roman province. The Jewish kingdom was left nominally independent, but reduced to little more than the area around Jerusalem plus Galilee and a few nearby territories. With a minimum cost to the treasury, Pompey had brought peace to the eastern

Mediterranean for the first time in centuries and gained huge riches for Rome as well as himself. The lesson was not lost on Caesar. Freed from interference by the Senate, a capable general could accomplish magnificent deeds that would assure his status at Rome and place in history, in addition to making him fabulously wealthy.

Caesar was not idle while Pompey was in the East. As a patrician, he could never serve as a tribune of the plebs, so he took the alternate step on the Path of Honors when he was elected as an aedile for the year 65 B.C. The aediles served as curators of Rome for a year, handling everything from street repairs and temple maintenance to urban crime, but the position was attractive to aspiring politicians because aediles also managed the public festivals. Two aediles organized a weeklong celebration in honor of the great mother goddess Cybele in April and fifteen days of festivities for Jupiter in September. In addition to state money, an aedile hoping to impress the common people and gain electoral advantages in the future was expected to spend lavishly from his own pocket. In this Caesar outdid anyone before him, though all on borrowed money. He decorated the whole Forum as well as the nearby Capitoline Hill, hosting public banquets, wild beast contests, and stage productions for all of Rome. One of Caesar's colleagues as aedile was Marcus Calpurnius Bibulus, a sworn optimate who would be a thorn in Caesar's side for years to come. Bibulus later complained that everything he accomplished as an aedile was overshadowed by Caesar, who claimed credit for the deeds of both of them.

Caesar further eclipsed Bibulus when, in addition to the two required festivals, he sponsored gladiatorial games of unprecedented splendor in honor of his late father. No fewer than 320 pairs of top-rank gladiators were shipped in by Caesar, causing not a few Romans to worry about an uprising by some latter-day Spartacus. But as always, Caesar was in firm control of events.

He had, however, developed a taste for the finer things in life so

long denied him in the poverty-stricken Subura. Caesar became an
avid collector of fine art with exquisite and extravagant taste in jew-
elry, sculpture, and paintings. His sense of perfection coupled with
his extravagance led him to build an expensive country house at
Lake Nemi in the Roman countryside only to tear it down when it
failed to meet his exacting standards. The debts that Caesar was in-
curring both as an aedile and in his private life were staggering.

Caesar's masterstroke of publicity during his year as an aedile
was accomplished in a single night. Four years earlier during his
aunt Julia's funeral, he had paraded the family images of Marius
through the streets, much to the chagrin of the optimates in the Senate. Now he had more elaborate displays of Marius constructed and
collected the dazzling trophies of Marius's victories over the Germans that had been banned by Sulla. With his followers, Caesar secretly carried all these forbidden objects to the Capitoline Hill under
the cover of darkness and set them up outside the half-finished temple of Jupiter. When the sun rose the next morning, all of Rome
could see the trophies of Marius glittering above the Forum. Word
spread throughout the city and crowds gathered on the Capitoline to
marvel at both the brilliant display and the audacity of Caesar. The
optimates were aghast and cried out that Caesar was putting himself
above the law by setting up forbidden objects in public. But the common people who loved Marius now wept and cheered for his
nephew, filling Rome with their shouts and applause. The Senate
held an emergency meeting, which Caesar attended, and the upstart
aedile was denounced by Lutatius Catulus, the optimate leader:
"This Caesar is no longer trying to undermine the Republic secretly,
but is now attacking the state openly with machines of war."

Caesar rose to answer and calmly explained to the Senate that his
intentions were not threatening to the state at all. Though his speech
to them is now lost, it must have been a masterwork of oratory since
the hostile Senate, even the optimates, were convinced of his noble
intentions. Caesar's supporters in the Forum were thrilled at these

events and urged him never to give in to the opposition in the Senate. Even though he was a mere aedile only thirty-five years old, the populists now began to see in him someone who could become the most important man in Rome.

Some ancient sources, however, suggest that the optimates may have been right to fear Caesar. The biographer Suetonius mentions a plot against the state while Caesar was serving as an aedile that promised a bloody end to the Senate's rule. Suetonius records that Publius Autronius and Publius Sulla, the two consuls who had been elected for 65 B.C., were disqualified from service before taking office because of corruption charges. In their place, Lucius Torquatus and Caesar's cousin Lucius Cotta were chosen to serve as consuls. The original consuls determined to have their revenge by murdering Torquatus and Cotta at their inauguration, then handing power to the millionaire Marcus Crassus as dictator. Crassus would supposedly then reorganize the government and return power to Autronius and Publius Sulla. The chief assistant of the dictator Crassus was to be none other than Caesar. Suetonius says the plot fell through when Crassus lost his nerve at the last minute and Caesar failed to let his toga fall off his shoulder, the pre-arranged signal for the slaughter to begin.

But there are several good reasons for thinking that Caesar was not involved in this conspiracy, if it happened at all. First, the sources that Suetonius gives for his information on the plot include the plodding anti-Caesarian historian Tanusius Geminus as well as Caesar's persistent rival and fellow aedile Marcus Bibulus. Second, Cicero, who rarely missed a chance to condemn Caesar in his later years, never claimed that he was involved. Third, Caesar was capable of bold action, but he is unlikely to have been involved in a poorly planned insurrection that included murdering his own cousin. Caesar would one day defy the Senate and lead Rome into civil war, but everything we know about his nature argues against bloody revolts and conspiracy theories. Caesar had for years been carefully, step by step, building his credentials as a proven military leader and sensible populist politician. Even though his enemies would naturally look back at his career in later years and accuse him of revolutionary plans from the cradle, Caesar was not the kind of man who would unnecessarily risk his career by supporting a violent coup d'état.

A much more believable plan for increasing the power of both Crassus and Caesar at this time centered on the ancient kingdom of Egypt. Crassus had been nursing a grudge against Pompey since the younger man had stolen the glory of his victory over Spartacus. Even though the two had made peace and worked well together as consuls in 70 B.C., Crassus had watched impotently as Pompey was lauded by the Roman people for sweeping the Mediterranean of pirates, defeating Mithridates, and conquering the Near East. Crassus realized that in spite of his own vast riches, he needed a spectacular prize to offer Rome if he were ever to equal Pompey in the eyes of the Senate and common people. Crassus saw a golden opportunity in Egypt, the one kingdom of the eastern Mediterranean that Pompey had left untouched. Rome had long meddled in Egyptian affairs, but the land of the Nile still remained independent—and immensely wealthy.

Egypt in the first century B.C. was a far cry from the mighty civilization it had been in earlier ages. The glorious early dynasties of the third millennium B.C. had built the pyramids and Sphinx, while the second millennium saw an Egyptian empire stretching from the Euphrates to Nubia under kings such as Rameses II. In following centuries, however, internal decline and foreign rule weakened Egypt until it was seized by Alexander the Great in the fourth century B.C. After his death, Alexander's general Ptolemy took over the Nile valley and established a family dynasty of Greek rulers of Egypt—each bearing the name Ptolemy—ruling from the cosmopolitan city of Alexandria on Egypt's Mediterranean coast. In 80 B.C., Ptolemy XI died, leaving his kingdom to Rome, though the Senate could never agree on whether or how Egypt should be annexed. The Egyptians had maintained their shaky independence since then, though the Alexandrians despised their new king Ptolemy XII (nicknamed Auletes, "flute player") for being too friendly to Rome.

Crassus now proposed that Rome at last make Egypt a proper Roman province. It was a reasonable proposal given that Rome had a legal claim to the kingdom through the will of Ptolemy XI, and that annexation would mean a considerable influx of gold into the treasury. Crassus wanted to send Caesar to Egypt to handle the details of the takeover, a plan that Caesar wholeheartedly supported. Such a commission could give Caesar enormous popular standing in Rome as well as erasing all his debts. But the Senate quite reasonably concluded that, as much as they disliked Pompey, allowing Crassus control over Egypt would make him far too powerful. The optimates also opposed any move that would increase Caesar's growing influence in Rome. The bill was soundly defeated when presented to the people because of maneuvering by the optimates and by the well-spoken opposition of Cicero, who was carefully defending the interests of his patron Pompey.

The year 64 B.C. dawned with Pompey still in the eastern Mediterranean, Crassus in Rome counting his money, and Caesar quietly planning his next move up the Roman political ladder. But the one man in Rome most ready to seize the day was Marcus Porcius Cato, five years Caesar's junior, who had just been elected as a quaestor. Caesar's quaestorship in 69 B.C. had been spent in Spain, but Cato's assignment was to manage the treasury in Rome. Previous quaestors had served in this capacity in a loose supervisory role. They were content to let the professional clerks manage the day-to-day paperwork and dull duties of revenue and expenditures, occasionally popping in for a cursory inspection or friendly chat with the treasury supervisor. Cato, however, was not a typical quaestor. A remarkable man of discipline and duty, as well as a sincere student of Stoic philosophy, Cato had spent the weeks since his election carefully studying the minute details of treasury management.

When Cato arrived at the treasury at the start of his term, the clerks and bureaucrats expected just another young Roman politician who had little real interest in the position and who would leave them alone to carry out their dull jobs while skimming state funds as before. But Cato entered the doors of the treasury on the Capitoline Hill like a mighty storm. He immediately put a stop to corruption and mercilessly lectured the clerks on their improper procedures and sloppy bookkeeping. For the lax civil servants of the treasury, Cato's quaestorship was a nightmare. They appealed to the other quaestors to curb their relentless colleague, but no one could stand up to the righteous fury of Cato. The new quaestor soon spread his crusade beyond the treasury walls when he discovered that many of the Roman nobility owed money to the state that they had somehow forgotten to pay. Cato brought them up on charges without regard for their political standing. He even dug up the records on those who had received blood money during the proscriptions of Sulla almost twenty years earlier and charged these men, on somewhat dubious legal grounds, with murder. The courts designated to handle such cases overflowed with defendants, so special judges were appointed from among ex-aediles, including Caesar, to hear testimony. No respectable member of the Senate admired Sulla's murderous old henchmen living out their comfortable retirement on blood money, but none before Cato had dared to charge them. Throughout the long and painful year of the trials, the ghosts of the past were exorcised. Caesar, who had little reason to love Cato, could only approve of the quaestor's decisive actions.

III

CONSPIRACY

> Catiline planned to ignore the laws of Rome, over-
> throw the government, and unleash chaos everywhere.
> — PLUTARCH

Good news arrived the next year when Caesar's niece Atia gave birth to a baby boy named Octavius, the future emperor Augustus, but events outside the family marked 63 B.C. as the most eventful and formative time in Caesar's early political career. For ten years Caesar had served as a *pontifex* (priest) supervising religious affairs of the Roman state, but he was only one of a dozen or more minor religious officials in the college of the pontiffs. The most important priest in Rome was the *pontifex maximus,* who led the pontiffs, supervised the Vestal Virgins, and published the decrees governing religious life that had the force of law. The pontifex maximus also acted as spokesman for the pontiffs before the Senate. The chief pontiff lived in an official state residence, called the Domus Publica, and had his office in the Forum at the Regia. This ancient building, across from the temple of the Vestals, held the archives of the pontifex maximus and many sacred objects of great antiquity. The pontifex maximus at the start of 63 B.C. was Quintus Metellus Pius, a distinguished old gentleman who had been one of Sulla's chief supporters. When

Metellus died that year it was expected that a senior statesman of impeccable standing would be chosen for the office as custom had long dictated. The two candidates for the job, Quintus Lutatius Catulus and Publius Servilius Isauricus, both fit this description perfectly. Caesar knew both men well, Catulus having condemned him when he set up the trophies of Marius on the Capitoline two years earlier and Isauricus as a former commander in Asia Minor.

But in one of the most risky moves in a lifetime of unconventional choices, Caesar declared himself a candidate for the office of pontifex maximus. Caesar was only in his thirties and the highest office he had held up to this point was as a lowly aedile. For him to have the temerity to run against two of the most respected members of the Senate for the exalted position of pontifex maximus was bold beyond belief. And yet, Caesar was anything but a fool. He must have carefully surveyed the Roman political scene at this moment, weighed his options, and decided that the gamble was worth the price. Already deeply in debt, Caesar borrowed even more money to lavish bribes on the electors who would choose the chief priest. Only seventeen of the Roman tribes voted for the pontifex maximus and of these Caesar needed a simple majority of nine to win. Since the election was weighted in favor of the urban tribes, he could focus his payments on a relatively small group of voters. Bribery such as this was technically legal and acceptable in practice as long as one wasn't caught passing money—and Caesar was nothing if not discreet. Through his supporters and agents, he managed to grease the palms of enough voters so that his rival Lutatius Catulus began to seriously worry. The elder senator knew of Caesar's desperate financial situation and offered a substantial sum to the young candidate if he would withdraw from the race. Caesar responded by stretching his credit to the absolute limit and borrowing even more money for bribes. On the morning of the election, Caesar's mother, Aurelia, was in tears because she understood the situation her son had put himself in. If he lost the election, his creditors would force him into financial ruin and his political future would be destroyed. As he left their house in the Subura, he kissed her and said in all seriousness: "Mother, today you will see your son as pontifex maximus—or as a fugitive."

As the votes came in, Caesar outpolled the other two candidates by large margins, even in their home districts. At the end of the day, Caesar indeed returned home as pontifex maximus. Soon he moved his mother and daughter, together with servants and thirty-seven years of memories, from their small house in the Subura to the Domus Publica in the center of Rome. Caesar's gamble had paid off. Risking everything, he had let the dice fly high and was now positioned as a leader in Roman politics.

▣

Caesar's success in attaining the high priesthood of Rome did not deter his legislative and legal career. One of Caesar's most useful allies in further tearing down the optimate system that Sulla and his followers had so carefully constructed was a tribune of the plebs named Titus Labienus. Like Pompey, Labienus hailed from the rough Picene region along Italy's Adriatic coast and was an ardent supporter of the absent general while he was still settling affairs in the eastern Mediterranean. Labienus was the same age as Caesar and had served with him briefly in Cilicia as a young officer fifteen years earlier, fighting the pirates under Isauricus. Labienus had already worked with Caesar to change the rules for his election as pontifex maximus, allowing the chief priest to be chosen by popular vote rather than by insider selection within the college itself as Sulla had arranged. Now the two cooperated closely on other schemes to wrest power from the privileged world of the Senate. Reform, however, was a risky business. The popular Gracchi brothers, respected members of the nobility, had both been killed late in the previous century while trying to change the power structure at Rome. The same fate could easily await Caesar.

Crassus and his followers had recently introduced a bill on agricultural reform and land distribution, but this bill had little support and was doomed to failure by Cicero's stinging oratory. Then Caesar and Labienus struck the optimates in a most unexpected way. They brought charges of high treason against an aged backbench senator and optimate named Gaius Rabirius. In the year that Caesar was born, Rabirius had participated in the killing of a rebellious tribune of the plebs named Saturninus. The Senate had at that time issued a decree reluctantly authorizing Marius to restore order to the state by any means necessary. Marius imprisoned Saturninus and his followers on the Capitoline Hill, but before the Senate could decide their fate, a mob including Rabirius broke in and slew Saturninus. Neither Marius nor the Senate had raised any objections to this quick delivery of justice at the time and indeed had supported Rabirius. Now almost forty years later, Caesar and Labienus charged Rabirius with the murder of a sacrosanct plebeian tribune. Neither really cared what Rabirius had done to Saturninus long ago—their action was instead meant as a direct challenge to the Senate and its power to issue decrees that permitted the condemnation of Roman citizens without due process.

To avoid a drawn-out court case they might well lose, Caesar and Labienus resorted to an archaic form of trial conducted by only two judges, one of the two being chosen by lot to pronounce the sentence. Such a court proceeding was long outdated, but as the Romans fiercely respected tradition they rarely rejected any custom no matter how antiquated. By no coincidence, Caesar was selected as one of the two judges and as the man who would determine the sentence. Rabirius was of course found guilty, after which Caesar sentenced the old man to be crucified on the Field of Mars outside the walls of Rome. Fortunately for Rabirius, this ancient form of judgment allowed an appeal directly to the Centuriate Assembly, which was promptly done. The lower-class Romans who made up the bulk of the assembly were angry enough at the optimates to confirm the death sentence against Rabirius, but Metellus Celer, one of the aged senator's defenders, then remembered another archaic custom. Since the Centuriate Assembly was military in origin, there was an arcane rule that a flag had to fly during meetings from Janiculum Hill on the west of the city to signal that the Samnites, Etruscans, or other enemies long since subdued were not about to attack. Metellus ran all the way to the Janiculum and pulled down the flag, thereby preventing a lawful vote. The assembly was then adjourned and Rabirius was saved from the cross. Rabirius was tried again in a more standard fashion before a tribune, but with Cicero as his defense attorney he was acquitted. Caesar and Labienus, however, had made their point. The Senate was now on notice to take care in issuing sweeping decrees that violated the rights of citizens. Even though Caesar had not really wanted Rabirius dead—he may, in fact, have encouraged the lowering of the Janiculum flag—he had played a cruel game with an old man's life to curry favor with the common people.

The trial against Rabirius was just one of Caesar's legal actions during 63 B.C. as he also continued his traditional role as a gifted defender of the oppressed provincials against the rapacious Senate. Around this time Caesar acted as prosecutor of his old foe Marcus Juncus, the man who as governor of Roman Asia had tried to sell Caesar's captured pirates for his own profit. The Bithynians, like the Macedonians before them, had suffered ill at the hands of the Roman administration and now sought out Caesar to plead their case. Given the eagerness of his political enemies to raise the issue of his supposed illicit affair with the late Bithynian King Nicomedes at every opportunity, it was courageous of Caesar to hand his foes an occasion to dredge up old accusations once again. But to Caesar, it was a matter of honor. As he himself said at the trial:

> *Because of my friendship with King Nicomedes and with those who are bringing this case against you, Marcus Juncus, I could not refuse to take up this cause. For those closest to a man ought not to allow his death to end their loyalty to him. Just so, it would be a*

*disgrace for us to abandon our friends in need even if they have
been wronged by our own families.*

Caesar also offered his services as prosecutor of the optimate
Gaius Calpurnius Piso for unjustly executing a Gaul during his governorship in northern Italy, then served as defender of an ill-treated
Numidian nobleman named Masintha. During his speech in favor of
Masintha, Caesar grew so animated that he even grabbed the beard
of the Numidian prince Juba who was at the trial to oppose Masintha
and represent the interests of his father. Caesar lost the case, but hid
the convicted Numidian in his own house for two years until he
could secretly smuggle him out in a covered litter and spirit him
away to Spain. Prince Juba, who never forgot the indignity of having
his facial hair grabbed in public, became an implacable enemy of
Caesar.

The year 63 B.C. also marked the rise of Cicero, one of Caesar's
most brilliant foes, to the highest office in Rome. This man from a
small hill town south of Rome had fought his way to the top of the
Senate in spite of incredible odds, using the sheer power of his intel-
lect along with his famously golden tongue. Cicero was no military
hero like Marius or Pompey, nor did he have the patrician ancestry of
Sulla or the vast wealth of Crassus, but when he rose to speak in the
Forum, all of Rome stopped to listen. In an age of outstanding orators, Cicero was the very best. But even with these talents, it is unlikely Cicero ever would have risen above a midlevel magistracy
except for the fortuitous threat posed by a nobleman named Catiline.

Catiline, like Caesar, was from an ancient patrician family that
had fallen on hard times in recent years. Catiline had served together
with Cicero and Pompey under Pompey's father during the Italian
War. He had also been an ardent supporter of Sulla and an enthusiastic participant in the bloody proscriptions that rocked Rome, but
we hear little of him again until he served as a governor in Africa after his praetorship in 68 B.C. He tried to run for consul in 66, but a

lingering charge of corruption from his term in Africa rendered him ineligible. He reportedly conspired to murder the newly elected consuls that year in revenge, but there was little hard evidence against him. Backed by Crassus, Catiline made another run for the consulship of 63 B.C., the same year that Cicero declared his own candidacy for the office. Most of the nobility considered Cicero a superb orator and competent administrator, but to promote a new man from an obscure country family to the consulship was like inviting one's horse home to dinner. Catiline gained the backing of many senators, including Caesar and Crassus, who preferred a noble of middling competence who could at least be easily controlled. Cicero, however, began a whispering campaign against Catiline that played up his rival's revolutionary tendencies, provoking just enough concern among the senators to overcome their snobbish dispositions and allow Cicero to win the race.

Catiline did not give up easily. During Cicero's consulship in 63, Catiline once again presented himself as a candidate to serve as consul in the following year. His platform this time was a general cancellation of debts—a radical notion that had great appeal to struggling farmers and senators stretched beyond their means, like Caesar, but anathema to the powerful creditors among the equestrian class, like Crassus. For the second time, Cicero raised the specter of Catiline as an unstable and dangerous threat to traditional Roman order and succeeded yet again in forcing his defeat at the polls. Catiline's patience for the political process was now at an end. He began to plot a genuine revolution that would overthrow the state and murder his opponents, chief among them Cicero.

Catiline's plan was to gather his forces among the disgruntled poor and restless nobility, then march on Rome in late October of 63. Once there, he would set fire to the city, kill his enemies, and establish himself as ruler while Cicero's head looked on mutely from a pike in the Forum. But Catiline had misjudged the mood of Rome. Even though there were many unhappy citizens among the different classes, few yearned for a return to the bloody days of Sulla. Crassus, whose paid informants prowled every palace and street of Rome, quickly heard about the plot and passed on incriminating information to Cicero in an anonymous letter. Cicero rushed to the Senate and persuaded them to declare a state of emergency. A guard was organized to man the city walls against any sign of approaching revolutionary armies, but as Cicero lacked solid evidence, Catiline continued to wander Rome freely and attend Senate meetings. Some among the Roman leaders began to think that Cicero was greatly exaggerating the whole affair in a bid to increase his own standing and establish a legacy as defender of the Roman state. Catiline bided his time for a few days apparently innocent as a lamb, but then secretly issued new orders to his followers that called for simultaneous uprisings throughout Italy. These would distract the Senate so that he could lead his army against the city.

Cicero heard of these new plans almost immediately and turned to his skill as an orator to win his case. With Catiline present, Cicero carefully laid out the plot to the Senate, then turned to the conspirator himself:

> O Catiline, for the safety of the Republic, for your own detriment and destruction, for the ruin of those who have joined themselves to your evil plans—Get out! Go to your wicked and impious war!

Catiline listened unperturbed to Cicero's invective. The Senate was concerned, but still unconvinced by the consul's accusations. Utterly frustrated at the inability of the senators to see danger staring them in the face, Cicero retired for the night. But by the next day, Catiline had vanished and soon reappeared among his troops in Etruria, just north of Rome.

Catiline's fellow conspirators inside Rome were not as careful as their leader. They contacted a delegation from the Celtic Allobroges tribe in Gaul, who were visiting Rome at the time. The warlike Allobroges had been thoroughly defeated by Rome sixty years before and since that time their tribal lands southwest of Lake Geneva had been the northernmost part of the Roman province of Mediterranean Gaul. Like most provincials, they were burdened with heavy taxes and debts to Rome, which they could not pay. The conspirators thought they would make perfect allies in a revolt against Rome and so listened sympathetically to their complaints against Rome, then at last revealed Catiline's plan for a revolution. The Allobroges were certainly tempted. If Catiline won, they could be rid of their debts and gain valuable booty serving in a Roman civil war. But instead, the Gauls weighed the odds of success and decided instead to pass on their new information to Cicero. The consul arrested the leading conspirators in Rome and called an emergency meeting of the Senate. Finally, in early December, even the most reluctant senators acknowledged that Catiline and his band of malcontents were indeed planning to overthrow the Roman state. The conspirators were entrusted to senators, including one to Caesar, so that they might guard them in their own homes.

Cicero finally began to receive the praise he had so long craved from the Senate. At the next Senate meeting held to decide the fate of the arrested conspirators, he blushed at the accolades heaped upon him for preserving the Roman state. In the general fervor against the revolutionaries, some of the optimates decided it would be a good time to clean house by implicating other populist leaders in the uprising. A witness came forward claiming that Crassus and Caesar had been in touch with Catiline and had been planning to use their populist influence on his behalf. It was a transparent attempt to sully the optimates' leading opponents with the stench of Catiline's revolution. Caesar was no more likely at this point to support a violent overthrow of the government than he had been in the past, while the last thing Crassus wanted was a cancellation of all the debts owed to him. Cicero too, in spite of his natural enmity to Caesar and Crassus, saw things rapidly getting out of hand. Even if he thought Caesar might have been involved with Catiline, he did not want the Senate to waste time on distracting witch hunts. The leading conspirators were in his hands and ready for punishment. If he could see justice done to them quickly, his place in Roman history would be secured, and there would be no more whispers from senators wondering if the new man was really up to the job of leading Rome. Cicero managed to have the accusations against Crassus and Caesar dismissed, instead calling the Senate to a debate regarding the punishment of the arrested conspirators.

Cicero wanted Catiline's henchmen executed immediately, but the situation was a delicate one for the consul. As Caesar and Labienus had recently shown in the case of Rabirius, the Roman people had no patience for leaders who condoned the killing of citizens under questionable legal circumstances. The conspirators were under arrest and posed no immediate threat to Rome, so exile or some other harsh punishment short of death could be a reasonable alternative. Therefore Cicero had to be absolutely sure he had the Senate firmly on his side before ordering any executions. He even had the Senate proceedings recorded in shorthand and distributed publicly so that everyone in Rome would know he had acted with the full backing of Rome's leaders. Cicero opened the debate by summarizing the situation, then turned to the most senior senators for their opinions. All of these, including the consul-elect Decimus Silanus, outdid each other in calling for the harshest possible penalty (*ultima poena*), which everyone clearly understood to be immediate execution. When the senior magistrates had finished speaking, it was at last Caesar's turn.

Caesar began what all considered a masterful speech by reminding the senators that decisions made in anger are often faulty. He pointed out instances in the past when the Senate had wisely acted with prudence rather than passion, thereby strengthening their position and the whole state. Caesar accepted that the conspirators were guilty and had absolutely no sympathy for any man who would overthrow Rome: "As I see it, Senators, there is no punishment too harsh for these men."

But he emphasized what mattered the most in this situation was how the actions of the Senate would be judged by the common people and posterity:

The problem is that people only remember what happens last. Thoughtless men will consider not the evil deeds these criminals have committed but instead the punishment they have received from us—if that punishment is unusually harsh.

Caesar praised the magistrates who had spoken before him for their spirited condemnation of the conspirators, but he reminded them that death was really no punishment in itself, just an end of suffering. He raised the dubious legal grounds for condemning Roman citizens to death without a full trial. Exile, he pointed out, and similarly severe punishments had long been an option in Roman law. Consider, he urged them, that you could be establishing an important precedent here today. Consuls such as Cicero, he continued, and men such as yourselves would never abuse power, but a future tyrant may arise, as did Sulla in the past, who could twist today's actions to suit his own evil purposes. Caesar then recommended that the conspirators be sent to various Italian cities, which would imprison them the rest of their lives. Their property would be confiscated and it would be forbidden for any senator ever to suggest they be released.

The senators were deeply impressed by Caesar's words. This man who had not yet even served as a praetor had presented an impeccable argument for clemency for the conspirators. The Senate realized that his warning about the reaction of the common people was very perceptive. As much as the majority of the Senate couldn't care less what the man in the street thought of them or their actions, the senators knew they could be provoking a full-scale riot by ordering the execution of the conspirators without trial. They also remembered that Catiline and his army were as yet at large just north of Rome. A mutinous city mob joined with a radical populist and his soldiers could form an irresistible force that would destroy the Senate's power.

Silanus, who earlier in the debate had called for the ultimate penalty, now back-tracked and claimed that he actually meant what Caesar had proposed, lifelong exile. Other senior magistrates, including Cicero's brother, Quintus, agreed that Caesar's proposal was an excellent idea. The Senate seemed poised to vote in favor of exile when Cato rose to speak. If the Roman gods had deliberately fashioned an opponent to rival Caesar in brilliance, daring, and tenacity, it would have been Cato. He began his speech by berating Silanus, who was his brother-in-law, for bending like a reed in the wind, but saved his harshest words for Caesar himself. Cato claimed Caesar was in fact trying to destroy the Roman state under a pretense of mercy. Caesar, he alleged, was simply trying to spare the members of a conspiracy in which he was a likely participant. He chastised the weak-willed senators for giving in to such blatant manipulation and showing any compassion for the conspirators. Clemency was exactly the wrong message to send to Catiline and his gathering army:

The more harsh the punishment you give, the less will be their courage. If they see even a hint of weakness on your part, they will descend on us ferociously.

Cato urged that the conspirators be executed immediately and their property handed over to the state.

At this point in Cato's fiery speech, someone brought in a message from outside the chamber and quietly slipped it to Caesar. Cato jumped on this as proof that Caesar was receiving secret information from Catiline and demanded that Caesar read the note to the whole Senate. An uproar ensued, but instead of reading the message aloud to all, Caesar calmly handed the note to Cato. It was, in fact, a love letter to Caesar from Servilia, a married woman with whom he was engaged in a heated affair. Servilia was none other than Cato's own stepsister and wife of the inconstant Silanus. (She was also the mother of young Brutus, Caesar's future murderer.) Cato read the note with increasing embarrassment, then threw it at Caesar in disgust and continued his speech.

In spite of the awkward interruption, Cato's oratory had its desired effect. Cicero now wanted to put the proposals of Caesar and Cato to a vote, but Caesar tried to salvage his cause by suggesting a compromise. There was such an angry uproar against him that the knights who had been called to guard the session rushed in waving their swords at Caesar, assuming he was a danger to the senators. Cicero rescued Caesar from this debacle and had him escorted out of the chamber for his own safety. The last thing Cicero wanted was to have Caesar slain under his watch during a Senate meeting. The Senate then voted to execute the conspirators without delay.

There was no appeal for the ragged group of conspirators as they were led one by one to their place of execution in the Forum. This ancient building, called the Tullianum, was probably an old wellhouse built over a spring. It was a circular structure with a hole going down to a small, dark, underground room with a hideous stench of death. Each conspirator was forced one by one down the hole into the dank chamber where a *carnifex* (executioner) was waiting to strangle them. When they were all dead, Cicero spoke the required words—*"They have lived"*—to those assembled around the Tullianum.

In the aftermath of the executions, Caesar stayed away from Senate meetings for the rest of the year. In keeping a low profile, he was saving his political capital for another day rather than becoming bogged down in petty quibbles with the optimates. Caesar was instead busy preparing for his upcoming term as praetor, the next step on the Path of Honors, to which he had been elected earlier in the year. Catiline and his army, just as Cato had predicted, quickly lost heart and tried hopelessly to fight their way to safety outside of Italy. He and his dwindling forces were cut down as they tried to flee across the Apennine Mountains. The Senate conferred on a joyful Cicero the title of *pater patriae* ("father of his country"), an honor that he would bear with pride for the rest of his life. But to Cicero's dismay, when the newly elected tribunes for the next year took office in December, some from their ranks began to rail against the Senate for the executions of the conspirators as unconstitutional, just as Caesar had foreseen (and now, perhaps, had helped to arrange). The common people were furious at Cicero and the senators for their actions, though well disposed to Caesar as a champion of their rights. Accordingly, the populist party decided to punish Cicero with one final insult. When the proud consul on the last day of his term rose to make his triumphal valedictory speech before laying down his office, a tribune of the plebs named Metellus Nepos interposed his veto and forbade Cicero to say a another word. The deeply frustrated Cicero was allowed to make only a customary short declaration that he had fulfilled his duties honorably—though he added quickly at the end of his oath that he had, in fact, saved the city from ruin.

Caesar returned to the public arena with a vengeance on his very first day as praetor. The temple of Jupiter on the Capitoline Hill overlooking the Forum had burned down in 83 B.C., but there had been no serious effort to rebuild it until Caesar's old nemesis Lutatius Catulus had been given the job in 78. Even then, Catulus had only partially restored the central temple of Rome by 62 when Caesar took office. Acting both in his role as high priest of Rome and as a newly elected praetor, Caesar called an assembly of the people in the Forum on the first morning of his term. The senators at this very moment were above the Forum on the hill of the Capitol celebrating the inauguration of the new consuls for the year. When they looked down, they could see a great crowd gathering below with Caesar on the speaker's platform. The new praetor addressed the people and lamented the fact that after fourteen years and plentiful funds from the public treasury, Lutatius Catulus had still not managed to rebuild the centerpiece of Roman piety and power. There were then dark hints of state money finding its way into Catulus's own pockets. Caesar proposed that the commission for finishing the temple of Jupiter be given to Pompey, soon to return from the East, a man who had shown he could get things done, unlike the self-serving, foot-dragging, nose-in-the-air optimates of the Senate. The people roared their approval. All the senators rushed down from the hill, Catulus demanding that he be allowed to address the crowd. Caesar granted the senior statesman this privilege, but deliberately insulted him by not letting him mount the speaker's platform. Caesar had not forgiven Catulus for condemning him concerning the display of Marius's images three years earlier and for opposing him during the debate on Catiline. When Caesar saw the Senate's followers would soon break up the meeting with violence, he dismissed the assembly—but his point was made. Caesar the praetor, who now held the ultimate Roman power of *imperium* that allowed him to use force if necessary, was putting the optimates on notice that he was a man to be reckoned with.

Caesar continued his attack on the optimates early in his year as praetor by wholeheartedly supporting the agenda of the newly elected tribune Metellus Nepos. Pompey had bought and paid for Nepos to serve as his agent in Rome in preparation for his return from the East later in the year. When Catiline and his army were still at large that winter, Nepos had proposed that the conqueror of Asia be given a broad commission to destroy the conspirators and restore order to Italy. The Senate had been down this path with Pompey before and decided it was finally time to bring the upstart Picene general to heel. It was a dangerous gamble, since Pompey had a massive army at his back and could, if he wished, simply march into Rome and declare himself dictator. But Cato and his optimate supporters had dealt with Pompey long enough to take the measure of the man. Pompey wanted glory, respect, and recognition as the greatest general in Roman history, but, unlike Marius or Sulla, he had not shown any signs of desiring to rule Rome as a bloody tyrant.

The morning Nepos brought his bill for a vote before the people, Cato marched to the Forum only to find Nepos and Caesar sitting on the platform of the temple of Castor and Pollux, surrounded by a large gang of ruffians and off-duty gladiators. Other tribunes would have taken the hint and retired quietly to the back of the crowd, but Cato, along with his friend and fellow tribune Minucius Thermus, pushed his way through the mob, then taunted Caesar by asking loudly if all the guards were there just to keep him away. Even the populist crowd loved Cato's boldness and shouted to him not to back down. For one of the few times in his life, Caesar was unnerved, having lost control of a situation he himself had carefully staged. Cato threw himself into a seat right between Caesar and Nepos, while the delighted crowd waited for what would happen next.

Nepos motioned to his clerk to read the bill aloud, but just as he started, Cato stood up and in a ringing voice bellowed, *"Veto!"* The clerk stopped, unsure of how to proceed, so that Nepos took the bill to read it to the assembled people himself. Cato tore it out of his hands. Nepos then began to recite the bill from memory when Thermus shoved his hand over his mouth to prevent him speaking. Nepos finally signaled his bully boys standing around the temple to intervene. The gladiators and small-time thugs came running with their swords and cudgels swinging, shouts and screams filled the air, and everyone, including Caesar, quickly withdrew—except for Cato. The obstinate tribune stood his ground until a senator named Murena, whom Cato had earlier charged with bribery, came to his defense and wrapped his toga around the battered tribune, leading him to safety inside the nearby temple.

Caesar and Nepos had overplayed their hand. As the swelling mob in the Forum grew out of control and violence descended into urban chaos, the Senate met and conferred power on the consuls to restore order to the city by any means necessary. Nepos fled the city to join Pompey, and Caesar, realizing he had foolishly let a populist rally turn into pointless riot, took off his praetor's robes, dismissed the lictors guarding him, and retired to his home. But Caesar had an uncanny talent for turning a bad situation to his advantage. The next day, when an unruly mob of populists appeared at his door in the Forum shouting that they were ready to march against the Senate and restore him to his office as praetor, Caesar calmly said they were to do no such thing and dispersed them without incident. The Senate was so grateful for his prudence in not provoking an insurrection that they brought him immediately to their meeting place and heaped endless praise on him. They even withdrew their emergency decree and begged Caesar to take up his office as praetor again, to which he graciously agreed. Cato, his bruises still aching, must have marveled that only Caesar could have nearly burned Rome to the ground and still received the Senate's adulation.

After his acceptance back into the good graces of the Senate, Caesar was content to spend the remainder of his year as praetor quietly carrying out his duties in Rome and avoiding controversy. But events in both his public and private life soon thrust Caesar back into the limelight. After Catiline and his forces had been defeated on the battlefield, the surviving conspirators were hunted down and brought before a special investigator appointed for the task, named Novius Niger. A former Catilinian, the knight Lucius Vettius, who had betrayed the conspiracy to the Senate for a substantial reward, came before Novius and declared that he had letters in Caesar's own handwriting linking him to Catiline. This was little more than a rehashing of the earlier accusations tying Caesar to the conspiracy, but Caesar had lost patience with such needling assaults on his dignity and integrity. He rose before the Senate and defended himself superbly, invoking Cicero's own testimony that he had immediately passed all information he possessed to the consul to aid in destroying the conspiracy. The Senate supported Caesar, but he was determined to stop these petty attacks against him by making a public example of these latest adversaries. Caesar employed his power as a senior magistrate to manhandle Vettius in the Forum, confiscate his property, and throw him into prison. The investigator Novius he merely sent to jail for allowing a frivolous case against a praetor to be presented at his tribunal. It was a long time before anyone bothered Caesar again.

The juicy scandal that hit Caesar next soon made him forget about any conspiracy accusations. There was an ancient religious gathering for Roman women each year called the Bona Dea festival. The true name of this "good goddess" is unknown, but she was probably a nature divinity otherwise known as Fauna, who was worshipped throughout Italy. In the Roman version of the cult, the Vestal Virgins gathered women at the house of a senior magistrate for a night of celebration and fellowship. Men were absolutely forbidden to attend. The year before, Cicero's home had been the site for the festivities, and now Caesar's mother, Aurelia, was the hostess for the celebration at the house of the pontifex maximus. There were similar women's festivals throughout the ancient Mediterranean world. Stories, promulgated by men, often grew up around such worship claiming the secret female festivities were occasions for lewd debauchery, but in reality they were a much-needed chance for women to relax without the tiresome presence of men. It was an evening of music and dancing, with vineyard decorations and abundant wine—discreetly called "milk" for the night as ancient Roman law frowned on wine for women. Caesar's wife, Pompeia, was of course present at the celebration, along with all the leading Roman matrons. Aurelia had cheerfully ushered Caesar from the house earlier in the day, ordering him to take all the males of the household along, a command he gladly obeyed.

Once the festivities were well under way and many cups of wine had been drained, a servant of Aurelia came upon a shy young maiden hiding in the shadows. She called the stranger out to dance, but the heavily veiled figure declined in a surprisingly deep voice. The servant dragged the mysterious person forth and then screamed, shouting to the whole household that she had caught a man violating their worship. Aurelia immediately stopped the celebration and ordered all the doors of the house barred. She led a search through Caesar's home until she cornered the intruder, stripped him of his disguise, and drove him out of the house.

Word of the sacrilege quickly spread throughout the city. The culprit was a man named Publius Clodius Pulcher, an irreverent young noble who led Rome's avant-garde Bohemian set and who delighted in thumbing their noses at authority and tradition. Clodius had even changed the spelling of his family name Claudius as a fashionable affectation. Clodius had long been in love with Caesar's wife Pompeia—or at least had decided it would be great fun to seduce her if he could. With this in mind, he had dressed as a lute girl and entered Caesar's house. He was trying to get Pompeia alone in her bedroom when he was discovered. Rome was in an uproar, both because of the sacrilege against the gods and because Clodius was a notorious rake who had reportedly engaged in incest with his sisters. He was also a favorite among the urban populist party because of his staunch defense of their interests and his continual annoyance of the prim and proper senatorial class.

Caesar's response was decisive and immediate. He sent Pompeia a letter of divorce, even though it was unclear whether or not she had been a willing participant in the scandal. When asked why he would put his wife aside without firm proof, he responded that Caesar's wife must be above suspicion. Even if Caesar loved Pompeia, he could not afford to play the cuckolded husband for the amusement of his political enemies. But he also could not alienate the populists who saw Clodius as a hero, so he declined any attempts at personal revenge or legal prosecution. Caesar knew that Clodius, in spite of his recklessness, could be very useful to him in years to come if they maintained good relations. Instead, Caesar left soon after for his pro-praetorian governorship in the familiar province of Further Spain, allowing others, including Cicero and the Senate leaders, to bring Clodius to trial.

Just as Caesar was preparing to leave for Spain, Pompey finally returned triumphantly to Italy after six years conquering and organizing the eastern Mediterranean. To the surprise of everyone and the great relief of the Senate, Pompey almost immediately dismissed his troops to return to their homes. He then walked to Rome accompanied only by a few friends as if returning from a vacation abroad. Pompey could have easily repeated the actions of his mentor Sulla twenty years earlier, sweeping into Rome, ruling as dictator, and beheading his political enemies. Crassus certainly expected this, removing his children and especially his money out of Rome just as Pompey landed in Brundisium. But Cato had cleverly understood Pompey's mind and goals when he had opposed the legislation of his agent Nepos just a few months before. Pompey believed he had earned the position of first man in Rome through his achievements and thus had no need for a bloody coup. He fully expected to enter Rome as a hero, accomplish his legislative aims, and then live out his life as a respected statesman and leader of the Senate. If not, Pompey believed he could always call up his loyal veterans throughout Italy, though he had no plans or desire to do so.

When Pompey arrived in Rome at last and presented his legislation to the Senate several months later, he discovered just how obstinate and obstructionist the optimates could be. His two proposals were very reasonable—a ratification of his eastern settlement and a grant of well-deserved land to reward his veteran soldiers. The Senate, however, bogged down the bills in procedural limbo until an exasperated Pompey took the proposals to the people in assembly. But there the optimates used their allies to block Pompey until he finally withdrew his bills in frustration and decided to wait for a better day. Sulla would have never allowed himself to be defeated this way, but Pompey had lost his will to fight, at least for the present.

While Pompey was still making his way to Rome, Caesar had set off at breakneck speed for his province in Spain. The debts he had been accumulating since his service as an aedile four years earlier were now reaching epic proportions, prompting Caesar to appeal to Crassus for help. Rome's richest man pledged himself as security to the most insistent of Caesar's bankers, but a quick exit was prudent as there was still a mob of angry creditors snapping at his heels. Caesar didn't slow down until he came to the Alps. At a wayside village high in the mountains, one of Caesar's traveling companions looked around at the squalid huts and laughingly wondered if even in such a woebegone hamlet there was a struggle for power and influence. In words eerily similar to those of Satan in Milton's *Paradise Lost,* Caesar declared:

> *I would rather be first man here than second in Rome.*

Caesar's exploits in Spain were a preview of his future conquests in Gaul. Caesar knew that his political career depended on his success in Further Spain, both as a chance to gain the attention he would need to run for consul and as a means to raise desperately needed cash to pay his enormous debts. Fortunately for Caesar, the Iberian peninsula was ripe with potential military victories and rich in silver. Caesar began by ordering the Lusitanian bandits who had long infested the Herminian Mountains northeast of modern Lisbon to leave their highland homes and settle in the plains. Caesar knew very well they would not, but their refusal gave him the perfect chance to launch a war against them. After hastily raising more troops, Caesar led his army into the hills. The native tribes expected to defeat this new Roman governor as easily as previous incompetent generals, so they sent away their families and prepared for war. The mountain raiders then tried to distract the Romans by sending their herds be-fore them, hoping Caesar would seize the cattle as booty so that they could swoop down on him while he was distracted. But Caesar had not come all the way to Spain for a few cows. He ignored the herds and pushed through to attack and quickly defeat the bandits. He chased the survivors all the way to the Atlantic coast, where they crossed over to a nearby island. Caesar then sent a band of troops across to the island in the few small boats he possessed. The soldiers were forced to disembark at a breakwater some distance from the is-land and wade across, but they had not reckoned on an unfamiliar factor. In the Mediterranean, the tide varies no more than a few inches, but on the Atlantic seaboard the water can swiftly rise several feet. The Roman soldiers were trapped and all but one cut down by the Spanish rebels. Caesar cursed his luck, then sent to Gades for more ships while maintaining a blockade on the island. When the ships arrived, the Romans sailed across the channel and quickly de-feated the surviving brigands. The rebellious natives were learning that Caesar was maddeningly persistent in war.

Caesar next led his new fleet against the troublesome Callaici in the northwest corner of Spain. These proud tribesmen of Celtic ori-gin had never been conquered by Rome, but when they saw Caesar's fleet approaching their port town of Brigantium, they were shocked by the novel prospect of a full-fledged naval attack and quickly sur-rendered. Caesar had now accomplished a major pacification of western Iberia in just a few weeks, bringing peace and stability to a region that had been a thorn in Rome's side for decades. But Caesar's skill was not limited to the battlefield. He quickly ended the inces-sant disputes between native cities and reorganized the dismal fi-nances of the province, especially the bitter quarrels between Roman creditors and Spanish debtors. Caesar could not afford to alienate the Roman knights who loaned money to the Spaniards, so he could not propose a cancellation of debts as Catiline had promised. Instead, he limited the amount of money a creditor could garnish from a debtor to two-thirds of his annual income. This was still exorbitant, but it allowed the natives to avoid complete financial ruin.

Caesar was not above the Roman tradition of enriching himself during his service in a province. Later classical historians, many of whom were hostile to Caesar, claim that he solicited hefty contributions from native towns and sacked a few only for their riches. Whether or not this is true, Caesar without a doubt finished his term in Spain as a wealthy man. He also generously shared the profits with his men, who hailed him as *imperator,* the coveted title of a conqueror who was then eligible for a prized public triumph on his return to Rome. In Spain, Caesar also gained the friendship of many influential businessmen, including Lucius Cornelius Balbus, a native of Gades. The wealthy and influential Balbus had been made a Roman citizen by Pompey years before and worked closely with the Picene general, but in time became an important supporter of Caesar.

After the winter snows had melted, Caesar quickly made his way back to Rome to begin campaigning for the consulship, the final office on the Path of Honors. He had been reluctantly granted a triumph by the Senate for his victories in Spain, a dream of Caesar for years that would guarantee his enduring status as a successful military commander. A triumph was the highest honor Rome could grant a general and so was not conferred lightly on any man. The Senate was full of optimates who hated Caesar and the populist politics he championed. They knew that a triumphal parade would only help his standing among the common people. But in spite of their animosity, the optimates shared with the rest of Rome a genuine admiration for an excellent soldier. Not enough of Caesar's enemies could bring themselves to deny him a well-earned victory parade, even if it was to their own detriment. Caesar would mount his four-horse chariot in the Field of Mars dressed in glowing robes and accompanied by his lictors as a guard of honor. Trophies of his conquest would be heaped on carts before him and notable prisoners captured in the war would march in chains with heads bowed low. Even in the midst of such glory, however, the Romans dared not offend the gods. A slave would stand in the chariot behind Caesar during the whole parade whispering in his ear, "Remember you are mortal." Caesar's soldiers would bellow obscene songs as their commander drove through the Forum and up to the top of the Capitoline Hill, where he would sacrifice to Jupiter.

But Caesar faced a conundrum. As a general awaiting a triumph, he had to remain outside the walls of Rome. His *imperium* as a commander would be lost, as would his triumph, if he entered the gates of Rome before the morning of the parade. Yet it was also a law that a candidate for consul had to appear personally within Rome's walls as a private citizen before the election. Caesar sent a message asking the Senate if they would bend the rule this once and allow him to run for consul while remaining outside the city. The senators debated the matter with many willing to grant Caesar his request. But when Cato saw that the Senate was going to vote in favor of Caesar, he invoked an ancient privilege allowing him to speak without interruption as long as he wished. As Senate meetings could be held only during the day, Cato filibustered for hours until the summer sun set over the Tyrrhenian Sea. Since there were no days left for further debate, Cato and his optimate allies congratulated themselves on at least postponing Caesar's rise to the consulship for another year— and in a year, anything might happen. Of course, as a triumph was an incredible honor to be remembered for generations, no Roman in his right mind would ever trade it for the chance to run for any political office, not even consul.

But early the next morning, Caesar left his tent on the Field of Mars clad in a shining white toga and walked deliberately toward the city gate just north of the Capitoline Hill. The few who were awake at that hour must have stared openmouthed as they realized what he was about to do. Passing under the gate, he crossed the sacred boundary of the city and thereby forfeited his triumph. No one could believe that Caesar would give up such an honor, but once again he proved to friends and foes alike that he was unique.

One of the consular candidates for 59 B.C. was none other than the optimate Bibulus, Caesar's bitter foe who had earlier been paired with him both as aedile and praetor. It seemed as though Bibulus would forever be an albatross around Caesar's neck. In a move to secure the defeat of his old rival, Caesar made a clever pact with another candidate named Lucius Lucceius, who had plenty of money but no broad constituency. Lucceius agreed to form an alliance and use his own wealth to bribe voters on behalf of both himself and Caesar. In turn, Lucceius, as a relative unknown, would benefit from association with a famous and popular candidate, greatly increasing his own chances of election. The response of the optimates was not to fight Caesar's election—that would have been futile—but to make sure he was paired with a fellow consul who would obstruct, obfuscate, and hopefully block any reformist actions Caesar tried to undertake. Of course, the only man for the job was Bibulus. The optimates distributed their own bribes on a massive scale, even winning the approval of the priggish Cato for such blatantly illegal electioneering. It was, as Cato grudgingly admitted, all for the good of the Republic.

The optimates also thought ahead to the year after Caesar's consulship. Normally, a former consul would be rewarded with a prestigious governorship in one of the most important and wealthy provinces of the empire. In a bid to hamstring any ambitions of Caesar well ahead of time, the optimates pushed a bill through the Senate mandating that the consuls for the year 59 B.C. on completion of their office would both be charged with overseeing woods and pastures. This ridiculous job would guarantee that Caesar neither profited from a governorship nor had any troops at his disposal after his year as consul.

When the election was over, Caesar had easily taken first place with Bibulus beating out the now considerably poorer Lucceius to serve as co-consul. Caesar was painfully aware that his year as consul, the high point of his long struggle up the Path of Honors, would all be for naught unless he managed to secure powerful allies fast. The optimates, however, were determined to destroy his political and military career at any cost. They would doom him to an insignificant consulship followed by a year inspecting cow pastures. Caesar's only hope for a productive magistracy and later military glory lay in reaching a mutually beneficial accord with one or more significant players in the Roman power game who would help him defeat the entrenched conservatives of the Senate. But who would be open to a grueling battle with the optimates? Or more precisely, who had the most to gain? The first choice was obvious—Pompey. Ever since he was a young lieutenant of Sulla, the Senate had laughed at the Picene upstart behind his back even while they occasionally used him as a military leader. Pompey had recently failed to pass the legislation ratifying his settlement in the Near East and granting land to his veteran soldiers. He needed a skillful magistrate like Caesar, who understood the subtle uses of power in the Senate and Forum. The second choice was more of a challenge—Crassus. Rome's resident financial magnate despised Pompey and had aided the optimates in blocking him on a number of occasions. But the Senate still viewed Crassus as an upstart knight to whom they would not grant real power, especially the major military command he so coveted. After his previous alliance with Pompey, the optimates made it their policy to keep the two feuding populists constantly at odds. Now Caesar revealed yet another quality of his genius by skillfully and with tremendous insight into human nature bringing these two bitter enemies together. Caesar also labored to win the support of Cicero, but the former savior of the Republic hesitated, then declined. He felt it was important for him to maintain a strategic neutrality to preserve the harmonious concord of the different factions in Rome. But this concord was largely a figment of Cicero's imagination.

Thus Rome's greatest general along with its wealthiest citizen joined together with a supremely talented and ambitious consul in a secret three-man (*triumviri*) pact to run the Republic. With solemn oaths administered by Caesar as high priest of Rome they bound themselves not to undertake any action opposed by any one of them. The optimates did not realize what they were about to face—the First Triumvirate was now in business.

IV

CONSUL

Caesar had a very kind nature and was not easily angered, but he nevertheless struck back at many of his
enemies . . . His vengeance pursued most of his opponents without them even knowing it.

— DIO CASSIUS

Caesar was unusually tall for a Roman man and had a fair com-
plexion in spite of so much time spent under the Mediterranean
sun. He also had piercing dark eyes and was fastidious to an extreme,
regularly having his body hair plucked out. He could be quite vain, especially regarding his baldness. Like many men through the ages, he
attempted to hide his shiny crown by combing his hair over from the
sides of his head, though like every man through the ages, he fooled no
one. He also wore a laurel wreath in later years not so much out of
pride in military victories, but simply to cover up his thinning hair.
However, the women of Rome seem not to have minded. He was a notorious ladies' man who carried on many affairs with the leading beau-
ties, most especially Cato's stepsister Servilia. Since Servilia was the
mother of Brutus, some historians have wondered whether Caesar
could in fact have been the father of his own murderer. This is unlikely, however, as he was only fifteen years old when Brutus was born.

Caesar struggled with poor health, regularly suffering crippling headaches and recurring bouts of epilepsy. The ancients knew this latter condition as the falling sickness or sacred disease, because victims would collapse to the ground in seizures that seemed to onlookers like divine or even demonic possession. Epilepsy was well known and widely discussed in the ancient world, especially in Greek medical texts. Even in the gospels, Jesus heals a severely afflicted epileptic boy who is believed to be possessed by an evil spirit. Caesar's epilepsy did not strike him until adulthood, and then it seemed to have been particularly frequent during military campaigns. But as Plutarch says:

> *He never allowed his weakened health to slow him down, but instead used the life of a soldier as therapy. He marched endlessly, ate simple food, slept outside, and endured every hardship. In this way, he strengthened his body against illness.*

Caesar did not let any health problems interfere as he prepared to take up the consulship for 59 B.C. Aside from his alliance with Pompey and Crassus—a closely guarded secret as yet—Caesar sought out other senators and magistrates who might help him counter the impending assault from the optimates. More than anything he needed a cooperative and fearless tribune of the plebs who would be willing to use his veto to block his enemies and help him pass legislation through the popular assembly. Caesar was determined to follow tradition and present his reforms first to the Senate, but he knew this was unlikely to succeed. If he were going to force his reform bills into law, he would almost certainly need to bypass the Senate and instead appeal directly to the people. One bold tribune for sale was Publius Vatinius, but even Caesar (no stranger to doling out lavish bribes) was shocked at how much Vatinius was going to cost him. As Cicero later said, "Vatinius the tribune did nothing for free."

On the morning of January 1, 59 B.C., Caesar became senior consul of Rome, the most important magistrate in the greatest empire Europe had ever known. He had exactly one year to stage a peaceful revolution that would bring desperately needed changes to the Roman world. Beside him stood the junior consul Bibulus, who made it abundantly clear that he was going to stop Caesar at all costs.

Caesar borrowed a trick that Cicero had used during the Catilinian debates and ordered that all Senate and assembly proceedings were to be recorded and published each day. Now neither populists nor optimates could hide behind the veil of secrecy and deniability, but were forced to speak and act as if all of Rome were watching. He then offered an olive branch to Bibulus by reviving an ancient custom. Roman consuls alternated as chief executive each month, so that Caesar bore the symbol of power, the fasces, in January, then Bibulus in February and every other month thereafter. But even in the months when Bibulus held prominence, Caesar, as senior consul, would normally have had his own lictors march before him as an intimidating sign of power. Caesar, however, ordered his lictors to march behind him when Bibulus reigned as a show of respect to the junior consul. In a world of ritual and symbolism, it was the kind of small but significant gesture that Romans appreciated, but Caesar soon discovered that such concessions were wasted on the optimates.

Caesar's first significant action as consul was to propose a land distribution bill—a volatile type of legislation that had destroyed many reformist politicians before him. But none of Caesar's predecessors had ever introduced such a thoroughly detailed, impeccably reasonable, and skillfully crafted law. More than ever, the city of Rome was bursting at the seams with landless farmers and discharged soldiers, including Pompey's veterans, who were draining the public coffers and adding to the riotous instability of the capital. Caesar calmly explained to the Senate that Rome would be much better served if these urban dwellers and their families were relocated to plots of state-owned agricultural land throughout Italy. As a concession to the nobility, the rich public lands of Campania around

the Bay of Naples would not be touched since they provided important income for the treasury as well as many wealthy senators. A land
commission—made up of a wide cross section of Romans—would
be formed to handle all the details (Caesar exempted himself from
serving to avoid a conflict of interest). No one would be removed
from his land involuntarily. All current land ownership would be
recognized without need of tedious documentation. Any extra land
the commission required would be bought at assessed value, but only
if the owners wished to sell. This money for purchase would come
from the taxes and tribute of Pompey's conquests in the eastern
Mediterranean. The entire land bill would cost the Roman treasury
not a single denarius.

When he was finished, Caesar urged all the senators present to
voice any objections they might have to the bill. If anyone found fault
with any article of the legislation, he promised to alter or delete it.
One by one, Caesar called on the respected members of the Senate
for their opinion. No one—not even Cato—could find a single criticism to make concerning this model of clear and necessary legislation. In spite of this, the optimates were not about to let Caesar pass
his bill. They knew perfectly well the dire situation of Rome's urban
poor, but they also knew that the legislation would make Caesar even
more popular with the people. Regardless of the enormous benefits
to Roman citizens, they were determined to block Caesar. Several
senators, while still having no criticisms of the bill, recommended
that the vote be delayed. Cato then began to speak at length until it
was obvious his plan was to continue until sunset when the Senate
would have to adjourn. At this point Caesar lost his patience. He had
introduced the best land reform bill in Roman history, only to find
that the nobility preferred an untenable status quo to the slightest in-
novation. Caesar ordered one of his lictors to seize Cato and haul him
off to jail. As a consul, he was within his legal rights to do this, but it
was a foolish move on Caesar's part. The optimates, in a show of soli-
darity, immediately followed Cato to prison. Even some of the more

moderate members of the Senate were shocked at Caesar's breach of Senate protocol and rose to leave. When Caesar angrily demanded of one of them, Marcus Petreius, why he was leaving, the senator shot back: "I would rather be in jail with Cato than here with you." These words brought Caesar to his senses and he ordered Cato's release, since the last thing he needed was a optimate martyr. As he dismissed the meeting he gave the Senate notice—he had tried to work with them to gain their approval as custom required, but from now on he would go directly to the Roman people.

When Caesar presented his new land proposal to the popular assembly, he invited Bibulus to address the people and again present any arguments against the law. Caesar's colleague obstinately refused to say anything except to mutter that he was not going to allow any innovations that year. Caesar then implored the huge crowd, calling on them to beseech Bibulus to support the land bill. "The law will pass," Caesar cried, "but only if he supports it." Then Bibulus lost his composure and shouted at the crowd in outrage as he left the assembly, "You will not have your law this year—not even if all of you want it!"

Caesar could now claim—with all of Rome as a witness—that he had tried his best to work with the stubborn optimates and had gone the extra mile to be fair with his fellow consul. But Caesar's political theater for the day was not finished. He next asked Pompey and Crassus to come forward and give their opinion of the legislation. Pompey was especially vehement in support of the bill and promised he would take up his own sword to defend Caesar against the obstructionist senators. The mob roared its approval, led by hundreds of Pompey's veterans, who had packed the Forum that morning. As wave after wave of cheers swept over the platform where the three men stood, Cato watching from afar suddenly realized what Caesar had done. The populist consul had formed an unprecedented alliance right under his nose with the two most powerful men in Rome. Aside from the support of thousands of clients and the enormous wealth Pompey and Crassus had to offer Caesar, their backing would nullify any optimate attempt to paint Caesar as a dangerous revolutionary bent on destroying Roman tradition. The man on the street, already sympathetic to Caesar, would now see him not as a lone voice of radical reform but as the leader of a powerful political team with broad support.

Bibulus, meanwhile, although not the equal of Caesar by any measure, was nevertheless a tenacious adversary. When he and the optimates realized Caesar's triumvirate was likely to win any legislative battles during the year, they set about laying the groundwork to nullify the laws Caesar would surely pass. Bibulus found three like-minded tribunes and decided on a clever strategy. Since one of the duties of the consuls was to determine which days of their year would be dedicated to the gods as sacred, Bibulus simply declared that every remaining day until the end of Caesar's consulate was now holy. As no meetings could legally be held on holy days, no assembly could pass any binding laws. It was clear to everyone that Bibulus was blatantly abusing his consular power, but he had thrown a wrench into Caesar's plans that could technically negate all his achievements for the year if and when the optimates could regain the upper hand. In public Caesar laughed at Bibulus and his foolhardy schemes, but among his allies and friends he confessed they posed a serious threat in the long term.

Caesar fixed a day for the assembly to vote on the land bill, filling the Forum with triumvirate supporters the night before to assure an enthusiastic crowd. Caesar was addressing the assembly the next day from the steps of the temple of Castor and Pollux when he saw a resolute Bibulus, accompanied by Cato and others, marching toward him. The crowd made way for the junior consul and his companions, partly from respect for his office and partly because they couldn't imagine he would be foolish enough to oppose Caesar among a multitude of his own partisans. Bibulus, however, showed his mettle by pushing his way to the platform and rebuking Caesar. In moments the crowd erupted and began assaulting Bibulus and the optimates. Someone quickly found a basket of animal droppings and dumped it on Bibulus's head. Beaten, bruised, and covered in manure, his fasces torn apart by the crowd, Bibulus fled the Forum with Cato at his heels. Caesar then had no problem passing his land distribution act into law—with Pompey and Crassus appointed as leading members of the land commission.

Bibulus was incensed by his treatment at the hands of Caesar's mob and appealed to the Senate the next day to stand up to his fellow consul. But the senators were hesitant to act against the triumvirate backed by an angry mob. In bitter frustration and embarrassment, Bibulus withdrew to his own house and was not seen in public for the rest of the year. His conspicuous absence as junior consul became a joke to all of Rome—documents normally dated according to the names of both consuls for the year were wittily amended to read, "Done in the consulship of Julius and Caesar." Then a comical tune arose on the streets:

> *There was a deed just now done by Caesar, not by Bibulus.*
> *For I remember nothing done in the year of Bibulus.*

The worst fears of the senators came to pass after this first agrarian bill was approved. Caesar soon realized that the restrictions of his land legislation meant that there would not be enough farmland available for the neediest citizens of Rome. As a result, he introduced a new bill to the people that opened up the previously sacrosanct public land in Campania for distribution. Cato objected, of course, but Roman families with three or more children would now be granted a parcel of this prized land on which to raise cabbage and offspring. It was painful for the ruling classes to see what they regarded as their own private preserve being given away to the rabble of Rome, but the settlement of landless families was immensely beneficial for the state as a whole. To make sure the senators did not

tamper with the land settlement once he was out of office, Caesar inserted a curse clause that all future candidates for office had to swear
before the gods they would not introduce any legislation contrary to
his own.

With Bibulus out of the way and most of the optimates intimidated for the moment, Caesar and his partners began to pursue their
agenda in earnest. Some of their proposals were shamefully self-
serving, but much of the legislation was badly overdue. Pompey had
returned from the eastern Mediterranean two years earlier yet his
settlement still had not been ratified by the Senate. The importance
of this landmark agreement for Roman political interests can hardly
be overstated since to the east lay the mighty Parthian empire.
Stretching from the deserts of Mesopotamia to the mountainous borderlands of China, Parthia was an aggressive military kingdom fully
capable of taking on the legions of Rome. These fearless warriors
had already made forays into Armenia and were perilously close to
Roman territory. It was not lost on thoughtful Romans that four centuries earlier, another Persian empire had rapidly conquered all of
Asia Minor, Syria, and Egypt before invading Greece. The last thing
Rome needed was an eastern Mediterranean that was weak and disorganized, practically inviting the Parthians to intrude.

Pompey had brought peace to Asia Minor and made important
treaties with Tigranes of Armenia, a land that could serve as a crucial
buffer state between Rome and Parthia. The Roman general had
also removed the ever-quarrelsome Seleucid princes from Syria and
established the rich land as a full Roman province. With the addition
of the Maccabees of Judea as a client kingdom, the Romans now had
a strong eastern frontier stretching from the Black Sea to the deserts
of Arabia—but only if the Senate would ratify the settlement of
Pompey. If not, it was likely that the Parthians would soon take advantage of the resulting instability and intervene.

Most of the Senate saw that there was little point in resisting the
triumvirate on the eastern settlement, but the aged Lucullus—a no-

torious hedonist who had looted much of Asia before being replaced by Pompey—stood to speak against the bill. Caesar quickly cut him off and began to list all the crimes he had committed in the East, with the none-too-subtle implication that he would be brought up on charges unless he kept quiet. At this, the old man fell to his knees before Caesar, weeping and begging forgiveness. It was a shameful display that shocked Caesar; he had simply wanted Lucullus to cease his opposition, not grovel before him like a slave. It was a disturbing sight as well for optimates and populists alike to see the respected ex-consul lying at Caesar's feet. Lucullus was quietly removed and the bill passed into law, but the scene long endured in the minds of the senators.

When the Greek historian Herodotus called Egypt the gift of the Nile he meant that the longest of the world's rivers brought a fertility to the barren desert that other civilizations could only dream of. The rich soil carried down annually from central Africa by the flooding Nile had nourished Egypt's fields and yielded fabulous wealth for its rulers while the ancestors of the Romans were still living in mud huts beside the Tiber. The Romans could have marched into Egypt and taken over decades earlier, but the fact that they did not must have been due at least in part to the vast amounts of money the Ptolemaic kings spent bribing the various factions of Rome. It may also be that Egypt was a country unlike anything the Romans had ever known. Spain, Sicily, and even Greece were lands similar to the climate and culture of Italy in many ways. But to walk beneath the towering pyramids and gaze at ruins that were more ancient to the Romans than the Romans are to us today must have struck the sons of Romulus with awe.

Caesar and Crassus had managed to overcome any sense of wonder they may have felt when they proposed annexing Egypt as part of their money-raising scheme six years earlier. That move had been defeated by the Senate, but now Caesar the consul was ready to press the Egyptian question. Rome had a tenuous legal title to the desert kingdom through the will of Ptolemy XI, but the current unpopular ruler, Ptolemy XII "the Flute Player," had managed to hang on to power for twenty years through extravagant bribes and close commercial ties to Rome. Caesar now pushed through legislation ratifying Ptolemy's rule of Egypt and alliance with Rome after two decades of neglect by the Senate. This quick settlement was partially due to Caesar not wanting to take on the complex incorporation of a huge kingdom at this busy moment in his political career, but the major factor seems to have been an enormous bribe he and Pompey received from Ptolemy.

Caesar completed his eastern legislation with a clever move to clean up the tax-collecting mess in the Roman province of Asia. Several years earlier, the Roman tax collection agencies had carelessly overbid the amount of revenue they hoped to collect from the province. When they discovered it was impossible to pay the treasury as much as they had promised, they asked the Senate to reduce the amount they owed by a generous one-third. Crassus naturally backed this proposal as he was heavily invested in tax-farming companies, but the opposition led by Cato killed the proposal and left the tax collectors owing the full amount. A year later, the owners of the collection firms were still up to their necks in debt they could not pay the state. This impasse was broken by Caesar when he brought forward a bill before the popular assembly granting the tax collectors their reduction of debt. Just as he had done two years earlier in Spain, Caesar managed to smooth out the financial troubles of a distant province with a quick deal. This legislation didn't particularly benefit the natives of Asia since they had already been squeezed out of every coin the agents could find, but it left the Roman tax collectors and their financial investors in a much more solvent position. Not by coincidence, Caesar was one of these investors. But the real advantage to Caesar came not from the profits he made on the bill but in the goodwill and increased support it garnered among the knights. All the legislative successes of Caesar, in spite of their practical benefit for Rome, sent a shiver down the spine of Cicero. "We should all be very afraid," said the orator in a contemporary letter to his friend Atticus. "He is surely making himself into a tyrant."

By the late spring of 59 B.C., Pompey had secured most of the laws he wanted. His monumental settlement of the eastern Mediterranean had been ratified while his veterans were provided with land as a reward for their loyal service. Caesar recognized that this was a moment of crisis for the triumvirate because Pompey might well decide he no longer needed to throw his considerable political weight behind the remaining goals of Caesar and Crassus. To counter this possibility, Caesar came up with a plan to bind Pompey to him that strikes modern readers as more at home in the courts of medieval Europe than the Roman Forum. Caesar offered his daughter, Julia, now about twenty years old, to Pompey as his bride, even though the general was almost thirty years her senior. This came as something of a shock to Caesar's loyal supporter Servilius Caepio, who was engaged to Julia and preparing for their wedding in only a few days' time. But as much as Caesar appreciated Caepio, he needed Pompey more. Still, Pompey appeased Caepio's fury somewhat by promising him his own daughter, Pompeia. Though the marriage was hastily arranged by her father, Julia soon came to love Pompey just as he became a devoted husband to Julia. Caesar could now rest assured that as long as Julia and Pompey were together, he could count on his colleague's indispensable support. Caesar himself now married Calpurnia, daughter of Lucius Piso, who would be consul the next year. Surveying this dizzying web of family alliances, Cato proclaimed that it was disgusting that Roman power should now be based on the trading of women.

Caesar's next crisis came not from Pompey's camp but from Cicero. During the spring the ex-consul Gaius Antonius was put on trial for misconduct during his administration of Macedonia a few years earlier. Since Antonius had been Cicero's fellow consul in 63 B.C., the orator felt obligated to defend his former colleague in court. Even though the triumvirate supported the persecution of Antonius, they were not at all offended that Cicero would support him—that was only proper—but Cicero could not resist this opportunity to stray beyond the facts of the case to criticize Caesar and his partners in an open setting. The words of his scathing speech do not survive, but they were sharp enough to strike Caesar to his very core. He had worked diligently to accommodate and mollify Cicero, offering him a share of power and always treating him with the honor the prickly statesman felt he deserved. However, when Cicero spoke viciously against him to the delight of the optimates, Caesar felt betrayed and decided he had had enough of Rome's most famous lawyer. Everyone acknowledged that Caesar had a mild and forgiving nature, but he could be pushed too far—when he was, he could strike out in fearful and ingenious ways against his foes.

Publius Clodius, who had scandalized all of Rome by violating the Bona Dea celebrations three years earlier, was a bitter enemy of Cicero. Clodius may have been an undisciplined radical who believed in nothing but jeering at the establishment and furthering his own ambitions, but he could hold a grudge like no one else. Cicero had led the charge, unsuccessfully, in trying to punish Clodius for his previous sacrilege. In turn, Clodius had made it his mission in life to annoy, aggravate, and denigrate Cicero at every opportunity. The previous year he had also taken the almost unprecedented step of attempting to abandon his patrician standing so that he could be elected as a tribune of the plebs. The pride that most patricians felt in their ancient blood meant nothing to the iconoclastic Clodius if, by abandoning his heritage, he could advance his political career and private vengeance. But his attempt to join the plebeians in 60

B.C. through traditional means was thwarted by his many opponents.

Now, thanks to Caesar's anger with Cicero, Clodius was about to see his dream come true. Although his goal of becoming a plebeian was almost impossible to achieve through normal avenues, there was another option open to Clodius. If he could be adopted as the son of a plebeian, he would then be rid of his patrician standing forever. But even this was a difficult process as it required an examination before the college of pontiffs and final approval by the ancient *comitia curiata* assembly. Caesar cut through the religious red tape in his authority as pontifex maximus, then called his thirty lictors together at an ad hoc meeting of the *comitia curiata* to approve Clodius's adoption. Pompey even acted as augur for the transferral ceremony. Clodius, now about forty years old, was adopted by a young plebeian man only twenty years of age named Publius Fontius. The whole affair was a scandal that would collapse under examination in any Roman court, but Caesar had managed to discard tradition and install an enthusiastic Clodius in his new role as a plebeian in a matter of only a few hours. The ex-patrician began his campaign for tribune of the plebs almost immediately.

In spite of Caesar's smug satisfaction at granting Clodius his wish in defiance of convention, he had made a serious mistake in acting so quickly out of anger against Cicero. Caesar wanted to teach Cicero a sharp lesson and mute his criticism, but he had no desire to harm or even seriously trouble a man whom he genuinely respected. Pompey as well pointedly warned Clodius not to use any tribunate powers to attack his old friend Cicero. Clodius, however, was the original loose cannon who could not and would not yield to anyone, even Caesar or Pompey. The triumvirate also hoped that in preparing his way to be a tribune, Clodius might be grateful and prove useful to them in the future against the optimates—but the only voice Clodius ever listened to was his own.

The administration of the Roman provinces had reached a low point by the time of Caesar's consulship through criminal mismanagement, exploitation, and crushing taxation. As many far-thinking Romans had realized since the time of Hannibal, no empire spanning thousands of miles and containing millions of people could be safe and prosperous if it were run for the exclusive benefit of a few wealthy citizens. Caesar determined to change this once and for all—not because of any altruistic love for the oppressed natives, but because Rome would fail miserably to live up to its tremendous potential as a world power unless it revolutionized how it controlled the lands beyond Italy. Caesar's monumental *lex Julia de repetundis*— the Julian law of extortion—contained over one hundred chapters of incredibly detailed rules for administering provinces, prosecuting crooked governors, preventing bribes, and generally keeping the senatorial class in line when they were abroad running the empire. The full text of the legislation is lost, but Cicero called it *justissima atque optima* ("most just and best") and even Cato could find nothing to complain about. This infuriated Cato so much that in coming years whenever he referred to what everyone else praised as the Julian law, he could never bring himself to attach Caesar's name to it. This law was so carefully crafted and effective that it was used as the foundation of provincial governance throughout Roman history and even into the Byzantine era.

Caesar might have given Rome the legal framework to rule its empire responsibly for centuries to come, but it was not going to do him much good personally if the optimates had their way. Once Caesar had completed his year as consul and was again a private citizen he would lose the immunity from prosecution he enjoyed as a magistrate. At the start of the new year, Cato and his allies would pounce. He would be brought before tribunals and charged with every crime they could think of to punish him for his impudence and destroy his political career. He would be accused of acting against established tradition and trampling the hallowed Roman constitution to push through his radical agenda. Bibulus would testify that every law passed by Caesar was invalid since he had declared most of 59 B.C. to be a sacred holiday. No one really believed the gods had made the days of Caesar's consulship unpropitious, but Bibulus was technically correct—if the courts followed the letter of the law, everything Caesar had accomplished would vanish like smoke.

Without a doubt Caesar had made a mockery of the constitution by violating sacred customs, bypassing the Senate, and even using force to achieve his revolutionary goals. His supporters would argue that Caesar had no choice since the alternative was to let the empire slip further into chaos all in the name of preserving tradition. The Rome of Cincinnatus and Scipio, they would argue, was long gone, and the sooner the Senate realized this, the better. The ancient republic founded by Romulus had ceased to exist when the little village on the Tiber took control of a vast domain stretching across the Mediterranean. The Senate was still trying to govern this realm as a private fiefdom based on archaic rules, ignoring the fact that the most powerful force in Rome was now generals with professional armies behind them. Future leaders in the mold of Marius, Sulla, and Pompey would soon make the Senate irrelevant unless it opened its eyes and agreed to a reformed and responsible governance of the empire. Caesar had tried to effect some of the changes to bring about this new order—painful changes, yes, but they were absolutely necessary and only the beginning. Much more needed to be done to establish a new form of constitutional rule or Rome would inevitably collapse into a tyranny led by ruthless generals.

Caesar's immediate concern, however, was how to avoid prosecution after his consulship and at the same time further his career. The obvious answer was to obtain a proconsular governorship of a promising frontier province, not a year overseeing the woods and pastures of Italy as the Senate had intended. As a governor, he would be immune from court action until his term was completed. It was crucial that his province would allow him to expand the territory of the empire as a conquering general since this would earn him both military glory and riches to finance his continued political goals. As Caesar's younger contemporary Sallust said of him: "He desperately wanted great power, an army, and a new war so that his talents could shine forth." The problem was finding the right war. Pompey had already brought peace to the eastern Mediterranean and would not appreciate his junior partner trying to steal his glory in that region. Even if he allowed Caesar to campaign there, the only viable option was an invasion of the Parthian empire. Caesar was smart enough to know such a war could quickly be his last. Egypt had enormous potential, but Caesar had just sealed a treaty of friendship with King Ptolemy. The rest of Africa was also at peace unless he wanted to strike out across the endless Sahara or sail up the Nile to attack distant Nubia or Ethiopia. Spain was wealthy, but already controlled by the Romans aside from a few poverty-stricken mountain tribes. Caesar knew therefore that Europe beyond the Alps was the best choice for fortune and glory.

Rome's northern frontier in the days of Caesar ran from the Pyrenees Mountains of Spain eastward across southern Gaul to the deep, blue waters of Lake Geneva. From there it followed the crest of the snowy Alps along the northern Balkans and across Macedonia and Thrace to the Black Sea. Beyond these borders lay the restive kingdom of Dacia above the Danube River, the vast dark forests of Germany, the rich lands of the fearless Gaulish tribes, and even the fabled island of Britain. But Caesar could not simply declare war against some northern land and march forth from the gates of Rome. He needed to gain the governorship of a frontier province bordering on the Gauls, Germans, or Dacians, then wait for one of the inevitable raids these tribes were always launching against Roman territory. As governor, it would then be his duty to strike back against the barbarians and teach them a lesson. If he went a little deeper into enemy territory than was really necessary and if the natives responded by attacking his troops prompting further actions by the legions, well, such were the fortunes of war.

Caesar began his plans for a northern campaign by first seeking the governorship of Cisalpine Gaul. This populous land in the Po Valley of northern Italy was ideally located as a gateway either west to Gaul proper, north to Germany, or east to the Danube. Not to be ignored was the fact that it also lay just a quick journey over the Apennine mountains from Rome itself. The governor of Cisalpine Gaul, significantly, commanded the legions closest to Rome. Whoever controlled this province could use it as a base for war beyond the Alps while still keeping a close eye on events in Rome. It was a region Caesar knew well and had championed in the past. He had many friends among the Romanized Celts along the Po and numerous clients among the Roman colonists in cities such as Milan and Verona. But what made Cisalpine most attractive of all to Caesar was the enormous wealth of manpower the province held. Whoever ruled this fertile land could draw on an almost endless supply of brave and capable young men for his legions.

In the late spring of 59 B.C., Caesar's well-paid tribune Vatinius laid a proposal before the plebs to grant Caesar governorship of not only Cisalpine Gaul but the mountainous province of Illyricum along the eastern Adriatic coast facing northeast toward Dacia. The command would last for five full years, until 54 B.C. Pompey backed the legislation and the bill was approved, completely bypassing the furious Senate. Soon after, Pompey pushed through legislation of incalculable importance granting Caesar, in addition, the province of Transalpine Gaul along the Mediterranean coast. This rich land was known simply as the Province (in Latin, *Provincia*), thus the modern name for the region, Provence. Lying north of the Province was the unconquered land of Long-Haired Gaul (as the Romans often called it) and it was there Caesar decided to stage his war.

The vast tribal lands of Gaul stretching north from the Roman Mediterranean province to the Atlantic and the English Channel were immensely wealthy and deeply troubled. The Aedui, longtime Roman allies and a major power in Gaul, were battling the Sequani and their German allies just to the north of the Roman province. The Sequani had called in the German warlord Ariovistus to help them fight their fellow Gauls, but as with similar invitations throughout history, the Sequani got more than they bargained for. Ariovistus attacked the Aedui, but he also took over vast swaths of land from the Sequani on which to build his own kingdom in Gaul. This move had upset the fragile balance of power in the region and prompted the Aedui to send a prince and trained druid named Diviciacus to Rome to lobby Cicero and others for help. But the agents of Ariovistus reached the senators first and, with the support of Caesar, won the title of friend of the Roman people. This left eastern Gaul in a shambles with Germans pouring over the Rhine, threatening the Aedui and every other Gaulish tribe in the region. The Gaulish Helvetii north of Lake Geneva even began plans to move into Roman territory to escape the German threat. To the delight of Caesar, the Senate suddenly faced an invasion of the Roman province by Gauls with Germans on their heels. Caesar realized this was his opportunity to show the Roman people that he could win glorious victories just as his uncle Marius had done. The ancient stories of the Gaulish sack of Rome in 390 B.C. and the invasion of the Germanic Cimbri and Teutones less than fifty years before now seemed frighteningly real to everyone in Italy. Ambassadors were hastily dispatched to Gaul and armies were recruited to fight the teeming hordes pressing on the border, while Caesar did his best to keep the threatening image alive in the minds of the public. Nevertheless, the danger to Rome was quite real.

With Caesar's postconsular plans now settled, he could focus on preparation for his upcoming campaign, while settling affairs at Rome before his departure. Caesar was not above boasting to the optimates that he had now gained his heart's desire in spite of their opposition and would use his newfound powers as governor and general to "jump on their heads." A murder plot against Pompey was soon uncovered in which Caesar was incriminated by some, though it is highly unlikely that he would stoop to such base behavior, especially against a man he still very much needed. Still, the optimates and even Cicero made as much of the matter as possible to cast lingering suspicions on Caesar. Clodius finally began his long-awaited term as tribune in December of 59 B.C. and proceeded to pander to the mob in an unprecedented fashion with guarantees of free grain at state expense. This helped him gain support for a private vendetta against Cicero that would last into the next year, when he forced the orator into exile. Caesar had no love for Clodius, but he must have been secretly delighted when on December 31, after making his farewell speech as consul to the assembled crowd, Bibulus rose to deliver his own address only to be silenced by Clodius' veto. Soon, however, Caesar was to be far away from the petty squabbles of Roman politics—news had reached Rome that the Helvetii were about to move into the Roman province of Gaul. Caesar quickly packed his gear, bade farewell to his family, and set out to face the greatest challenge of his life.

V

GAUL

> All of Gaul is divided into three parts—the first is oc-
> cupied by the Belgae, the second by the Aquitani,
> and the third by those called Celts in their own lan-
> guage, but Gauls in ours.
>
> —CAESAR

Long ago in the mountains of central Europe arose a people
known as the Celts. They spoke a language related to Greek,
Latin, and Sanskrit, but they lived a very different life from their civilized cousins to the south and east. The Celts had no cities, no empires, no books or monumental temples. They were instead a fiercely
independent collection of tribes who delighted in heroic warfare
while at the same time being masters of poetry, art, and metalwork.
About the middle of the first millennium B.C., just as Athens was
embroiled in the Persian Wars and Rome was expelling her last
Etruscan kings, the Celts burst out of their Alpine homeland to
spread like wildfire throughout Europe and even into Asia. One of
the earliest Celtic groups to leave their mountainous cradle migrated
to Spain and fused with the native culture to become known as the
Celtiberians. Other Celts moved west to occupy the fields and forests
of Gaul, and on across the sea to Britain and Ireland. Some warriors

and their families were lured to the Po Valley of northern Italy, while others moved east to Bohemia, Transylvania, and the northern Balkans. The holy shrine of Apollo at Delphi in Greece was attacked by these wandering Celts in 279 B.C., while at the same time thousands crossed into central Asia Minor to survive for centuries as the "foolish Galatians" of the New Testament. The Galatians and other mercenary Celts even served as much sought-after soldiers in the armies of Syria and Egypt.

Thus in the days of Caesar the Celts were spread far and wide throughout Europe and the Mediterranean lands. Those in Spain and Italy had been brought under the control of Rome and served as formidable soldiers in the Roman army, but the Celts of the British Isles and Gaul north of the Province still remained free. Caesar says Gaul was divided into three parts, but actually it was divided into five. In the Po Valley of northern Italy (Cisalpine Gaul to the Romans), Celtic tribes had long dominated the countryside from the Alps to the Adriatic coast. The Gauls of this region spoke the same language and worshipped the same gods as their cousins on the Loire and the Seine. The Italian Gauls had been conquered by the Romans over a century before Caesar and were well on their way to becoming part of classical civilization, but they were still Celts at heart. The second part of Gaul was the Province, stretching along the Mediterranean coast from the Pyrenees past Massalia (Marseilles today) to the Alps and up the Rhone to Lake Geneva. Here were the Gaulish Tectosages, Vocontii, and especially the Allobroges around modern Lyon—fierce warriors all but long exposed to Greek and Roman civilization. The Gaulish people of the Province were settling down nicely into a life as Roman dependents.

The final three parts of Gaul—where warriors battled in the ancient fashion and druids performed human sacrifice to the gods—lay beyond the Mediterranean watershed to the north and west. Aquitaine, north of the Pyrenees and along the Garonne River to modern Bordeaux, was a relatively small but richly productive land of tribes such as the Elusates and Tarusates. The fourth and largest part of Gaul was the enormous region beyond the Garonne and the mountainous Massif Central of southern France to the Atlantic on the west, the Rhine on the east, and the Seine to the north. Here lived dozens of the most organized Gaulish tribes, including the Arverni, Aedui, Sequani, and Helvetii in the south and east, the Carnutes around Chartres, the Veneti in Brittany, and the Parisii around Lutetia, modern Paris. Hundreds of miles north of the Province was the fabled land of the Belgae, the final region of Gaul. The Belgae were the fiercest, toughest, and least compromising of all the Gauls. Tribes such as the Nervii, Remi, and Treveri occupied the woods and dales of northern France, the Rhineland of Germany, Luxembourg, the Netherlands, and their namesake, Belgium. From north to south and east to west the unconquered lands of Gaul stretched over five hundred miles over swift rivers, impenetrable swamps, bitterly cold mountains, and endless dark forests.

For centuries the classical world had heard stories of the Gauls brought back by merchants and explorers. Massalia itself was the hub of a vast trade network in tin, gold, amber, and slaves that spread up the rivers of Gaul to northern France, Germany, Britain, Ireland, and the North Sea. The Celts eagerly imported Mediterranean goods in turn, especially wine. In the decades before Caesar, Roman merchants had even begun to establish permanent trading posts among the major Gaulish tribes. These outposts were often located in fortified tribal hill forts, known in Latin as *oppida*. From fortresses such as Alesia of the Aedui and Gergovia of the Arverni, Gaulish leaders and warriors ruled over their tribes.

Most Gauls were simple farmers, but the wealthy military aristocracy formed an elite class that battled their enemies in a manner more like the Greek heroes on the plains of Troy than Roman legionaries. To a Gaulish warrior, honor and bravery were paramount. They would fight with dashing bravado (sometimes naked to intimidate their foes) seeing war as a chance to win eternal glory and decorate their walls with an enemy's head. They were notoriously difficult to organize into a united force since they preferred individual combat to coordinated group actions.

Most ordinary Gauls lived in isolated farms or small villages, peacefully growing their crops and herding sheep. Houses were usually round or rectangular structures made of interwoven wood and sealed with mud. A central hearth fire served for both heating and cooking, with a small hole in the roof to allow smoke to escape. Women dominated home life and raised the children, while on the whole enjoying more freedom than their Greek and Roman counterparts. Craftsmen in the villages created amazingly sophisticated and beautiful art with abstract animal figures that echoes a thousand years later in Christian Irish manuscripts. But they also produced practical weaponry and armor that rivaled anything in the Mediterranean world. The Romans in fact had long ago adopted the Gaulish short sword called a *gladius,* the origin of the word *gladiator.*

The Gauls were polytheists and worshipped a great variety of gods, just like the Greeks and Romans. Chief among them was a divinity Caesar equates with the Roman god Mercury but known to the Gauls as Lugus ("the Shining One"). Inscriptions to him are found throughout Gaul as well as in other Celtic lands. The Irish knew him as Lug and danced before him at the summer festival of Lughnasadh. Among the countless other Gaulish gods were Belenus (the healer), Matrona (the divine mother), Cernunnos (an animal divinity), and Epona (a horse goddess later adopted by the Roman cavalry). These gods were worshipped with sacrifices at temples throughout Gaul and in small sanctuaries scattered amid villages and forests. All worship was overseen by the druids, a priestly caste of the Celts who were found in Britain and Ireland as well. Ancient authors, often eager to cast the Celts in a negative light, claimed the druids engaged in frequent human sacrifice. Archaeology has indeed shown that human sacrifice took place, but it was a rare event conducted only under extreme circumstances—and practiced by the Romans themselves on occasion. The druids, as Caesar relates, trained for up to twenty years, believed passionately in reincarnation, and were highly respected throughout Gaulish communities. These priests could even step between warring armies and call a halt to any battle. Along with the professional class of poets known by the Celtic name *bardoi* (hence our word *bard*), the druids acted as a unifying force among the quarrelsome and constantly fighting Gaulish tribes.

⊡

The Gaulish tribe of the Helvetii had long lived in the beautiful alpine valley bound by Lake Geneva on the west, the Jura range to the north, the Rhine on the east, and the soaring Alps around Mont Blanc to the south. For years they had fought to hold back fierce Germanic tribes such as the Suebi, who were relentlessly pressing on their territory. The Celts had originally controlled the area to the north of the Alps, but by the second century B.C. the Germans were pushing the native Gaulish tribes out of the region. The Helvetii had resisted this pressure by virtue of their numbers and skill at warfare, but by the late sixties B.C. even the bravest of the Helvetian warriors were tired of constant battles against the Germans. The increasing population was also putting tremendous pressure on the farmers of the tribe to produce enough food from their mountain valley.

In 61 B.C., a wealthy Helvetii nobleman named Orgetorix proposed a solution to the tribe's dual problems of constant warfare and growing population—mass migration. Orgetorix urged the Helvetian leaders to pack up the entire tribe and resettle in the rich land of southwest Gaul near the Atlantic. Yes, he admitted, there was already a Gaulish tribe there, the Santones, who would resist such a takeover, but they were no match for the mighty Helvetian warriors, who were raised from childhood fighting the barbarous Germans. The Helvetii thought this was a marvelous idea and began their preparations. They planned to stay in their valley for two more years to give themselves time to lay in a surplus of grain for the three-hundred-mile journey. They also decided to invite their nearby Celtic neighbors to join them, including a group of Boii tribesmen who had recently been driven out of their home in eastern Europe by Germans and Dacians. The two-year delay would also give the Helvetii time to negotiate peace treaties with their rivals the Aedui and Sequani to the west so that they would not be harassed during their migration.

Orgetorix, however, had much more in mind than a simple journey across Gaul. He was already a mighty voice among the Helvetii, but he longed to rule the tribe as a king. His dream was to forge an alliance with the powerful Aedui and Sequani to take over all of Gaul. Thus, under the guise of negotiating safe passage for the Helvetii on their march, he conspired with the leaders of the Sequani and Aedui to conquer Gaul. One important faction of the Aedui at the time was led by Dumnorix, brother of the druid Diviciacus, who had served as ambassador for his people to Rome. Diviciacus was staunchly pro-Roman, but his popular brother, Dumnorix, despised the empire to the south. Dumnorix saw the alliance proposed by Orgetorix as a force to counter Rome's increasing influence in Gaul and to increase his own power (*Dumnorix* is, after all, Gaulish for "king of the world"). With the Helvetii and Sequani on his side, they could form a mighty Gallic empire stretching from the Alps to the sea. Like Caesar, Crassus, and Pompey at about the same time, the Gaulish leaders swore a secret oath to seal their bargain, with Dumnorix likewise giving Orgetorix his daughter in marriage.

But the eternal truth of conspiracies is that they never remain secret. Informers reported the plans of Orgetorix to the Helvetian leaders, who promptly had him put in chains. He was brought before the tribal assembly to face judgment for his misdeeds but, in a move worthy of a Roman politician, Orgetorix packed the assembly with his followers and forced a mistrial. The Helvetian elders were so incensed at this breach of tradition that they determined to punish Orgetorix and so began collecting warriors to storm his stronghold.

At this point Orgetorix suddenly died. Some said it was suicide, but most of the Helvetii, and Caesar, suspected foul play.

Even though Orgetorix was dead and his conspiracy shattered, the Helvetii were still determined to follow his plan and abandon their valley for a new homeland across Gaul. They gathered together the food and transport they would need for the long journey and decided to make a permanent break with their old land by burning down all the hill forts and villages in their mountain home. In this way, no one would be tempted to turn back if the migration became too difficult. They set a date of March 28, 58 B.C. to set forth, just as the last of the winter snows were melting from the lower valleys. There were only two possible routes of escape open to the Helvetii. The first was a narrow road northwest through the Jura Mountains, along ravines wide enough only for a single cart, and down into the land of the Sequani. But such a slow and perilous passage along mountain paths could be hampered by only a few determined enemies blockading the way or attacking from above. The second choice was to head southwest out of their valley until they reached the border of the Allobroges at the lakeside town of Geneva. The tribal leaders decided that this was by far the preferable route as they could cross the Rhone there by bridge or even ford the river if necessary. But Geneva was also the beginning of Roman territory. The Helvetii, however, felt they could persuade the Allobroges as fellow Gauls to allow them passage through their lands and across the northern tip of the Province on their way to the Atlantic. If the Allobroges were not cooperative, the Helvetii felt sure they could convince them by force of arms.

Warfare in Caesar's time was a bloody, face-to-face affair in which men hacked, stabbed, and killed their opponents. It was also a normal and natural part of life. If your city possessed fertile land, abundant crops, or valuable goods, there would always be an enemy who wanted to take them from you. If you sensed weakness in a neighboring town, more likely than not you would try to conquer them or at least force them to serve your state as subordinate allies. If you wanted to maintain your independence, you kept your army strong. In this the Romans were like the Greeks, Germans, Celts, and everyone else in the ancient world. But unlike everyone else, the Romans perfected an army that allowed them to conquer the world.

The keys to the legendary power of the Roman military were flexibility and organization. The Romans dearly loved tradition and might celebrate religious rituals long after their meaning was forgotten, but they were quick to learn new ways of fighting and to discard outdated military techniques. If the Parthians defeated them in battle using a new type of spear, Roman forges would soon be glowing bright as they copied the new weapon for themselves. What ultimately made the Romans unbeatable were not weapons, however, or well-trained leaders (since Roman generals, like politicians, were essentially amateurs), but the Roman genius for fighting as a unit. Homer might sing of individual heroes challenging each other to battle on the plains of Troy, but the Roman army was a machine.

Our sources for the Roman military in the earliest days of the Republic are sparse, but we know that at least by the late third century B.C. the Roman army had developed the basic characteristics that would define it for centuries to come. At the heart of the Roman army was the heavy infantry formed by men who possessed enough wealth to outfit themselves with armor and weapons. From the beginning the Roman military was a citizen army that fought more or less willingly to protect their city and gain a share of the spoils of war. Each infantryman wore metal armor over a tunic to protect his upper torso. Chain mail of linked iron rings was best but frightfully expensive, forcing most to use cheaper rigid armor. On his head was a padded helmet, sometimes with cheek pieces to protect the jaws or capped with a feathered plume. The vulnerable legs gained some protection from greaves over the shins, but Romans' limbs were

largely left uncovered to allow freedom of movement. Each infantryman carried more than one *pilum* or javelin that was used for stabbing rather than throwing. This heavy weapon, over six feet long
with a large barbed head, was designed to punch through an opponent's shield and skewer him. If it missed his body, it would at least
break off and lodge in his shield making it heavier and more awkward to wield while the Roman grabbed his second javelin and tried
again. The Roman sword was short and used for stabbing rather
than swinging. Each Roman soldier also carried a large shield about
four feet high and two feet wide. Secured on the left arm, it was constructed of layered wood covered in thick leather and weighed at
least twenty pounds. This hefty shield provided effective protection
from all but the fiercest blows, but was also useful as an offensive
weapon to knock opponents to the ground.

No matter how well-equipped the individual Roman soldier, it
was the army's arrangement and discipline on the battlefield that
won or lost a fight. The military was organized in legions of four to
six thousand infantry. These would advance across a battlefield in
three lines of thirty staggered units called maniples—so that a Roman legion looked much like the squares of a checkerboard moving
ever forward. Unlike the solid lines of other armies, these gaps gave
the Romans great flexibility in rough terrain. Each maniple consisted
of two centuries (a century equalling 100 men), each led by a centurion and a standard bearer. The maniples in the front line were the
hastati ("spearmen"), all younger soldiers who clashed with the enemy first. Behind them were the *principes* ("first men"), made up of
seasoned warriors in their twenties and thirties, followed by the *tri-
arii* ("third-line") maniples of the most experienced fighters. A
skilled commander could use this checkerboard system to great advantage, shifting forces around the battlefield as needed. Legions also
included allied infantry forces and cavalry ready to assist. This basic
structure of the Republican army would last until the end of Roman
rule in Europe.

Caesar received word of the Helvetian plan and their departure date as he lay camped outside of Rome in mid-March. Clodius was busy at the time stirring up every kind of imaginable trouble in Rome, especially for Cicero, but Caesar had no time to waste on Roman politics. He moved from Rome to the northern tip of the Roman province of Gaul at astonishing speed, arriving at the Allobrogian town of Geneva scarcely before anyone knew he had left Italy. On the way, he began recruiting troops from Transalpine Gaul because there was only one legion in the Province at the time. He immediately ordered the bridge across the Rhone at Geneva demolished and waited for the Helvetii to approach him. Caesar was anxious for a victory to strengthen his military credentials at home, but he had legitimate reasons as well for resisting the Helvetii. Any march they made across the Roman Province would throw the land of the Allobroges into chaos as the Helvetii could scarcely be expected to behave themselves properly and refrain from pillage. Once they reached a new home in southwest Gaul, they would be a constant danger to Roman towns on and near the Mediterranean, such as the Roman center at Tolosa (modern Toulouse). In addition, the vacated alpine homeland of the Helvetii bordering the Roman territory would almost certainly be occupied by German tribes, who would pose an even greater threat to peace in southern Gaul than the Helvetii. Finally, it was not lost on Caesar that the Helvetii had deeply shamed the Romans by defeating them in battle fifty years earlier and forcing the survivors to march under a yoke. The Roman sense of justice demanded retribution.

The Helvetii soon sent two of their elder noblemen to parlay with Caesar at Geneva. They presented their case saying they did not seek a fight with the Romans, only passage through their lands. Caesar replied that he would have to think about their request and that they should return on April 13 for his answer. Of course Caesar had already made up his mind, but he needed more time for his troops to arrive at Geneva and to strengthen his defenses. As soon as the Helvetii ambassadors left, Caesar demonstrated one of his keenest talents, that of a combat engineer, by rapidly constructing a massive earthen wall nineteen miles long to seal off the entire Alpine valley of the Helvetii from Roman territory. From the Jura Mountains all the way to Lake Geneva, sixteen feet high with ditches in front and forts along its length, this forerunner of later works such as Hadrian's Wall across Scotland stood as an impenetrable barrier to the migrating Gauls.

When the Helvetian elders returned on the appointed date, they stared in awe at a formidable barricade as high as three men stretching across the entire plain. Just a month earlier their way had seemed clear and easy, but now this upstart Roman general had dared to fence in tens of thousands of Gaulish warriors. Caesar told the ambassadors what by now was obvious—he rejected their request to pass through Roman territory and he would repel them by force if necessary. The Helvetii were not about to give up easily and so began to test the Roman defenses along the wall by day and night, always seeking a weak spot. Caesar, however, did not believe in weak spots. His men on the wall repelled all Gaulish attempts to break through, while his troops along the river and lake stopped anyone trying to sneak across by boat.

The Helvetii were infuriated by this point, but were utterly frustrated by Caesar's unexpected defensive tactics. In desperation, they turned to the narrow mountain path through the Jura and the land of the Sequani as their only other option. But as the Sequani could easily block this trail if they wished or attack them once they descended, they determined not to try this northern route unless they first secured the agreement of the Sequani leaders. It was no surprise when the Sequani leaders also forbade them passage across their land, believing, as did Caesar, that the Helvetii would bring turmoil to any territory they entered. The Helvetii then turned to Orgetorix's former coconspirator, the Aedui leader Dumnorix, to intercede for them. Dumnorix was friendly with both the Sequani and Helvetii, having a reputation for fairness and generosity. Dumnorix cheerfully agreed, but like most politicians he had his own reasons for cooperating, namely his burning desire to increase his already significant power in eastern Gaul by acting as a powerbroker between hostile tribes. Dumnorix arranged for the Helvetii to give important hostages to the Sequani as a guarantee of their good behavior. If they ransacked the land as they passed through, the Sequani could then kill the Helvetian hostages. The Sequani would also give their own hostages to the Helvetii as a guarantee they would not betray them and attack as they crossed their territory.

Caesar soon learned of the new plans of the Helvetii and realized he was facing a much larger problem than battling one tribe of angry Gauls along a defended wall. If the Helvetii broke loose into central Gaul they could cause untold havoc that would threaten the Province and destabilize the whole country, encouraging further German movements into Gaul. The troops he possessed were not sufficient to handle this threat, so Caesar handed over defense of the wall to his old comrade Labienus, who was serving as his chief lieutenant in Gaul. Caesar himself rode quickly back to northern Italy and collected three legions he had kept there in reserve. He also made good use of his long patronage of Italian Gaul by recruiting two further legions from among the Celtic natives of the region. With five legions of Romanized Gauls, he set off to fight their untamed cousins beyond the Alps.

There was no time for a leisurely march along the Mediterranean past Massalia and up the Rhone to the land of the Allobroges. Instead, in a move typical of Caesar, he led his troops west past the modern Italian city of Turin into the snow-covered Alps by paths and passes no other Roman general would have even considered.

Wild mountain tribes blocked his advance, but Caesar broke through and forced his way down into the Rhone valley. Already he was making his young recruits believe in themselves and him by moving faster and harder than anyone thought possible.

In the time that it had taken Caesar to bring troops from Italy, the Helvetii had already moved out of the mountains, past the Sequani, and down into the lands of the Aedui. As predicted, they were looting and burning as they went, prompting the Aedui leaders to dispatch an embassy to Caesar requesting his intervention to protect their lands. As the Aedui had long been on friendly terms with Rome and had aided them in their wars against the Allobroges and Arverni in southern Gaul, they had a compelling case for expecting Roman help. The Helvetii, the Aedui claimed, were ravaging their lands, enslaving their children, and causing devastation and chaos just over the borders from the Roman province. Caesar could not have been happier. Here was the perfect excuse to intervene in Gaul—a formal plea for help from a long-standing Roman ally. Even the most obstructionist senators back in Rome could only approve if Caesar intervened to protect Roman interests in Gaul. Indeed, if he did not, they would surely condemn him for not carrying out his duties as a provincial governor. Even Dumnorix was happy, since the Helvetian invasion of his own tribal lands and subsequent Roman intervention bred just the sort of chaos he needed to overthrow the established order.

Caesar quickly led his army beyond the Rhone and north past the modern city of Lyon. At the sluggish Saône River, thousands of Helvetian warriors and their families were busy crossing to the western side over a rickety bridge made of rafts bound together. As Gauls were not known for their engineering skills, it had taken them twenty days of hard labor to construct this bridge. Caesar watched from afar until three-quarters of the tribe had moved across, then the Romans pounced. The bridge itself was easily blocked to prevent any assistance from their countrymen, then the legions turned to the

Gauls still on the eastern shore and began cutting them down. Many of the Helvetii were slain on the spot, while others managed to flee exhausted into the woods. To the Gauls watching from the west bank, it was a cowardly and dishonorable attack. But Caesar was not interested in Gaulish notions of heroic warfare—he was heavily outnumbered and determined to win by any means necessary. He was often merciful to a vanquished enemy, but only after the battle.

With a quarter of the Helvetii now either dead or scattered, Caesar quickly moved to pursue the rest who had already marched northwest into the heartland of the Aedui. Whereas it had taken the Gaulish invaders twenty days to build a bridge across the Saône, Caesar did it in one and immediately began moving his army across. The Helvetii were so unnerved by the destruction of part of their tribe and by the incredible speed of the Romans that they sent a respected elder named Divico to speak with Caesar. Divico had been a young commander of the Helvetii army almost fifty years earlier when they had defeated the legions sent against them and slain a Roman consul. Divico brought a very generous proposal to Caesar—if he would make peace with the Helvetii, they would be willing to settle down in any reasonable part of Gaul he selected. But if he continued to make war on them, he should remember that only by treachery had the Romans defeated a small portion of their people on the banks of the Saône. The Helvetii, he pointedly reminded Caesar, had learned from their ancestors to fight with courage like true men and did not rely on tricks. They had easily crushed a Roman army half a century before and were perfectly capable of doing it again.

Caesar listen politely, then told Divico that he was well aware of the Helvetii victory years past. For that very reason the Romans were determined to seek revenge. In addition, he could not allow the Helvetii to settle peacefully among the Gaulish tribes after they had already caused so much havoc. However, Caesar continued, he was a generous man and would allow the Helvetii to return home to their mountain valley if they would surrender hostages to the Romans to guarantee their good behavior in the future. In addition, they must pay a large reparation to the Aedui, whose lands they had ravaged. Just as Caesar knew he would, old Divico reddened in fury and spat back at Caesar that the Helvetii might take hostages from the Romans, but they would never give them. With that, the Gaulish embassy stormed out of the Roman camp.

The Helvetii had good reason to be confident since, even though they had lost a quarter of their warriors, they were still a formidable force far outnumbering the Romans. Because of this Caesar took a cautious approach and followed the Helvetii at a distance as they moved north over the hills deep into Aedui territory. The Romans relied almost exclusively on foreign allies for cavalry support in their wars, so Caesar had recruited four thousand horsemen from the Gauls of the Province and from the Aedui. He chose as their captain none other than the popular Aeduan leader Dumnorix, a man he had no reason to distrust as he knew nothing of his secretive dealings with the Helvetii. As the cavalry followed the Helvetii closely, Dumnorix spurred his men on to attack the enemy rearguard, contrary to Caesar's orders. Since the ground was unfavorable to horses, the Helvetii routed the allied cavalry. As Dumnorix had intended, the Helvetii were greatly encouraged by this victory just as the Romans were thoroughly disheartened.

Caesar was also having serious supply problems. Since Roman troops routinely lived off the land and relied on grain requisitioned from nearby tribes, Caesar had counted on his Aeduan allies to provide his troops with most of the food they needed during the campaign. But the Aedui were full of excuses why this wasn't happening—the weather was too cold, the grain wasn't ripe, there were problems with transport—but they assured him the rations would be at the Roman camp soon. After being put off repeatedly, Caesar realized his army was now in a dangerous situation far from

Roman territory and cut off from any reliable supplies. He called a council of the Aeduan leaders, including his friend Diviciacus and his brother, Dumnorix. Among those at the council was the Aeduan magistrate named Liscus, who warned Caesar darkly of treacherous plots against his army by some of his Aeduan countrymen. Liscus explained that as elected leader of the Aedui, he was doing everything he could to bring grain to the Romans, but that certain powerful, unnamed figures in the tribe were blocking his efforts. These conspirators were claiming that if they helped Caesar defeat the Helvetii, the Romans would then take over Gaul for themselves.

Caesar suspected Dumnorix at once. He dismissed the meeting but kept back Diviciacus and questioned him privately about his brother's actions. Diviciacus broke down and confessed that he also had heard such stories about Dumnorix, but had been bound by family loyalty not to betray his brother. He told Caesar that Dumnorix hated the Romans and wanted to be king of the Aedui. His brother was a charismatic figure adored by the common people who saw him as a champion of their rights against the entrenched nobility. Caesar must have marveled at how politics was the same whether in Rome or among barbarian tribes. He called in Dumnorix and told the would-be Catiline to his face that he knew all about his treacherous actions. Any other Roman general would then have promptly separated Dumnorix's head from his body, but Caesar, out of respect for his brother, Diviciacus, instead pardoned Dumnorix and placed him under guard.

Meanwhile, Caesar's situation was growing ever more dire as he moved farther into the hills and forests of central Gaul. He desperately needed to maneuver the Helvetii into a battle where he could use his smaller number of troops to the best advantage. The ideal opportunity soon arose when his scouts reported that the Helvetii had made camp at the base of a hill about eight miles to the north. If Caesar could get some of his troops on top of that hill, they could advance against the enemy from above—always an advantage in war. He could then bring the rest of his army from the opposite direction and trap the Helvetii between his soldiers descending from the hill and his main force in the valley. It was a perfect plan, but it all depended on speed and secrecy. Caesar immediately sent Labienus by night with two legions on a fast march to the opposite side of the hill from where the Helvetii were camped. In absolute silence, eight thousand men climbed over ridges and around trees until they reached the summit, at last gazing far below at the campfires of the Helvetii. At the same time, Caesar led the rest of the army through the night along the valley floor until they were a little over a mile from the Helvetii. Caesar quickly sent one of his most experienced veterans, Publius Considius, to confirm that Labienus was ready to spring the trap. It wasn't long until Considius was galloping back into the Roman camp to report that he had seen Gaulish troops swarming over the hill that Labienus should have taken. Cursing his luck, Caesar retreated with his army to a small hill nearby and drew up his troops in line to await the attack he knew was coming. Hour after hour, Caesar's troops stood ready for their first and perhaps last major battle. But as the day wore on, there was no attack. Finally, a messenger from Labienus rode into camp asking why Caesar had not launched an assault, as Labienus was under strict orders to do nothing until he saw the main army storming the Helvetii camp. It turned out that Considius had been completely mistaken as Labienus's troops had been holding the hill undetected for many hours. To make matters worse, the Helvetii had now moved their camp from under the hill and far away to the north.

It is to Caesar's credit that in his *Gallic War* he never hesitates to reveal the many mistakes he made during his campaigns. A military genius he was, but even the best generals can be confounded by the fog of war. Caesar was now in a truly perilous situation as his troops had only a two-day supply of food remaining and—more to his chagrin—had seen their commander let a golden opportunity for victory slip through his fingers. His pride would heal, but Caesar knew he had to find food for his troops quickly. His only chance lay almost twenty miles north at the hill fort of Bibracte, chief city of the Aedui. This enormous citadel loomed over the surrounding fields and held more than enough grain to feed his troops for many weeks. Thus Caesar ceased his pursuit of the Helvetii and turned his men towards Bibracte.

The Helvetii heard of Caesar's change of plans almost immediately from Gaulish deserters who had decided the Romans were a lost cause. The Helvetii had already learned of Caesar's fiasco beneath the hill the previous night; now they believed the Romans were panicking and could be easily finished off. The Helvetian leaders turned their army after Caesar and struck the Roman rearguard before Caesar's troops could reach Bibracte. While his allied cavalry held back the Helvetian advance for a few precious minutes, Caesar quickly stationed four of his legions halfway up a steeply sloping hill. He placed the rest of his troops on top of the hill along with all their equipment and remaining supplies. The Roman army then stood in formation while tens of thousands of Helvetian warriors marched up the valley and finally turned to face the smaller Roman force. The Helvetii knew the Roman soldiers were hungry, tired, and still inexperienced, most of them farm boys from the Province and northern Italy. Now the grim-faced Helvetian warriors, veterans of countless victories against the Germans, stood gazing with contempt at the Roman troops and thirsting for revenge.

Caesar was about to lead the first great fight of his life. Of course, he had directed many minor skirmishes in Spain and had supervised the previous ambush of the Helvetii, but never before was he responsible for the lives of thousands of men in a formal battle. He and every one of the troops with him knew that if they failed to defeat the Helvetii on this hillside, there was little chance any of them would ever see home again. The first thing Caesar did after drawing up his men was to send away his horse—and to make sure all his men saw him doing it. Caesar's horse was a unique animal born with cloven hoofs that looked almost like human toes. Soothsayers had declared at its birth that its master would someday rule the world, so Caesar had taken the greatest care in rearing the foal. The horse adored Caesar and would not allow anyone else to ride it. The affection was returned by his master, who would one day dedicate a statue of the beast at the temple of his ancestral deity, Venus, but for now the horse was led away along with the mounts of the other officers. Caesar wanted his men to know that he would face with them whatever fate lay ahead. Finally, he used his oratorical skills to deliver a short but powerful speech of encouragement to his troops—then the battle began.

The Helvetii were not pleased to be fighting an enemy that had the advantage of the high ground, but they so outnumbered the Romans that they must have felt confident. They could, however, expect the Romans to use their position to a defensive advantage, forcing the Helvetii to march up the hill to them. The Gauls were therefore surprised when they saw the Roman troops moving swiftly down the slope toward them. When they were just a few dozen yards from the mass of Helvetian warriors, the legionaries launched their deadly javelins at the Gauls. A few Helvetii fell, but most of the javelins stuck firmly into their large wooden shields. More volleys from the Roman lines sent countless javelins toward the Gauls until their shields were weighted down with the heavy iron points that could not be removed even after the wooden shafts had been broken off. In frustration, most of the Helvetii in the front lines simply threw away their shields and fought without cover. This gave the Romans a tremendous advantage as they drew their swords and charged in close formation straight at the Helvetii.

The Gauls broke under the Roman charge and retreated as they fought, many with serious wounds, across the bottom of the valley then up the opposite hillside. The Romans had managed to win the first part of the battle, but they slowed as they were now forced to fight while charging uphill. At this point, the Boii and the other allies of the Helvetii who had stood in reserve up the valley attacked the Romans on their right flank. This forced Caesar to split his already smaller force in two to attack the Helvetii on the hill in front of them and the fresh Boian troops who were now hitting them from the side. The Romans were hard pressed to fight on two fronts, but Caesar managed to hold his men together as the battle turned into a grueling struggle for survival that lasted long into the evening. At last the Helvetian defense collapsed, with some retreating north into the forests while others made a final stand around their baggage carts. As the last of the light was dying in the west, the Romans finally destroyed the remaining Helvetian warriors who, according to Caesar, had not once turned their backs on the Romans in an attempt to flee.

Caesar captured several daughters of the late Helvetian leader Orgetorix among the baggage carts as well as one of his sons, but many thousands of their fellow tribesmen had managed to escape. Still, when the count was completed, at least half of the Helvetii who had faced the Romans with such confidence that morning were now either dead or captured. Those who had fled sought refuge among the Lingones tribe just to the north, but Caesar had already dispatched messengers to the Lingones warning that if they aided the Helvetii in any way, he would treat them as enemies of Rome. Shut out of the Lingones' land and facing the victorious Romans at their back, the Helvetii were sure they would be overwhelmed at any moment by Caesar. But Caesar's troops were so exhausted and so many were suffering from wounds that they could not have pursued the Helvetii if they had wanted to. It took Caesar three whole days to tend to the wounded and bury the dead before he could move his army north to follow the escaping Gauls.

The embassy from the Helvetii found Caesar's army marching north. They threw themselves at his feet and sought his mercy, saying that they had no food and only wanted peace. Caesar granted their petition, insisting that they return to their mountain valley and serve there as a defense against German encroachment into Gaul.

They would be granted enough grain and seed to begin their lives again, provided that they surrender hostages to him as a guarantee of their good intentions and that they hand over any slaves who had deserted to them from the Roman army. The Helvetian legates agreed at once and returned to their camp to fulfill the terms. But during the night some of the tribe broke away and made a dash to the Rhine to seek sanctuary among Germans, fearing that Caesar would slaughter them all once they had lain down their arms. The Romans quickly rounded up these fugitives and Caesar—not one to show clemency twice—had them all enslaved or killed.

Among the remains of the Helvetian camp Caesar found tablets written in the Gaulish language but using Greek letters. The druids were forbidden to record any of their secrets in writing, but ordinary Gauls used the Greek, Etruscan, and Roman alphabets to write down everything from tax records and epitaphs to erotic messages and magic spells. The tablets that Caesar uncovered were a census of all the Helvetii and their allies, recording that over three hundred thousand men, women, and children had set off from Lake Geneva weeks before to seek a new land in western Gaul. Caesar now conducted his own census and discovered that barely a third of them would be returning home.

Caesar had won the first great military victory of his career and could report to the Senate that the Province and Italy itself were finally safe from the marauding Helvetii. Since slaves taken in a war traditionally belonged to the victorious commander, Caesar could also make a tidy sum selling his captives to the eager slave traders who followed ancient armies on campaign. But the Romans were not the only ones pleased with the Helvetian defeat. Caesar writes that representatives from most of the Gaulish tribes converged on his camp and expressed their gratitude for his victory over their rapacious countrymen. Undoubtedly, the enthusiasm for a major Roman victory in the heart of Gaul was not unanimous as Caesar records, but there was genuine relief from most tribes that the Helvetii were out of the way. The prospect of thousands of Helvetian warriors running amok through the countryside was terrifying even to those Gaulish tribes who hated Rome. The Gauls had to admit that the mighty empire to the south had so far shown no interest in expanding its territory north of the Mediterranean basin. The legions might march into Gaul on occasion to punish an unruly tribe or stand up for an ally such as the Aedui, but they always returned to the warm lands of the Province as winter approached. The Gauls saw no reason why Caesar should be any different.

Confident that Rome had no long-term interest in conquering Gaul, the tribal leaders asked if they could hold a private meeting with Caesar to discuss a pressing matter of mutual concern. They chose Caesar's trusted friend Diviciacus as spokesman and swore an oath to the Celtic gods that no one would reveal what they were about to say. Diviciacus then explained to Caesar that two of the major Gaulish tribes, the Sequani and the Arverni, had conspired with the Germans to gain power over the rest of Gaul. They had invited the brutal Germanic chieftain Ariovistus to intervene against the Gaulish Aedui and their allies. At first, this had gone well since only a small number of German warriors had crossed the Rhine. But Ariovistus had refused to return to Germany when he was no longer needed and had instead brought more than a hundred thousand of his wild countrymen to settle in Gaul. He had forced many of the Gaulish tribes to surrender children to him as hostages—if the Gauls failed to do his bidding, he tortured their sons and daughters in the most unspeakable ways until they changed their minds. Now more and more Germans were pouring across the Rhine every year, so that soon all of Gaul would be overrun by these barbarians. The Gaulish tribes could not fight the Germans alone. Many were in fact already making plans to emigrate just like the Helvetii, threatening massive instability in western Europe that was sure to spill over into Roman territory. The only hope of the Gaulish people was if the Romans would intervene and drive the Germans out. Even the Sequanian delegates at the meeting were now anxious for Caesar to come to their aid. If the previous request of the Aedui for Roman assistance had been convenient for Caesar's plans, a plea from a whole confederation of Gaulish tribes to protect them from the Germans was a dream come true.

In Caesar's report of this council to his Roman readers, he is at great pains to explain why it was necessary for him to fight the Germans in Gaul. His previous war against the Helvetii was less controversial as they had clearly threatened the Province, but German incursions across the Rhine were still far to the north of Roman territory. Caesar argues his case step-by-step like the lawyer he was. First, the Gauls, most especially the longtime Roman allies the Aedui, had formally requested his assistance. Second, the act of mistreating hostages from among the friends of the Roman people was a slur against Rome itself. Third and most importantly, Ariovistus was leading Germans by the thousands into Gaul. It was only a matter of time, Caesar stresses, before they moved south to threaten the Province and even Italy just as the dreaded Cimbri and Teutones had done half a century before. The Germans could soon be at the gates of Rome unless he stopped them.

Caesar conveniently downplays the fact that he himself had been a major supporter of Ariovistus when the Germanic leader had earlier sought Roman friendship. Nevertheless, as disingenuous as Caesar is in his narrative at this point, he was absolutely right to call the Germans a threat to Rome. For many years the Germanic tribes had been spreading steadily southward out of their homeland in northern Europe. With their exploding population and unmatched skill in war, they had already pushed the Celts out of southern Germany and were now threatening Gaul. The Alps would be no real barrier to the Germans if they decided to cross into Italy. But if Caesar could stop them at the Rhine, Rome would be safe for many years to come.

The Germans, dwelling as they did in the dark forests and distant shores of northern Europe, were a great mystery to the Romans. In fact, aside from a few scattered remarks by traders and explorers, Caesar gives us the earliest extensive description of the Germanic people. Like the Gauls, the Germans never saw themselves as a nation but rather as independent tribes with a related language and culture, who were more often than not at war with each other. Caesar speaks from experience when he describes them as fierce warriors with little use for farming or luxuries such as wine. Instead, they prided themselves on bravery in battle and toughness developed by bathing in freezing streams from childhood. They were especially skilled at cavalry warfare, though they scoffed at anyone who used a saddle. Those who betrayed their people or showed cowardice in war were subject to execution by the warriors of the tribal assembly, either by hanging from a tree or drowning in a bog.

There were tribal kings among the Germans, but real power lay with military leaders such as Ariovistus, who could inspire and reward any warriors who chose to follow them. The Germans worshipped a multitude of gods and were especially devoted to divination conducted by priestesses, who would cut branches from a nut-bearing tree, strip them of bark, then cast them on a white cloth. If the lots promised good fortune, then business could proceed; but if the branches were ill-omened, nothing—not even battles—could take place.

Caesar was determined to try diplomacy with the Germans before he committed himself to war. He invited Ariovistus to a meeting at a neutral spot halfway between their two armies, but the German leader sent back a message saying that if Caesar wanted to talk, he would have to come to the German camp. Ariovistus haughtily added that it was no business of Caesar's what he or any other German might do in Gaul. Caesar refused to be provoked and instead sent a letter laying out three conditions of peace between Ariovistus and Rome—first, he would bring no more Germans across the Rhine; second, he would return all Gaulish hostages; and third, he would no longer make war on any Gaulish tribe. Caesar added that if these conditions were not met, he would be forced by honor to defend the interests of the Gauls in battle. It is notable that Caesar did not demand that Ariovistus return back across the Rhine. Unlike the Helvetii, he would be permitted with his people to remain in Gaul.

Ariovistus, however, did not see Caesar's conditions as generous. He sent back yet another message asking who on earth Caesar thought he was issuing demands and threatening him with war when he had done no more than the Romans themselves had accomplished all over the Mediterranean. Rome conquered any land that suited its fancy and never asked permission in doing so nor suffered interference from any third party. He would not release any Gaulish hostages and, if Caesar knew what was good for him, he would withdraw his troops back to the Province before he was taught a bloody lesson on just how unbeatable the Germans really were.

As Caesar was reading the message from Ariovistus, he received a report from the tribes of the Aedui and the Gaulish Treveri to the north that a German people called the Harudes were ransacking their lands. In addition, a huge number of Germans were gathering on the eastern bank of the Rhine ready to cross into Gaul. Rightly expecting that Ariovistus was behind these new threats, Caesar realized that if additional Germans joined Ariovistus in Gaul, his task of driving them out might become impossible. The time for talk was over, so he set out immediately for the Gaulish fortress of Vesontio (modern Besançon) halfway to the Rhine to seize this strategic and well-supplied base before Ariovistus could lay claim to it. By forced marches day and night, Caesar reached the town ahead of the Germans and posted a garrison there to hold the citadel for the Romans.

Through dark, silent forests unlike anything the Romans had ever seen, Caesar led his army from Vesontio toward the Rhine and Ariovistus. His men found themselves marching through endless woods so thick the trees blocked out the sun for days at a time. Soon a cold panic began to spread through the army. Those few who had seen Germans before whispered around campfires that these barbarians were giants, ferocious in battle, with eyes so piercing you couldn't look them in the face. Some of the wealthy young men Caesar had brought along from Rome to gain experience in war suddenly began to think of reasons they were needed at home. Others, too ashamed to leave, were found weeping in their tents or exchanging the latest grim rumors with their companions. The common soldiers were soon overcome by the same fear and began to make out their wills. Even older experienced soldiers—proven centurions and cavalry commanders—who had fought in battles throughout the Mediterranean started to feel panic creeping up their bones. Some tried to hide their fear by claiming it wasn't really the Germans they were worried about but the impenetrable forest or the uncertain grain supply. Murmurings even arose among some who declared they would not move a step closer to the Germans no matter what Caesar ordered.

Caesar realized this mutiny was potentially the most difficult challenge he had ever faced. If he could not control his own army, he was finished as a military leader and would be laughed out of public life by Cato and the optimates back in Rome. But like most challenges, Caesar approached this crisis boldly in an unexpected fashion. He immediately called together not his officers and tribunes, but the dozens of veteran centurions who were the true backbone of his army. These sergeants of the Roman legions were all seasoned soldiers who directed life in the camp and on the march—and most importantly, stood by their men on the line in the heat of battle. Caesar knew if he could persuade them, the rest of the army would follow. Spoiled young tribunes from the nobility of Rome he could deal with or even do without, but he had to have the centurions on his side.

Instead of negotiating or promising them rewards as other generals might have, he struck at the centurions with a furious passion—
who do you think you are, he demanded, to question where I am
leading you? You are Roman soldiers, part of the greatest army the
world has ever seen. Your job is to obey the orders of your commander and lead your men into whatever battle I deem fit. You
might not even have to fight Ariovistus if the fool will listen to
reason—but even if you do, what are you afraid of? Marius destroyed a much larger German army in the time of your grandfa-
thers. And you yourselves just conquered the Helvetii, a tribe that
had defeated Germans countless times before. Ariovistus is a coward
who hides in swamps and strikes like a bandit out of the woods. He
will collapse before our army on the battlefield. You won't follow
me? Fine, we're packing up and marching against Ariovistus
tonight. If you don't know the meaning of Roman duty and honor—
if you are cowards—then stay here. I'll march with the tenth legion
alone, brave lads who have always stood by me, and we'll conquer
the Germans on our own while you lot crawl home in disgrace.

Caesar's centurions were so shamed by his words that they immediately declared their willingness to follow him anywhere. Legates
and officers then fell all over themselves explaining that their hesi-
tancy had all been a misunderstanding and that their loyalty to Caesar was unwavering. Caesar graciously accepted their explanations
and considered the matter closed. When they struck camp that night,
not a single man stayed behind. On the other hand, Caesar was wise
enough to have Diviciacus lay out a new path toward the Germans
that avoided the dense forest, even though it added an extra fifty
miles to their journey.

After a weeklong march the Roman army drew near to the camp
of Ariovistus and the Rhine. The German leader sent a message that
he was now willing to meet with Caesar, but he was very cautious
and sent numerous deputies back and forth to the Roman camp to
negotiate the details of the talks. His key demand was that Caesar

bring no infantry with him to the meeting, only a cavalry escort. As Ariovistus well knew, all of Caesar's cavalry were Gauls and could not necessarily be trusted to follow orders or guard their commander wholeheartedly. To remedy this, Caesar had members of his trusted tenth legion mount the Gallic horses instead and accompany him to the meeting. These legionaries laughed, saying that Caesar certainly had great faith in them since he was demoting them to common horse soldiers, but they were genuinely touched that he entrusted his life to them.

Ariovistus was so edgy when they arrived at the appointed meeting place at a mound in the center of a nearby open plain that he insisted they bring forward only ten men each to the negotiations and that both he and Caesar should converse on horseback. Caesar began by telling Ariovistus face-to-face what he had said in his previous message—that the Germans must stop their movement across the Rhine and treat the Aedui honorably. Ariovistus contemptuously replied that he was acting according to the laws of war and would do as he wished with what he regarded as his portion of Gaul. He didn't need Caesar's approval and would gladly have their armies settle the whole matter on the battlefield. Then he let slip a telling piece of information—he had received private messengers from the optimates in the Roman Senate implying they would be only too happy to have the Germans slaughter Caesar and his army.

If Ariovistus had intended to unnerve Caesar with this disclosure, it didn't work. He continued to insist that the Germans must abide by his terms if they desired to remain on this side of the Rhine. While this exchange was taking place, Caesar received word that the horsemen of Ariovistus were harassing his cavalry on the edge of the plain, throwing stones and the occasional javelin at them. Caesar, of course, knew that Ariovistus was trying to provoke him, but he withdrew himself and his men back to their camp rather than be accused of violating a flag of truce.

A couple of days later Ariovistus sent a message to Caesar sug-

gesting they meet again or that he at least send some senior deputies
to him that they might discuss matters further. Caesar smelled a trap
but was reluctant to pass up any opportunity for negotiations, so he
sent two of his most trusted men to the German camp. Once there
they were immediately accused of spying and thrown into chains.

As much as Ariovistus was trying to annoy the Romans, he curi-
ously did not seem anxious for a full-scale conflict as yet. This puz-
zled Caesar greatly as he could see no advantage for Ariovistus
delaying, especially as the German leader had the advantage of numbers and was clearly itching for a fight. The Germans had already
moved their camp two miles to the west of the Romans so that they
could cut them off from any reinforcements or supplies from Gaul.
Now the Romans were wedged between the Germans and the
Rhine, a situation Caesar would have used immediately to his advantage if he had been Ariovistus. Caesar wasn't afraid, however, and
marched his troops out of camp five consecutive days to face the Germans and offer battle, but Ariovistus did nothing except to send
forth a few of his cavalry. Caesar could not understand what the Germans were waiting for.

On the sixth day Caesar decided to leapfrog past the Germans
and establish a second Roman camp to their west to ensure they
could not block his grain supply from Gaul. To make sure his men
were safe while building this camp, he marched them to the new site
in triple-line formation. The front two lines stood guard against the
annoying cavalry of Ariovistus while the third line pulled out their
shovels and constructed an impregnable fort. He left two legions in
this second camp only a few hundred yards from the Germans and
moved the other four legions back to their original position. This
was a clever move on Caesar's part because even though he was far
outnumbered by the Germans, he effectively had them pinned between his two camps.

The next day Ariovistus launched a fearsome raid on the new
Roman base, but still refused to commit his troops to a major battle.

Thanks to several Germans captured during the foray, however, Caesar was finally able to discover why Ariovistus was hesitating. The captives said that their priestesses had cast lots forbidding them to attack with the entire army until the new moon. The German warriors were in such awe of these diviners that they refused to disobey them for fear of losing the war. Caesar must have smiled when he heard this news, because the prisoners had just handed him a powerful weapon.

The next day Caesar left just enough men in each camp to guard against a surprise attack and then marched the rest of his army right up to the German camp. Caesar was going to compel the Germans to fight him no matter what their priestesses ordered. Thus when Ariovistus and his men came storming out of their camp, each was fearful that they were fighting against the will of their gods. In a culture where divination was a deadly serious business, this hesitation gave Caesar a compelling psychological advantage.

Whatever religious scruples they may have had, the Germans fought with great bravery. They rushed against the Romans so fast that the legions had no time to launch their javelins. These were cast aside and swords were quickly drawn, commencing a fierce struggle among thousands of men at close quarters. The Germans formed closely packed groups protected by their shields and pushed the Romans back, until a few legionaries actually leapt on top of the Germans and began tearing their shields away. The bloody conflict raged back and forth with the living stepping over the bodies of the dead. Finally, a young officer named Publius Crassus, son of Caesar's triumvirate partner, rallied the troops on the far side of the line and began to force the Germans back. At this crucial moment, the Romans knew they would win.

The Germans broke and ran toward the Rhine, though precious few ever made it across the river. Some, like Ariovistus, managed to escape by boat, but most were slain at the riverbank by the pursuing Roman cavalry or drowned in a futile attempt to swim to the other side. The Romans were so caught up in victory that they spared almost no one, including women and children. Ariovistus abandoned two of his wives and one of his daughters to be slain by the Romans. Caesar himself was at the fore of the cavalry pursuit when by chance he came across one of his deputies who had been treacherously seized by the Germans days before. The young man was being dragged in chains by his captors as the Romans cut them down. Caesar says he was as thrilled to find his friend safe as he was to win the battle. The weary but elated officer told Caesar how the Germans had planned to burn him alive, but the lots they cast three times kept telling the priestesses to wait.

With the battle won, news quickly spread to the German tribes on the east side of the Rhine that Ariovistus was defeated. Since many of the Germans hated the upstart warlord, they were only too happy to slay any of his men they could find hiding in their territory. Thus in a few months' time, in the summer of 58 B.C., Caesar had triumphed in two great wars against both Gauls and Germans, the two most feared enemies of Rome. It was a remarkable achievement in Roman military history, but it was only the beginning of Caesar's plans. The Gaulish allies who had urged Caesar to save them from the Helvetii and Ariovistus were immensely grateful and were now ready to escort him back to the Province with full honors. Instead, Caesar made a winter camp for his troops among the Sequani, far to the north of Roman territory, and left Labienus in command. It now dawned on the Gauls what was happening. This Roman camp deep inside their lands served no military purpose except as a forward base for Caesar to use the next spring in further campaigns. The Romans were in Gaul to stay.

VI

THE BELGAE

The enemy never gave up even when they had no
hope of victory. When those on the front line had
fallen, those behind moved forward and stood on the
bodies of their comrades to fight.

—CAESAR

With the Germans defeated and the legions firmly ensconced
at their winter quarters in central Gaul, Caesar now journeyed back to his province in northern Italy. Governors were expected to be present in their home territories at least part of the year
no matter how many wars they were waging beyond the borders.
There were always cases to be heard and decisions to be made that
required a governor's attention—reviewing citizenship petitions, supervising public works, crucifying criminals. Caesar handled most of
these administrative matters during his campaigns with the help of
his many secretaries and messengers. Even while he was riding between camps, he would keep a scribe at hand so he could dictate
notes and dispatch orders back to Italy. But some problems could
only be solved in person. Caesar never regretted his time in the Po
valley away from the army since the convenient proximity of the
province to Rome allowed him to participate in Senate politics al-

most as if he were present in the city. For confidential communications with his supporters in the city, he used a code based on switching letters of the alphabet, guaranteeing frustration for anyone who might intercept his mail. During these winter months there was a constant stream of high-level visitors from Rome to Caesar's headquarters just over the Apennine mountains.

The new force on the Roman political scene during Caesar's absence in Gaul was the unpredictable ex-patrician tribune Clodius. Before Caesar had left to fight the Helvetii, Clodius had already passed an unprecedented free-grain bill to the horror of the Senate. Previous food distribution in the city of Rome had been at a discounted price to the truly needy, but Clodius was establishing a welfare state gone wild by passing out grain at no cost to a large portion of the city's population. A substantial share of the government revenue suddenly shifted to paying for the largesse of Clodius. It was an obvious ploy to garner the favor of the urban masses, but it worked nonetheless. Clodius was rapidly building up a huge base of populist support to use in his many devious schemes.

But unlike other optimates or populists, no one could ever be sure which side Clodius would take on any particular issue. For the first few months of his tribunate, he followed a generally populist line, but his prime motivation seemed to be furthering his personal vendettas. He managed to have Cicero exiled for his questionable execution of the Catalinian conspirators, just as Caesar had warned at the time. Clodius even had Cicero's house destroyed and a temple to the goddess Liberty erected on the site. Now Clodius, with Caesar's wholehearted support, devised an ingenious plan for removing Cato from the Roman political scene as well. Many years earlier, Clodius, like Caesar, had been kidnapped by Cilician pirates, who held him for ransom. Clodius had arrogantly demanded that the nearby king of Cyprus pay the required gold, but the island ruler had not been enthusiastic about ransoming such an ill-mannered Roman youth. When Clodius finally was released from the pirate camp, he vowed he would have his revenge against the king someday. Now Clodius put before the popular assembly a bill for Rome to annex Cyprus. Included in the legislation was a provision that Cato be given extraordinary powers to oversee the takeover. This was a particularly Clodian twist of the knife since Cato had long been Rome's chief opponent of granting extraordinary powers to anyone. If Cato refused, he would be guilty of defying the will of the Roman people. In the end, Cato grudgingly agreed to depart for Cyprus, much to Caesar's delight.

But Caesar's support of Clodius soon waned when the volatile tribune turned against the general's triumvirate partner and son-in-law. Clodius first attempted to assassinate Pompey and, failing in that endeavor, blockaded him in his own house. The optimates saw in this recklessness a possible wedge to drive Pompey from Caesar and destroy the triumvirate, even proposing that Pompey divorce Caesar's daughter, Julia, and join their side. But Pompey rejected this ploy and remained firm in his loyalty to Caesar, though he did begin working with the optimates to recall Cicero from exile.

Caesar soon had much more to worry about than politics in Rome. All during the winter while his army remained in camp in central Gaul, the fearsome Belgic tribes in northern France, Belgium, and the Netherlands had been watching and making plans to destroy the Romans. The Belgae had reasonably concluded that since the Romans had previously conquered southern Gaul and were now clearly starting a takeover of central Gaul, the north would soon be next. Better to face the Romans now, the Belgic tribes reckoned, than wait for them to consolidate their power over all the lands south of the Seine River. The Belgae were also being stirred up by refugee nobility from central Gaul, who were upset that the Romans had ruined their plans for gaining political sway over their home tribes. Many of these would-be kings were perfectly content with the chaotic infighting that had dominated Gaul for centuries and relished the chance to play different tribes against each other to increase their own personal power. But the Romans were a new and unwelcome factor. If Rome gained ascendancy in Gaul, the entire game of who controlled the resources and manpower of the land would shift from a fractured tribal model to a centralized government run by distant governors and magistrates. Some Gauls, such as Diviciacus, were quick to realize that they could profit if they were part of the new Roman system. They would have to surrender their tribe's independence, but the Romans always rewarded local noblemen who cooperated with its empire. The Belgae, however, were a fiercely independent collection of tribes who wanted nothing to do with peace, commerce, or the fruits of civilization. With one notable exception, the tribes of the Belgae were prepared to face the Romans on the battlefield.

News of Belgic war preparations reached Caesar in northern Italy during the early spring, so he quietly began to recruit and train two new legions at his own cost from the Celtic farmlands of the Po valley. The Gaulish nature of his recruits from northern Italy was evident in many ways, including their language. One group from Italian Gaul even chose the nickname *alauda* (Gaulish for "lark") for their legion. Caesar dispatched these soldiers in the early summer to join his six veteran legions already stationed in central Gaul. Caesar soon followed and took command of his army just as the first grain began to ripen. What no one seems to have noticed at the time—and which Caesar never mentions—is that his force of eight legions was twice the number the Senate had actually authorized for the army of Gaul. Since Caesar had paid for half of these with his own money, they significantly felt more loyalty to Caesar than to the state. Although Celtic by birth and culture, the recruits from northern Italy were equipped with the best Roman arms and thoroughly trained in Roman tactics and discipline. They were proud to call themselves Romans and would one day by rewarded by Caesar with the coveted citizenship.

Caesar now moved the legions north to the borders of the Belgae. He had charged the nearby Senones tribe with keeping him informed of Belgic movements—and all reports were that the Belgae were gathering to fight the Romans. This was especially troubling to Caesar as the Belgic tribes had never previously agreed on anything except perpetual warfare with each other. Now they had laid aside their differences and were prepared to cooperate against the Romans. Caesar knew that if they maintained their united front his army would be in serious danger. He was therefore delighted when a delegation from the Belgic tribe of the Remi, from around their namesake city of modern Reims northeast of Paris, arrived at his headquarters. The Remi were the Belgic tribe closest to central Gaul and therefore the best informed about the Romans. The leaders of the Remi had met during the winter and devised a practical response to the Roman threat. The Remi had shrewdly calculated that the Romans were the rising power in Gaul and were unbeatable on the battlefield; thus they offered themselves to Caesar as allies against their Belgic kinfolk. They would provide him with any information he might desire and assist him with food supplies, auxiliary troops, or anything else he might require. They agreed to surrender to Caesar as hostages the children of their own chieftains as proof of their loyalty. Caesar was thrilled with the Remi's offer and quickly agreed to welcome them as friends of the Roman people. This firm base of support in northern Gaul was to prove an incalculable advantage to Caesar throughout the war.

Caesar learned from the Remi that the Belgae had originally lived to the east of the Rhine, but had migrated from Germany long ago in search of better land. They were a fiercely proud people who boasted that they, alone of the Gauls, had repulsed the dreaded Cimbri and Teutones invaders in the previous century. There were many Belgic tribes, but the Bellovaci and the Nervii were counted as the bravest. The Bellovaci claimed they could muster a hundred thousand warriors and had insisted on overall command of the Belgic forces fighting Rome. Other tribes, such as the Atrebates, Morini, and Caleti, each pledged tens of thousands of warriors. The Suessiones, neighbors and friends of the Remi, promised fifty thousand men.

Caesar called the Aeduan chief Diviciacus to his tent and laid out his plan for fighting the Belgae. It was imperative, Caesar insisted, that the Belgic tribes be prevented from gathering as a single force. He therefore ordered Diviciacus to lead the Aeduan auxiliaries into the lands of the Bellovaci and lay waste to their crops. Caesar was betting that this most powerful of the Belgic tribes would soon abandon the coalition if they saw their own fields burning. Caesar then set out to meet the approaching enemy. Time and again in the Gallic war, Caesar displayed a genius for picking the right ground for a fight. In this case, he moved just beyond the Aisne River on the border of the Remi so that his camp was on the far side with the river to his rear. There on top of a hill next to the Aisne, he entrenched a formidable camp looking down on a swampy stream to his north, through which the Belgae would have to approach if they wanted to attack. He secured his supply lines to the Remi with a bridge over the Aisne guarded by a small fort on the southern bank. Then he waited as the Belgae drew near.

The leaders of the Belgic forces were no fools and quickly attempted to bait Caesar out of his camp by instead launching an attack on the Remi town of Bibrax only eight miles away. The Belgae had a very effective technique for taking a town, though they lacked the massive towers and siege works favored by the Romans. The army surrounded the site and drove the defenders on the walls to seek cover by a constant and overwhelming barrage of stones. While the walls were cleared, a group of warriors locked shields above their heads and moved to the weakest point of the town, attempting then to quickly undermine the wall. The ferocious assault on Bibrax lasted throughout the day, but the townspeople were able to beat back the invaders before nightfall. The Remi commander sent a message to Caesar warning him they would not survive another attack without help.

Caesar knew he could not play into the enemy's hands and abandon his secure position. His thirty- or forty thousand men could not beat a Belgic army at least five times that size if he let the Belgae choose the time and place of battle. He therefore decided to send something against the enemy that they had never encountered before. He had no elephants like Hannibal, but he did have a number of Cretan archers and Balearic slingers in his auxiliary units. These soldiers were from distant islands on opposite ends of the Mediterranean, but they shared an uncanny skill at hitting their targets from unheard-of distances. When they sneaked into Bibrax later that night, they brought hope to the besieged Remi just by their presence; but the next morning, when the Belgae attacked yet again, they showed their true worth. The Belgic warriors standing at what they thought was a safe distance from the city walls suddenly heard shrill whistles cutting through the air all around them—and men began to fall as the missiles shattered their skulls. Some slingers used smooth stones, but others preferred molded lead balls that were almost impossible to see in flight and could debilitate a man even if they didn't penetrate his armor. Then arrows from the Cretan archers on the walls found their targets among the warriors of the Belgic lines. The Belgae were totally unnerved by these strange and deadly new attacks. They abandoned their siege and headed instead toward Caesar's camp, burning every Remi farm they could find along the way out of sheer frustration.

The Belgae arrived just north of Caesar's fort and pitched their own camp on a broad hill at the far side of the narrow swamp. About two miles separated the camps, so the Romans could easily see the vast hordes of the Belgae stretched out before them. That night, the Belgic campfires burned across the hill like thousands of stars in the Gaulish sky. Even taking into account the Roman habit of exaggerating enemy numbers for effect, Caesar was no doubt vastly outmanned. The site of countless Belgae was so terrifying and their reputation for warfare so formidable that Caesar hesitated at first to meet them on the battlefield. But after a few days during which the Roman cavalry skirmished successfully with the Belgic horsemen, Caesar decided to risk an open battle. He was still cautious, not willing to unduly risk the lives of his men, but he knew he could not defeat the Belgae by remaining in camp. Caesar positioned his men on the hill in front of his camp that sloped gently down to the swampy stream. On both sides of his troops he had dug a deep protective trench at right angles to his line so that the enemy could attack only from the front. This would in effect funnel the Belgic multitude into a narrow space no wider than Caesar's own front line and seriously reduce their advantage in numbers. At the near end of each trench he positioned his artillery to guard against a flanking movement and to fire deadly volleys at the Gauls as they charged the Roman lines. The dreaded *scorpiones* ("scorpions") were a particularly effective piece of Caesar's artillery that were basically large crossbows with the capacity to fire oversized arrows with incredible force at great distance. Stone-throwing *ballistae* capable of decapitating a man may also have been set up along the trenches even though these were normally used for assaulting towns.

The Belgae brought their troops out of camp and stood facing the Romans on their own hill on the far side of the muddy, reed-covered stream. The Romans waited; the Belgae waited. But neither side was willing to cross the narrow swamp to attack the other. Now and then horsemen from both sides clashed between the lines and provided a bit of a distraction as the hours wore on, but still neither army moved. Finally, Caesar led his troops back to the protection of the Roman camp. Caesar was smart enough not to be provoked into exposing his men to a fight under unfavorable conditions, but he was disturbed to find that the Belgic leaders and warriors were equally self-controlled.

But the Belgae were not finished for the day. As soon as the Romans disappeared behind their walls, the warriors moved in mass far around the Roman camp using the hills and trees as cover. Their plan was to secretly ford the Aisne River, destroy the small Roman fort guarding the southern approach, then storm the Roman camp unexpectedly from behind. Fortunately for Caesar, his scouts reported the enemy movements in time for him to lead a force of cavalry, archers, and slingers across the bridge to the small fort. From there they spread along the river and were waiting on the southern bank when the first Belgae appeared on the opposite shore. Even Caesar admits that the battle at the river was unbelievably fierce. The Roman cavalry rushed the Belgic warriors while they were still in the river and cut many down. Others were killed by arrows and missiles from the Cretan archers and Balearic slingers who had returned from the siege of Bibrax. The few Belgae who managed to cross the river were slain with the greatest difficulty by Roman cavalry. But still, the Belgae on the north side of the Aisne kept coming, using the bodies of their dead comrades as a bridge across the bloody river.

At last the Belgic leaders realized their plan had failed. They retreated to their camp and held a council that evening on what to do next about Caesar. Since their strategy of luring Caesar into open battle against their massive army had failed, it seemed best to let him make the next move. The Belgae decided that each tribe should return home and wait to see where the Romans would strike. Whichever tribe the legions attacked, the Belgic leaders pledged they would all immediately bring their troops to their aid. Just as Caesar had planned, the Bellovaci were particularly anxious to leave since Diviciacus and his Aeduan troops were busy ravaging their lands.

The Belgic forces departed that very night tribe by tribe to their respective homes amid great disorder and commotion. Caesar naturally heard the uproar of their departure, but kept his men in camp fearing that this was a trick to lure his men into a trap. He couldn't believe any army would deliberately break camp in such a raucous fashion unless they were up to no good. But when morning came,

Caesar's scouts confirmed that the Belgic tribes were indeed in retreat with no signs of an ambush laid for the Romans. Not one to let
such an opportunity pass, he ordered his cavalry to pursue and attack
the departing warriors. The rear guard of the Belgae put up a brave
fight so that their comrades could escape to safety, but by the end of
the day many of them had been slain.

During the first two years of the war in Gaul, Caesar was quite con-
sciously training his troops to a new standard of military performance
and personal loyalty. No Roman general ever pressed his troops
harder than Caesar, but no army ever followed its leader more willingly. Caesar didn't care what kind of background his men came
from, whether they were Roman patricians by birth or the sons of a
goatherd. All that mattered to him was how they conducted themselves in war. He didn't address his men by the standard term *milites*
("soldiers"), but as *commilitones* ("comrades"). During the season
when they were not on campaign he indulged his men shamelessly,
turning a blind eye to minor violations of camp rules and regulations.
He even provided them with the finest in armor and weaponry, often
decorated with inlaid silver and gold. But when his army was on the
march, no one was stricter than Caesar. Punishment for shirking duty
was severe, and deserters were promptly executed. He also made a
habit during campaigns of not announcing the hour of the army's departure beforehand as he expected his men to be prepared to follow
him at any time. Sometimes, especially on rainy days or during holi-
days when soldiers might hope to relax, he would break camp at a
moment's notice and march his men long distances for no reason
other than to build up their endurance. But after a great victory, Caesar would allow his men a well-earned night on the town, boasting
that his army fought bravely even when they smelled of perfume.

Even with the Belgic retreat, however, there was no time for his
army to relax. They were still vastly outnumbered and deep in enemy

territory, with a dozen tribes threatening to annihilate them if they let down their guard for a moment. The day after the Belgae began returning to their homes, he led his army on a forced march from the land of the Remi down the Aisne River to Noviodunum (modern Soissons), a stronghold of the neighboring tribe, the Suessiones. The Gaulish word *dunum* means "fortress" and is found in names throughout the Celtic world, but Noviodunum ("new fortress") deserved the suffix more than most sites. Caesar says its trenches were so deep and its walls so high that he abandoned any idea of storming the citadel as he had originally planned, even though there were relatively few defenders at first. He established a camp nearby and studied the fortress carefully. The next day he sent soldiers into the nearby woods with axes and began felling trees. The carpenters among the men set to work building what looked like small sheds on wooden wheels. Each of these was roofed and sided with thick boards and hides capable of withstanding rocks and arrows raining down on them. While the Gauls watched in wonder, Caesar also began constructing enormous towers and filling in the ditches around the town. Even though the Suessiones had never seen anything like this before, they quickly realized the purpose of these siege engines and knew their fortress could not withstand this new kind of warfare. The town surrendered to Caesar the same day, with the Remi interceding on behalf of their wayward neighbors. Caesar's rule was that if an enemy opened their gates to him before his siege works touched their walls, they would be allowed to surrender peacefully and maintain their way of life. If, however, they forced him to seize their city by force, they were subject to the cruel laws of war.

The first siege of the Gallic war was a great success—and no one was more happy than Caesar that he didn't have to storm the town. The Roman army could take any town given enough time, but such efforts used up weeks he could not waste during the summer fighting season. Much better to quickly intimidate a town into surrender and spare his men the risk of a battle. True, a sacked town could yield a great deal of immediate booty for his army, especially in the form of slaves, but even towns that surrendered peacefully could be highly profitable through tribute and taxes.

Caesar now moved west to the Bellovaci tribe near the English Channel. The Bellovaci were the most numerous of the Belgic tribes and were famed for their skill in war, but they didn't put up much of a fight when Caesar arrived. About five miles from their main fortress of Bratuspantium, north of Paris, he met a crowd of old men from the tribe stretching their hands to him in supplication. The women and children did the same when Caesar arrived at the town. Diviciacus stepped forward to speak on behalf of the Bellovaci, who he explained were longtime friends of the Aedui. It was not their fault they set themselves against Rome, he declared. The blame lay with their fickle leaders, who had now escaped to Britain, shamefully leaving their women, children, and old people at Caesar's mercy. In accordance with his policy of clemency, Caesar agreed to accept their surrender provided they turn over six hundred hostages and all of their weapons. In one day and without any blood spilled, the Romans had conquered the largest of the Belgic tribes.

One tribe after another had surrendered, but Caesar knew the most formidable of all the Belgae still remained—the Nervii. The Bellovaci were the largest of the Belgic tribes, but the Nervii were the toughest warriors in all of Gaul. Like the Spartans in ancient Greece, the Nervii prided themselves on their austerity at home and discipline in war. They shunned cavalry and relied instead on heavily armed infantry. They alone of the Gaulish tribes banned merchants from their borders lest their fighting spirit be weakened by wine and other luxury imports from the Mediterranean. They despised the Aedui, Remi, and now the Bellovaci for making peace with the Romans and swore they would never come to terms with Caesar.

According to cavalry scouts, the Nervii were waiting for the Ro-

mans on the southern bank of the Sambre River. They had persuaded the neighboring Atrebates and Viromandui tribes to stand
with them and were waiting for reinforcements from the Aduatuci
to the east. All the women, children, and older members of the tribes
had been taken to a nearby safe area surrounded by marshes, but
every able-bodied man stood ready for battle. The Nervii had made
their camp inside a forest just south of the Sambre so that their numbers and movement could not be easily observed by the Romans.
Caesar knew he would face a formidable force at the Sambre, but he
didn't realize he was walking into a trap.

Some of the Belgic hostages Caesar had taken earlier in the campaign had escaped and now passed on valuable information to the
Nervii. The Romans, they said, marched with their legions widely
separated with their supply wagons in between. If the Nervii attacked the supply train after the first legion had reached camp, they
could destroy the Roman grain stores and drive back the approaching troops, isolating the first legion.

Caesar decided to make his camp on this hill above the river opposite the forest, but as he approached the site he became suspicious
and decided to rearrange the order of his march, bringing six legions
in front and leaving the baggage to follow guarded by two legions.
Even though the Nervii watching from the woods noted this unfortunate change, they decided to press ahead with their attack as
planned. They had drawn up their forces under the cover of the
trees, so that when the signal trumpet sounded, they burst from the
woods toward the Romans in full battle array. The six legions that
had started to entrench the camp were caught totally off guard by the
speed and force of the Belgic attack. There was no time to form up
lines or organize by units—each Roman soldier drew his sword and
fought where he stood as the host of screaming Belgae came rushing
over the river and up the hill.

Caesar says he had to do everything at once—sound the trumpet
call, stop the entrenchment, gather the men together, form a line, en-

courage his troops, and launch a counterattack. He had been caught unprepared for a surprise assault of such force and speed; his army would surely have been overwhelmed had it not been for the training and experience they had gained during the past year. There was no time to call his officers together and form a plan, so each organized whatever men were nearest and struck back at the Belgae. With a herculean effort, the Roman troops on the eastern side of the battlefield were able to push the Atrebates and then the Viromandui back across the river with heavy losses on both sides, but the Nervii on the western end would not yield and pressed the Romans until they fell back in a hopeless struggle to save their camp. The Nervii stormed over the uncompleted walls of the Roman stronghold, killing many of the legionaries and threatening to outflank the Roman forces who had already crossed the river. Caesar had been rushing madly to every corner of the battlefield, but when he saw the dire threat at the camp, he leapt from his horse, grabbed a sword, and joined the fray:

> He rushed to the front lines, calling the centurions by name and urging on the troops. He told them to spread out so they might have more room to use their weapons. His presence breathed a new life into his soldiers.

Caesar rallied his men by fighting along side them, but they were still in grave danger. Slowly, however, the lines began to reform and the Nervii were prevented from encircling the Romans. At this opportune moment, the two legions that had escorted the baggage arrived to reinforce their comrades. Across the river, Labienus also saw the danger Caesar was in and rushed back with his men. His arrival brought such hope to the beleaguered men around Caesar that even those who had been seriously wounded propped themselves against their shields for support to continue the fight. The Nervii were now trapped on all sides by the Romans—but none of them fled or surrendered. As the hours passed, the Romans slowly tightened the circle on them, hacking and killing as each Belgic warrior fought with all his might. In the end, the few Nervii who were left stood on a mound formed by their fallen comrades and—pulling the Roman spears from the dead bodies of their friends—threw them back down at the legions.

When the battle was finally over, the Roman soldiers collapsed in exhaustion while the surviving officers began to count the dead. Caesar describes the battle as a marvel of Roman courage and leadership under horrific conditions, but he cannot hide the fact that his own carelessness had almost destroyed the entire Roman army in Gaul.

Soon the old men of the Nervii emerged from the swamps where they had hidden with the tribe's women and children. They approached Caesar knowing they had no hope for mercy, but pleaded nonetheless on behalf of those left alive. The Nervii, they declared, were utterly destroyed as a people—from their six hundred leading tribesmen, only three remained alive. From the sixty thousand warriors that had faced Caesar at the beginning of the day, only five hundred had survived. Later events show the Nervii had more men than they claimed, but there is no doubt their numbers had been drastically reduced. By the ancient laws of war, Caesar should have killed all the remaining men and sold the women and children into slavery. But as a gesture of mercy he hoped would encourage other Belgic tribes to yield, he sent the surviving Nervii home and ordered that none of their neighboring tribes take advantage of their weakness— if they did, they would feel the wrath of Rome.

The Aduatuci warriors who had been on their way to join the Nervii in battle heard of the defeat and quickly returned to their homeland near the Rhine delta. All the tribe then gathered at a stronghold surrounded on three sides by steep cliffs and a towering, double wall on the fourth. Caesar relates that the Aduatuci were a remnant of

Rome's ancient nemesis, the marauding Cimbri and Teutones, that had been left behind in northern Gaul fifty years previous to guard the livestock and goods stolen during their rampage. The plan was for the Cimbri and Teutones to send for the loot once they had defeated the Romans, but Caesar's uncle Marius had instead destroyed them in the south. Thus the 6,000 warriors left behind as a garrison became the Aduatuci, the stranded descendants of the Cimbri and Teutones.

Caesar was surely aware of their ancestry as he approached the Aduatuci citadel and must have felt the pull of history. Marius had saved Rome from their invasion decades earlier; now his nephew could win glory in Rome by writing the final chapter of the ancient Cimbri and Teutones saga. Caesar soon had the town cut off from reinforcement and supplies with a fortified rampart, but the tribesmen had plenty of food. The Aduatuci stood on their walls and laughed at the Romans building a giant tower in the distance. They shouted that the besiegers would never be able to move such a monstrosity up to the fortress. Caesar says the jeering suddenly stopped when the siege tower began to roll toward their walls. Like the Suessiones earlier, the Aduatuci had never seen such a marvel but knew their city would not be able to stand the coming Roman assault.

A deputation from the citadel soon arrived at Caesar's camp and offered the tribe's surrender. They asked only that they might be allowed to keep their weapons to protect themselves from hostile neighbors. Caesar accepted their surrender, but insisted that all weapons be handed over immediately. The Aduatuci reluctantly agreed and began throwing piles of spears and swords over the walls—but the men secretly hid a third of their arms deep inside the fortress. Caesar ordered the tribe to remain in the stronghold that night, but instead, they burst out of the gates in the early morning hours fearing that the Romans were preparing to slaughter them all the next day. Caesar's troops hunted them down by torchlight and killed about four thousand of the men in a rare nighttime battle, but the rest managed to flee back into the fortress. At dawn, Caesar broke open the city gates with a battering ram, sent in his troops, and sold every surviving Aduatuci, including the women and children, into slavery. The merchants who followed the legions paid Caesar personally for the fifty-three thousand captives. Thus the last descendants of the Cimbri and Teutones were marched south to spend the rest of their lives laboring in the fields and quarries of the Mediterranean world. Caesar did not show mercy twice.

Caesar's problems in Gaul, however, were not quite over for the year. Just after the battle against the Nervii, the twelfth legion under Caesar's protégé Servius Galba had been sent to secure what we know as the Great St. Bernard Pass into Italy before winter set in. Roman merchants had long been accustomed to traveling through these heights, but the natives of the area demanded outrageous tolls for the privilege. Caesar knew that if he could gain control of this strategic pass, he would have a shortcut from northern Italy straight into the heart of central Gaul that would cut many days of travel from the normal coastal route. Galba was given this commission even though his legion was still short of men. Securing the pass went well at first with only a few minor skirmishes, which the Romans easily won. The local tribes grudgingly provided hostages from among their children, then Galba settled most of his troops in the Alpine village of Octodurus nestled just below the soaring heights of Mont Blanc and the Matterhorn. To keep peace with the natives, he restricted his men to a fort on one side of the village while the townspeople remained on the other side, separated by a rushing river. The grain he had ordered to be brought up the mountains had not yet arrived, but he was confident the supply trains would appear soon and that the cold mountain winter would be peaceful. The next morning, however, he learned that all the natives had ominously vanished from their side of the village. Looking up at the crags above his camp, he saw thousands of warriors gathered from neighboring tribes. The natives of the Great St. Bernard Pass had decided that the Romans were bent on outright conquest, not merely securing a passage to Italy. They were also furious at being forced to hand over their children to the Romans as hostages. With only a few thousand legionaries in the camp, the tribesmen felt confident they could bury the Romans beneath rocks and spears in the first assault.

Galba knew he was in a desperate situation. He considered a hasty retreat down the mountain, but, in the manner of Caesar, decided instead to fight against difficult odds. The enemy began its attack by hurling stones and spears at the Romans, then rushing the walls of the fort. The legionaries were vastly outnumbered and could not afford to leave their place on the wall even if they were grievously wounded. The natives on the other hand had plenty of reserves to replace any man who fell. In this impossible situation for the Romans, a centurion named Baculus proposed the outrageous idea of rushing boldly from the fort and attacking the enemy. The Roman troops were in such straits at this moment that they were willing to do anything rather than wait for the fort to be stormed. At a signal from Galba, all the troops burst from the gates of the fort at once and charged the natives. The Alpine warriors were so shocked by this unexpected counterattack that they fell back, then began running headlong down the valley in retreat. The Romans alledgedly killed ten thousand men in the scramble, returning exhausted to their camp that night along with all the weapons they could collect from their fallen enemies. Galba was proud of his victory, but he knew he couldn't hold the pass with so few troops and no reliable supply line. The next day he burned down the whole village, then moved his men back to the lowlands of the Province.

▣

Caesar reports in the *Gallic War* that while he had been engaged defeating the Belgae in the summer of 57 B.C., he sent his lieutenant

Publius Crassus west into Normandy and Brittany to subdue the tribes along the English Channel and Atlantic coast. Now Crassus returned to headquarters and reported that the Veneti, Osismi, and all the other maritime states had surrendered to Rome. Caesar passes over this episode with notable brevity since events of the next year were to prove the conquest of the western tribes was anything but complete.

Nevertheless, Caesar declared in his annual dispatch to the Senate that all of Gaul was finally at peace, with even some German tribes on the far side of the Rhine sending emissaries declaring their submission to Rome. Caesar soon established his legions in winter quarters in western and central Gaul, as well as several among the Belgae and Galba's battered legion in the south. He then began preparations to leave for Italy and Illyricum confident that the conquest of Gaul was practically finished. Even his enemies in the Senate were impressed as they declared an unprecedented fifteen days of thanksgiving for Caesar's achievements. The consensus among the more moderate senators, including Cicero, was that Caesar had washed away the blemish of any unconstitutional actions during his consulship by his victories in Gaul.

Not everyone in Rome that winter was happy with Caesar's success. Pompey had been slowly distancing himself from the triumvirate during the last year—not going as far as to side with the optimates, but lending them an increasingly sympathetic ear. Cato and the rest were working very carefully to pry Pompey away from Caesar and Crassus. The major reason for Pompey's discontent was simple jealousy of Caesar's victories. Pompey never deluded himself that he was a master politician, but he took pride in his unmatched accomplishments in war. The adulation now heaped on Caesar for his military triumphs hit Pompey hard as everyone seemed to forget his own exploits in Asia. He began to mutter against Caesar, urging the Senate not to read his dispatches from Gaul in public and even hinting that someone, perhaps himself, should be sent to Gaul to replace Caesar.

The optimates played on Pompey's discontent for all it was worth, listening to his complaints and agreeing that Rome needed a way to counterbalance the rising power of Caesar. When food riots broke out in Rome in September of 57 B.C., the Senate voted, at the urging of Cicero, to give Pompey extraordinary powers to administer the grain supply throughout Roman lands for five years. This appointment, like his mandate to end piracy several years before, carried with it military power to enforce his authority even above governors throughout the Roman world, including Gaul. Many senators were genuinely concerned about securing the food supply for Rome, but those who opposed Caesar saw this as a perfect opportunity to curb his influence and to break up the triumvirate. Most of the optimates detested Pompey, but they hated Caesar even more.

A few months later, Pompey discovered how shallow his support in the Senate really was when he attempted to add to his portfolio the mandate to reinstate the now-exiled king of Egypt. Ptolemy XII had been driven out of Alexandria by his eternally discontented subjects and had fled to Rome with bags of gold. With these he bribed senators and hired assassins to kill the delegates the Alexandrians had sent to Rome to explain their side of the story. Intrigue to regain the Egyptian throne became so heated that the Senate grew weary of the matter and rejected Pompey's bid to retake Alexandria for Ptolemy. They were afraid that giving Pompey effective control of Egypt as well as the grain supply would make him a virtual emperor of the Mediterranean. Pompey took this rebuff with ill humor and soon became convinced that there was a conspiracy not only against his power but his life as well. He even brought in armed guards from his home region of Picenum to protect him in the unruly streets of Rome.

Caesar was, of course, keeping a close watch on all these events from Cisalpine Gaul. The proceeds from plunder and slave sales among the Belgae had provided him with enormous amounts of cash that he now applied liberally to his political problems in Rome. Any potential tribune or other would-be magistrate knew Caesar would lavishly finance his campaign as long as he swore to support Caesar's agenda. He was also working behind the scenes to rebuild the triumvirate. In utmost secrecy, Caesar met with Crassus at Ravenna that winter, then welcomed Pompey at the small town of Luca just over the border in Cisalpine Gaul. Caesar once more demonstrated his consummate skill in personal politics, wooing his two partners into a reaffirmed pact that would benefit both of them greatly. It was agreed that Crassus and Pompey would serve as joint consuls once more in the year 55 B.C. They would unite with Caesar to form a solid front against the optimates and anyone else who stood in their way, including Cicero. The prize for both Pompey and Crassus would be unprecedented military commands after their year as consuls. Both would have the opportunity to conquer enemies far more glorious and lucrative than Caesar's Gauls. For his part, Caesar wanted to continue his war in Gaul unfettered and serve again as consul in 48 B.C., the earliest year he would be eligible. Caesar's deference to his two senior partners won over both to a new alliance that chilly winter. Pompey soon sent a message to Cicero warning him that he would oppose Caesar at his own peril.

Cicero, a proud man, but also devoted to self-preservation, agreed not only to support Caesar but to speak in his favor on the Senate floor. The orator swallowed his pride and advocated an extension of Caesar's power in Gaul as a matter of national security since changing leadership before the war was completed would put Rome at unnecessary risk. In addition, money should be provided to support Caesar's new legions and his *imperium* from Illyricum to the English Channel must be prolonged for several years. The Senate concurred despite the clamor of the outraged and outmaneuvered optimates. The winter of 57 B.C. had begun with Caesar in great political peril, but with the spring of 56 now drawing near, his future had never looked brighter.

Caesar spent most of that winter in northern Italy, but he traveled to nearby Illyricum, where he also served as governor. Since deciding to wage war in Gaul, he had left the rule of Illyricum to subordinates, but he maintained constant contact with the Province and now visited it in person. This mountainous territory on the east coast of the Adriatic Sea had once served as a haunt of pirates and as a buffer state between Rome and Macedon, but now the land was at peace. Caesar had insisted on the governance of the province when he was still pondering an invasion of Dacia to the east—and though he was currently occupied in Gaul, he maintained a lively interest in Illyricum with an eye to future campaigns beyond the Danube.

The bad news from Gaul came early that spring of 56 B.C., just as Caesar had settled affairs in Rome and was touring Illyricum. Young Publius Crassus, who had earlier assured Caesar that the Gaulish maritime tribes on the west coast had been subdued, now reported that his emissaries had been seized by those very tribes. Crassus had settled into winter camp on the northern bank of the Loire River, near the Atlantic. Since food was scarce in the immediate area, he had sent legates to nearby tribes, including the Veneti of Brittany, to requisition supplies. Even though the Veneti had given hostages and assured Crassus just a few weeks before that they would willingly submit to Caesar, they now decided that spending their lives as Roman subjects was not for them. They put the legates in chains and sent an embassy to Crassus demanding that he exchange the Veneti hostages in his keeping for his own men. They then sent messengers to the other maritime tribes encouraging them to join the rebellion against Rome and were pleased with the enthusiastic response from their Gaulish kindred. With little forethought—as Caesar says was typical among the Gauls—the Veneti and their allies had now started a war with Rome.

In spite of the poor record of Gaulish tribes in the previous two years, the Veneti were well positioned to succeed in a prolonged conflict against Rome. Like the Phoenicians and Athenians before them, the Veneti were a people of the sea. Skilled at sailing the dangerous waters of the north Atlantic, they also dominated trade between Gaul and Britain. Unlike the Helvetii or Belgae, the Veneti could maintain an endless supply line by sea and had the mobility to sail unimpeded from one fortress to another if threatened. They knew they could not defeat the Romans in a pitched battle on land, but they could wear them down using their unchallenged dominance of the sea.

As soon as the message from young Crassus arrived in Illyricum, Caesar ordered a fleet of warships to be constructed on the Loire and rowers, seamen, and pilots to be recruited from the experienced sailors of the Province. Caesar himself quickly finished his business in the Balkans, then headed west to meet the fleet in early summer. The Veneti heard news of Caesar's armada and began to make their own preparations. Ships were readied for battle and more allies were recruited, including the Venelli of Normandy and the Morini and Menapii tribes along the Belgic coast. The Veneti even recruited fighters from across the sea in Britain. The Veneti leaders realized the formidable nature of the Roman military machine, but they were confident that their own skills at open ocean sailing combined with Roman ignorance of the coastline would see them through the summer until the Romans ran out of supplies and were forced to withdraw. The Veneti fortresses were all located on precipitous spits of land reaching out into the sea and could be attacked from land only with the greatest difficulty. The force of the ocean waves pounding constantly beneath the walls and the potent force of Atlantic tides also made a sea attack by the Romans unlikely. All the Veneti coastal forts were soon well stocked with grain and ready to withstand a protracted siege.

Caesar inserts an amazing statement in his *Gallic War* just before he begins the campaign against the Veneti, in which he describes why the maritime tribes revolted against Rome: "Human nature everywhere yearns for freedom and hates submitting to domination by another." This kind of refreshing honesty is typical in Roman writers from the earliest days of the Republic to the fall of the empire. The Romans never pretended that they were bringing freedom or a better way of life to the peoples they conquered. They frankly admitted that they were only interested in increasing their own power, wealth, and security through conquest. They had no particular desire to spread classical culture throughout the world unless it served their own plans to better control a province. Caesar freely admits that the Veneti were simply fighting for liberty, just as he would have done in their place. Nevertheless, he was determined to crush them.

Caesar recognized that a war in Brittany could spark rebellions among tribes throughout Gaul if they believed he was distracted by the Veneti and their allies. He therefore first secured potential problem areas, including the border with Germany. His chief lieutenant, Labienus, took up station along the Rhine to prevent any Germanic warriors crossing into Belgic territory. Next, he sent Crassus to Aquitainia in southwest Gaul to quell any uprisings among the tribes near Spain. Finally, he dispatched Quintus Titurius Sabinus with three legions to crush the revolt among the Venelli in nearby Normandy. Caesar had put a young man named Decimus Brutus in charge of preparing the Roman fleet along the Loire. Not to be confused with the Brutus who would one day deliver the death blow to Caesar, this Brutus nevertheless, after being much honored by Caesar, would also participate in his assassination.

But those events were still twelve years in the future. Now Decimus Brutus threw all his considerable energy into constructing and outfitting the ships Caesar would use to attack the Veneti. When Caesar arrived with the soldiers who would serve as siege troops on shore and as marines on the ships, the fleet was ready. The Romans had learned the hard way how to fight sea battles two hundred years earlier, during the First Punic War, but that was a naval conflict fought with similar ships by two mighty empires. The Veneti, as they had planned, challenged the Romans in a new way. Instead of playing by the normal rules of combat, the Veneti in a seaside fortress would watch patiently while the Romans toiled to construct massive towers and walls to blockade them from escape by land. Then, just as the siege towers were about to breach their walls, they would call in their sturdy ships and escape by sea to another fortress. Caesar couldn't stop the Veneti ships because his own fleet was too fragile to handle the crashing waves around their strongholds. It was a maddening game for the Romans that lasted throughout the summer.

Caesar was learning a lesson that Roman generals had been taught many times in previous centuries—new foes often have unexpected weapons and techniques that must be overcome through ingenuity and adaptation. Unlike the Roman ships designed for warfare in the calm, deep waters of the Mediterranean, Veneti ships were flat on the bottom so that—like Viking longboats—they required very little water underneath them. This allowed the Veneti to maneuver in shallow coves and over rocky shoals that grounded Roman ships. The sides of Caesar's ships were low to accommodate rowers and allow quick boarding of an enemy vessel, but Veneti ships rose many feet above the waterline. This made it extremely difficult for the Romans to use their trademark grappling hooks and almost impossible for them to climb up the sides of a Veneti ship. The Romans tried building small turrets on board to reach the Veneti, but these made their own boats unstable and even so were still not tall enough for them to look the enemy sailors in the eye. The Veneti fleet was also made of sturdy oak, with hefty crossbeams for support and held together by nails as thick as a man's thumb. Roman ships on the other hand were designed to be light and fast, since ramming an enemy craft was standard procedure. But when the Romans tried smashing into a Veneti ship, they either bounced off or shattered their own prows. The Veneti also used leather rather than cloth sails as these stood up much better to the punishment meted out by Atlantic storms. However, the Veneti fleet did have one weakness Caesar realized he could exploit—since their ships had no rowers, they were totally dependant on the wind in their sails to move.

By the end of the summer Caesar had captured several empty Veneti fortresses, but he was getting nowhere on either land or sea. True to his nature, he then decided to risk everything on a major naval battle just off the coast. The whole Roman fleet under Decimus Brutus was brought up while the Veneti eagerly sailed forward to meet them. Here was their chance to destroy the Romans at last. Over two hundred fully outfitted Veneti ships engaged the Romans in what they were sure would be a crushing defeat for Caesar. On the cliffs above the sea, Caesar watched the battle unfold just as the Persian king Xerxes had gazed down on his own fleet fighting the Athenians at Salamis four centuries earlier. The Roman fleet was savaged at first by spears and arrows from the taller Veneti ships, but Caesar had a trick up his sleeve. Each Roman ship had been equipped with several long poles with a sharp hook on the end. The Romans now rowed close to a Veneti ship, hooked the lines holding the enemy's sails, then reversed direction and rowed with all their might until their lines were cut. This left the Veneti ship without usable sails and immobilized. Several Roman ships would then converge on a disabled Veneti craft and fight their way on board with ladders. It was an exhausting battle that lasted all day, with many casualties to the Romans, but finally the Veneti began to flee. It was just at that moment the gods smiled on Caesar as the brisk wind suddenly ceased. With the air dead calm, the Veneti ships were sitting ducks. By nightfall, only a handful of the enemy ships had escaped.

The Veneti knew that with their fleet destroyed and most of their warriors slain, they could no longer offer any resistance. Since the sea was now off-limits to them and the Romans were dominant on land, they had no choice but to surrender. If they hoped for any mercy from Caesar, they soon realized their error. Not only had the Veneti broken Caesar's cardinal rule by rebelling after surrender, but they had violated the sacred status of his ambassadors when they had held the legates of Crassus for ransom. To make an example of them, he executed all the surviving Veneti leaders and sold the rest of the population into slavery.

◙

While Caesar was fighting in Brittany, his lieutenant Sabinus was engaging the Venelli over a hundred miles away in Normandy. Nearby tribes from the area west of Paris had also joined the Venelli in rebellion after their warriors had killed their own elders for refusing to lead their people against Caesar's army. In addition, fighters from all over Gaul were arriving in Normandy every day to take up the anti-Roman cause. Caesar says some of these were true patriots while others were simply ruffians seeking plunder or young men weary of life on the farm.

Sabinus refused to meet the Venelli and their allies in open battle and instead withdrew behind a well-fortified camp on top of a long, sloping hill. Day after day the Gauls emerged from their own camp two miles away and taunted the Romans for their cowardice. Soon the Venelli were even approaching the walls of the Roman camp itself and hurling abuse at the legionaries standing guard. A storm of discontent began to rise among the frustrated Roman troops in the camp, but all was going according to the plan of Sabinus. The general then chose one of the Gaulish auxiliary soldiers among his men and made him an offer—he would receive a great reward if he would pretend to desert to the Venelli and tell them what Sabinus instructed him. That night the man slipped quietly over the walls and made his way to the Gaulish headquarters. The story he told the Venelli was exactly what they wanted to hear—Sabinus was a sniveling coward who was planning to withdraw his whole army secretly that next night to join Caesar in Brittany. The Venelli decided to launch an attack the next day before Sabinus could escape. At dawn the Venelli warriors and their allies were so excited at the prospect of spoils and glory that they ran the entire two miles uphill to the Roman camp in full battle gear. By the time they reached the top, they were exhausted. It was then Sabinus sent his own soldiers out of the gates. The fresh and eager legionaries began cutting down the weary Gaulish fighters, while those Gauls who managed to escape the slaughter on the hill were hunted down by the Roman cavalry. The spirited rebellion in Normandy evaporated as quickly as it had begun. As Caesar himself commented:

> *The Gauls are by nature very eager to begin a war, but they have no perseverance. If a setback or calamity befalls them, they cannot carry on.*

While Caesar and Sabinus were leading their campaigns, young Crassus was locked in a fierce struggle against the Gauls of Aquitania near the Pyrenees Mountains. The Romans had crossed into this land from the Province in previous decades, but had always been driven back by the martial skill of the natives. In spite of setbacks, Crassus led his men first against the cavalry of the Sotiates tribe near Bordeaux, then surrounded their stronghold with towers and siege equipment. The Sotiates were experienced copper miners and attempted to tunnel under the Roman army, but in the end to no avail. After taking their city, Crassus moved against the Vocates and Tarusates, who had wisely recruited veterans from Spain who had served with a Roman rebel named Sertorius twenty years earlier. These men were trained in Roman-style warfare and gave Crassus a difficult time, but by the end of the summer he had subdued all of Aquitania from the mountains to the sea.

Caesar himself finished out the campaign season with a quick strike against the Morini and Menapii along the modern Dutch coast. Seeing that all the tribes that had stood their ground against Caesar had been defeated, the Morini and Menapii prudently gathered supplies and hid deep in their impenetrable forests. Caesar tried repeatedly to attack them, but his men were constantly ambushed while the Gauls only fled farther into the woods. In frustration, Caesar adopted the novel if impractical strategy of leveling the entire coastal forest. But as the summer was rapidly coming to an end, Caesar abandoned his woodcutting campaign and, burning all the native villages in the area, left the Morini and Menapii for another day. He gave orders for his legions to make winter camps throughout Gaul, but especially in those areas that had taken part in that year's rebellion. These vanquished tribes had not only suffered defeat and a considerable reduction in population, but they were now forced to feed the Roman army that winter from their meager supplies. Caesar was teaching them a very deliberate lesson on the cost of rebellion.

After three summers of war in Gaul, Caesar had conquered—and in some cases reconquered—an enormous ring of land stretching from Lake Geneva down the Rhine to the North Sea, then through the lands of the Belgae to the English Channel and Brittany, and finally south to the Loire valley and the Pyrenees Mountains. If any Gauls or Romans had been unsure of his ultimate intent, it was now clear. Caesar had drawn a net around Gaul with only the center left untouched. With the boundaries of Gaul secure, he believed the heavily populated and prosperous central area would submit peacefully to Roman rule. If there was any trouble in the future, it was simply a matter of sending in his legions to close the net.

VII

BRITAIN

What a wonderful letter you sent me about Britain! I was terrified for your sake concerning the sea and coast of that island . . . You write about such amazing things you saw there—the countryside, wonders of nature, interesting places, customs, tribes, battles— and of course your commander himself.

—CICERO TO HIS BROTHER, QUINTUS

Caesar returned to northern Italy in the autumn of 56 B.C. to supervise affairs in Cisalpine Gaul, but more importantly, to keep a close eye on events in Rome. Cato was still venomous in his opposition to Caesar, but with the conqueror of Gaul wrapped in his proconsular immunity, the leader of the optimates was unable to strike at him directly. Instead in September of 56, Cato brought charges against Caesar's trusted counselor Balbus, claiming that he had obtained his Roman citizenship illegally from Pompey sixteen years earlier. The charge was spurious, but was a typically Roman maneuver designed to attack an opponent through his subordinate and force one's enemy to waste his political capital on trivialities. The triumvirate responded by twisting Cicero's arm until he agreed to defend Balbus in court, which he did successfully.

During the previous winter, the triumvirate had laid plans for Pompey and Crassus to be elected as joint consuls and begin service at the start of the new year. The optimates, however, were once again ready to demonstrate that they could cause considerable trouble for Caesar and his colleagues even if they could not block them outright. Marcellinus, one of the two consuls for the current year, declared that Pompey and Crassus had violated the law by canvassing for the magistracy outside of the strict campaign season and were therefore ineligible for election. The violation was a minor technicality, but Marcellinus was determined to thwart the triumvirate's agenda as long as he held the consulship. Pompey and Crassus, undoubtedly with Caesar's collusion, responded by hiring a tribune of the plebs to veto the entire election process for the year so that no one could be chosen for any office. This activated a clause in the Roman constitution providing for an *interregnum* (transitional government) followed by a special election early in 55 B.C. after the term of Marcellinus had expired. This action secured several extra months for the triumvirate to plan a strategy of intimidation and dirty tricks to overcome their opposition.

In January of 55 B.C., as the special elections drew near, Cato fought tooth and nail to promote his own brother-in-law, Lucius Domitius—a fierce optimate with the family cognomen Ahenobarbus ("Bronze Beard")—as an alternative candidate for consul. As Domitius and Cato worked to secure last-minute votes the night before the election, Pompey ordered his well-paid thugs to attack the optimate leaders in the dark streets, wounding Cato and killing his torchbearer, while Domitius fled to the safety of his own home. The next morning, the center of Rome was packed with triumvirate supporters. Caesar had conveniently granted leave to young Publius Crassus to lead a force of loyal soldiers back to Rome for his father's election. The presence of hundreds of Caesar's veteran legionaries in the Forum was enough to assure the consulship for Pompey and Crassus. Once Caesar's partners were elected to Rome's highest of-

fice, they easily manipulated the selection of the remaining magistrates. When the bruised Cato came forward for the vote on his candidacy as praetor, Pompey declared that he had heard thunder and
promptly dissolved the assembly for the day. But imaginary omens
did not interfere soon thereafter when the triumvirate bribed
enough voters to elect their supporter Publius Vatinius in Cato's
place.

Pompey and Crassus spent the next few weeks pretending they
wanted nothing for themselves, but were all the while arranging for
others to promote their agenda before the Roman people. The tribune Trebonius pushed through a bill granting the two consuls a proconsular governorship of five years each for Spain and Syria. Cato
objected, of course, but the optimates were bested once again by
bribery, intimidation, and outright violence. Pompey's choice of
Spain as for his governorship shows surprisingly little enthusiasm on
his part for new conquests, but the selection of Syria by Crassus
plainly meant that Rome's most famous tycoon was setting his sights
on the mighty Parthian empire. Crassus had made his immense fortune in Rome and had led troops in combat with Spartacus, but he
craved a glorious military campaign on a par with Pompey's eastern
war and Caesar's conquests in the north. Soon after this legislation
was passed, the partners lived up to their earlier agreement and secured a further five years for Caesar in Gaul. With these affairs settled, the remainder of the triumvirate consulship was fairly quiet,
though the year ended with an optimate victory when Domitius
Ahenobarbus was at last chosen as consul along with Cato as praetor.

When the messenger bearing news from the north arrived at Caesar's headquarters in Italy, he broke the seal and quickly read the dispatch. He must have wondered then if he was ever going to enjoy a
peaceful year in Gaul. The report said that the Usipetes and Tencteri,
Germanic tribes from just east of the Rhine, had crossed the river

into Gaul near modern Düsseldorf, fleeing from the powerful Suebi. Caesar writes that the Suebi, who dominated western Germany, were the most numerous, warlike, and toughest of the Germans, living chiefly on milk and beef while shunning such luxuries as wine and warm clothes. The tribe had been a thorn in Caesar's side since his conflict with Ariovistus and now they were pushing other Germans into the still-troubled lands of the Belgae. The Usipetes and Tencteri had moved into the territory of the Menapii near the mouth of the Rhine. Then, after looting what supplies they could find, they headed south toward the heart of Gaul.

Because of these troubling developments Caesar decided to depart northern Italy while snow still covered the Alps. He was particularly worried by the German incursion into Gaul since it threatened to destabilize the whole country. Caesar writes that some Belgic tribes had even sent recruiting parties across the Rhine seeking other German tribes who might aid them in a new revolt against Rome. As soon as he arrived from Italy, Caesar summoned leaders from all the Gaulish tribes to a conference reportedly to "soothe their spirits and encourage them," but he undoubtedly issued some stern warnings as well against any treachery. He then requisitioned auxiliary cavalry from among the Gauls, added them to his legions, and moved swiftly against the Germans.

Caesar soon received an embassy from the Germans declaring that they had no wish to fight him, but that they were not a people who avoided armed conflict when it was thrust upon them. The one exception, they ruefully admitted, were the dreaded Suebi, who had driven them into Gaul—not even the gods could resist such titans. The ambassadors told Caesar they were willing to settle as Roman allies anywhere in Gaul he might direct them, but they were definitely not going back across the Rhine. Four hundred years later, the Romans would probably have jumped at such an offer, as the policy in late imperial times was to settle friendly tribes along the frontier to guard against more hostile groups across the border. Caesar, however, was not interested in a compromise. As with the Helvetii three years before, he told the representatives of the two tribes that there was no room for them in Gaul—their only option was to cross back into Germany. He graciously offered to help settle them among the Germanic Ubii on the east bank of the Rhine. Together, he suggested, their united armies might be able to resist the Suebi.

The envoys of the Usipetes and Tencteri were understandably cool to this proposal. They said they needed to consult with their tribes and promised to return in three days. In the meantime, they asked Caesar not to move his camp any closer to theirs. Caesar was quite suspicious of this request, especially since his scouts had told him that most of the German cavalry were several days distant on a raiding mission. If they could keep Caesar away until their cavalry rejoined the army, the Germans would be a potent force.

The next day Caesar resumed his march toward the German camp and again met a German embassy beseeching him to wait. They had thought about his offer, they claimed, and were seriously considering the idea of settling across the Rhine among the Ubii. They just needed a few days to work out the details. Caesar knew this was again a ruse to buy time, but agreed to move his army forward only four miles to be near water. The envoys then promised not to attack his men—but when Caesar's cavalry moved out ahead of his main force, the Germans struck. Startled by the speed of the German charge, the Roman cavalry was caught completely off guard. The Germans rushed forward, leaped off their mounts, and quickly stabbed the Roman horses, forcing the ill-prepared cavalrymen to fight on foot. In this way the Germans managed to kill many horsemen, including two Gaulish noblemen Caesar counted as friends.

Caesar felt betrayed by the Germans and vowed he would show them no mercy from that point forward. When their ambassadors approached the Roman camp the next day to explain that the battle had been a misunderstanding and that they needed just a few more days to consider his proposal, Caesar had them arrested. He then personally led his eager men against the enemy camp. His soldiers, hostile to Germans at the best of times, were bitterly angry at their violation of the previous day's truce. Caesar himself was determined to make a frightening example of these marauding tribesmen so that no others would be tempted to cross the Rhine. When legions of heavily armed Romans burst into the German camp that morning, it was a slaughter on a scale unknown during the last four years of the Gaulish war. Some of the Germans tried to make a desperate stand amid the baggage carts, but tens of thousands were cut down as they fled, including many women and children. The few who escaped were pursued relentlessly by the Roman cavalry until they plunged into the Rhine and drowned. Caesar does not mention taking any prisoners.

After the crushing defeat of the Usipetes and Tencteri, Caesar decided to cross the Rhine into Germany itself. He gives his Roman readers several reasons why he thought this unprecedented action was necessary. First, he wanted to demonstrate to the German tribes that the Romans were willing and able to enter their homeland whenever they might choose. Up until that time it had always been the Germans who had crossed the Rhine into Gaul, but a Roman army on the east bank of the river would send a powerful message that armies could move in both directions. Second, the cavalry of the defeated Usipetes and Tencteri that had failed to join their countrymen before Caesar destroyed them had now taken refuge across the Rhine with their old neighbors the Sugambri. Caesar had sent a message to this tribe demanding they turn over these horsemen to him for punishment, but they had refused. The Sugambri had responded that if Caesar thought it wrong for Germans to interfere in Gaul, what gave him the right to claim any authority in Germany? A reasonable argument, but one Caesar rejected. The third motive Caesar gives for crossing into Germany was that the beleaguered Ubii had formally requested his presence there to show the bellicose Suebi that

Rome stood behind them. As they said, his unmatched reputation in war had spread even to the most distant corners of Germany since his defeat of Ariovistus three years earlier.

The one reason Caesar doesn't give for crossing the Rhine was probably the most compelling of all—it would be a spectacular publicity stunt. In the decades since the Cimbri and Teutones had threatened to overrun Italy, the barbaric Germans had become the ultimate bogymen in the Roman imagination. Senators and commoners alike lived in fear of the day the next wave of German hordes would cross the Rhine and sweep south to pillage and burn their land. But no one—until Caesar—had ever considered the possibility of actually taking the fight to the Germans. Caesar had no plans to conquer Germany, but if he could be the first general to raise the standards of the legions on the far side of the Rhine, he would go down in history. More immediately, it would keep his name on Roman tongues at a time when his triumvirate partners Pompey and Crassus were much in the public eye as consuls.

The Ubii had offered to ferry the Romans across the Rhine, but to Caesar this simply wouldn't do. The sight of his legions crossing the river in a flotilla of little boats was not the image he wanted to leave with the Germans. In any case, he deemed it a bad strategy since it made his army dependent on unproven allies for their very survival. What Caesar needed was a means for his army to cross the Rhine that was safe, under his control, and—perhaps most important—impressive. It was then that he conceived his audacious plan to build the first bridge across the Rhine.

The Romans had been building substantial bridges for many centuries, but what Caesar was proposing was unprecedented. In a period of just a few days, he proposed to span a swift-moving river at least eight hundred feet wide and up to twenty-five feet deep. Moreover, he was determined to build this bridge during a war in the middle of a vast wilderness. This was a far more difficult task than building a bridge across the much smaller Saône in the early days of the war to pursue the Helvetii. That project had taken only a single day, but any competent Roman engineer would have told Caesar that spanning the Rhine—if it were possible at all—would require many weeks of hard labor.

Any doubters in the Roman camp, however, did not reckon on Caesar's own engineering skills and his talent for accomplishing seemingly impossible tasks. His soldiers immediately set to work in the surrounding forest near modern Koblenz felling countless trees and shaping them into timber. These were brought to the riverbank, where rafts fitted with hoists and cranes were waiting. The current of the Rhine was so strong that Caesar drove the first piles into the riverbed at an angle facing the flow of the stream and further secured them on the downriver side with bracing supports. When facing piles had been placed in the river upstream, crossbeams were fixed on top to connect them. The soldiers then rowed out into the river to drive in the next piles and linked them to the previous pair with sturdy timbers. On top of all this planks and woven branches formed the roadway on which the troops would march. Caesar even drove additional piles into the Rhine just a few feet upriver from the bridge to act as a barrier against any floating debris that might damage his masterpiece.

From before sunrise to after sunset each day thousands of Roman soldiers labored to construct the bridge section by section across the Rhine. The Suebi scouts watching from the opposite bank were amazed by what they saw and rushed to report the news to their chieftains. After only ten days, Caesar's bridge across the Rhine was complete. Caesar left strong garrisons on either end of the long wooden bridge to defend against any Gaulish or German attempts to destroy it and trap his army; then he and his men marched boldly into Germany.

Caesar's intention in crossing the Rhine was never a full-scale war, only a brief foray to intimidate the natives. In this goal, he succeeded admirably. The Sugambri, who had been sheltering the cavalry of the Usipetes and Tencteri, were so frightened they evacuated all their towns and hid deep in the forest. Caesar satisfied himself with burning their empty villages and razing their crops. Even the mighty Suebi ordered all their women and children into the woods while their warriors huddled together far from the Rhine to await the coming Roman army. But after almost three weeks of marching unopposed through the German countryside, Caesar felt he had made his point. He returned with the army to his bridge on the Rhine and crossed back into Gaul. He then destroyed the bridge to prevent any enemy from using it and left the dark forests of Germany behind him.

The summer of 55 B.C. was almost over, but Caesar was determined to solidify his hold on the Roman imagination by staging one more military spectacle before the winter began—a foray across the sea to the mythic island of Britain. He writes that his primary reason for the campaign was to punish those Britons who had aided the Gaulish tribes in their previous rebellions, but he also notes that a brief reconnaissance of the island would be most helpful in any future operations there. Caesar was undoubtedly sincere, but again the true value in such an expedition was the publicity it would generate back in Rome. How could Cato and the optimates—not to mention Pompey and Crassus—hope to complete with a man who could lead his troops to a land as mysterious to the average Roman as the far side of the moon?

The fact that Britain was so exotic to the classical world also made any military campaign there risky. Gaul and even Germany had been visited by Greeks and Romans for centuries, but Britain was almost completely unknown. Some Romans even claimed that the island didn't exist except in fables. Caesar therefore summoned the handful of Gaulish merchants who had traveled there to learn what he could about the island, but with few substantive results:

He could not discover the size of Britain, nor the names or num-
bers of the tribes there, nor their tactics in war, nor their customs,
nor the ports that might be suitable for landing a large fleet.

Ignorance about Britain was no surprise since to the civilized cul-
tures of the Mediterranean it was truly at the end of the earth. The
only way for explorers or merchants to reach the island before Caesar
was a long and dangerous trek across Gaul or an even longer and
more perilous voyage through the Pillars of Hercules, up the Iberian
and Gaulish coasts, and finally across the stormy English Channel.
Caesar had a few pieces of information about Britain brought back
over the previous five hundred years by those few voyagers who had
managed to travel there and return. Chief among these was the
Greek scientist Pytheas of Massalia, who had sailed to Britain, Ireland, and perhaps even Iceland during the age of Alexander the
Great. From Pytheas, Caesar knew that the Britons used to call their
island *Albion*—a Celtic term meaning "the upper world"—though by
the first century it was called *Britannia,* "land of the painted people."

Armed with so little information, Caesar felt it expedient first to
survey the south coast and to establish ties with British tribal leaders.
For the former task, he sent his aide Gaius Volusenus to search out
the best harbors. As events would soon reveal, the young man did a
rather poor job since he was afraid to leave his ship. At the same
time, Caesar sent a Gaulish nobleman named Commius from the
Belgic Atrebates tribe to meet with the kings of the southern British
tribes. Caesar held him to be a trustworthy man of great courage and
discretion who was known and respected among the Britons. Since
many of the southern British tribes were Belgic in origin and spoke
the same language as their cousins in Gaul, Caesar hoped to use
Commius to stress the practical benefits of yielding to Rome without
a fight. But although Commius was braver than Volusenus, he was
no more successful—as soon as he arrived in Britain, he was thrown
into chains.

With this inauspicious start to Caesar's British adventure, things soon began to get still worse. The Roman army advanced across Gaul to a camp around the modern seaport of Boulogne on the English Channel and there gathered enough ships for two legions, plus a large cavalry contingent. Caesar was so anxious to set sail during a break in the stormy weather that he weighed anchor with only his infantry, giving orders for the cavalry to follow immediately. Unfortunately, the ships assigned to transport his horsemen across the channel were prevented from reaching the Gaulish port by a contrary wind. Undoubtedly cursing his luck, he nevertheless decided to launch the invasion without cavalry support, trusting to fate that they would arrive in Britain close behind him.

Thus it was on a clear morning in the late summer of 55 B.C. that Julius Caesar became the first Roman to see the white cliffs of Dover. This impressive sight must have awed the general and his troops, until they drew closer to shore and noticed the thousands of British warriors gathered along the top of the cliffs for miles in each direction. Realizing at once that it would be suicide for his men to storm the cliffs, Caesar anchored off the coast until the rest of his infantry transports arrived. He then headed seven miles up the coast of Kent to a level stretch of beach that seemed more suitable for landing his troops, probably around present-day Deal. The British warriors, observing the Romans from on top of the headlands, followed them along the coast and were waiting as the first ships reached their shore.

Caesar soon discovered that the heavy Roman ships that had performed so poorly in the shallow waters against the Veneti were even more of a liability on the gently sloping British beach. All the landing craft bearing his troops suddenly ground to a halt far from shore in water several feet deep. The amused British, familiar with the beach and sitting high on their horses, quickly rode out and cut down the Roman soldiers from the first ship as they struggled to shore. With a heavy load of equipment on their backs and the waves knocking them off balance, the Romans were no match for the British cavalry. Even more intimidating were the British charioteers, who tore through the surf launching spears at the Romans and cutting down any man they could reach. The Romans had heard about war chariots from the ancient tales of Homer, but they were terrified to see such a weapon actually being used against them.

When Caesar saw that his first landing on British soil was turning into a bloody fiasco, he brought some of his lighter ships around to the side of the enemy forces and launched a continuous volley of arrows, stones, and deadly artillery to drive the Britons away from his struggling men. This brought some relief to the troops, but they were still reluctant to throw themselves into the deep, pounding surf. At this point, the unarmed standard-bearer of Caesar's prized tenth legion said a quick prayer to the gods and shouted to his comrades: "Soldiers, follow me unless you want this eagle to fall into the hands of the enemy. I at least am going to do my duty for my country and general." He then leaped into the water and began struggling to shore. There was no greater disgrace than for a legion's eagle to be captured by an enemy, so the Romans reluctantly jumped off their ships and began fighting their way to the beach.

In spite of the renewed spirit the standard-bearer had given the troops, their fight to gain the shore was a chaotic struggle hampered by the more maneuverable British warriors. After what seemed like hours of hand-to-hand fighting, the two legions finally forced their way onto dry land. They were then able to form a line with their shields and push the natives off the shore to form a secure beachhead. Caesar, who had been directing the battle from a nearby ship, at last set foot on British soil and surveyed the dismal scene. Many off his best troops lay dead in the surf, others were seriously wounded, and everyone was exhausted. Still, he was thrilled to have reached Britain at last and claimed it was only his lack of cavalry that forced him to remain near the beach that evening instead of pressing inland.

The British knew that they were no match for the Romans in a prolonged land war, so the same war leaders who had attacked Caesar at the shore now came to him with offers of peace. Caesar must have been weary of hearing defeated Celts claim that battles were just a misunderstanding, but the British chieftains said it was the common mob who had foolishly pushed them into an unmerited conflict with Rome. They brought forward their prisoner Commius and returned him unharmed with their apologies. If Caesar had been in Gaul with his full army and abundant supplies, he probably would have stormed the nearest citadel and sold all the natives into slavery. But he knew his position in Britain was tenuous at best, since winter was fast approaching and he had no cavalry support. He therefore accepted the surrender of the British and only demanded hostages from their tribes.

The missing Roman cavalry that had been waiting in Gaul finally set sail four days after Caesar arrived in Britain. The wind was light and fair as they left Gaul, but as they were almost across the channel a violent storm arose and blew the ships in all directions. Some ended up back on the Gaulish coast, while a few were driven far to the west of Caesar's position. These ships made a valiant effort to reach their commander, though after enduring a tempestuous night in the channel they abandoned the attempt and also returned to Gaul. At Caesar's camp, the same storm struck his own troop transports drawn up on shore. With more bad luck for Caesar, the tempest hit at high tide during the full moon, creating the highest possible surge for the storm to ride on. Caesar should have learned more about the fury of the ocean from his war with the Veneti, but all he could do now was watch his precious ships battered against rocks and each other. By the time the storm cleared in the morning, several ships were completely destroyed and many of the rest were badly damaged. The Roman troops came down to the beach and stared in dismay at the remains of their fleet. They were perfectly aware that their only link to the civilized world was gone. They now faced a long, cold winter in Britain with few supplies and little food, surrounded by hostile tribes who could pick them off at their leisure.

The Romans were obviously in desperate straits, so the British secretly begin gathering their troops. They continued to visit the Roman camp over the next few days and spoke of their unwavering loyalty. The promised hostages were unexpectedly delayed, so they claimed, but assured Caesar they would be forthcoming. All the while warriors were pouring into the area from all the neighboring tribes. If they could defeat Caesar and his two legions, they were confident that Rome would not trouble their island again.

One lesson Caesar had learned from Roman military history was that the best commanders knew how to recover from disaster. He was suddenly everywhere at once organizing and encouraging his men. Well-armed foraging parties were dispatched to nearby fields to gather grain, while timber and bronze was stripped from the most severely damaged ships to repair those that could be saved. The few transports that were still in working order were dispatched to Gaul to bring supplies, sails, rigging, and anchors. With only a few days of diligent work, Caesar was confident that most of the damaged ships would be sufficiently seaworthy to limp back across the channel.

While the ship repairs were still ongoing, Caesar sent his seventh legion into the British countryside to seize whatever food they could find. They came across one large field that was still uncut, so the soldiers set to work harvesting grain. They didn't realize that the British had deliberately left this field untouched as bait to lure the Romans into a trap. The busy soldiers were suddenly surrounded by thousands of native warriors circling them on horseback and in chariots, hurling spears at the Romans all the while. Miles away at the Roman camp, the guards on the walls noticed an unusual amount of dust rising from the direction in which the soldiers had set off. Caesar immediately knew he had been betrayed by his newfound British allies and ordered his troops to follow him to the dust cloud.

The besieged soldiers were meanwhile learning just how devastating Celtic war chariots could be. The drivers did not charge into the Roman ranks, but instead created an unnerving noise and confusion rushing past the troops while the warriors they carried cast spears into their lines. With practice, the British could rush down steep hills in their chariots, turn on a moment's notice, and even dash out onto the yoke while their horses galloped at full speed. Warriors would often leap out of their chariots and attack the enemy on the ground while their drivers hung back to pick them up in an instant. As Caesar says, fighting in chariots gave the British the mobility of cavalry with all the advantages of heavy infantry.

Fortunately for his troops, Caesar arrived just in time to drive the British into the forest and prevent a crushing defeat. The Romans then returned to camp while the native chiefs sent messengers far and wide collecting even more troops to push Caesar and his men into the sea. Storms raged across the land for the next few days, keeping Romans and British alike huddled in their tents, but with the first break in the clouds they attacked the Roman camp in full force. As in Gaul, however, the natives were no match for the disciplined legions drawn up in tight ranks in front of their walls. The British broke and scattered into the countryside, later sending emissaries promising Caesar they would keep the peace and send him double the original number of hostages once he reached Gaul. Caesar had little faith in their promises (only two tribes ever sent hostages) but he had no further time to waste in Britain. With his repaired ships at last ready, Caesar's two legions sailed back across the channel to Gaul. The Senate announced twenty days of public thanksgiving when they heard the news of Caesar's safe return, graciously over-looking the fact that he had almost lost a quarter of his army on an ill-conceived and poorly planned venture at the end of the world.

Cato, as usual, was not impressed by Caesar's achievements. While all of Rome was celebrating Caesar's victories in Germany and Britain, Cato rose to denounce him on the Senate floor. The optimate leader claimed that Caesar had in fact provoked the wrath of the gods by attacking the Usipetes and Tencteri during a truce and therefore should be handed over to the Germans themselves for punishment. This speech was a purely political move as Cato cared no more for the Germans than he did for the common people of Rome, but it elicited a bitter reaction from Caesar. No one was able to get under Caesar's skin like Cato—a fact that Cato knew well and used to his own advantage on a number of occasions. When Caesar's letter responding to Cato's charges was read to the Senate a few weeks later, it was full of vicious abuse and unworthy insults against his accuser. Cato calmly listened to the dispatch, then by his composed demeanor and point-by-point rebuttal proceeded to make Caesar look like a spoiled and vulgar child. Even Caesar's friends who were present wished that he had not risen to Cato's provocation. In the end, nothing came of Cato's charges, but he had managed to tarnish Caesar's glory.

Caesar himself was still in Gaul preparing for a new invasion of Britain the following summer. He had learned from his pointed failures during the first expedition and was now determined to launch a successful campaign to avenge his embarrassment at the hands of the British. To leave the British tribes with the impression that they had driven him off their island was not only a black mark on his military record but was an invitation for trouble in the future. Britain could easily become a major inspiration and source of support for Gaulish rebels.

Caesar knew that his preparation and ships had been inadequate for the first invasion, so he set about designing an entirely new kind of vessel for war in the stormy seas off Gaul. The plans he presented to his lieutenants in Gaul called for ships that were an ingenious combination of Roman and Veneti craft, along with some innovative touches of his own. The sides of his new ships would ride low in the water to allow for quick unloading of men and material. They would also be broader to handle more cargo, especially cavalry horses, and have less draft so that they could be beached in shallow water. Unlike Veneti ships, they would be fitted with both sails and oars to allow for rapid movement with or without wind. Caesar did not want a repeat of either the interminable Veneti campaign or his disastrous landing the previous summer in Britain.

Having set his legions to work on the English Channel constructing his new fleet, Caesar quickly made his way south to his Italian province for the winter. He traveled to the Po Valley settling legal disputes and supervising civic projects, all the while strengthening ties with a land that was an important political base and the source for most of his troops. During this tour he learned that an Alpine tribe called the Pirustae were raiding his nearby province of Illyricum. This was little more than an annoyance at present, but he could not afford to allow the situation to worsen and distract him from more pressing ventures in Britain and Gaul. Caesar quickly reached Pirustae territory, then called their leaders to a conference, warning them that unless they wanted him to wage a crushing war on them as he had done against troublesome tribes in Gaul, they would immediately cease their raids and make reparations. Caesar's reputation was such that the Pirustae did not hesitate a moment— they assured him the incursions would stop, quickly settled all damages, and surrendered hostages to ensure their good behavior in the future.

Caesar soon returned to northern Italy, where he faced a more delicate problem. He had long been a friend of the influential family of the poet Catullus in Verona. Whenever he passed through the area on his tours of Italian Gaul he always stayed at their home and enjoyed their warm hospitality. Young Catullus had long since left his rustic town at the foot of the Alps for the cosmopolitan air of Rome, where he was now a well-known poet in the city's most fashionable literary circle. Catullus, who would die later that year, had suffered a heartbreaking romance with a woman he calls Lesbia in his poems— almost certainly Clodia, sister of the unpredictable Clodius. Unlucky in love, Catullus had also failed to reap any expected profit from recent service on the staff of the Roman governor of Bithynia. The poet had nursed a bitter and jealous feud with a third-rate bard named Mamurra, who for years had been growing rich on Caesar's staff, first in Spain, then in Gaul. As long as Catullus aimed his invectives at Mamurra alone, his verse aroused little but amusement at his clever wit:

> *Who can look at this, who can bear it,*
> *unless he's a shameful, greedy gambler,*
> *who can bear that Mamurra holds the riches*
> *of long-haired Gaul and distant Britain?*

But recently he had decided to include Caesar himself in his biting satire:

> *They're a pretty pair of sodomites,*
> *Mamurra bent over and wretched Caesar behind.*

The family of Catullus was mortified that their son would slander their longtime patron so viciously for public amusement. Caesar was indeed deeply offended by these poems, especially as they called to mind his alleged affair with King Nicomedes—a bitterly resented slur that he had been battling all his life. But Caesar was not a man to hold a grudge, especially as he admired the poet's obvious talents. When Catullus was persuaded by his father to apologize that spring, Caesar invited him to dinner the same day to let the young man know all was forgiven. His relations with the poet's family in Verona continued for many years as warmly as ever.

Caesar also cultivated a new relationship with Cicero during the winter between his two British campaigns. The triumvirate had pressured Cicero to support its plans two years before, but Caesar went well beyond treating Cicero merely as a useful tool. For so many years the man who had risen to the consulship from obscurity had been held in bemused contempt by the Roman nobility. Caesar recognized Cicero's hunger for respect and began honoring the famed orator accordingly. The two became frequent correspondents during Caesar's campaigns in Gaul and Britain. Cicero even sent samples of his poetry over the Alps, which Caesar compared to the best of Greek verse. Caesar also welcomed Cicero's brother, Quintus, into his service that winter as a senior military legate. Although Quintus was a literary man who translated the Greek plays of Sophocles into Latin during spare moments in the field, he proved to be a gifted soldier.

It was probably during his journey back to Gaul in the spring of 54 B.C. that Caesar again demonstrated his own literary talent by composing a now-lost work entitled *On Analogy,* recommending clarity and simple language as the chief goals for orators and writers rather than the elaborate ornamentation then in style. One surviving fragment of the book puts it bluntly: "Avoid strange and unfamiliar words as a sailor avoids rocks at sea." The fact that he was able to dictate this work to secretaries while riding on horseback or jostling in a cart in the midst of pressing military duties makes the book all the more remarkable. Caesar dedicated the work with genuine admiration—and perhaps a touch of irony—to the loquacious Cicero.

When Caesar arrived back at the Channel in the early summer of 54 B.C., he was thrilled to see that the fleet was almost ready to sail. His men had built six hundred transport vessels and twenty-eight ships designed for naval combat—a virtual armada that would soon carry over twenty thousand men to Britain. He summoned the leaders of all the Gaulish tribes to assemble together at his camp with a prearranged number of cavalry from each as auxiliary units for the invasion. From every part of Gaul, men streamed to Caesar's camp to join the grand adventure in hope of plunder—gold, pearls, slaves. The one tribe that had refused Caesar's summons were the Belgic Treveri

near the border with Germany. Caesar not only needed their contri-
bution to his invasion force as they had the best cavalry in Gaul, but
he could not afford to leave a rebellious tribe in his rear to stir up
trouble. One group of the Treveri, led by Indutiomarus, had set
themselves against Rome, while a pro-Caesar faction rallied around
a noble named Cingetorix. Since it would be several weeks before the
fleet was ready, Caesar set off with his army across Gaul to quell the
Treverian rebellion. Indutiomarus had prepared for the upcoming
Roman attack by gathering his men in the broad Ardennes forest,
but as the legions approached, many warriors of the tribe began to
slip away and declare their loyalty to Caesar. By the time the Romans
reached Treverian territory, Indutiomarus was seeking terms of surrender. Caesar spared his life—a kindness he would later regret—
and appointed Cingetorix as ruler in his place.

Caesar soon returned to the Channel to resume his preparations
for the British invasion, chief of which was to ensure that every
Gaulish leader of questionable loyalty would accompany him to
Britain. Caesar believed in keeping his friends close and his enemies
even closer. At the top of the list of potential troublemakers was
Dumnorix of the Aedui, a man who had troubled Caesar since the
beginning of the Gallic War. Caesar knew very well that Dumnorix
was a courageous and influential man bent on seizing power for
himself in Gaul if given half a chance. Dumnorix came to Caesar and
begged to be left in Gaul—he was afraid of sea travel, he had religious obligations at home—but Caesar demanded that he prepare to
sail. Dumnorix then tried a different strategy by spreading rumors
throughout the camp that Caesar wanted to transport the Gaulish
leaders to Britain so that he might kill them there with impunity.
Whether the tribal leaders were foolish enough to believe this or not,
many began to question the wisdom of following Caesar any farther.

When the day of departure finally came, however, the Roman
troops and all the Gaulish auxiliary boarded the ships—except for
Dumnorix and a contingent of the Aedui. They had managed to slip

away from camp in the confusion of departure and were now heading south toward home. Caesar halted the ships when he heard the
news and sent back a large force of cavalry to chase down Dumnorix.
Their orders were to bring him back alive, if possible, but to stop him
at all costs. The Aeduan leader was much too dangerous a man to
leave untended in Gaul while most of the Roman army was across
the sea. When the pursuers caught up with Dumnorix, they surrounded him and ordered his surrender. Dumnorix refused and
shouted as they cut him down:

I am a free man of a free people!

His words would soon become a rallying cry for all of Gaul.

A gentle southwest breeze blew Caesar's fleet steadily across the
Channel that evening until the wind suddenly died around midnight. The ships now rode the tide through the darkness as they
drifted blindly to the east. When the sun rose, Caesar saw that he had
overshot Britain, which lay far on the western horizon, and ordered
his ships to row for the coast as fast as they could. With tremendous
effort by all, the fleet finally arrived in Kent by midday. This time
their arrival was greeted by an eerie silence, with not a British warrior to be seen anywhere. Leaving a sufficient contingent on the
beach to make a fortified camp and guard the ships, Caesar marched
inland that same afternoon with most of his troops.

Somewhere near what would one day be the cathedral town of
Canterbury, Caesar finally saw the British. The natives were much
more cautious than the previous year, dashing out of a thick forest on
horseback and in chariots to strike the Roman lines, then rushing
back for the cover of the trees. The legions easily repulsed these attacks but Caesar, rightly fearing an ambush, forbade them to pursue
the enemy into the woods. The army instead built a well-fortified

camp and prepared to continue its march the next day. But at sunrise, word arrived from Caesar's fort on the beach that nearly all the ships had been damaged yet again by a sudden squall during the night. Instead of taking this second catastrophe to his fleet in as many years as a warning sign from the gods, Caesar returned with his army to the shore and ordered shipwrights to be brought from Gaul along with whatever supplies they needed to mend the vessels. Caesar did, however, finally take to heart that ships could not be left lying unprotected on North Sea beaches. He spent the next ten days in a round-the-clock construction project to secure his fleet against damage from either storms or enemy attacks. When he next left camp with his army, he was confident that his means of transport back to Gaul was finally safe.

Caesar then headed across Kent toward a broad river called the Tamesis, now the Thames. He knew that on the far side of this stream somewhere to the west of modern London was the citadel of Cassivellaunus, king of the Cassi. Caesar had learned that Cassivellaunus held a loose hegemony over all the tribes of southern Britain. This united front made Caesar's job much more difficult, but he was determined to crush all resistance in the south before returning to Gaul for the winter.

At this dramatic point in his yearly report to the Senate, later published in his *Gallic War,* Caesar interrupts his own description of battles and naval disasters to highlight his talents as an ethnographer and scientist. Caesar obviously enjoyed using what he learned about Britain and its natives to stir the imagination of his Roman audience and thereby increase his own prestige. Much of what he says has been verified by modern scholarship and archaeological excavations, but regardless of his accuracy his readers in Rome would have been fascinated by the strange and wonderful world he describes across the sea.

Caesar knew almost nothing about Britain when he planned his

first invasion in 55 B.C., but by the time of writing his report he had
visited the island twice and interviewed many British natives to
gather information. He begins his description with the different
types of people found on the island:

> *The parts of Britain far from the sea are inhabited by tribes who*
> *claim to be indigenous, but those along the coast are recent mi-*
> *grants from Belgic Gaul who came for profit and war.*

The claim that the southern Britons had close cultural ties to Gaul is
undeniable. What little linguistic evidence we possess of the ancient
British language, the ancestor of Welsh, shows that it was a variant of
the Celtic tongue spoken in Gaul. Archaeologists have also shown
that weapons, art, clothing, burial practices, and many other features
were similar on both sides of the Channel. Excavations also provide
abundant evidence of trade between Gaul and southern Britain, including wine. The Britons in turn exported grain, cattle, precious
metals, hunting dogs, and slaves to Gaul and beyond. We can be certain that however little Caesar knew of the Britons before his first expedition, the inhabitants of at least the southern part of the island
were well aware of Rome.

Caesar also mentions that the Britons used coins, again confirmed
by archaeology, and that their weather was more moderate than that
of Gaul (thanks to the then unknown Gulf Stream). He comments on
the roughly triangular shape of the island and is tolerably accurate on
its overall size, even though he saw only a small portion of the southeast. He notes that a large island called Hibernia lies just to the west,
providing one of our earliest descriptions of Ireland. He also was
keenly interested in variations of daylight hours according to latitude
and so imported from Gaul a *clepsydra*—an ingenious water clock
used by the ancients to measure time in all weather, day or night.
Through careful experiments he discovered that summer nights in
Britain were indeed slightly shorter than those on the continent.

Some of his most fascinating comments on the island for both ancient and modern readers concern the customs of the inhabitants themselves. Caesar records that the Britons considered certain birds, along with all hares, sacred and would never eat them. This may well be true since there are countless tales of sacred birds in Celtic mythology. The reference to hares is also borne out in the next century when the rebellious British queen Boudicca released a hare as part of a divination ceremony before battle. He notes that all British warriors, north and south, dye their skin with a bluish coloring derived from the leaves of a plant called *vitrum* (woad) that gives them a terrifying appearance in battle. Finally, Caesar claims that on their native farms, up to a dozen related men could live in a communal lifestyle freely sharing wives. As this has no parallels in other early Celtic societies, it may be that Caesar misunderstood the inner workings of British households or was deliberately pandering to his Roman readers, who quite expected such scandalous behavior from distant barbarians.

Caesar proceeded with caution through the early autumn countryside of Kent on the way to his battle with Cassivellaunus and his British allies. The native warriors struck at the Romans on the march but always in small hit-and-run attacks designed to lure the legions into the confines of the dense forests. On one occasion they did assault a small group of soldiers setting up camp and managed to slay a number of Romans in the melee, but they were pushed back and never tried such a daring attack again. What drove Caesar to distraction was the uncanny way the British warriors would divide themselves into multiple assault teams and strike at different parts of the Roman lines at once. The legions were trained to fight in set battles or protracted sieges, not dozens of simultaneous skirmishes.

When Caesar finally reached the Thames somewhere near London he discovered from native prisoners that there was only one spot on the river suitable for fording, and that only with great difficulty. He could see the warriors of Cassivellaunus waiting on the far side of the river eager for the Romans to press across so they could strike them down in the water. They had even fixed sharp stakes just below the waterline to impale the Romans as they struggled up the bank. With the autumn storms on the Channel fast approaching, Caesar knew he had no time to repeat his bridging of the Rhine nor did he have enough boats for his men. Instead, he decided on an extremely risky maneuver. Before the British knew what was happening, Caesar sent thousands of troops screaming across the Thames in water up to their necks. The British were so surprised that they broke ranks and ran as fast as they could away from the river.

Caesar was now north of the Thames (probably near modern Heathrow Airport) but Cassivellaunus still commanded a sizeable force to oppose him. However, with the Thames breached, the authority of Cassivellaunus was considerably weakened. It was now that the southern British kings, long resentful of Cassivellaunus, began to come forward and seek peace with Caesar. Especially important was a prince named Mandubracius of the Trinovantes of Essex, northeast of London. His father had been murdered by Cassivellaunus and the son had fled into exile to save his own life. Mandubracius offered Caesar his loyalty, hostages, and all the grain his troops could eat if he would help him restore his throne. Caesar was only too happy to oblige.

Caesar learned from these defectors that the headquarters of Cassivellaunus was nearby, though well-protected by swamps, thickets, and trenches. The Romans nevertheless snuck up on the fortress from two sides and rushed the stronghold, killing many of the British, though the king himself escaped. In a final attempt to rid himself of the Romans, Cassivellaunus ordered four subordinate kings in Kent still loyal to him to destroy Caesar's fleet, though the assault failed miserably. No fool, Cassivellaunus now began to make peace overtures to Caesar through the agency of Caesar's old ally Commius of the Gaulish Atrebates. In different circumstances, Caesar might have squeezed more concessions from Cassivellaunus than he did, but he was facing several pressing problems. He was not prepared to winter in Britain, the autumn seas would soon make the Channel impassible, and, in a telling remark, he reports that there was "suddenly trouble in Gaul." Caesar settled for a quick peace treaty, the usual hostages, and a promise from Cassivellaunus that he would not interfere with Mandubracius and the Trinovantes. With these terms reached it was a fast march back across Kent to the waiting ships. With storm damage to his fleet and so many British hostages, as well as slaves, to convey back to Gaul, Caesar split the invasion force into two groups to ferry them across the Channel in turns. Undoubtedly Caesar's last word to the British kings was to be on their best behavior as he and the legions could return at any time to punish troublemakers or even annex the whole island. However, as events unfolded, no Roman soldier would touch British soil again for almost a century.

The news awaiting Caesar on his return to Gaul could not have been more grim. A drought had severely reduced the grain harvest for the Gaulish tribes and therefore made supplying the Roman troops quartered among them even more taxing. Caesar was forced to spread his legions thinly throughout Gaul to reduce the strain on the local populations, making it all the more difficult for the commanders to aid each other in the event of trouble. The frustration soon broke into open revolt among the Carnutes tribes around modern Chartes when they murdered their king, Tasgetius, a solid ally of Caesar. It was only a matter of time, Caesar feared, until the whole country would explode. So great was his concern that he immediately abandoned his usual plans to return to northern Italy that winter and chose instead to remain in Gaul with his troops.

But the most crushing blow to Caesar that autumn of 54 B.C. was a personal matter he omitted from his official reports to the Senate. When he stepped off the ship in Gaul, a messenger handed him a sealed letter from his friends in Rome. He opened it and learned that his beloved daughter, Julia, his only child and the wife of Pompey, had died in childbirth just days before. The infant granddaughter of Caesar had survived only a few days after her mother's death. A general such as Caesar could not afford to break down in front of his troops, but his mourning for his Julia was profound. Pompey too was crushed beyond all consolation. Caesar ordered public gladiatorial games and a banquet in her honor in Rome—an honor unprecedented for a woman. Over the objection of the optimates, she was buried on the sacred ground of the Field of Mars by the people of Rome. But Caesar's supporters—and especially his enemies—realized that it had been Julia who held together the alliance of Caesar and Pompey. Without her, they feared—or hoped—the days of the triumvirate were numbered.

VIII

VERCINGETORIX

There was such a passion among the Gauls for liberty and for renewing the ancient glory of war that
no Roman rewards, no alliances, not even any
friendship with Caesar could hold them back from
throwing themselves with all their heart and soul
into the fight for freedom.

—CAESAR

The first blow in the Gaulish war for independence came from an
unexpected source. The Eburones were a small Belgic tribe of
little significance that had played no great role in the war against
Caesar, dominated as they were by their far more powerful neighbors. Their leader, Ambiorix, was an amiable man who had been as
friendly with Rome as possible under the circumstances and was
honored by Caesar in turn. The Roman leader had placed several
thousand of his men in the Eburonian territory for the winter under
the command of the generals Sabinus and Cotta. Ambiorix was no
doubt vexed to feed so many additional mouths during the upcoming months, but he willingly agreed and supplied the legions with
grain he had collected from his meager harvest that year.

Scarcely had the Romans settled in their winter camp when Ambiorix was approached by Indutiomarus, the chieftain of the Treveri who had rebelled the previous year but whom Caesar had pardoned. The disgruntled Indutiomarus had sought support among the neighboring kings for action against Caesar, but it was with the seemingly peaceful Ambiorix that he at last found a sympathetic ear. Drawing on a keen intelligence and devious side of his personality no one had ever suspected, Ambiorix devised an ingenious plan for destroying the Romans quartered among his tribe and hopefully igniting a revolt that would spread across Gaul.

Ambiorix ordered some of his warriors to attack a small Roman force gathering firewood, then sent his troops against the nearly impregnable fort manned by the soldiers of Sabinus and Cotta. The Eburones were easily driven back, at which point Ambiorix asked the Roman leaders for a parley. He apologized profusely for the assault and swore that his feelings for Caesar and the Romans were as warm as ever. He explained that the weak Eburones had been bullied into attacking the Romans by the dire threats of the larger Gaulish tribes surrounding them, who even now were engaged in a vast conspiracy against Rome. The Gaulish leaders had all agreed to fall on the isolated winter camps of the Romans simultaneously so that the legions might not be able to send aid to one another. Moreover, the Gauls had hired hordes of fierce German warriors, who would be present among them in less than two days. He pleaded with Sabinus and Cotta, for their own safety and the lives of the troops under them, to abandon their camp and march as quickly as possible to the stronger positions held by Quintus Cicero or Labienus. He tearfully swore by all the gods that they would be granted safe passage through his territory, but they must hurry while there was still time to reach safety.

The Roman leaders quickly held a council to discuss the matter, in which the generals, tribunes, and centurions present were of two minds. Both sides agreed that it was most unlikely for a minor tribe led by a man like Ambiorix to attack the Romans unless there was a much larger rebellion afoot. But one group, led by Cotta, argued against doing anything rash and for staying in camp until ordered otherwise by Caesar. They had plenty of troops, abundant supplies for the winter, and their walls could hold back tens of thousands of Gauls and Germans if necessary. The other contingent, led by Sabinus, warned that they had no time for deliberation and must seek safety while they could. The Rhine was nearby and if the fierce Suebi chose to cross over and fight with the Gauls, even a well-fortified Roman camp might not survive. In any event, he claimed, Caesar was probably already far away in northern Italy. They would have to take decisive action immediately and move the troops without waiting for his orders. Speedy and decisive action was the only hope for survival.

The bickering continued until midnight when Sabinus finally claimed that Cotta was going to get them all killed because of his caution. Cotta then yielded with the warning that this was a most foolish decision. The soldiers packed through the night and headed out of the camp gates the next morning in a long column heavy with the booty of four years of war. They comforted themselves that their safety had been guaranteed by Ambiorix himself, a proven friend of Caesar. About two miles from the camp the road led through a narrow ravine—and it was here that Ambiorix sprang his trap. One group of his warriors attacked the Romans from the front while another hit their rear, sealing them in a narrow valley in which they could barely maneuver. Sabinus panicked and ran among the troops, shouting conflicting orders to his terrified men, but Cotta held firm and commanded those nearest him to form into protective squares. The confusion of the battle was such, however, and the confines of the ravine so limited, that the concentrated squares only hampered the movement of the Romans and made it easier for the Gauls to strike them down at a distance with spears.

As the hours passed, the exhausted Romans were slowly worn down. Cotta was wounded in the face but continued to lead his men bravely. Sabinus, in an utterly foolish move, called out to Ambiorix for a conference, hoping he could still salvage the situation. Ambiorix agreed provided that Sabinus and his officers lay down their arms before approaching his lines. Sabinus ordered his reluctant men to comply. Ambiorix welcomed the general and his men with a warm smile and open arms, then signaled his men to slaughter them all. Cotta and his officers fought on in the ravine, but the wiser leader soon fell along with most of his troops. When darkness at last descended, the few Romans who had survived the day held a final council, then slew each other to deny the Gauls any further victory. Only a handful of Roman soldiers that night managed to slip away from the terrible valley where the bodies of thousands of their comrades lay. A few escaped through swamps and forests to reach the camp of Labienus and eventually pass on to Caesar the story of their crushing defeat.

After destroying the army of Sabinus and Cotta, Ambiorix set off at once toward the lands of the Aduatuci and Nervii. These Belgic tribes were easily fired by the tale of the recent slaughter of Caesar's troops and eagerly joined in the rebellion. Gathering together more neighboring tribes until they had a force of perhaps sixty thousand warriors, the rebel army approached the winter camp commanded by Quintus Cicero, brother of the famous orator, deep in the forests of northern Gaul. Encirclement and total surprise were the watchwords of the Belgic commanders as they moved quickly to cut off the camp from any possible contact with Caesar, who was, in fact, still in his own winter quarters a hundred miles away. The Eburones, Nervii, Aduatuci, and their allies all burst out of the woods and rushed Cicero's camp in hope of taking the Romans off guard, but the surprised troops quickly manned the ramparts and held firm against the first Gaulish assault. Quintus Cicero now showed that he was as good a general as he was a scholar by inspiring and organizing his few thousand men against a determined army perhaps ten times their size. All through the frantic first night of the siege the Romans erected over a hundred towers along their walls and deepened the trenches surrounding the fort. Weak spots in camp defenses were strengthened and weapons made ready, but every man on the walls knew they were facing the fight of their lives.

And so a grim routine began. Each morning the Gaulish army would surge forward against the Romans' fort, filling in trenches, launching fiery missiles, and trying the storm the walls. By late afternoon each day, the exhausted Romans had driven them back, but at a terrible cost in casualties. The Gauls could draw on practically unlimited replacements to fill in their front lines, but the Romans could not afford to lose a single man, so that the wounded served their turn on the ramparts alongside those few legionaries still unharmed. Quintus Cicero was everywhere among his men at all hours of the day and night until they forced him to rest for a few moments.

Ambiorix and the Gaulish leaders then decided to try the same trick on Quintus Cicero that had worked so well at the previous Roman camp (Quintus Cicero had not yet heard the fate of Sabinus and Cotta). They called a meeting and told Quintus Cicero of the supposedly widespread rebellion throughout northern Gaul. The Germans, they claimed, had already crossed the Rhine and were now on their way to attack Cicero's camp. They confided to the commander that they had nothing personal against the Romans but merely wanted them to remove their winter quarters farther south so that they could have enough grain to feed their own tribes. The Gaulish chieftains offered the Romans safe passage anywhere they might choose to go, as long as it was out of their territory. Quintus Cicero rejected their offer outright—and boldly advised them to surrender to him instead. Caesar, he declared, might show them mercy if they did so, but he himself would never negotiate under threat nor would he move one inch from his camp.

The enraged Gauls then redoubled their efforts to take the camp. Learning from their own service among the Romans over the last few years and from Roman prisoners, they began to construct a siege wall around the camp. The result was a poor imitation of a Roman effort, but it served well enough to trap Cicero's men. The Gauls then heated balls of red-hot clay and launched them over the walls onto the thatched roofs of the camp buildings, but the Romans refused to abandon their posts even to save their burning huts. Next the Gauls moved wheeled towers up to the walls to climb onto the ramparts, but were forced back by the Roman troops. When one tower did approach close enough for the Gauls to leap across onto the walls, the Romans invited them to come over and try their luck—but none of the Gauls dared. Old rivals in the legions fought to outdo one another in bravery and honor. The centurions Pullo and Vorenus, bitter adversaries for years, fought side by side against tremendous odds, each gladly saving the life of the other.

Throughout the endless days and nights of battle Quintus Cicero had been dispatching riders in hope of getting a message through to Caesar, but each of these men had been captured and tortured to death by the Gauls in full view of the Roman soldiers on the walls. Now, a nobleman of the Nervii inside the camp who was still loyal to Rome presented a plan to Cicero. He had a faithful slave he was willing to send across the lines that night with a message inserted in the hollow of his spear. In exchange for his freedom and a large reward, the slave agreed to risk his life blending in among the Gaulish troops besieging the camp. He would then quickly make his way west to Caesar. Cicero gladly accepted the offer, and to make sure the note could not be read if discovered, he wrote it in Greek—a language he and Caesar understood but no Belgic Gaul knew.

At Caesar's camp at Samarobriva a few days later, an aide came bursting into the command tent with the slave's message. After scanning the few lines, Caesar immediately sprang into action. He ordered all the available legions in northern Gaul to join him, sparing only enough men to guard the scattered camps against further Belgic attacks. He was able to gather together only two understrength legions of perhaps seven thousand men total to form the relief force for Quintus Cicero, nevertheless, he quickly led his army out into the freezing Gaulish winter at a forced march toward Quintus Cicero's camp.

Caesar had sent his own messenger back to Quintus Cicero to deliver the news—again in Greek—that help was on the way. However, the loyal Gaulish horseman who carried the letter panicked when he approached Cicero's camp. Instead of dashing past the hostile Belgae and through the gates, he tied the message onto a spear and threw it with all his might toward the camp wall. There it lay stuck in the rampart for two days until one of Quintus Cicero's men noticed it and brought it to his commander. Cicero quickly called together his beleaguered men and read the letter from Caesar—cheers of joy then rang throughout the camp.

Caesar soon drew near and realized it would be foolish to attempt a direct relief of the camp with his vastly outnumbered men. He therefore led the attacking Belgae away from Cicero with a series of feints and pretended cowardly moves until he was able to maneuver the Gaulish host into a setting of his own choosing and crush them in battle. Later that day, the gates of Quintus Cicero's camp were opened as Caesar marched through with his men. Scarcely a man among Quintus Cicero's troops was unscathed, but they stood proudly for review. For his part, Caesar said he had never been more pleased with any soldiers and honored many of them personally for their extraordinary bravery.

At about this same time, Caesar at last learned the fate of his men under Sabinus and Cotta. The blow to Caesar was so terrible that he adopted the traditional Roman signs of mourning for the dearest of friends, leaving his hair and beard uncut. It was clear to all who saw him and heard his few terse words that Ambiorix and the tribe who had betrayed and slaughtered thousands of his men were going to pay a terrible price for their actions.

Caesar spent the few remaining weeks of 53 B.C. and the first few months of the next year in preparation for his punitive campaign. There was no thought of even a brief return to northern Italy that year as there was so much to do in Gaul. He brought Quintus Cicero and his battered troops back to his headquarters at Samarobriva and began recruiting new troops from northern Italy to replace those lost by Sabinus. Three new legions soon joined him in Gaul, one of which was on loan from Pompey. This more than made up for the slaughter of his men by the Eburones and gave him a total of ten legions or roughly fifty thousand troops on the ground in Gaul. He called together a council of all the Gaulish tribal leaders to threaten them into submission. Several tribes ignored his summons completely, tantamount in Caesar's eyes to a declaration of war. Caesar knew from his spies that news of the massacre of his troops under Sabinus had spread throughout the land and heartened the discontented tribes. Even many of those leaders who answered his call to a council were plotting with each other against Rome behind his back. Of all the Gaulish tribes, Caesar trusted only the Aedui in the southeast and the Remi of Belgic Gaul, the first because of their longstanding alliance with Rome and the latter because of their steadfast support. This short list of firm allies coupled with the poor harvest and general discontent throughout Gaul gave Caesar many a sleepless night throughout the long northern winter.

One bit of good news for Caesar that winter was the success of his chief lieutenant Labienus against his old foe Indutiomarus of the Treveri. After stirring up Ambiorix and the Eburones against Sabinus and Cotta, Indutiomarus had returned to his own people and held a secret war council. He deposed his rival and Caesar's friend Cingetorix from the tribal leadership by invoking an ancient Celtic tradition. When the warriors of a tribe were summoned to a military council, the last one to arrive was publicly tortured to death. This not only discouraged tardy attendees in general, but served as a pretext in this particular case for Indutiomarus to declare the life of the absent Cingetorix forfeit. Indutiomarus had little luck persuading German mercenaries to cross the Rhine and join his cause, but he was successful in recruiting disgruntled warriors to his standard from all the tribes of Gaul.

Once his forces were gathered together, Indutiomarus led them west to destroy the winter camp of Labienus. Caesar's best general in Gaul was as tough a soldier as Rome had ever produced, but he was also a clever strategist. When he saw the massive army of Indutiomarus approaching, he shut his troops inside his camp walls and gave every impression of being terrified of the Treveri and their allies. The Gauls should have learned this particular Roman trick after so much experience, but they flattered themselves into thinking they had terrified the great Labienus. Each day the Gaulish troops moved a little closer to the Roman camp, taunting the soldiers with spears and insults. The Romans shrank from any conflict until the Gauls were beyond contempt for the legionaries. One particular evening after the Gauls had spent the whole day mocking the Romans, they broke up in a disordered mass and began sauntering back to their own camp for a hearty meal and a mug of beer. The two gates of the Roman camp suddenly sprang open and out poured the entire cavalry of Labienus to fall on the surprised Gauls, who quickly scattered in all directions. Labienus had given them orders not to attack the entire army, but to aim for Indutiomarus alone. The Treveri leader watched in horror and frustration as hundreds of horsemen separated him from the rest of his army and moved in for the kill. In the best tradition of Gaulish war trophies, his body was left on the field but his head soon graced the wall of the Roman camp. The Treveri lost the nerve to fight after the death of their king and returned home, at least for the present.

Caesar's campaign of terror and revenge in Gaul began early in the spring of 53 B.C. while snow still covered the ground. Four legions moved to Nervian territory with lightning speed and devastated the countryside as punishment for their attack on Quintus Cicero's camp. What the Romans didn't burn they seized as booty, including thousands of cattle and slaves distributed by Caesar to the troops. Next, Caesar moved south against the rebellious Senones and Carnutes, led by a rebel named Acco, who were caught totally off guard by the speed of Caesar's approach. They quickly surrendered and were spared the devastation of the Nervii through the intercession of the Aedui. Caesar satisfied himself with hostages rather than pillaging in this case as his more pressing desire for revenge lay east along the Rhine.

The truculent Menapii, who dwelt in the Rhine delta, were next on Caesar's list. They had never sent deputies to any of Caesar's councils and had always disappeared into their endless swamps when the Romans drew near. This time, however, Caesar was determined to teach them a lesson. When the Menapii predictably hid deep in the marshes, Caesar outwitted them by ordering his legions to build long causeways to connect their islets to the mainland. Without their usual protection, the Menapii were completely vulnerable to the legions, who stripped the region of cattle and took many slaves before the Menapii finally surrendered.

The powerful Treveri, who had fought against Labienus just weeks before, were a more difficult case. Caesar's chief lieutenant took the lead in chastising his old foes and again tricked them into fighting in an unfavorable position. The result for the Treveri was a crushing defeat that resulted in the restoration of Cingetorix as their king. A group of Germans who were on their way to aid the Treveri quickly returned to their own country when they heard the news of the Roman victory. Caesar was so infuriated that the Germans had not yet learned their lesson about aiding his Gaulish enemies that he built a second bridge across the Rhine in just a few days and marched across to terrorize the nearby tribes. After only a few days he returned to Gaul but left the bridge mostly intact and heavily guarded as a warning to the Germans that he would be back if they failed to stay on their side of the river.

All of these brutal strikes during the summer of 53 B.C. drew an ever-tightening circle around the territory of the Eburones. More than anything Caesar wanted to capture Ambiorix and destroy the tribe that had killed thousands of his men. With this goal in mind, he issued an invitation throughout Gaul to come and help him plunder the land of the Eburones. However much the Gauls hated the Romans, the chance to seize cattle, slaves, and rich booty from a doomed tribe was too tempting to resist. Thousands of Gauls from the Atlantic to the Rhine descended on Eburonian territory and began to strip the land like locusts.

By early autumn, the Eburones were only a memory. Their land was completely devastated and their people sold into slavery, so that the name of their tribe utterly vanished from history after this point. But Caesar's greatest disappointment was that Ambiorix himself managed to escape the dragnet of Gauls and Romans searching for him. With only four loyal comrades left to him, the king of the Eburones disappeared, never to be seen again.

The summer campaign season ended with a grand tribunal held by Caesar in the land of the loyal Remi. Some rebellious leaders were outlawed while Acco, chief conspirator in the uprising of the Senones and Carnutes, was sentenced to the *fustuarium*—the traditional form of Roman military execution. While all the Gaulish leaders watched, Acco was beaten to death with a club.

Caesar established his legions in strongly fortified winter camps and set out for northern Italy. After an absence of two years it was time to devote himself to provincial affairs and neglected duties at Rome. He hoped that at last Gaul might be at peace, but the bitter Gaulish chieftains returning home after Acco's tribunal now had no doubt of their place in the new Roman world.

Caesar's return from Gaul to northern Italy in the winter of 53 B.C. provided him with the opportunity to again be close to the political action in Rome. He had never been out of touch with developments at home even during his most difficult times in Britain and Gaul, but the proximity of his headquarters just across the Apennine Mountains from Rome allowed him to receive frequent visitors, communicate more quickly with his supporters, and supervise a new series of public works in the city. As early as 54 B.C., Caesar had been working to endow Rome with magnificent buildings using the spoils he had taken from Gaul. His first major project was the new Basilica Julia on the southwest side of the Forum, between the temples of Saturn and of Castor and Pollux. A Roman basilica was a large hall used for a variety of purposes, including judicial functions, commerce, and public gatherings. The standard layout included a long, high-roofed central hall separated from side chambers by columns, with a semi-circular apse for speakers at the far end (the basilica is the direct ancestor of most Christian churches). At over three hundred feet long, Caesar's basilica was enormous, paved with the finest marble, and decorated with beautiful artwork. As was Caesar's intention, it came to dominate the Forum as a center of activity and constant reminder of his benevolence. Caesar also planned and financed an entirely new forum just to the northwest of the Capitoline Hill, though construction was delayed for several years. The crumbled remains of both projects can still be seen today by visitors to Rome.

Caesar's primary concern that winter, however, was not mortar or marble but politics, especially the sudden end of the triumvirate and Pompey's rising power. The most drastic change in Caesar's web of political alliances had come the previous summer while he was conducting his campaign of revenge in Belgic Gaul. On that fateful June day, Marcus Crassus, the silent but powerful third member of the triumvirate along with Caesar and Pompey, was killed during battle with the Parthians in Mesopotamia. Crassus had long been jealous of the military success of his two partners, so as proconsular governor of Syria he had lost no time in provoking a confrontation with Rome's greatest enemy. He invaded the Parthian empire with over thirty thousand infantry troops but almost no cavalry aside from a contingent of homesick Gauls brought to the desert by his son Publius. Crassus intended to make for the city of Seleucia on the Tigris River, near modern Baghdad, but unwisely took a shortcut across the parched plains of northern Mesopotamia, where he met ten thousand mounted Parthian archers. The mobility and deadly accuracy of these famous bowmen sealed the doom of the Roman infantry. The younger Crassus, who had served Caesar so well, was cut down along with his hopelessly outclassed Gaulish cavalry. The elder Crassus was soon slaughtered as well, with barely a third of his men surviving to return to Roman territory led by a young lieutenant named Cassius. It was an ignominious end for a man who had served Sulla, defeated Spartacus, and been a major player in Roman politics and commerce for decades. His death, following so soon after the demise of Julia, strained the partnership of Caesar and Pompey to the breaking point. It was, of course, the perfect opportunity for Cato and the optimates to sever the remaining ties between Rome's two most powerful men.

The split between Caesar and Pompey began with a chance meeting of two of Rome's most infamous thugs along the Appian Way. The veteran troublemaker and ex-patrician Clodius was returning from a small town south of Rome in January of 52 B.C., when he and his bodyguard of thirty armed slaves passed his rival in urban gang warfare, Milo, heading south to his hometown to participate in a local ceremony. Milo was accompanied by his wife, a friend named Saufeius, and a band of hired guards that included at least two off-duty gladiators. Near the small village of Bovillae—across the road, ironically, from a shine to the goddess Bona Dea—the two parties met. Milo and Clodius seemed content at first to go their separate ways exchanging just a few choice words of derision, but the bodyguards in both parties started a brawl that ended with one of the gladiators hurling a spear into Clodius's shoulder. While the gangs battled on the road, Clodius was rushed to a nearby inn in Bovillae for medical attention. Milo quite rightly realized that Clodius would be a more far serious threat wounded and vengeful than dead, so his men dragged him from his sickbed and slew him, leaving his body on the road. Thus Clodius, the man who had defiled the Bona Dea mysteries in Caesar's own house, met his end in the dust at the foot of her shrine.

Rioting broke out in Rome when the supporters of Clodius heard of his murder. The Senate house was burned and even the optimates now began to call on Pompey to restore public order by any means necessary. Cato could not bring himself to support Pompey for the office of dictator, but he did nominate the general as consul without a colleague at least to assure some accountability from him when his term was complete. Pompey was duly elected and began recruiting troops throughout Italy to put down mob insurrection. Cicero, incidentally, jumped at the chance to defend Milo for killing Clodius, a man who had been nothing but trouble to the orator for years.

The optimates now began to work steadily on the newly empowered Pompey to distance him from Caesar. A law was passed with Pompey's approval requiring candidates for office to be present in Rome for election, a bill aimed at ruining Caesar's chances at a future consulship. Caesar attempted to renew family ties with Pompey, offering to marry Pompey's daughter and give his own grandniece Octavia (sister of the future emperor Augustus) to his colleague as a bride. Instead, Pompey married the daughter of Quintus Metellus Scipio, one of Caesar's most bitter enemies. Still, Pompey did not completely break with Caesar. He maintained cordial relations with his old partner while frustrating the optimates with his lack of enthusiasm for their agenda. Pompey was certainly jealous of Caesar's military victories and wanted to teach the younger man who was really in charge in Rome, but he had no thoughts at this point of an open break. Such a rupture would have inevitably led to civil war between Rome's two greatest generals, an outcome neither desired. Caesar's position in Gaul was secure for the immediate future, as was Pompey's in Rome, but both men now looked at each other with growing suspicion and mistrust.

The unrest in Rome, especially the threatened political situation of Caesar, did not escape the notice of the Gauls. The chieftains who gathered together in secret councils that winter hoped that events in the city would force Caesar to remain in Italy during the coming summer. They believed, with good reason, that the fickle nature of Roman politics guaranteed that Caesar would either be recalled by his enemies or become embroiled in a distant civil war, during which he and Rome would have more pressing matters to attend to than Gaul. If by chance he did return to Gaul for the campaign season, the leaders reasoned they could still stage a successful rebellion if he could be cut off from his army stationed in the north. The Gauls realized that this year would be their last chance to throw off the Roman yoke and live as a free people.

The tribe of the Carnutes south of Paris struck the first blow by murdering all the Roman merchants resident in the Gaulish town of Cenabum. Their willingness to challenge Caesar and Rome in this drastic fashion may have been due to religion, since their territory was considered the sacred center of Gaul, the holy gathering place each year for all druids. If the druids felt threatened by a Roman takeover, as is likely, it was clearly in their interest to stoke the fires of war. With their contacts throughout Gaul, they could also be a vital element in any widespread rebellion. In any case, with the slaughter of the Roman citizens of Cenabum, the Carnutes had taken an irreversible step towards freedom or destruction.

The Arverni, on the other hand, were generally pro-Roman. This large and powerful tribe occupied the rich lands just north of the mountainous Massif Central above the Province. They had clashed with the Romans in the late second century B.C., but had shown little interest thus far in Caesar's Gallic war and had consequently been left untouched by the Romans. The Arverni had dutifully contributed their share of cavalry to Caesar's auxiliaries and faithfully attended his annual councils, turning a deaf ear to any calls for rebellion. Being near the Mediterranean, they had long been accustomed to Greek and Roman visitors and were closely connected to the classical world. Their nobles enjoyed a level of prosperity and culture unknown among the more distant tribes of the north. The Arverni were also led by cautious and conservative men who were dedicated to maintaining the status quo with Rome.

But among the Arverni was a tall young warrior named Vercingetorix, who did not fit the mold of his peaceful tribe. Coins show him as a striking figure with long flowing hair and a bushy mustache typical of the Gaulish aristocracy. His father had once held the tribal leadership, but had been deposed and executed when he aimed for greater power than the elders thought prudent. Vercingetorix himself had probably served under Caesar and was considered a friend by the Roman general, but when the siren call of rebellion reached his ears that winter he responded with a passion, calling together the more hot-blooded warriors of his tribe and firing their imagination with dreams of casting the Romans out of Gaul. His uncle Gobannitio and the council of Arverni elders promptly exiled him.

Undeterred, Vercingetorix borrowed a page from Roman history and, like Romulus and Remus, gathered together the outcasts of society to forge them into an army. He used these troops to depose the old leadership of the Arverni and take over the entire tribe. He then sent forth a call throughout the land to join him in a crusade against Caesar and the Roman occupation. Warriors from every part of Gaul flocked to his standard and hailed him as their king. For the first time in history, the Gauls put aside their bitter rivalries and united behind a single leader.

In spite of the initial enthusiasm of his followers, Vercingetorix realized that they would soon collapse into a ungovernable mob unless he applied some Roman discipline to his new army. It is testimony to the leadership of Vercingetorix that he was able to forge thousands of unruly and fiercely independent Celtic warriors into a coordinated military force. Discipline came first, so that any soldier who committed a minor infraction of the rules was sent home in shame with his ears cut off or eyes gouged out. Major crimes were punished by burning the offender at the stake. Vercingetorix had also learned from Caesar that the acquisition and distribution of supplies were essential for military success. He told each tribe exactly what they were going to contribute, whether horses, grain, or weapons, and demanded they meet their obligations.

Caesar soon heard of these developments through his intelligence network and decided to cut short his stay in northern Italy. He calculated that his troubles with Pompey and the Senate were less of a danger to his career than a massive rebellion in Gaul. With just a handful of troops, Caesar crossed to the Province while it was still winter, but there faced a difficult decision. If he summoned his legions out of their camps to join him, they would have to fight their way through Gaulish territory without his leadership. But on the other hand, he did not have enough troops with him to safely reach his army in the north.

To make matters even worse, Vercingetorix devised a brilliant plan worthy of Caesar himself to keep him occupied in the Province. While Vercingetorix led part of his army north, he sent his chief lieutenant Lucterius south. There Lucterius persuaded the smaller Gaulish tribes along the Roman border to join the rebellion, then led them in a daring invasion of the Province. Vercingetorix had no intention of liberating the long-tamed Gauls of the coast from Roman rule; he simply wanted to cause widespread panic along the Mediterranean and force Caesar to deal with an unexpected threat. The plan worked beautifully. Although Lucterius never reached the coast, the mere presence of thousands of wild Gaulish warriors in lands that had known peace for decades threw the natives into a frenzy. Instead of finding a way north to his legions, Caesar was forced to organize a local militia to drive the invading Gauls away from the border. Caesar was compelled to waste time shoring up defenses in the Province when he was urgently needed in the north. But, cut off by the armies of Vercingetorix and the winter snows of the Massif Central, how could he hope to reach his legions in time?

The solution was typical of Caesar. Everyone knew that the mountains of the Massif Central were covered in six feet of snow and impassible, therefore Caesar led his small force of infantry and cavalry directly across them:

> *The Romans opened up a path through the mountains with the greatest of difficulty and reached the border of the Arverni. The Gauls were caught totally unprepared as they believed these peaks guarded them like a wall. Not a single traveler had ever crossed them in winter.*

Caesar ordered the small cavalry force that had accompanied him to strike north at the soft underbelly of Arvernian territory, spreading panic. He then dashed down the mountains, through the territory of the loyal Aedui, and on to the lands of the Lingones, where two of his veteran legions were quartered. His troops were amazed that he had crossed the mountains in winter and arrived at their camp so quickly. Caesar immediately sent orders for most of the remaining legions to gather together. This was risky since Caesar knew even the Aedui might revolt if he quartered fifty thousand men on their lands, so he devised a strategy of sacking rebellious towns for supplies. This would not only feed his troops, but would, he hoped, demoralize the Gauls and undermine the authority of Vercingetorix.

Aeneas and his son Julus arriving in Italy. (© The Trustees of the British Museum)

Sulla, dictator of Rome. (© Glyptothek,
Munich, Germany [The Bridgeman Art Library])

ABOVE: The ruins of the Roman Forum today. (© Janey Lee)

The Temple of Vesta in the Roman Forum, sanctuary of the Vestal Virgins, who served under Caesar when he was *pontifex maximus*. (© Janey Lee)

Bronze figurine of a lector, the guards for Caesar and all senior Roman magistrates. (© The Trustees of the British Museum)

Bronze statuette of a typical legion infantryman of Caesar's time. (© The Trustees of the British Museum)

Julius Caesar. (© Museo e Gallerie Nazionali di Capodimonte,
Naples, Italy [The Bridgeman Art Library])

Pompey, Caesar's political partner and son-in-law, who later became his greatest military foe.
(© Ny Carlsberg Glyptothek, Copenhagen, Denmark [The Bridgeman Art Library])

Crassus, one of Rome's wealthiest men and the third member of the triumvirate with Pompey and Caesar. (© The Louvre, Paris, France [The Bridgeman Art Library])

Cicero, Rome's most gifted orator and a frequent critic of Caesar.
(© Museo Capitolino, Rome, Italy [The Bridgeman Art Library])

Coin of the Remi tribe from Belgic Gaul. (© The Trustees of the British Museum)

Roman silver denarius showing a Gaulish warrior (*left*) and Celtic chariot (*right*).
(© The Trustees of the British Museum)

Head of a woman resembling Cleopatra, Egyptian queen and mistress of Caesar. (© The Trustees of the British Museum)

Ring etched with a portrait of Mark Antony, Caesar's ruthless but loyal lieutenant. (© The Trustees of the British Museum)

The Death of Cato of Utica by Charles Le Brun (1619–90). (© Musée des Beaux Arts, Arras, France [The Bridgeman Art Library])

Octavius, Caesar's great-nephew and heir, who ruled
the Roman Empire as Augustus.
(© The Trustees of the British Museum)

The Death of Julius Caesar by Vincenzo Camuccini (1773–1844). (© Museo e Gallerie Nazionali
di Capodimonte, Naples, Italy [The Bridgeman Art Library])

Caesar soon reached Vellaunodunum in the territory of the Senones and surrounded the town. After learning what would happen if they resisted, the inhabitants surrendered and furnished Caesar's army with food and pack animals, as well as six hundred hostages. Two days later Caesar was at Cenabum on the Loire River, where the Roman merchants had been murdered. The townspeople didn't even bother to ask for terms as they knew what their fate would be. Instead, about midnight, the men of Cenabum slipped out one of the gates and began crossing the river to escape in the darkness. Caesar, however, had been expecting just such a move and had his men waiting by the bridge. They rushed the open gates, stormed the town, and slaughtered the whole population. The next morning Caesar distributed everything of value in the town to his troops as booty, then burned Cenabum to the ground.

Caesar moved to sack the nearby town of Noviodunum, but the residents, fearing the fate of Cenabum, surrendered immediately. They were in the process of turning over supplies to the Romans when someone on the walls saw the cavalry scouts of Vercingetorix approaching. The townspeople suddenly had a change of heart and slammed the gate shut in Caesar's face. The Romans easily drove away the Gaulish scouts using their auxiliary band of German cavalry, fearless men with a well-earned reputation for brutality. Caesar then returned to the town, where the inhabitants fell before him and begged his forgiveness. His response is not recorded, but given his record on granting second chances he was unlikely to have been merciful.

Caesar had now captured three Gaulish towns while Vercingetorix watched impotently. Any other leader in Gaulish history would have been deposed or worse after such setbacks, but not Vercingetorix. He was held in such respect by the tribes that he not only survived the disasters of that spring but now drew on his authority to propose a far-sighted but radical change in strategy. He ordered all the towns, farms, hamlets, and barns anywhere near Caesar to be burned along with any stores of grain the Gauls could not carry away. By doing so, Caesar's army would starve, while Roman foraging parties would have to scatter far and wide to seek supplies, making them easy targets for the Gaulish cavalry to pick off. As Vercingetorix grimly explained to the exasperated nobles:

> *If this plan seems drastic or cruel to you, consider that it will be worse if instead your wives and children are dragged away into slavery while you are slaughtered—for that is the fate of the conquered.*

The council agreed and that day set fire to more than twenty towns of the Bituriges. The leaders of this tribe begged only that their capital, Avaricum, be spared. It was, they pleaded, the grandest city in Gaul and absolutely safe from siege because of its location, surrounded as it was by rivers and swamps save for one small and easily defended approach. Vercingetorix argued that sparing Avaricum was a foolish indulgence, but in the end yielded to the pressure of the Bituriges.

Caesar soon arrived at Avaricum and examined the city closely, realizing immediately that it was unlike town any he had stormed in the past. It could not be approached from any direction save one narrow slice of land protected by immense fortifications. Nevertheless, Caesar immediately ordered his troops to begin constructing a huge ramp of wood and earth three hundred feet wide and eighty feet tall, as well as towers for the assault. For almost a month Caesar's starving men labored through late winter rain and bitter cold while many of those assigned to search the countryside for food were picked off by Vercingetorix and his cavalry. On the walls, the warm and well-supplied Gauls showered the miserable Romans with artillery, fire, and endless abuse. Being a master of military psychology, Caesar encouraged his men by offering them the opportunity to lift the siege and withdraw from the town if the task was too grueling. Their pride forbade the Roman soldiers even to consider such a suggestion and they begged Caesar not to give up, no matter the cost.

After twenty-five days, the ramp was at last complete and almost touched the top of the town walls. The same night there was a pounding rain that drove all but the most steadfast Gaulish sentries on the walls to seek cover. Caesar saw his opportunity and ordered his men milling about the ramp to act as if they longed for nothing except a dry bed. Slowly, quietly, and under cover, the legions armed and prepared to assault the town. At Caesar's signal thousands of men dashed up the muddy ramp and bridged the final gap to the town walls. The Romans quickly seized the entire circuit of walls and gazed down at the terrified townspeople, no mercy in their eyes. The Romans were so angry at having labored in wretchedness for almost a month to take Avaricum that they killed every man, woman, and child they could find. Only a few hundred of the forty thousand inhabitants of the town escaped to reach Vercingetorix.

Caesar captured enough grain and supplies at Avaricum to supply his army for the next few weeks. Surprisingly, the fall of the town only enhanced the standing of Vercingetorix. The Gauls now saw that he had wisely advised them to abandon the town. With renewed energy and dedication, the tribes of Gaul recommitted themselves to Vercingetorix and the war against Caesar.

The terrible fury of Caesar against Avaricum was barely spent when he was distracted by petty politics among his Aeduan allies. After a bitter contest, two nobles of the tribe both claimed the title of chief magistrate for the year. Convictolitavus was an up-and-coming young warrior favored by the druids, while Cotus hailed from a powerful family with long experience in government. Normally, Caesar would not have broken off a war to deal with such squabbles, but concord among the Aedui was essential to his campaign. Their ancient ties with Rome and their steady support of his army demanded his atten-

tion to settle the dispute. On the other hand, he knew the situation had
to be handled delicately. Whichever party he rejected might seek support from Vercingetorix, splitting the tribe. After hearing the arguments of both sides, he chose to back Convictolitavus, largely, it seems,
because he had the backing of the religious authorities. Caesar did not
want to alienate Cotus and his supporters, but it was even more important that he not make enemies among the druids of the Aedui.

With this matter settled, Caesar asked the Aedui for more cavalry
support and ten thousand additional auxiliary troops for his war
against Vercingetorix. He then sent four of his legions north with Labienus to the rebellious region around Paris, taking the other six to
the citadel of Gergovia, the home town of Vercingetorix, deep inside
the lands of the Arverni. Unfortunately for Caesar, he was still five
days' march from Gergovia with the raging Allier River, fed by melting snows from the mountains to the south, blocking his way. Moreover, Vercingetorix had gotten wind of Caesar's plans almost before
he made them and had beaten him to the few bridges spanning the
swollen stream. These he quickly destroyed, trapping Caesar and his
army on the east side of the river. One look at the torrents of the Allier
convinced Caesar that it would be suicide to ford the stream. The
camp of Vercingetorix lay within sight of the Romans on the far bank
of the river, with the Gauls watching closely to make sure Caesar's
engineers did not attempt to rebuild any bridges. In apparent frustration, Caesar withdrew his camp into the dense forest away from
the river. The next morning Vercingetorix followed the Romans on
the opposite bank as they left the woods and headed south along the
stream toward Gergovia. But that night, with the Gauls far away,
Caesar and two legions that had remained secretly hidden in their
forest camp crept toward the river. Before Vercingetorix received any
word from his scouts, Caesar had already built and secured a new
bridge on the piles of one of the old structures the Gauls had torn
down. His main force then returned north and crossed the Allier.
Vercingetorix knew he had been outmaneuvered yet again, but rather

than being forced into battle on unfavorable ground, he quickly marched his army to the fortifications of Gergovia.

Caesar arrived near Gergovia soon after Vercingetorix. Surveying the city from afar, the Roman leader despaired at taking it by storm or siege. The citadel rose over the plain on a steep-sided plateau almost a mile wide with no easy approach for engines of war such as he had used at Avaricum. The Gaulish fortress also had ample food in its stores and easy access to water. Given unlimited time and manpower, Caesar knew he could eventually seize the city, but it would require months of arduous labor. With most of Gaul in rebellion and his Aeduan allies divided and wavering still, he could not afford a protracted siege. Thus he put his faith in good fortune and the quality of his men.

He began the next night by securing a small hill that lay closer to the citadel than his main camp. He posted two legions there, then built a long wall between the two camps to give safe passage to his troops. Just as things were starting to look up for Caesar, he received word that a large number of nearby Aeduan warriors were now in open rebellion, having tortured and slaughtered the Romans in their company. Caesar immediately left his camps at Gergovia under heavy guard and marched over twenty miles at lightning speed to the Aeduan rebels. He quickly surrounded the Gauls—who rightly feared revenge at the hands of the angry legions—but Caesar forbade his men to take any action. Instead Caesar spoke to the Aedui and convinced them they had been deceived by their leaders into turning against Rome. Caesar knew not all the Aeduan soldiers were innocent, but he was willing to overlook their misbehavior as he desperately needed them on his side. In what had become a regular performance among the Gauls, the tearful Aedui threw down their arms and begged Caesar's forgiveness. They swore eternal loyalty to Rome and joined his army on the fast march back to Gergovia.

Soon after his return, Caesar made an inspection tour of his smaller camp below the citadel and noticed that the heights between his camp and the city itself were less well defended than in days past. Seeing an opportunity to edge his forces closer to the town and perhaps cut off the Gauls from supplies and reinforcement, he decided to take the heights that night. First, he dressed the camp mules and their handlers to look like armed cavalry from a distance, then paraded them noisily around his lines to confuse the enemy. Then he quietly moved his real troops into position at the small camp and ordered them forward with a stern warning that they were to stop at the heights and by no means attempt to take Gergovia itself. But because of the difficulties of communication over broken ground and the eagerness of the troops for glory and spoils, the Roman soldiers pressed forward to the walls of the town. At first it seemed they might actually take Gergovia when a few of the legionaries managed to scale the walls, but soon the battle turned sorely against the Romans. Spears and rocks poured down on the troops and those few who had climbed to the top of the walls were hurled to their deaths below. By the time Caesar was able to recall his troops to a safe position he had lost almost 700 men, including forty-six veteran centurions.

Caesar assembled his army the next morning and raked them over the coals. Your reckless stupidity, he declared, has cost us a certain victory and endangered everything we are fighting for. As if the Gauls needed any more incentives to rebel, they can now point to the defeat of Caesar's fabled legions at Gergovia. Vercingetorix could not have been handed a more powerful recruiting tool. What I require from my soldiers, Caesar concluded, is discipline and restraint as much as bravery and courage.

But being the shrewd leader of men he was, once he had chastised his troops Caesar then strove to encourage them and restore their confidence by arranging a few easy victories in skirmishes with the enemy cavalry over the next few days. Nevertheless, Caesar knew that his hopes of taking Gergovia had been dashed on the heights beneath its walls. There was nothing he could do but order a humiliating retreat back to the lands of the Aedui.

Caesar could not imagine how things could get much worse—but soon they did. The crucial Aedui now abandoned Caesar altogether and joined forces with Vercingetorix. At the town of Noviodunum in their territory, they first murdered the Romans they could find inside the walls, then stole the Roman horses and supplies, and finally liberated all the Gaulish hostages Caesar had kept there for safekeeping. What food they couldn't carry off, they burned along with the town, threatening Caesar's army with starvation. The Gauls rightly believed that unless fortune favored Caesar very soon, he would be forced to abandon Gaul and withdraw south to the Province. But instead of heading toward the Mediterranean, Caesar marched his army north to the Loire, which the Gauls had deemed impassable. There at last he found a ford across the raging river. By stationing his cavalry just upstream to break the current, his infantry was able to cross in water up to their necks, holding their weapons high above their heads.

The Gaulish rebels meanwhile had gathered at Bibracte in the lands of their new allies, the Aedui. There they unanimously confirmed Vercingetorix as commander in chief even though some of the Aedui believed they could better lead the alliance. Vercingetorix ordered a continuance of his slash-and-burn policy to deny the Romans any supplies, then sent forces south to attack the borders of the Province and put even more pressure on Caesar to withdraw. The Romans were soon in such trouble that Caesar appealed to the Germans for cavalry support and gave them horses requisitioned from his own officers. Caesar knew that unless he could perform a miracle in the next few days, his Gaulish war was over. He would be forced to pull back to the Province and pray that Vercingetorix didn't decide to press on to the coast or even into Italy. The Senate, led by Cato and the optimates, would gleefully strip him of his command. The remainder of his miserable life would be spent defending himself against punitive lawsuits or in wretched exile in some distant land.

Vercingetorix was well aware of Caesar's predicament and now prepared to crush his enemy once and for all. Somewhere near modern Dijon, a far superior number of Gauls suddenly descended from the hills against the legions on the march. There was little time for Caesar to draw up his lines since he was attacked on all sides at once. The Gauls were so confident of victory that their cavalry had vowed to ride through the Roman lines twice or never go home again. Caesar rushed everywhere encouraging his men to stand against the onslaught. After a grueling fight, the Romans at last began to press the Gauls back just as the German cavalry drove Vercingetorix from a nearby hill. The Gauls, afraid that they would be encircled and trapped, abandoned their attack and ran, only to be cut down by the pursuing Romans. Caesar had won an unexpected victory just when he needed it most.

It was now that Vercingetorix made his fatal mistake. Stunned by this relatively minor defeat, he ordered his men to take refuge behind the towering walls of nearby Alesia. As the last of the Gauls entered the gates of this impregnable town, Caesar arrived on the scene and knew that he would win the war. Vercingetorix had led his army into a citadel surrounded by rivers and steep cliffs. There was no way for Caesar to storm the fortress, but there was also no way for the Gauls to escape if Caesar could find a way to entrap them. He immediately ordered his engineers to begin construction of an enormous wall over ten miles long that would completely encircle Alesia. The astonished Gauls looked on in dismay as they realized Caesar's intentions. At alarming speed, a twelve-foot-high palisade backed by deep trenches on both sides and manned by guard towers every eighty feet sprang up around the town. The Roman soldiers also rammed thousands of sharpened stakes, nicknamed "tombstones," into the ground along the wall to discourage attacks. As if this remarkable feat of construction under adverse conditions wasn't enough, Caesar built a second wall over a dozen miles in circumference facing outward to ward off any hostile forces sent to relieve Alesia. Caesar had soon completely cut off Vercingetorix and his army, but he had also sealed his own forces inside a gigantic double-ringed camp.

Just before the trap closed, Vercingetorix sent messengers out to recruit a relief force. He knew he had little chance of breaking out of Alesia on his own and, with only thirty days of food in the citadel, he needed help quickly. The call was answered by a vast army of Gauls from almost every tribe, but cut off from the outside world, Vercingetorix had no way of knowing help was on the way. He therefore called an assembly inside Alesia and asked the tribal leaders gathered there for advice. Some urged surrender and an appeal to Caesar's clemency, others, immediate attack before they were too weak to fight the Romans. One chieftain, Critognatus, even advocated cannibalism to sustain their men. This latter suggestion was unthinkable to Vercingetorix, but he did take the drastic step of expelling all the unfortunate townspeople of Alesia, including the women and children, to seek mercy among the Romans. When this crowd of civilians reached the inner wall of the Roman camp and begged to be sold into slavery if only they would be fed, Caesar sent them back to Alesia to starve.

At this desperate hour, the Gaulish relief army arrived at last and began assaulting the outer walls of the Roman camp. Vercingetorix and his men soon joined in, pouring down from Alesia to attack the inner walls. From noon to sunset, a two-sided battle raged as the Gauls tried to scale the Roman walls from both directions, but Caesar and his men held their positions. With the help of his German cavalry, Caesar at last managed to push the relief force back to their own camp a mile away, but it was a hard-fought battle. At one point, Caesar even lost his sword while fighting on the front lines. (After the war, when he saw it displayed as a trophy in an Arverni temple, he smiled and refused the request of his officers to remove it.)

The Gauls from Alesia had retreated in despair but were not

beaten yet. After giving his men a day to rest and prepare, Vercingetorix again attacked the inner walls with scaling ladders and grappling hooks, but was beaten back at last by a young Roman officer
named Mark Antony. After this second defeat, Vercingetorix knew
his men had only enough strength and courage left for one last assault. He learned from those familiar with the area that there was
one weak spot in the Roman fortifications on the north side of the
town, where a steep ridge had prevented a solid enclosing wall. He
sent a large force of his men by night to this spot and the next morning led the rest of his army in a diversionary attack against the main
walls to the south. The Gaulish relief force joined in against the outer
walls until thousands upon thousands of warriors on both sides of the
Roman camp were joined in a final, frenzied struggle to destroy Caesar's army. For a few hours, it seemed that the Gauls might win.
Then Caesar dashed to the front lines, clad in his crimson commander's cloak, to inspire his men. A shout went up from the Roman
troops as they rushed the Gauls with their swords drawn until at last
the relief army was destroyed.

The next morning, Vercingetorix called together the survivors of
Alesia and declared he would now offer himself to the Romans, alive
or dead, as they wished. He ordered all the weapons from the citadel
to be brought to Caesar's camp and surrendered. At last Vercingetorix himself rode proudly through the gates of the town and came
before Caesar, falling silently to his knees. Some of the Roman officers at hand were touched by his humility, but if he had hoped for
mercy from the man who had once named him a friend, it was in
vain. Caesar ordered all the defenders of Alesia to be taken into slavery, aside from the Aeduan and Arvernian tribesmen, whom he
spared for political reasons. Vercingetorix was taken to Rome, where
he would be held prisoner for six long years until he could be displayed as an ornament at Caesar's triumphal parade and then executed.

⊠

Much to the disappointment of his enemies in the city, the Roman Senate declared a public thanksgiving of twenty days to celebrate Caesar's victory at Alesia. However, the destruction of Vercingetorix and his army did not bring an immediate end to the Gallic war, though only the most ardent Gaulish patriots still pressed for independence. Caesar's mercy in sparing from slavery the Aedui and Arverni captured at Alesia went a long way to pacifying these two powerful and influential Gaulish tribes. Only in the north and in the far south was there any serious continued resistance to Roman rule. The Bellovaci near the English Channel fought bravely against the legions during 51 B.C., but were at last crushed by Caesar. His clemency to them soon won over the remainder of the Belgae, and even the recalcitrant Commius eventually surrendered to Mark Antony on the promise that his life would be spared.

Still, the southern fortress of Uxellodunum held out against Caesar. The stubborn natives hoped they could stave off the Romans until Caesar's governorship was over. Caesar, however, brought an end to their dreams when he diverted their water supply by undermining the citadel's only spring. The hapless citizens then surrendered to the Romans and begged Caesar's forgiveness. But in this instance he was determined to make a profound statement to end the Gaulish rebellion once and for all. He therefore spared the lives of all those who fought against him at Uxellodunum, but ordered that both their hands be cut off. The war in Gaul was now over, but for the rest of their days the mutilated men of Uxellodunum would serve as a living warning that Caesar's mercy had its limits.

IX

RUBICON

When I look at Caesar with his carefully combed hair and watch him casually scratching his head with a single finger, I can't imagine this man would ever do something as monstrous as destroying the Republic.

— CICERO

After eight long years, the war in Gaul was finally over. But as the ancient historian Tacitus was later to say, it was as if the Romans had created a desert and called it peace. Hundreds of towns had been destroyed, fields and forests were laid waste throughout the land, and hundreds of thousands of men, women, and children had been torn from their homes and sold into slavery throughout Rome's vast empire. The number of Gaulish dead is hard to estimate, though Caesar's own figure of over one million souls may not be far off the mark.

Caesar's defense of his devastating actions was simple—instability in Gaul was a threat to Rome. The only way to guarantee security for the civilized people of the Mediterranean was to bring Gaul under complete Roman control and fortify the Rhine as a barrier against the Germanic tribes to the east. This argument, it must be noted, was supported by almost every Roman. People throughout the towns and farms of Italy were thrilled to live free from the danger of invasion by northern barbarians and shed no tears for Gauls or Germans. Even the optimates of the Senate, who deeply resented Caesar's conquests in Gaul, did so only because of the power and riches they brought him personally. None of them ever suggested giving the land back to the Celts.

Justified or not, the Gallic war had enormous benefits both for the Roman state and for Caesar himself. Rome now controlled all the lands from the Rhine to the Atlantic—a rich new province over 3,000 miles in circumference. Even depleted and devastated, Gaul paid 10 million denarii in taxes each year into the treasury, a denarius being the average daily wage for a Roman worker. In time the province could pay much more.

Caesar's personal wealth from the conquest of Gaul was so immense that he endowed magnificent temples from Spain to Asia, sent slaves and soldiers by the thousands to provincial kings throughout the Mediterranean, and loaned vast amounts of money to needy senators. He gathered so much Gaulish gold in tribute and booty that he sold it in Italy for half the usual price. But even more than treasure, Caesar's most valuable asset from his campaign in Gaul was the army that now followed him. Caesar had never been able to win the hearts of the nobility. His power base was firmly set among the common people he had served as a magistrate and the soldiers he had recruited and fought along side in battles across Gaul. It was Caesar's army—made up of no-nonsense, dependable, and absolutely loyal men he raised from the farms and small towns of Italy and the Province—that would determine his future.

The experience of leading an army in a distant war for eight years also shaped Caesar into someone very different from the senators of Rome. Almost all the leading men in Rome had served in the army at some point and many had led soldiers into battle, but none, with the possible exception of Pompey, had achieved the autonomy that Caesar gained in Gaul. Beyond the Alps he was a virtual king, unham-

pered by factions, politics, and courts. Caesar faced no tiresome
checks and balances as a general in Gaul—his word was law. But
now that the Gallic war was over Caesar was expected to reenter the
contentious world of the Senate and play by the arcane rules of the
Republic. With good cause many in Rome worried that civil war was
fast approaching.

The chief predicament Caesar faced was that as soon as he lay down
his military command and governorship he would lose immunity
from prosecution guaranteed by his *imperium* and face endless lawsuits that would undoubtedly destroy his political career. Cato had,
in fact, long been threatening, under oath, that Caesar would face
prosecution in a court full of armed guards the moment he disbanded his army. Caesar thought he had solved the problem by a
popular decree two years earlier, allowing him to retain control of his
provinces until he was—he hoped—elected consul for 48 B.C. Such a
seamless transition would maintain his immunity until he could gain
the consulship and face down his optimate opponents from a position
of power in Rome. But new legislation was threatening to strip him
of his governorship and troops at an earlier date, while barring him
from seeking the consulship in an absentee campaign. If this plan
was carried out according to the optimates' design, he would be
buried under lawsuits the moment he crossed under the city walls to
run for consul, making him ineligible to campaign for office. Cato
and his supporters had devised the perfect trap for Caesar—if only
they could make it work.

Unfortunately for the optimates, they had plenty of ill will toward Caesar but no military muscle to back it up. It was useless for
them to fume and fuss against a man with an army at his back unless
they had an even bigger force. This meant they had to deal with
Pompey. With an ongoing governorship in Spain and plenty of
troops available in Italy as well, Pompey's army was the only force

available that could stand up to Caesar. Although the optimates hated Pompey only slightly less than they hated Caesar, they were convinced the older general could be manipulated into opposing his younger rival to serve their own purposes. Once Caesar had been stripped of his troops and was facing criminal prosecution, they believed Pompey could be disposed of as well and the Republic returned to their capable hands.

Caesar spent the remainder of 51 B.C. in Gaul rewarding his faithful supporters and organizing the country as a proper Roman province. Those Gauls who had served him well were granted large estates of confiscated land and rich shares of the spoils of war. Some were even marked for eventual membership in the Roman Senate. Trustworthy Gaulish nobles from every town and tribe were given limited local authority and privileges to bind them to Rome. Soon, of their own free will, the nobles of Gaul were adopting Roman customs and employing Latin tutors for their children. The Romans could not countenance human sacrifice by the druids, but as in other provinces the locals were otherwise left alone to follow their ancestral religion as long as they paid their taxes and caused no trouble. Gaulish troops spread throughout the Mediterranean as a mainstay of the legions, just as Romans moved north into Gaul as merchants, landowners, and government administrators. Gauls who had thought of themselves only as Aedui, Helvetii, or Veneti kept their tribal affiliation for centuries to come, but in time came to see themselves first and foremost as Romans.

With Gaul settled, Caesar could now give Roman politics his full attention. Cato had tried and failed to gain the consulship for the next year, but the equally belligerent and capable optimate Marcus Marcellus was selected. He dedicated himself enthusiastically to Caesar's downfall. Marcellus's opposition should not have been surprising: Caesar had earlier tried to steal Marcellus's wife—Caesar's own grandniece Octavia—and present her as a bribe to Pompey after Julia's death. Caesar, however, struck first with a surprisingly modern propaganda tool aimed at the Roman public. He had previously forwarded to the Senate annual reports of his Gaulish campaigns, as was customary, but now he quickly edited these dispatches into a an exciting memoir. The publication of his *Gallic War* made a huge splash on the Roman literary and political scene as no one had ever read such a compelling story written in clear and simple language. Thrilling battles against brave but inferior barbarians, exotic lands and gods, the triumph of the Roman spirit—it was a book guaranteed to excite the minds of Roman voters. The tone was seemingly objective, yet it was clear that the hero of the tale was Caesar, who had courageously saved Rome from the savage Gauls and Germans. The Roman populace loved it, while even Cicero praised the work as a masterpiece of lucid history.

Although the optimates could not produce exciting accounts of their glorious deeds to influence the Roman electorate, they had powerful weapons of their own. Marcellus cleverly countered that since Caesar had won such a magnificent and complete victory against the Gauls, it was no longer necessary for him to maintain his army. Caesar's forces should be disbanded, he declared, and a new governor appointed so that Caesar could return home and campaign for consul as a private citizen. Marcellus also attacked Caesar's power base in Italian Gaul by declaring that the residents of Caesar's colony at Comum (modern Como) north of the Po were ineligible for Roman citizenship. He personally beat with rods a new senator from Comum who was present in Rome, telling the man that he should return home and show the marks to Caesar.

As the optimates well understood, granting citizenship to the inhabitants of Italy north of the Po was central to Caesar's vision for the future of Rome. To Caesar it was a question of expanding the benefits of full membership in the Roman state to new territories that had proven their loyalty and worth. To be sure, it didn't hurt that these new citizens were his clients and supporters, but to see his actions merely as short-term political gain belies his proven commitment to ending the cycle of senatorial exploitation of provincials.

Caesar managed to block the legislation of Marcellus by using well-paid tribunes to veto his proposals, but it was now clear to him that the optimates were declaring war not just on his actions but on his very dignity. For a man who had risen from the slums of the Subura to the heights of Roman power, it was more than his pride could stand. Caesar rightly or wrongly believed that his conquest of Gaul had earned him the rank of first man in Rome and so was not about to meekly submit to the Senate as Pompey had done when returning from his eastern campaign. More than once in these troubled months Caesar was heard to say:

Now that I am the greatest man in Rome, it will be more difficult to push me down to second place than it would be to push a second-rank man to the bottom.

Still, Caesar would not be provoked into open rebellion against the Senate.

The optimates continued to pressure Pompey to declare his opposition to Caesar, but the veteran general would not make a firm commitment to their cause. Yet he made clear that he would soon request the return of the legion he had loaned Caesar two years earlier and voiced his opinion that the Senate must be obeyed in all matters. The optimates, meanwhile, worked to portion out the provinces in the coming year so that Caesar would be deprived of his governorship and army before he could seek election as consul. When Pompey was asked what he would do if Caesar tried to keep his legions, he snapped back: "What do you think I would do if my son tried to beat me with a stick?" It was a reply that brought joy to the hearts of the optimates who believed Pompey was moving still closer to their side.

The Senate, however, was not simply divided into optimates and supporters of Caesar. Many, if not most, senators sought a middle ground that would avoid civil war. These moderates admired Caesar's military accomplishments but remembered how he had overturned cherished traditions during his consularship. Now they feared that with more power than ever, he might shatter the very foundations of the Republic. On the other hand, they saw the optimates as reactionaries whose unreasonable devotion to the status quo was pushing Caesar and the populist movement into open rebellion. Might it be possible, the moderates wondered, to buy off either Pompey or Caesar with the promise of a new campaign against the Parthian Empire? Feelers went out to both sides, with Pompey taking a particular interest, but in the end the proposal only fanned the flames of dissension as neither camp was willing to allow the other such glory.

It was becoming clear to Caesar that his contest with the optimates might have to be settled with arms rather than diplomacy. It was a clash he earnestly wished to avoid, not just because he wanted peace, but because he would have few supporters among the Senate and would be greatly outnumbered by Pompey's forces on the battlefield. However, if the rulers of Rome were determined to crush him he would fight back. In preparation for any military conflict he transferred thousands of soldiers from Gaul to northern Italy under the dubious rationale of protecting the Province from raids by Illyrian brigands. He dismissed no troops, but instead doubled their pay, made sure they were well fed, and gave each soldier a Gaulish slave. More ominously, he continued to stockpile weapons and recruit additional soldiers in spite of the war's end.

Caesar continued his maneuvering on the political front by attempting to place his supporters among the Roman magistrates to serve the following year, in 50 B.C. He was successful in winning the tepid backing of the optimate consul-elect Lucius Aemilius Paullus with an enormous bribe of 9 million denarii. An old foe of Cataline, Paullus was desperately in need of funds to complete a showcase basilica in the Forum. But the other entering consul, Gaius Marcellus, a cousin of the previous year's consul, would not be moved.

But by far the most important magistrate Caesar was able to buy that year was Gaius Scribonius Curio, one of the new plebeian tribunes. Curio moved in the same raucous and irreverent circle as Clodius, even marrying Clodius's widow, Fulvia, after her husband was murdered. Recently, however, Curio had settled down to become a firm opponent of Caesar and the populists, like his father before him. But the young man had run up enormous debts with his prodigal lifestyle and by financing elaborate funeral games for his father, which included a two-stage wooden theater that could be converted into an amphitheater. Caesar now offered to cover his debts completely if Curio would change sides. The new tribune was only too happy to agree, soon revealing by his tenacity and political acumen that Caesar had made a very wise investment.

The spring of 50 B.C. began with bad news from the east. Caesar's lifelong adversary, Bibulus, now serving as governor of Syria, was having difficulties holding back the Parthians from the Roman frontier. He asked the Senate for two additional legions, which they promptly granted, but the problem was where to find the troops on such short notice. Pompey magnanimously offered to send one of his own legions to Syria as long as Caesar did the same. This seemed perfectly fair, except that the legion Pompey designated to send was the one he had previously loaned to Caesar. This would mean a net loss of two legions for Caesar and none for Pompey. To the surprise of many, Caesar agreed to these terms even though the new deployments left him significantly weaker. This more than anything he had done so far impressed the moderates in the Senate that he was a reasonable man who wanted to avoid military conflict with Pompey.

But to hedge his bets among soldiers he might have to face on the battlefield in the future, Caesar gave each departing legionary a substantial gift of money. As it turned out, the situation in Syria soon calmed down so that no additional troops were needed—but instead of returning one or both of the legions to Caesar, Gaius Marcellus insisted they remain in Italy under Pompey's command. Caesar shrugged off the loss and quietly recruited new troops.

Throughout this period Caesar never neglected the personal side of politics in his effort to build support among the moderate senators. One example is his continued wooing of Cicero, who had been serving as governor in Cilicia in eastern Asia Minor. Cicero was not a military man by any stretch of the imagination, but during his time in the province he had managed several minor victories in skirmishes with Parthian cavalry scouts and troublesome mountain tribes. He was immensely proud of his achievements on the battlefield and asked the Senate if he might be granted a small triumph on his return to Rome. Many of the senators, including Cato, felt Cicero's action did not merit a public parade, but Caesar ordered his supporters to push the bill through. After the petition was approved, Caesar wrote to Cicero congratulating him and pointing out that he, not Cato, had supported Cicero from the beginning.

Caesar was going to need every ally he could find in the political battle that began that March and raged for two months. Gaius Marcellus and the optimates now advocated sending new governors to replace Caesar immediately so that he would lose both his immunity from prosecution and his army. Caesar had been ready for this strike and had instructed his paid tribune, Curio, on the proper response. Curio rose from his bench in the Senate chamber and surprised everyone present by agreeing with the proposal of Marcellus—but then added that he would support the legislation only if Pompey also gave up his provinces and troops on the same day. The tribune argued that as undesirable as it was to have two well-armed generals threatening the land with civil war, it was worse to have only one. If

Caesar surrendered his army, Pompey would be the only man in Italy with thousands of troops at his disposal. It would then be an exceedingly short step, he declared, for Pompey to turn from protector of the Republic to tyrant of Rome. The optimates objected, but the moderates among the senators saw good sense in Curio's suggestion and applauded him warmly. Mutual disarmament was a risky strategy for Caesar as he would completely lose the military might he had so carefully built over the years, but he was betting that he could beat the optimates on a level playing field.

Debate raged week after week, but every time Gaius Marcellus proposed his bill anew Curio interposed his veto. On the other hand, whenever Curio put forward his compromise, the optimates blocked voting on the measure. Marcellus and his party next suggested a compromise—let Caesar keep his provinces and armies until November of that year. But Caesar knew this was meaningless since he would still be open to prosecution for over a year until he could take office as consul. Curio therefore rejected the offer outright and debate continued. Finally in May, Marcellus realized he lacked enough support among the moderates to push through his proposal and so he backed down. By willingness to compromise and stubborn determination, Caesar and Curio had won their battle with the optimates, at least for the moment.

Caesar turned fifty years old that July, but his vigor and drive were undiminished. He sponsored Mark Antony for the priestly office of augur, then maneuvered the election of Antony as a tribune of the plebs to succeed Curio as his spokesman in Rome. Caesar also returned to northern Italy that same summer to stage a whirlwind tour of the province, drumming up support for any coming conflict with the Senate. He knew that if he was to have any chance against Pompey and the optimates, he needed the full support and abundant manpower of the lands along the Po. This was Caesar's first visit to

Italy since the conclusion of the war in Gaul and he could not have been more pleased at his reception. The province Caesar had worked so hard to make equal with the rest of Italy spared no expense in welcoming the conquering hero. City gates and country roads were decorated with flowers as he rode by, children ran to greet him in every town square, and tables in the local marketplaces were overflowing with the best food for public banquets in his honor. Then after a warm handshake and kind word for all, Caesar quickly returned to his army in Gaul to make final preparations for the war he feared was coming.

Rumors flew throughout the autumn that Caesar and Pompey would soon drag all of Italy into a bloody struggle. Cicero, writing to his friend Atticus from Athens in October, reports that even there stories were spreading that Caesar was on the march from Gaul with four battle-hardened legions. At the same time, Pompey's supporters spread stories that morale in Caesar's legions was wretched and his soldiers yearned to be free of their rebellious master. Of course, neither report was true. Caesar was still in Gaul with his army, most of whom were quite ready to follow him through the gates of Hades if he gave the word.

But Pompey had plenty of reasons to take heart. He had just recovered from a serious illness in Naples and was heading back to Rome at last. The reception he received along the way rivaled that of Caesar's recent welcome in northern Italy. Villagers feasted him every night and threw flowers along his way as they marched beside him. Pompey had always assumed that the common people supported him, but this popular outpouring during his journey convinced him that he was unbeatable. He now believed that recruiting soldiers to fight Caesar would be simple: "All I have to do is stamp my foot anywhere in Italy for infantry and cavalry to rise up from the ground."

The clouds of war gathered rapidly as the winter of 50 B.C. drew nearer. Caesar continued to prepare his army to fight even as he worked furiously to avoid a conflict. Pompey and the optimates, however, were in no mood for concessions, especially after they scored a major coup against Caesar. Labienus, who had been Caesar's most trusted and competent general throughout the long years of war in Gaul, now defected to the side of the optimates. Labienus believed Caesar didn't stand a chance against Pompey, but Caesar's cold response to the haughty pride of Labienus also played its part in his change of allegiance. Caesar had made Labienus a rich and famous man, so much so that Labienus soon came to believe that victory in Gaul was as much his doing as it was Caesar's. The common origins of Labienus and Pompey in the rugged Italian region of Picentum together with careful cultivation by the optimates were enough to cinch the deal by December. Whatever the motives of Labienus, Pompey had now gained a lieutenant of tremendous military skill who was intimately familiar with Caesar's strategy and tactics. For his part, Caesar accepted the loss graciously and forwarded to Labienus all the money and baggage he had left behind.

Cicero hurried back from Greece to Rome in a frantic effort to find a peaceful resolution to the conflict. He expressed the sentiments of most moderate politicians and almost all the Roman public when he wrote to Atticus in mid-December:

> *The current state of affairs terrifies me. Almost everyone I know prefers to give Caesar what he wants rather than plunge the state into civil war. Caesar is certainly impudent, but he's really not asking for much.*

Even though Cicero personally favored peace at any price, he believed his political future and the safety of the Republic would force him to support Pompey in the end. It was a position more of the moderates were taking as the crisis came to a head. They would still jump at any chance for a peaceful resolution between Caesar and Pompey, but if they were forced to take sides, they had to back law and order rather than revolution. For all they knew, Caesar would stage another populist bloodbath against the Senate as Cinna and Marius had done almost forty years earlier. If war came, most Romans with money or political power would reluctantly support the optimates against Caesar.

A chance at compromise came that December just before the new tribunes were to take office. With considerable skill, Curio finally succeeded in forcing the Senate to vote on his proposal that Caesar and Pompey dismiss their armies simultaneously. Gaius Marcellus and the optimates railed against this plan that would end their dreams of crushing Caesar once and for all, but in the end the senators overwhelmingly supported the measure with 370 votes in favor and only 22 against.

It seemed at the last moment that civil war had been averted by the overwhelming desire of the Senate for peace. But if the optimates couldn't win fairly, they were quite willing to play dirty. After warning the senators that Caesar was on his way over the Alps with ten legions in spite of their foolish goodwill, Gaius Marcellus marched across the Forum to Pompey with optimate supporters trailing behind. When he met the general he granted him authority to defend the state and defeat Caesar by any means necessary. He was given command of the two legions originally meant for the war on Parthia with the promise of even more troops. That all this was totally illegal and contrary to the express will of the Senate did not stop Pompey from accepting.

Caesar had in fact returned to northern Italy from Gaul with only one legion and heard of the latest events in Rome almost as soon as they happened. He hoped to avoid conflict, but he was preparing to fight if necessary. All the pieces were in place for war by late December, when Caesar moved to Ravenna near the Rubicon, together with several thousand of his troops. He also secretly ordered two legions to begin marching from Gaul to Italy and for another three legions to stand ready in southern Gaul. Caesar believed he no longer

had anything to lose since the Senate seemed dominated by the optimates and afraid to stand up to the newly empowered Pompey. In
early January of 49 B.C., Caesar laid out his ultimatum to the Senate
in a letter. He began by calmly explaining all that he had done for the
Republic since he began his career many years before. He then repeated his offer to lay down his command at the same time as Pompey exactly as the Senate had previously voted. But, he warned, if his
demands to keep his army until he could become consul were not
met, he would uphold his personal honor by any means necessary.

Even moderate senators were shocked at the impudence of Caesar and considered his letter a declaration of war. Few believed he
posed much of a military threat, but they were outraged at his disrespect for the Senate. After several days of heated debate, they declared Caesar an enemy of Rome. The spurious mandate Gaius
Marcellus had given to Pompey just days before was now legally confirmed. The consuls then ordered Caesar's supporters, including
Mark Antony, to be removed from the Senate, but Antony jumped
from his chair screaming that they were violating the ancient sanctity
of a tribune. He called on the gods as witnesses to this indignity, pre-
dicting war, murder, and a dozen other calamities as they dragged
him from the chamber. He then immediately left Rome with Curio
to join Caesar at Ravenna.

In spite of the furor, Cicero labored over the next few days to
calm tempers and negotiate some compromise before it was too late.
The orator shuttled back and forth between the optimates and Caesar's men seeking a formula that would satisfy all parties. Would
Caesar consider dismissing some of his troops and leaving his
provinces? Yes, they responded, as long as he could keep two legions
he would at least withdraw from Gaul. Pompey rejected this proposal, but hesitated when Caesar's representatives countered that
their leader would be willing to keep just one legion and pull back to
Illyricum. It seemed for a moment that an agreement could be
reached, but Cato cried out that Pompey was a blundering fool if he

accepted Caesar's trickery. The talks collapsed and with them the last chance for peace.

On January 10, the news from Rome reached Caesar at Ravenna. He had hoped Cicero might be successful in changing Pompey's mind, but had rightly feared that Cato and the optimates would never allow a compromise. Caesar realized that Pompey and the Senate would now gather their forces and march on him in northern Italy. It would take them time to organize their enormous army from across the Mediterranean world, but when they did it would be almost impossible to beat them. Caesar therefore chose to risk everything on what the optimates were least expecting—an invasion of Italy with his single legion. It was, as any Roman commander would have agreed, a hopelessly foolish move. But Caesar was gambling that the element of surprise, coupled with his legendary speed, would throw the Senate forces off balance and push Pompey to withdraw from Rome.

That same evening Caesar rode to the banks of the Rubicon River. He had deliberately spent the day going about his usual activities in Ravenna and dining with friends so that senatorial spies would have nothing unusual to report. He hesitated at the bank of the swollen stream, knowing there would be no turning back once he crossed the boundary of his province, but at last he plunged forward into civil war.

X

CIVIL WAR

In all of life, but especially in war, the greatest power
belongs to fortune.

— CAESAR

No one expected that Caesar would dare invade Italy with only
a few thousand men, but once he crossed the Rubicon into
Italy Caesar advanced south against all odds. His rapid advance
caught Pompey and the optimates totally off-guard and threw Rome
into a panic. It was precisely the effect Caesar had intended.

Caesar's first stop was the old Umbrian town of Ariminum (modern Rimini) just ten miles beyond the Rubicon. Sulla had sacked the
town several decades earlier, but Caesar quickly occupied this strategic gateway to the south without any bloodshed. It was here that
Mark Antony caught up with his sponsor after fleeing from Rome.
Caesar played up his arrival for all it was worth to further motivate
his army and justify his move against the Senate. Look at him, he
cried, as he led Antony before his troops. This man is a sacrosanct
tribune of the people, manhandled by the Senate and driven from
Rome in defiance of all that is holy and just. Even Sulla, who had little respect for the common man, never dared to interfere with the
rights of the tribunes. Will you allow this to stand? Will you let a

small cadre of self-serving nobles who care nothing for the true welfare of the state destroy centuries of tradition and rob you of your freedom? As for me, Caesar exclaimed as he wept bitter tears and tore his robe in grief, will you let Pompey and the optimates destroy my dignity? We've fought bravely together for nine years against Gauls and Germans alike—and we won! Are you afraid to face Pompey and his ragged band of cowards? Are you afraid to follow me to victory?

It was a beautiful performance. The soldiers declared that they were ready to follow Caesar anywhere to defend his honor and restore the rightful power of the tribunes. Part of their enthusiasm may have grown from a rumor that he would make all of them knights, but they doubtless would have risked everything for him in any case. He had lifted them from poverty and taught them to believe in their ability to accomplish the impossible. They had beaten Ariovistus and his ferocious Germans, they had sailed beyond the edge of the world to Britain and returned, they had conquered Vercingetorix and the whole army of Gaul. Caesar had also put more money in their pockets than they had ever dreamed of back when they were struggling on the farm. Now they would restore the stolen honor of their commander and win undying glory for themselves, not to mention a tidy bit of loot.

Meanwhile in Rome, there was chaos in the streets. Countless frightened refugees were flooding into the city from the countryside, adding to the panic among the already terrified inhabitants of Rome. Stories flew among the crowds of dire portents—blood had fallen as rain from the sky, lightning had struck the holy temples, statues of the gods were sweating, and a mule had given birth to a foal. Fights broke out between partisans of Caesar and Pompey, mobs raged violently through the streets, and no one seemed to be in charge. The optimates turned on Pompey and berated him for letting Caesar cross the Rubicon. Where are the armies you had only to stomp your foot to raise? What are you going to do now? they demanded.

Pompey had an answer for them, but they didn't like it. Their only chance was to evacuate Rome and regroup in southern Italy. From there, it would probably be necessary to withdraw further across the sea to Greece. Then, like Sulla years before, the senatorial forces could gather their armies and retake Italy. Pompey pointed out that holding Rome meant nothing in the long term. It was men that won wars, not empty buildings. His scattered forces were still ten times the size of Caesar's army and would crush the upstart general in the end as surely as Sulla had destroyed Cinna and Marius. Pompey then warned them darkly that he would consider anyone who remained in the city a traitor to Rome. With that, Pompey took the Appian Way south, followed by almost every magistrate and senator in Rome. The refugees and common people of the city would have to face alone whatever horrors awaited them from Caesar's troops.

It wasn't long until Caesar received two visitors sent by Pompey himself. As Caesar writes, they came with a private message from the general expressing his regret to his former father-in-law that matters had reached such a sorry state. Pompey exclaimed that his recent actions were nothing personal against Caesar, but were merely the result of his lifelong desire to serve his country—a desire that always took precedence over his own wishes. Caesar, likewise, should put the welfare of Rome before his own pride, no matter how unjustly he believed he had been treated. Pompey urged Caesar to be reasonable and not let his bruised dignity lead Rome into civil war.

Caesar felt insulted by Pompey's condescending tone, but sent the envoys back to him with an olive branch. Caesar declared that he, too, had always put the needs of the state above his own desires, but he was fighting for the rights of the Roman people as well as his own honor. He therefore proposed that the Italian peninsula be demilitarized. He and his army would leave Italy if Pompey would at the same time withdraw to Spain with his troops. Then the Senate and the popular assemblies could meet in peace to settle everything without the threat of armed force from either side. Finally, he urged that he and Pompey meet face-to-face to work out the details of the agreement without the tiresome interference of politicians.

Cicero, who was in Pompey's camp at the time, reports that the message from Caesar arrived on January 23, 49 B.C. Whatever Pompey might have wished to do if left to his own devices, he was overruled by the optimates. They sent a letter back to Caesar agreeing that Pompey would go to Spain at some future date, but only if Caesar first withdrew from Italy. Until that time, they would continue to recruit and train their army to defend the state. And, of course, the optimates were not about to let Pompey meet privately with Caesar.

It's fascinating to see how the different parties viewed the negotiations. Caesar portrayed himself as an injured party: "It was an unfair offer," he exclaimed. But Cicero wrote to his friend Atticus that "Caesar would be mad not to accept, especially as his demands were so impudent." The practical result was that the discussions went nowhere and communications between the two parties ceased.

▣

Caesar now sent Mark Antony to hold the mountain passes north of Rome while he himself continued his advance south along the Adriatic coast. By early February, he had peacefully taken all of Picenum—an especially galling development to Pompey as it was his home region. Throughout the wider area of north central Italy, towns were flocking to Caesar's banner, much to the consternation of the optimates. Caesar portrays this support as sincere patriotism and affection for his just cause, though most townspeople cared little who won the war as long as they were left alone. The towns knew they were facing Caesar's army on their doorsteps while most of Pompey's troops were far away, thus the sudden swell of support. At Iguvium in Umbria, Pompey's lieutenant Thermus withdrew his few troops from the town in the face of open hostility. Even more telling was Caesar's reception at the ancient hill town of Auximum. There the local town council met with Attius Varus, the governor of Roman Africa, who was occupying their town with a garrison of Pompey's soldiers. The councilmen explained that they had no interest in imperial politics, but they felt it most unwise to resist the celebrated general Caesar and his veteran army. They urged Varus to consider his own safety and get out of town while he still could. Varus took the council's advice and quickly fled south. When Caesar learned of their actions, he warmly thanked the councilmen and promised he would not forget their support.

Pompey was near Naples at the time trying to rally his senatorial supporters, raise troops among the local farmers, and even recruit gladiators owned by Caesar from a nearby training camp, all to little avail. It was becoming clear to Pompey, if not to the optimates, that holding Italy was a lost cause. He would have to reach the fortified port city of Brundisium in Italy's heel as quickly as possible and from there sail to Greece. Pompey was confident he could win the war in the long run if he was allowed time to build an overwhelming force to return and invade Italy. Some of the optimates saw the good sense in this plan, but most detested the idea of yielding control of Italy to Caesar, even temporarily. The mood in Pompey's camp was accordingly contentious and dispirited as senators and soldiers alike packed their bags.

Meanwhile Caesar was having much better luck as he marched southward along the coast. Another legion from Gaul caught up with him near the town of Cingulum, doubling the size of his army. Cingulum itself threw open its gates and eagerly welcomed him, a deed particularly pleasing to Caesar since the town had recently been founded by his former comrade Labienus.

Lucius Domitius Ahenobarbus had been one of Caesar's most committed enemies for almost twenty years. He had watched Caesar's victories in Gaul with burning jealousy. His own grandfather had first beaten the Allobroges and Arverni seventy years before, thus he considered the northern lands by right a family fiefdom. The Senate had appointed Domitius the new governor of Gaul, but his plans had been ruined by Caesar's march across the Rubicon. Although Caesar had beaten him at every turn, Domitius would not back down, even if the rest of the optimates ran away to Greece. Promising rich rewards, he gathered a hearty band of local tribesmen and snake-worshipping Marsi warriors from the mountains of central Italy and set out to meet his nemesis. When Pompey ordered him to withdraw to Brundisium, Domitius refused.

Domitius marched with several thousand men to the strategic river crossing of Corfinium, a town less than a hundred miles east of Rome that had briefly been the capital of the Italian rebels thirty years earlier. Caesar's army arrived near the town soon after and clashed with soldiers of Domitius, who were frantically trying to tear down the bridge leading to the settlement. Caesar easily drove the men inside the walls of Corfinium. There Domitius drew up his forces and prepared for a long siege after sending a message to Pompey begging for help. Caesar spent the next few days surrounding the town with fortifications and securing his supplies. He also welcomed the arrival of his third legion from Gaul, plus thousands of Gaulish auxiliaries and 300 horsemen donated by the Celtic king of Noricum in the eastern Alps.

Domitius was quickly becoming desperate. He was no coward, but he was experienced enough to know he could not hold off Caesar for long. He called an assembly of his soldiers in the town square and told them that Pompey would soon be sending help and that they should defend the town with all their might. But secretly he had just received word from Pompey that no help was forthcoming. Pompey, in fact, reminded Domitius that he had foolishly acted against orders and advised him to break out of Corfinium before Caesar took the town. According to Plutarch, Domitius was in such despair at his hopeless situation and the shame of being captured by Caesar that he ordered his personal physician to prepare a draft of poison for him. He drank it stoically, then began to regret his action, wondering if perhaps it would have been better to slip out of town secretly or even surrender to Caesar. The physician told him not to worry—since he thought Domitius might change his mind, he hadn't actually put any poison in the drink after all.

Domitius knew that escaping with his army would be impossible, so he now decided to flee Corfinium that night with just a few of his officers. But since there are no secrets in an army, his soldiers soon heard of the plans and held a meeting among themselves. They decided that it was ridiculous to die for Roman honor while their general was planning to desert them. They burst into the headquarters of Domitius that very night and arrested him, then sent a message to Caesar saying they were ready to open the town gates and hand Domitius over to him.

Caesar was thrilled at this turn of events, but he was deeply concerned at what might happen if he sent his troops into Corfinium that night. It was imperative to Caesar that he present himself to the Roman world not as an outlaw and sacker of cities, but as a leader who respected law and order. With this in mind, he posted sentries around the gates but did not allow them to enter that night for fear they might sack the town in their eagerness for loot. Throughout the long night the army of Caesar stood waiting, more out of curiosity for the fate of the town and its inhabitants than any craving for booty. Inside the walls, Domitius and his officers waited as well, many contemplating suicide, knowing they would almost certainly be led out of town the next morning and killed. They all remembered how Sulla had treated his enemies and they knew that if the situation were reversed they would show Caesar no mercy.

At dawn Domitius and his followers were marched before Caesar. Many of them were senators, tribunes, and knights who had dedicated themselves to destroying Caesar. Now they stood before him

face-to-face for the first time in almost a decade and waited for the ax
to fall. Caesar rose to address them briefly, surely a final chance to
gloat before he ordered his men to kill them all. But Caesar merely
looked on them like a stern father and said they really should have
behaved better. Then he turned to his guards and gave the order—to
set them free. Domitius and his followers stood stunned as the words
sank in. Surely they had misunderstood or it was some kind of cruel
trick. But no, Caesar, declared they were free to go wherever they
wanted, even to rejoin Pompey if they wished. Moreover, Domitius
could take with him the treasure he had brought to Corfinium to pay
his soldiers. Even though Caesar needed cash badly, he wanted
Rome to know he was no thief. After Domitius and his officers were
dismissed, he incorporated the enemy soldiers into his own growing
forces. The capture of Corfinium had taken only few days; then Caesar headed south to beat Pompey to Brundisium.

The news of Caesar's mercy at Corfinium soon spread throughout Italy, just as he had planned. Cicero wrote to Atticus of the new
situation on March 1:

> *Do you see what kind of man we are dealing with? He has moved*
> *against the Republic with such cleverness, such care, such prepa-*
> *ration. I truly believe that if he continues to spare all lives and*
> *property he will convert his most bitter enemies into ardent sup-*
> *porters.*

All that remained was to reach Brundisium first and cut off Pom-
pey's retreat to Greece. Caesar's legions skirted the east side of the
Apennine Mountains as they swept down the coast towards Italy's heel,
while Pompey and his army raced past Mount Vesuvius and down the
Appian Way. In spite of Caesar's legendary speed, Pompey beat him to
Brundisium and occupied the well-fortified town. When Caesar
reached the port a few days later, he could only watch in frustration as
Pompey's men looked down on him from the high stone walls.

Caesar immediately began to surround the town with siege works, but the mouth of its harbor still opened to the Adriatic Sea. Pompey had already sent half his army to Greece and could sail away with the rest when his ships returned unless Caesar could find some way to block his access to the sea. Caesar had few ships, so a naval attack was out of the question, though it might be possible to seal the neck of the harbor if he could construct a barricade across its narrowest point. But even for men who had bridged the Rhine, blocking a wide, deep channel was an almost impossible challenge. On both sides Caesar constructed piers reaching toward one another across the harbor. When the water became too deep, he anchored huge rafts to the harbor bottom and connected them with a causeway. Each of these rafts was topped with a fortified tower to launch missiles against any ships that tried to break out.

But however weak Pompey was in the political arena, he was still a master of warfare. He commandeered several large merchant ships from the citizens of Brundisium and outfitted them with three-story towers to launch attacks against Caesar's blockade. Pompey's troops rowed out daily to tear down the wall across the harbor, while each night Caesar's troops labored to repair the damage.

Even while his troops were fighting to keep Pompey in Italy, Caesar pressed for a diplomatic solution. He fervently believed that if he could just meet with Pompey face-to-face they could reach an understanding that would allow both men to maintain their dignity and power. Caesar sent a messenger to Pompey asking for a conference to discuss terms for peace. The general stiffly replied that the consuls for the year had already sailed for Greece and he himself, as a humble servant of the Republic, could not negotiate in the absence of the chief magistrates.

After nine days of fruitless siege and failed peace initiatives, the ships that Pompey had previously sent to Greece returned to ferry across the rest of his army. They had no trouble breaking through Caesar's flimsy blockade and soon stood ready on the docks of Brundisium. Pompey laid his plans carefully and that night had his troops quickly and quietly prepare themselves to leave. He ordered barricades and pits with sharpened stakes constructed inside the gates and throughout the city streets to slow down Caesar's men once they entered the city. Then he positioned a rear guard of archers and slingers on the walls to cover the escape of his main force. His army was on board the ships and bursting through the harbor barriers before Caesar had time to stop them. Pompey had beaten the siege master at his own game.

Caesar was now ruler of Italy, but it was an empty victory. Pompey's army, though scattered throughout the Mediterranean, still vastly outnumbered his own. He had almost no navy and no reliable grain supplies for his men. He was threatened by Pompey's forces—especially his huge army in Spain—which could use its mastery of the sea to invade Italy at will. Worst of all in Caesar's mind, he had almost no senators on his side since most had followed Pompey to Greece. The few that remained in Italy, such as Cicero, offered him only a grudging neutrality. He had hoped to persuade some Roman officials to support his cause and give his actions at least a semblance of state approval. But with the whole Roman government absconded to Greece, he was just another rebel.

Caesar ordered ships to be gathered from Italy and Gaul in preparation for a crossing to Greece, but he knew this would take several months. In the meantime he could not leave Italy exposed to an invasion from Pompey's veteran armies in Spain. He therefore decided to strike his enemy first, quickly marching his troops all the way to the Iberian peninsula. He also secured his food supply by sending his own men to take Sardinia and Sicily from Pompey's forces. Pompey had put Cato in charge of Sicily, and Caesar's most implacable foe was busying governing the island with his usual efficiency. He had expected Pompey to stand fast in Italy and defend the homeland, but now felt betrayed when the general retreated to Greece. When Curio appeared offshore with two of Caesar's legions, Cato abandoned Sicily, cursing the fact that he had ever trusted Pompey.

Caesar meanwhile proceeded along the Appian Way toward Rome to spend a few days settling the affairs of the city before he continued on to Spain. Along the way he passed Cicero's country estate on the coast near Formiae south of Rome and decided to pay a personal call on the influential orator. For weeks Caesar had been corresponding with Cicero, trying to woo him from his stubborn position of neutrality. Cicero was no longer in office, but he held immense prestige among the Roman public and many senators. If Caesar could bring Cicero into his camp many others would follow. In early March, Caesar had written to Cicero:

> *I especially hope to see you when I return to Rome. I'm in great need of your help and sage advice, being the popular and influential man you are.*

Cicero had been impressed by Caesar's restraint at Corfinium. When Caesar heard of this he wrote:

> *You're right that cruel revenge is the farthest thing from my mind. Since mercy is so dear to me, I'm glad that you support me in this. It doesn't bother me that those I released are fighting against me again. All I want is for every man to follow his own conscience.*

Now at the end of March, Caesar and Cicero were about to meet in person for the first time in many years. Caesar may have wanted each man to be true to himself, but he very much wanted Cicero on his side.

After warm greetings and the usual inquiries about family, the two men settled down to business. Cicero bluntly informed Caesar that he would only make matters worse by going to Spain or Greece to continue the war against Pompey. He should, instead, submit to the authority of the Senate. In fact, he declared, he meant to put a bill before the senators demanding that Caesar do just that. Caesar quietly suggested that Cicero reconsider the matter. He then left a shaken but resolute Cicero behind at the villa. It was now clear to him that Caesar would never listen to reason and play by the ancient rules of the state. Cicero decided to join Pompey as he now realized the flawed general was the only hope left for preserving the Republic.

On April 1, 49 B.C., Caesar entered the city of Rome for the first time in nine years. Caesar never mentions visiting Calpurnia during his stay in Rome, but of course neither he nor any Roman man would consider it appropriate to write about his wife. He did call together the Senate, but the meeting was poorly attended—a fact Caesar also neglects to mention in his account. He spoke of his mistreatment by Pompey and the optimates, the injustice the tribunes had suffered, and his eternal desire for peace, He concluded his speech by calling on the senators to help bear the burden of administering the state, but warned that he would act alone if they refused to cooperate. After three days of tense discussions, the senators finally agreed to send a delegation to Pompey seeking negotiations, yet no one was brave enough to volunteer for this duty. In frustration, Caesar abandoned the Senate and went instead to the popular assembly, where he received an enthusiastic welcome after promising plentiful grain and a gift of cash to each citizen.

The one man in Rome willing to stand up to Caesar was the tribune Lucius Metellus. Caesar portrays Metellus as a pawn of the optimates, but if so, he was a very brave pawn. When Caesar went to the treasury with his soldiers to withdraw money for his troops, Metellus stood alone before the door and refused him entry. Caesar, as conqueror of Gaul and Italy, was now in the embarrassing position of facing down a single stubborn man in the heart of Rome. Matters were made even worse by the fact that Caesar had portrayed himself as a defender of the sacrosanct tribunes. As the situation quickly degenerated into the absurd, Caesar told Metellus to get out of the way or he would kill him. Metellus then stepped aside, but his point had been made. Caesar broke through the locked gates of the treasury and removed 15,000 bars of gold, 30,000 bars of silver, and millions of bronze coins. The common people, his traditional power base, were furious that he had looted the public treasury and threatened a tribune. His visit to Rome was, all in all, a miserable failure.

On his way to Spain, Caesar stopped at the ancient Greek city of Massalia on the Gaulish coast. Massalia was an old ally of Rome that had received the patronage of both Pompey and Caesar in years past. Caesar had undoubtedly done the most for the city by finally eliminating the barbarian threat and opening all of Gaul to its trading network, but if he had expected a warm welcome he was disappointed. He found the gates of Massalia shut and the walls manned against him. When Caesar demanded an explanation, the citizens sent a delegation to explain that they greatly honored him, but they wished to remain neutral in what was clearly an internal Roman conflict. They promised they would show equal goodwill to both sides and aid neither against the other.

Caesar probably would have accepted the neutrality of Massalia if the inhabitants had been sincere. In truth, the merchants of the city had shrewdly calculated that Caesar was a poor investment. They believed he stood no chance at all against Pompey and the combined might of the senatorial armies. Caesar was therefore not surprised when his old enemy Domitius Ahenobarbus—whom he had graciously freed at Corfinium just two months earlier—came sailing into Massalia's harbor and received a warm welcome from the city elders. The walls of Massalia had withstood attacks for 500 years, and the Greeks were confident that Caesar would fail as well. Caesar realized just how difficult it would be to take the city, but he could not leave such a powerful and strategic town in the hands of his enemies while he fought in Spain. He spent the next month strengthening the siege works and preparing the coming assault, but he knew that finishing the job would take more of his time than he could spare. Thus he left Decimus Brutus, veteran commander of the naval campaign against the Gaulish Veneti, in charge of the blockade fleet and Gaius Trebonius with three legions of infantry to besiege the city while he hurried on to Spain.

Caesar optimistically claimed he was going to Spain to fight an army without a leader and would return to face a leader without an army. In both cases, he was proven wrong. The Pompeian forces in eastern Spain were commanded by Lucius Afranius and Marcus Petreius, two of Pompey's most capable generals. Pompey, on the other hand, used Caesar's months in Spain to greatly increase his own forces in Greece. Caesar was familiar with Spain, having served in the western part of the peninsula as quaestor in 69 B.C. and again as governor eight years later, but his enemies were concentrated in eastern Spain, where he had little experience.

In late spring of 49 B.C., Caesar crossed the Pyrenees into Spain and arrived west of modern Barcelona near the town of Ilerda on the banks of the swollen Sicoris River. Afranius and Petreius were camped nearby with five legions of veteran Roman soldiers in addition to thousands of native recruits. Caesar's infantry was roughly equal in size to the Pompeian force, but he greatly outnumbered them in cavalry. Many of these horsemen were Gaulish nobles Caesar brought along because he did not quite trust them to remain at home. Apparently he had doubts even about his own men since he borrowed money from his tribunes and centurions to give extra pay to his foot soldiers, thus buying the loyalty of his army with cash and the faithfulness of his officers as debt holders—if they deserted him, they would not be repaid.

Caesar crossed the Sicoris and made camp near the enemy forces. But food for the animals was scarce on the western side of the river and he was compelled to risk his men daily on foraging expeditions to the eastern side. This was made even more difficult when one of the few bridges across the river collapsed in a torrential spring flood. Afranius and Petreius used their strong position to harass Caesar at every turn and wear down his men. When Caesar realized he could not hold out much longer he tried to lure the generals into battle, but they were too clever to take the bait. Only when Caesar attempted to seize a strategic hill between the town and their camp did the Pompeian forces move against him. The enemy legions had learned to fight against the fierce mountain tribes of western Spain and so were not intimidated by Caesar's bold uphill charge. The Pompeians fought ferociously, throwing Caesar's troops into confusion and retreat. After hours of combat, Caesar's men returned to camp battered and bewildered. In Gaul, they had grown accustomed to victory against heavy odds, but facing determined and disciplined Romans they had collapsed in panic. They had lost 70 men, including one of their best centurions, with over 600 badly wounded. The other side suffered heavy casualties as well, but had shown they could stand up to Caesar and win.

When news of Caesar's difficulties reached Rome a few days later, many of those senators who had remained neutral suddenly became enthusiastic supporters of Pompey. Few now believed that Caesar could win. It was six months since he had crossed the Rubicon, but he commanded almost no followers in Italy, was unable to take Massalia, and would soon be crushed by Pompey's generals in Spain. To make matters even worse for Caesar, another spring flood had just wiped out the remaining bridges across the Sicoris, cutting him off totally from forage and supplies from Gaul. Rumors also flew through Caesar's camp that Pompey himself was on his way across Africa to attack them from the south.

But Caesar was always at his best when faced with impossible odds. In Britain he had seen the Celtic natives using wood-frame boats covered with leather. This peculiar sort of craft, known as a currach, was easy to build and surprisingly stable, so he ordered his men to construct a small fleet of them. A few nights later, a convoy of wagons bearing the boats headed north along the Sicoris to a point about twenty miles above his camp. A whole legion was then ferried across and within two days had built a fortified bridge across the raging river. Caesar could now bring men and supplies across the Sicoris at will.

The new bridge set in motion a rapid change of fortune for Caesar. He could use his superior cavalry to attack the Pompeians and limit them to the foraging by night. Caesar then ordered the construction of diversion ditches close by his main camp to lower the level of the Sicoris. This would allow him to ford the river without a forty-mile detour north, then back along the eastern shore. He also began to win over some of the nearby tribes, who supplied him with fresh troops and grain. These Iberians had been among the strongest supporters of the rebel Roman general Quintus Sertorius thirty years earlier. Sertorius had served under Caesar's uncle Marius, but fled to Spain to lead a guerrilla war against Rome when he fell from favor. He was a gifted general who brought Roman organization to the Spanish natives, impressing them as well with his almost magical ability with animals. As a young man Pompey had unsuccessfully fought against Sertorius before the rebel leader was assassinated. Now the Spanish saw in Caesar a man of similar ability, who might lessen the burdens of Roman rule.

Afranius and Petreius grew uneasy at these new developments and decided to move south to more favorable territory. The Pompeians escaped across the Sicoris in darkness on a pontoon bridge made of rafts, destroying it after they passed. Caesar sent his cavalry after them as soon as they were on the other side, but the river was still so deep that it could be crossed only at great risk, even by men on horseback. There was no time to build a bridge for his infantry if he wanted to catch the enemy, so he rallied his men to cross in the same manner as his cavalry. Some were understandably reluctant to wade into a raging torrent that had almost swept away the horses, so Caesar left these hesitant soldiers as camp guards. The remaining thousands plunged into the freezing river up to their necks with packhorses stationed just upstream to break the force of the current and others below to catch those men who were driven downstream. Remarkably, none of his men drowned. Once across the Sicoris, Caesar found a shortcut and marched his soldiers, now eager for battle, in front of the Pompeian army. Caesar soon trapped the enemy in an unfavorable position where they had no access to supplies.

It was now simply a matter of time until the Pompeian army would be forced to surrender, but Caesar was anxious to see this accomplished with a minimum of bloodshed. He still had a long war to fight and did not want to risk the death of any of his men unnecessarily. Caesar also was determined not to kill any Roman soldiers on the enemy side unless absolutely necessary. If he showed mercy to his fellow citizens, it would greatly increase his standing among the Roman public; if not, he would be seen as a tyrant out to secure power at any cost. Caesar's men, however, had a different idea. They saw a golden opportunity for victory slipping away because of their commander's clemency. Some even declared that if Caesar didn't lead them into battle immediately they would not fight for him in the future.

Tempers calmed the next day when men on both sides took advantage of the lull in fighting to talk across the lines. Pompeians began to visit Caesar's camp to chat, expressing regret that they had ever signed up with Afranius and Petreius. Some of Caesar's men wandered over to the enemy camp to visit as well. Soon it seemed as if there was only one army camp instead of two with men from both sides swapping war stories and wineskins. Caesar's men now realized that their leader had been right not to lead them against the Pompeians—they were, after all, Roman soldiers one and all.

Afranius looked on the scene in dismay and shrugged, but Petreius ordered his personal guard to drive Caesar's men out of the camp and kill any they could catch. Then he addressed his disheartened men and begged them not to betray the cause of the Republic to a rebel like Caesar no matter how merciful he might seem. He ordered his men to bring forward any of Caesar's soldiers still in the camp for immediate execution—but they, instead, protected their recent guests by hiding them in the tents until they could escape by night. Caesar, in marked contrast, sent the Pompeians in his camp back to their generals unharmed, while many enemy soldiers remained with him of their own will.

Caesar returned to his strategy of patiently waiting for the enemy to give up. It didn't take long to achieve this result, especially when the Pompeians were reduced to eating their own pack animals for food. Soon Afranius approached Caesar's camp under a flag of truce and declared before both armies: "We have done our duty . . . and we confess that we are beaten. All we ask is that you spare our men, if there is any compassion left in your heart." Caesar was only too glad to spare both the men and the generals. The Pompeian army was disbanded, though many chose to join Caesar's ranks. Caesar then headed west to the Atlantic coast, offering clemency to any Pompeians who surrendered. The scholar Marcus Terentius Varro, whom Pompey had placed in charge of Further Spain, as this area was called, quickly handed the entire province over to Caesar. The town of Gades, where Caesar had once dreamed he would conquer the world, was even promised full Roman citizenship, though Caesar neglects to mention in his own account that he charged them a king's ransom for this privilege.

In just over a month of fighting, Caesar had beaten the best army the Senate possessed, but he still had not faced Pompey and the forces gathering in Greece. For Pompey, the defeat in Spain was disappointing but hardly decisive. He still commanded the eastern Mediterranean and Africa, along with the loyalty of any

Roman who really mattered. As the summer of 49 B.C. was drawing to a close, Pompey and his enormous army were fast preparing to crush Caesar.

Back in Massalia, Caesar's commanders faced determined resistance in their siege of the ancient Greek town. Decimus Brutus attacked the Massalians in their harbor with grappling hooks of a sort developed during the First Punic War against Carthage, but the Greeks were tenacious in defense of the city. Trebonius used Caesar's infantry to assault the walls of Massalia with siege works from the land side as well, but to no advantage. Week after week the stalemate dragged on until Pompey sent a relief fleet to help the Massalians, greatly boosting their confidence of victory. But as Caesar says: "Human nature is such that we become either too confident or too fearful when circumstances change."

The Massalians became too confident. The result was an overreaching by land and sea that soon had Pompey's men in flight and the townspeople prostrate before the gates of the city begging Caesar's troops not to destroy their city. Caesar had ordered his officers not to allow the men to sack the town since the destruction of such a respected Roman ally would considerably weaken his public image. The soldiers grumbled at his restraint, but Caesar confirmed his previous orders when he arrived on the scene soon after. He forced the city to surrender all its military fleet and weapons of war, its entire treasury, and part of its rich territory, but he did not kill the men and enslave the women and children. Yet just in case the Massalians changed their mind, Caesar left behind two legions to occupy the town as he marched back to Italy.

At the town of Placentia on the banks of the Po in northern Italy, Caesar faced a full-scale mutiny by his troops. Led by malcontents in the ninth legion, the soldiers demanded more pay, but the heart of their complaint was that there were no spoils in this war as there had been in Gaul. They would fight for months to defeat an army or conquer a town, then Caesar would forgive his enemies and march on. His soldiers craved gold, women, and slaves, not clemency for the vanquished.

The whole episode at Placentia is a fascinating study in Caesar's psychology of leadership. Caesar never mentions it in his own account—undoubtedly he didn't want to dwell on any discontent among his followers—but other ancient sources provide the details. The rebellious army had Caesar in a difficult position. He was waging a civil war against an empire with vast resources at its disposal. All Caesar had to counter Pompey and the Senate was his army. If he lost their backing, the war was over—and the soldiers knew it. They therefore expected concessions or they would pack their bags and go home. From the soldiers' point of view, it was a perfectly reasonable request. They were risking their lives and futures to follow Caesar. If he lost this war, they would receive no rewards. Any survivors, in fact, would be lucky to escape with their lives.

Most generals would have called the mutinous leaders together and worked out a compromise—but not Caesar. Instead, he ordered the whole army to assemble and then began to speak. He said he felt like a father faced by spoiled and unruly children. He had always seen to their needs before his own and had provided them with everything he had promised. Did they really want to see Italy laid waste like Gaul or Germany? Did they think they were better than their fellow Romans on the other side? They were proud soldiers fighting a war of principle, not a horde of ravaging barbarians sacking cities for plunder. They demanded their own way? They would not get it. Armies, he declared, cannot exist without discipline. He would therefore decimate the entire ninth legion, executing every tenth man among them as punishment and a warning to any who might question him in the future.

The whole army begged Caesar to reconsider and spare the ninth legion. They were wrong to defy him, they confessed, and earnestly beseeched him not to kill men who had served him bravely for many years. Caesar reluctantly agreed to show mercy on the condition that he was given the names of the ringleaders of the rebellion, twelve of whom he would choose by lot and execute. This he did, sparing the life of one innocent man and killing in his place the centurion who had vengefully accused him. Caesar had faced down thousands of his own men and won their respect and loyalty by not yielding an inch. The army now put aside all thoughts of insurrection and prepared to move against Pompey.

Caesar was facing other problems elsewhere in the western Mediterranean. He had placed Cicero's son-in-law, Dolabella, in charge of the Adriatic fleet, but Pompey's lieutenants now had him on the run. Mark Antony's brother Gaius rushed to his aid only to find himself besieged by Pompey's men on a small island off the Illyrian coast. Gaius and his troops soon faced starvation. A few soldiers managed to escape to the mainland on rafts, but Gaius and the rest of his men were forced to surrender.

But by far the greatest setback to Caesar during the first few months of the civil war was the loss of his army in north Africa. Caesar had placed the former tribune Curio in charge of three legions recruited from the Italian hill tribes who had surrendered at Corfinium. With these men the daring but inexperienced Curio had taken Sicily from Cato without a fight. He then landed on the African coast of modern Tunisia to fight Attius Varus, the governor of the province, whom Caesar had earlier driven from Italy. Curio had visions of himself as a second Scipio Africanus defeating Hannibal, but instead found himself battling, along with Varus, the ruthless Numidian king Juba. The king had never forgotten that years before Caesar had publicly humiliated him by pulling his beard during a trial in Rome. Now he was in a position to make Caesar pay dearly for that insult.

Curio established a camp near the shore, but the local tribes poisoned his water supply, leaving thousands of his men debilitated with vomiting and violent convulsions. But even in this deplorable condition, Curio inspired his ailing men to attack the army of Varus in a steep uphill charge and won a stunning victory. Full of confidence, Curio now received a report that a small detachment of Juba's forces was nearby. He led his men along a hot and waterless coastal road to what he hoped would be an easy victory, only to find the entire army of Juba waiting for him. Curio and his exhausted army were quickly surrounded by the Numidian cavalry and slaughtered like sheep. A few of the men serving under Caesar's friend Asinius Pollio escaped by ship to Sicily, but those who surrendered to the merciless Numidians were slain. Curio himself fought bravely till the end, but was killed and decapitated, with his head presented to the jubilant king as a trophy.

Caesar could not afford to dwell on his losses in the Adriatic and Africa as Pompey was increasing the size of his army in Greece at a furious rate. Unless Caesar moved fast, Pompey would invade Italy early the next year. One piece of good news that Caesar received during the waning months of 49 B.C. was that his backers in Rome had secured him the office of dictator. With this position, like Sulla before him, he could reorganize the state and act with impunity. All of Rome now trembled as Caesar approached the gates of the capital, fearing that he, again like Sulla, would use his dictatorship to launch a bloodbath against his enemies.

When Caesar arrived in Rome on the way to Brundisium, he had no time to waste on debate or political niceties. Caught between the warring parties, the city was in crisis with critical food shortages and a shattered economy. Caesar spent only eleven days in the capital, but during that time he set the government and financial system on a sound footing. He first had himself elected consul for the following year so that he could pursue the war with at least the veneer of constitutional respectability. As his consular colleague Caesar chose Publius Servilius Isauricus, a one-time supporter of Cato who was also the son of his former commander in the pirate wars. Next, he issued a rapid series of decrees, beginning with a grain distribution to the starving populace. He then assigned new governors to the western provinces, had Juba declared an enemy of Rome in payment for his slaughter of Curio, and allowed those sons of men condemned by Sulla years before to stand for public office. Nor did Caesar neglect his supporters in northern Italy, confirming at last that those dwelling on both sides of the Po River were now and forever Roman citizens. As he was still the chief priest of Rome, Caesar also celebrated the great festival of Jupiter that had been neglected during the turmoil of the previous year. It provided a rare moment of cheer for the people of Rome during those uncertain days.

Caesar's followers among the indebted knights and upper classes now licked their lips in anticipation of one last measure—a general cancellation of debts. But instead of wiping the slate clean on loans (and throwing the already fragile monetary system into chaos), Caesar passed a sensible law limiting repayments to a prewar level as determined by an impartial commission. Debtors howled that this was unfair, but the economy benefited greatly from Caesar's moderation.

Most important of all, there were no proscriptions. Caesar did not use his dictatorial powers to order the execution of anyone nor did he condemn Pompey or any of those gathering against him in Greece. The people of the city, as well as Caesar's enemies in Greece, were shocked that he did not seek revenge.

After less than two weeks in Rome, Caesar further surprised friend and foe alike by resigning his dictatorship. In conscious imitation of Cincinnatus centuries before, Caesar had taken on the mantle of ultimate power only to lay it down when the task was complete. Of course, Caesar had no intention of going back to his plow. As a consul of Rome with thousands of soldiers behind him he could afford a magnanimous gesture. But as he marched through the gates of Rome on the way to Brundisium, Caesar knew that few in the crowd that cold December believed he would return alive to the city. Pompey and his army were waiting for him just across the sea.

XI

POMPEY

If fortune doesn't go your way, sometimes you have
to bend it to your will.

—CAESAR

While Caesar spent all of 49 B.C. fighting in Italy, Gaul, and
Spain, Pompey had used the time to gather an enormous
international force in Greece. Such an assembly of soldiers from the
nations of the Mediterranean and beyond had not been seen since the
days of Alexander the Great.

Pompey dominated the sea with a fleet of 600 ships drawn from
Asia Minor, the Greek isles, Syria, and Africa, including 70 Egyptian
cruisers sent by Cleopatra. All these were placed under the command of Caesar's longtime nemesis and former consular colleague,
Bibulus. Pompey's army on land was composed of five full legions of
Roman citizens from Italy, three from Asia Minor, and a single legion of battle-hardened veterans from Crete and Macedonia. In addition to these regular troops, he had thousands of auxiliary infantry
from Greece, Asia Minor, Syria, and Africa. Allied kings brought
Celtic soldiers of Galatia and troops from Armenia beyond the Euphrates. There were Jews, Arabs, Gauls, Germans, Phoenicians, and
Egyptians in Pompey's ranks, along with several thousand archers

and slingers from Crete. Pompey's cavalry numbered an incredible 7,000 strong. Finally, Quintus Metellus Scipio was leading two additional legions overland from Syria to join Pompey in Greece. A meticulous organizer, Pompey had gathered plentiful supplies and money from the whole eastern Mediterranean for his troops. His plan was to place his army in winter quarters on the Adriatic coast at Dyrrachium opposite Italy and launch his invasion as soon as the calm seas of spring made sailing possible.

Caesar, on the other hand, commanded a formidable but considerably smaller army with perhaps a thousand cavalry as he again arrived at the port of Brundisium. His men were exhausted from endless marching and numerous battles over the last few months. Their supplies were almost gone and their pay was, at best, sporadic. To make matters worse, the dismal winter weather of Italy's heel soon had the whole army in various states of illness. Caesar was also bitterly disappointed to discover that his quartermasters had not been able to gather enough ships to transport his entire army to Greece. His only hope for victory in the war had been to move all his troops to Greece and strike Pompey early that spring before the enemy forces could cross to Italy. He was now faced with waiting out the winter months at Brundisium with his weary, sick, and hungry army. Across the Adriatic, Pompey's men sat by their fires warm and well fed as their commander and his optimate supporters looked forward to the spring, when they could sail to Italy and destroy Caesar.

Faced with this dire situation, Caesar followed his usual form and did something totally unexpected. No one sailed the wild Mediterranean waters in winter, especially with an army, but he decided to load as many men as possible on the ships at hand and cross to Greece immediately. Bibulus and his navy would never expect Caesar to risk transporting his troops in the dead of winter, especially as they knew he lacked enough ships to bring across all his legions at once. Caesar quickly assembled his men and told them his plan. He called on them to leave everything behind that was not absolutely necessary, including slaves and baggage. His faithful troops shouted their approval and urged their general to follow Pompey. Thus on January 4 of 48 B.C.—slightly less than a year after crossing the Rubicon—Caesar crammed seven legions onto his ships and set out into the Adriatic Sea.

By some miracle of fate or fortune, Caesar and all his men landed safely on an isolated stretch of the Greek coast the next day unhindered by storms and unobserved by the enemy fleet. Pompey was still on the march toward Dyrrachium with his main force, so Caesar used the opportunity to seize a number of smaller settlements to the south of the town. Dyrrachium itself lay at the western end of the Via Egnatia, the main Roman road across the Balkans to the Aegean. When Pompey heard that Caesar had actually landed in Greece and was on the march to the strategic port, he rushed toward Dyrrachium with his own troops. In spite of Caesar's legendary speed, Pompey again beat his rival to their goal. Caesar reports, somewhat dubiously, that many of Pompey's officers and troops were in a panic over facing his legions just arrived from Italy, but his former ally Labienus rallied the men and swore allegiance to Pompey no matter what fate might bring.

Both armies camped on opposite sides of the river south of Dyrrachium and waited for the other to move first. Pompey was forever cautious and resisted any urging by the optimates to attack Caesar at once, preferring instead to wear down his smaller foe. Caesar, on the other hand, knew that even boldness would fail to win the day if he attacked Pompey with the troops he had at hand. He therefore sent the ships back to Brundisium to bring over the rest of his legions before committing himself to battle—but this was just what Bibulus expected. Caesar's old enemy was furious with himself and his fleet for letting Caesar slip through to Greece and was determined not to let it happen again. He blockaded the coast for miles in either direction and kept a careful watch on the western horizon. When Caesar's legate in Brundisium attempted to send the rest of the troops across, he was forced to turn back to Italy to escape destruction. One unfortunate ship that attempted to make for the Greek coast was captured by Bibulus, who burned it and slaughtered all aboard, even the young boys, as a warning to any who might follow. Bibulus, in fact, worked with such intensity to deny his nemesis any relief that he soon succumbed to exhaustion and died on the coast of Greece. In spite of taxing his every step for decades, Caesar granted him due praise for his faithful service to Pompey and the optimate cause.

With no hope of military victory until he could reunite his whole army, Caesar decided to try diplomacy once again. Pompey's chief military engineer, Lucius Vibullius Rufus, had been captured and released at Corfinium many months before only to be taken a second time by Caesar in Spain. Instead of executing him, Caesar decided Rufus would be a useful envoy to Pompey. He therefore sent Rufus to the enemy camp with a message for Pompey. It is high time, Caesar wrote, that we both put aside our anger and lay down our weapons of war. You have lost Italy and Spain while I have suffered defeat in Africa and Illyricum. Let us spare the Republic any further suffering and allow the Senate and people of Rome to decide the matter, not our armies on the battlefield.

It was a calculated offer on Caesar's part as he had everything to gain and nothing to lose if Pompey accepted. The Roman people wanted nothing more than for both sides to stop fighting. Since Caesar controlled Rome and the magistracies, he could take advantage of this desire for peace and push through his agenda. Without an army behind him, Cato and his allies would be forced to concede and yield the victory to Caesar. When Rufus finally reached Pompey's headquarters and began to present Caesar's offer, Pompey immediately cut him off and declared:

> *What is the point of my life or citizenship if I hold them by the grace of Caesar?*

Pompey had seen the trap for what it was, as Caesar had undoubtedly expected. Still, the very fact that he could publicize that he had again offered Pompey the hand of peace could only help him in the court of public opinion.

Since he had failed in his peace efforts with Pompey, Caesar decided to take the matter directly to the opposing army. The two camps were near enough so that men on both sides conversed amicably across the river, much as Caesar's troops had mingled with the enemy in Spain a few months before. Caesar sent his longtime supporter Publius Vatinius to the river bank to address Pompey's troops and urge them to consider peace even if their leaders would not. Vatinius was a well-known figure who had served Caesar as a tribune and praetor before joining him in Gaul. He was a good-natured fellow who laughed along with the men at his own physical disabilities, but he was a powerful and persuasive speaker. A shout came back from Pompey's side that they would send an envoy the next day to begin talks. The next morning a huge crowd of troops gathered on both banks of the river in hope of successful negotiations. Caesar's spokesmen made their plea for peace, but an angry Labienus soon arrived and began to berate Vatinius. Suddenly, a volley of spears from Pompey's lines rained down on Caesar's men, wounding a number of officers, centurions, and soldiers. The conference fell apart as Labienus shouted at his enemies: "Don't bring us any more of your proposals—there can be no peace until you bring us Caesar's head!"

Caesar was fast running out of options as his negotiations had failed and he lacked the legions necessary to launch an attack on Pompey. In his darker moments he began to wonder if his supporters back in Italy, who had not sent word for weeks, were deliberately dragging their feet and holding back the rest of his army in Brundisium. There was also news of dissension and outright revolt among his magistrates in Rome.

Finally, he could wait no longer and rose from dinner one evening telling his friends he was going to bed early that night. Instead, he made his way down to the river mouth dressed like a slave, determined to slip across to Italy and bring the troops over himself. Thus disguised, he found the captain of a small boat and told him he bore a message from Caesar himself that must reach Brundisium immediately. The captain, perhaps a smuggler, was amiable but declared that the sea was thick with Pompey's ships. In any case a fierce winter wind was blowing that would make any crossing a nightmare. But Caesar was persuasive and soon the sailors were bearing him down the river and into the sea.

As darkness deepened, the wind howled from the west and threatened to overturn the tiny craft. The captain was no coward, but he knew they were risking their lives in the storm and ordered his crew to reverse course. Caesar then stood up and threw off his cloak revealing his true identity. The captain was now terrified of his passenger as well as the waves, but Caesar took him by the hand and urged him to abandon all hesitation: "Come now, my friend, be brave and fear nothing, for you carry Caesar and Caesar's good luck in your boat."

The captain and his crew, to their credit, turned the boat back toward Italy and rowed with all their might. But soon water was pouring over the sides and even Caesar realized they would never make it across the Adriatic. He reluctantly gave the captain leave to return to shore. When Caesar reached his camp, his friends and soldiers were outraged that he had risked his own life on such a dangerous mission. The troops proudly declared that they could beat Pompey on their own without any help from Caesar's legions in Italy.

Caesar's army had struggled and starved for three winter months on the bleak coast of Greece when, one day in April, they saw sails on the western horizon. After his failed attempt to reach Brundisium by boat, Caesar had managed to get a message through to Mark Antony ordering him to bring the rest of his legions across the Adriatic as soon as possible, even if the weather was poor. The long-awaited transports had now arrived, much to Caesar's joy, but the wind was blowing fiercely from the south. The ships were driven north past Dyrrachium and landed at last almost forty miles beyond the town. One tardy transport with over 200 fresh recruits aboard was overtaken by storm and darkness before it could reach safe harbor. The terrified men surrendered to one of Pompey's officers, who swore they would suffer no harm, but once on shore they were all massacred. At the same time, sixteen of Pompey's ships from the island of Rhodes that had pursued Antony up the coast were shattered on the rocks. Many of the enemy sailors were drowned, but Caesar rounded up all the survivors and sent them safely home.

Once Mark Antony's legions had joined his own, Caesar struck at Pompey by getting between the enemy and the town of Dyrrachium. This unexpected move cut off Pompey from supplies by land but still allowed him unfettered access to the sea. Pompey made his headquarters on a coastal citadel and waited for Caesar's army to starve to death in the surrounding hills. Caesar surveyed the grim situation from his own camp just a mile to the north. Pompey's superior forces were encamped on a well-protected hill near the beach surrounded by steep hills that ringed the well-watered plain. The nearby fields lacked enough fodder to sustain thousands of horses for weeks, but Pompey could send his horsemen into the hills whenever he wanted.

An audacious idea struck Caesar as he stood looking south—why not build a wall around Pompey? The notion seemed absurd at first since the enemy was more numerous, but the surrounding hills could be linked by ramparts if Caesar moved fast enough. A continuous wall would also give Caesar control of Pompey's water supply since he could cut off streams flowing to the sea. The same basic idea had worked at Alesia against Vercingetorix, but Caesar's wall would have to be even longer and built to hold in crack Roman troops instead of Gauls. The military value of the wall would be enormous, though it would be horrendous to defend, but the psychological benefit would be even greater. If Pompey, the great conqueror of the East, allowed himself to be hemmed in by an inferior army of rebels, his supporters in the camp and abroad would surely begin to question his leadership.

Caesar's wall soon stretched sixteen miles across the hills above Pompey's camp. Instead of attempting to break out of the trap, Pompey countered with a wall of his own facing Caesar's defenses. Between the two walls was a no-man's-land that, today, would resemble nothing more than a battlefield of World War I. As Caesar says, no one in the ancient world had ever seen such a conflict: "It was a totally new type of warfare with each side inventing new methods of fighting as they went along." One side would creep up on the other at night and fire a volley of arrows into the enemy's trenches, then pull back to safety. Others would light fires to draw their opponents into a trap, then attack with swords and spears. Week after week, from April until early July, men from both sides lived and died in mud and misery as they held the lines.

Caesar's men suffered most since they had a longer position to defend and could never gather enough food. Soon they were eating anything they could find. Some enterprising soldiers from Caesar's camp discovered a local root called *chara* and turned it into a kind of bread. A few of Caesar's men ran up to Pompey's wall and tossed over samples shouting that as long as they could dig roots out of the earth they would keep up the fight. When Pompey's officers showed some of the bread to their general, he exclaimed that if Caesar's army could eat such food they must be beasts, not men.

Pompey's troops began to look on Caesar's army as adversaries who could endure any hardship. Morale behind Pompey's line weakened every day as they launched petty raids and suffered attacks but did nothing to drive Caesar's men from the hills. There was enough food for Pompey's army as they had access to the sea, but the horses suffered greatly from lack of fodder and the men were forced to dig wells for a new water supply. Soldiers and civilians alike in Pompey's camp began to wonder if they had backed the wrong man. Caesar played on these feelings at every opportunity, once sending a letter to Cicero (who was with Pompey at the time) urging him to abandon a lost cause and accept instead a position of honor in Caesar's new government.

But there were also those, including Caesar, who never doubted Pompey's military instincts. The older general's plan of patiently biding his time until he found a weakness finally paid off that summer. Two brothers of the Gaulish nobility named Raucillus and Egus serving with Caesar had recently begun skimming the pay due their countrymen and pocketing the cash themselves. Caesar knew of their malfeasance, but felt an open confrontation would be unwise at the time. Instead, he took the brothers aside and scolded them privately, promising to forget the whole matter if they behaved themselves. The brothers, however, decided to take their ill-gotten gains and flee across the wall to Pompey's camp. There, in exchange for sanctuary, they gave the enemy valuable inside knowledge of Caesar's defenses, including weak spots in his lines.

In early July, Pompey used this information to attack Caesar in several places at once. These assaults failed due to the tenacity of Caesar's troops, including a contingent of fearless Germans, but many of his men were killed or badly wounded. The defenders at one spot on the wall counted thirty thousand arrows that had landed near them. One centurion named Scaeva came before Caesar with a shield pierced in over a hundred places.

About a week later, Pompey struck again. This time he concentrated his assault on the poorly defended southern end of the wall. At midnight, thousands of Pompey's soldiers poured across the lines and drove Caesar's men into a panicked flight. Caesar rushed to the battle and tried to rally his men as they streamed past him. He grabbed one towering soldier and ordered him to turn around, but the angry man raised his sword to slay Caesar rather than face Pompey's men. A bodyguard cut him down just in time, but Caesar could not stem the tide. Over a thousand of his best troops were slain that night and many more captured. Labienus took the prisoners, mocked them as old comrades who turned and ran, then killed them all.

Caesar withdrew to his camp and prepared for the worst. He spent the night in his tent berating himself for his poor judgment and failed leadership. He knew that Pompey could annihilate his dispirited army that very night and end the war in one blow. But amazingly, Pompey did nothing. As dawn rose the next day, Pompey's army returned to camp. Caesar knew he had escaped only by the grace of Pompey's excessive caution:

> Today the enemy would have won the war if only they had a commander who knew how to conquer.

There was now no hope that Caesar could achieve victory by remaining on the coast, his defenses shattered and his army in disarray. The triumph that had seemed so close only days before had been snatched away by fortune. As Pompey's army celebrated and word of his defeat began to spread across the Roman world, Caesar gathered his army, spoke a few words of encouragement to his exhausted men, then marched them sadly away.

After Caesar's retreat from the coast, Pompey could have easily crossed to Italy and reclaimed Rome. Nevertheless, he had known from the beginning that the goal of the war was not to hold Rome but to defeat Caesar himself. So hearing that his enemy had moved east to the plains of Thessaly, he gathered his army and followed him. Pompey knew that Caesar would have little support among the communities of Greece after his defeat. All he had to do was catch up with Caesar and harass him at every opportunity until his army fell apart.

It was a good plan, though Pompey once again underestimated both Caesar and his soldiers. They were beaten, hungry, sick, weary, and outnumbered, but they had been through worse in Gaul and still won the final victory. The men grumbled and swore, but their loyalty to Caesar was firm.

Caesar and his army moved over the mountains from the Adriatic coast, plundering farms as they went. The first settlement they came to was the town of Gomphi on the western edge of the great plain of Thessaly. The town had previously declared for Caesar and offered him their undying loyalty, but now they shut their gates to his army. They picked a bad day to defy Caesar. His soldiers were starving and he badly needed a victory, however small, to renew the spirits of his men. Caesar quickly ordered scaling ladders constructed and engines of war brought up to the walls. His men needed little encouragement to attack Gomphi, especially as Caesar had given them permission to sack the town. Caesar rarely allowed such license to his men as it was bad for discipline and contrary to his stated goal of mercy for all, but he knew in this case that the destruction of Gomphi would make a vivid impression on any other Greek towns that might resist him in the future. So in a very deliberate act of terror, the army of Caesar descended on the small settlement and utterly destroyed it. By sunset, the men had been killed, the women violated, and the houses and shops ransacked. The town elders were found dead in the local apothecary shop having poisoned themselves rather than face Caesar's wrath. The army ate every scrap of food they could find and drank sweet Greek wine until they lay unconscious in the streets. The next day Caesar's army continued their march with aching heads and packs bulging with loot. No Greek town now dared turn Caesar away.

A few days later Caesar and his army arrived at the small town of Pharsalus on the banks of the Epineus River. War had bypassed this quiet corner of Thessaly for centuries, though just over the mountains at Thermopylae the Spartans had famously fought to the death against the invading Persians four centuries earlier. Now Caesar gazed at the horizon and saw the entire army of Pompey—over 50,000 men—drawn up just south of the river. Caesar was outnumbered by more than two to one as he made camp west of the town and waited to see what Pompey would do.

In his tent nearby, Pompey was already fighting his own battle with the optimates. How could he hesitate to attack Caesar at once, they demanded, when his own forces were so much larger? Was he afraid of Caesar? Was he trying to delay conflict long enough to take over the state for himself? Domitius Ahenobarbus openly mocked him, comparing him to Agamemnon wavering before the walls of Troy. One of the senators asked if they would have to wait yet another year to eat figs from Tuscany. At last Pompey yielded to the overwhelming pressure from the optimates and agreed to meet Caesar on the battlefield even though it was against his better judgment. Pompey was a gifted general, but as Plutarch says, his leadership suffered from a fatal flaw: "He was a man who craved glory and hated to disappoint his friends."

The optimates were now so confident of victory they began squabbling over the spoils of war. Several powerful senators contended for Caesar's position as *pontifex maximus,* others doled out consulships for years to come. The avaricious divided the property of Caesar and his followers, the malicious planned proscriptions and executions:

> *They fought over honors or rewards or money or how to avenge themselves on their enemies, thinking only of what they could gain from victory and never how to win the battle at hand.*

For several days, however, Pompey continued to avoid an open fight. Each morning he would send his soldiers out to form a line just in front of his camp, while Caesar would bring his troops opposite Pompey's men a few hundred yards across the plain. But before any battle could begin, Pompey would always withdraw his troops back behind his walls. A few cavalry skirmishes took place between the lines during these days, but the infantry never came close enough to see the faces of their opponents.

Along with the optimates, Caesar was growing increasingly frustrated at this lack of action. On the morning of August 9, he decided to move his camp to a new site with better access to food for his men and grass for the horses. Suddenly, just before he ordered his troops to return to camp and pack, he saw Pompey's lines move away from their walls toward his army. His opponents halted on the plains south of the river and formed a deep line almost a mile in length. Pompey had at last decided to fight—and Caesar could not have been happier. Pompey might have twice as many men, but Caesar knew his own troops were more experienced, better disciplined, and spoiling for a fight.

On the northern part of Pompey's line were legions mostly from Asia Minor commanded by Afranius, who had surrendered to Caesar in Spain months before. In the middle were the soldiers newly arrived from Syria under Scipio, while Caesar's implacable adversary Ahenobarbus commanded the southernmost infantry. Pompey placed his entire cavalry at the bottom of the line under the control of Labienus. Pompey directed the operation from the rear.

Caesar took one glance at Pompey's enormous array and realized immediately what his opponent planned to do. Pompey knew his infantry was less experienced than Caesar's, so he had given orders for the foot soldiers to hold back Caesar's men like a human wall, not to rush forward and attack the enemy lines as was standard in ancient battles. He would then send his superior cavalry sweeping around the southern end of Caesar's lines to come up behind the enemy and force them to fight on two sides. The infantry would then cut them down in front while the horsemen crushed them from the rear.

Pompey's plan was brilliant, innovative, and sure to succeed, but Caesar saw a weakness. Everything in Pompey's plan depended on Labienus and his cavalry breaking through Caesar's southern lines. If somehow Caesar could hold back the horsemen, his infantry might have a chance against Pompey's legions. To counter Labienus, Caesar moved his best legion, the tenth, south to face Labienus. He also sent extra men from the other legions behind the tenth to a supporting position where they could not be seen by the enemy. In front of these he placed his own small force of cavalry. Publius Sulla, a young relative of the former dictator, led the southernmost legions. The former consul Domitius Calvinus held the center, while Mark Antony commanded Caesar's troops nearest the river. Caesar himself ranged over the whole battlefield, giving final directions to his officers and encouraging his men.

Caesar at last gave the order and his infantry began to run toward Pompey's lines with their spears at the ready. Twenty thousand weary veterans of Gaul swept across the plain of Pharsalus coming ever closer to almost fifty thousand troops gathered from the far corners of the Mediterranean. But when Caesar saw that Pompey's line refused to move against his men, he ordered the infantry to halt. Such was the discipline of Caesar's army that all his soldiers stopped just beyond spear range of Pompey's astonished army. The centurions told the men to take a break and catch their breath for a moment before continuing the advance. Then, when Caesar's men were rested, they gave a mighty shout and rushed against Pompey's lines, first throwing their spears, then drawing swords to fight at close quarters.

A hard-fought battle between the infantry on both sides raged as Labienus ordered his cavalry at the southern end of the plain to charge. Pompey's horsemen quickly overwhelmed Caesar's cavalry, but suddenly they came up against the tenth legion. Caesar had given his favorite soldiers very specific orders about what to do next. Normally they would have launched their spears against the cavalry

from a distance, then used their swords to try and cut at the legs of
the men and horses. But Caesar had the novel idea of brandishing
spears like bayonets to slash repeatedly at the heads and eyes of the
horsemen, knowing that they would instinctively pull up short to
protect their faces. Just as he had hoped, Pompey's cavalry panicked
at this new form of fighting and soon retreated in mass confusion.

When Pompey's infantry saw that their cavalry had collapsed,
they began to lose heart and finally fell back with Caesar's men in
pursuit. A certain victory by Pompey's forces turned into a rout with
Caesar's legions winning the day at a loss of only two hundred men.
Over twenty thousand of Pompey's soldiers were reportedly captured with another 15,000 slain. Domitius Ahenobarbus tried to rally
his men but died with them on the southern line. Most of the other
optimates turned and ran as fast as they could back to camp. Pompey
himself was among the first to leave when he realized the battle had
turned against him. He retreated to his tent to gather his belongings
only to have an aide rush in and declare that Caesar's men were almost on top of them. Pompey quickly shed his general's cloak and
put on civilian clothes before fleeing to safety.

When Caesar arrived at Pompey's tent he saw luxury beyond
compare—gourmet food, myrtle boughs, and couches strewn with
flowers, so that the scene looked more like a festival than an army
camp. Then while his men ate a well-earned meal and settled in for
the night, Caesar walked among the corpses on the battlefield and
shook his head at the pointless slaughter:

> This was their doing, not mine. They would have destroyed me,
> even after all my great deeds, unless I had turned to my army for
> help.

One consolation for Caesar was the number of senators on Pompey's side who had survived the battle at Pharsalus. Cicero, Cato, and
others had either remained behind at Dyrrachium or fled east with

Pompey, but many now willingly joined Caesar. The conquering general extended his clemency to his former enemies and burned the captured letters of Pompey lest they be used as evidence against anyone in the future. There would be no vengeance. Caesar was particularly glad to welcome into his circle Cato's nephew Marcus Brutus, the son of his lover Servilia. The affection Caesar had for Brutus was warm and genuine—he would trust the younger man wholeheartedly for the rest of his life.

Caesar had won the battle, but the war was far from over. Pompey was still at large and threatened to raise new armies at any moment. Cato, Scipio, and Labienus were preparing to cross the sea to rally Pompey's forces in Africa with the help of King Juba. And Spain, which had been stripped from Pompey just months before, was now in open rebellion due to the outrageous abuses of Caesar's appointed governor.

In spite of competing problems, Caesar knew that his first goal had to be the capture of Pompey himself. As long as the veteran general was free he posed a deadly threat to Caesar's plans. Caesar chased him up the Via Egnatia to the Greek port of Amphipolis, only to find Pompey had already sailed to the isle of Lesbos with all the gold he could carry. Caesar quickly hurried after him in a small passenger boat only to run into ten of Pompey's armored warships in the middle of the Hellespont between Greece and Asia. With perfect bravado, Caesar hailed the commander of the fleet and ordered him to surrender at once. The shaken captain—who could have ended the civil war then and there with the stroke of a sword—meekly complied and begged for Caesar's mercy.

Although he was in a terrible hurry, Caesar took time to visit the ancient city of Troy, the ancestral home of the Julian clan. The visit was much more than a sightseeing tour as Caesar was deliberately imitating a similar visit to the town made by Alexander the Great three centuries earlier. He also wanted to publicize to Greeks and Romans alike his connections to the ancient founders of Rome and through them his mandate to restore the Republic. From Troy he moved quickly south along the Aegean coast. Most uncharacteristically at this point in his *Civil War,* Caesar notes a number of divine signs that had occurred in the East at the very moment of his triumph at Pharsalus—a statue of the goddess Victory at a temple in Greece had turned on its pedestal to face the door, in Syria a great noise of trumpets and a clashing arms had terrified the citizens of Antioch, and the inner sanctuary of a temple in the Asian city of Pergamum reverberated with the sound of drums. Caesar was normally quite skeptical of signs from the gods, but in this case was willing to acknowledge them when they served his purpose. The Greeks of Asia Minor were certainly impressed by such reports, with the city of Ephesus dedicating an inscription to Caesar that survives to this day:

> The cities, people, and tribes of Asia honor Gaius Julius Caesar, son of Gaius, high priest and twice consul of Rome, a descendant of Ares and Aphrodite, a god who has appeared among us for the salvation of all mankind.

Caesar might record the occasional sign from heaven in his narrative, but he never mentions this inscription or similar divine honors. Such declarations of godhood had become common in the east since Alexander, but his Roman audience would recoil at such unseemly praise. Caesar, at least at this point in his career, was careful to present himself to Rome as a humble and very human servant of the Republic.

Caesar continued through the cities of Asia Minor, looking for news of Pompey and granting much-appreciated tax relief along the way. He heard that Pompey had been seen in Cyprus, then had sailed to Egypt along with his wife to seek new supporters. Wasting no time,

Caesar set off for Alexandria with only one legion and a few hundred cavalry.

Pompey arrived at the grand city of Alexandria on the Nile delta near the end of September. Egypt in the autumn of 48 B.C. was embroiled in its own civil war between the fourteen-year-old Ptolemy XIII—son of the recently deceased Roman ally Ptolemy XII Auletes—and his twenty-one-year-old sister, Cleopatra. The young Ptolemy held the advantage at the moment but was ruled over by two conniving courtiers, Pothinus the eunuch and Achillas, commander of the army. Having calculated that Pompey was now on the losing side of Rome's internal conflict, the king's two advisors schemed to earn Caesar's favor by murdering Pompey.

When Pompey's boat sailed into the harbor only one day after his fifty-ninth birthday, Achillas met him in a fishing boat along with a Roman expatriate named Septimius who had once served as a centurion under Pompey in the pirate wars. Septimius greeted him respectfully in Latin while Achillas welcomed him to Egypt in Greek. They apologized for the modest reception but explained that the fickle currents precluded a suitable warship with honor guard. Once ashore, however, they assured him he would be treated like royalty. Taking only two servants along, Pompey waved aside his suspicious wife and stepped into the transport. Pompey spent the few minutes on the way to the dock reviewing a speech he had written in Greek to greet the young king. At this point, just as Pompey was rising to wave to members of the court waiting for him on shore, Septimius ran him through from behind with his sword. Achillas and the rest then drew their daggers and stabbed Pompey repeatedly as he drew his toga over his face, his wife watching in horror from their ship. With no final words, Pompey the Great—general of Rome, conqueror of the east, and Caesar's most gifted foe—died in a torrent of blood at the bottom of a small Egyptian boat.

XII

CLEOPATRA

> They say her beauty was not so astonishing—those
> who saw her were certainly not swept away—but
> when you were in her presence and talked with her,
> she was irresistible.
>
> — Plutarch

Alexander the Great arrived in Egypt in the winter of 332 B.C., having defeated the Persian army in Syria and destroyed the cities of Tyre and Gaza. The Egyptians had watched these events closely and put up no resistance when the Macedonian general appeared on the banks of the Nile. Alexander was an inspired military leader, but he also dreamed of spreading Greek civilization to the lands of the East. So on a narrow spit of coastal land at the western edge of the Nile delta, he personally laid out a new city he hoped would become a shining example of Hellenic culture. The city he built—modestly named Alexandria—succeeded beyond his wildest dreams. The new town quickly grew into the commercial and intellectual capital of the eastern Mediterranean. Trade goods flowed into the city from Arabia, east Africa, and India. Immigrants arrived from the Mediterranean and beyond, including so many settlers from Palestine that Alexandria soon had the largest Jewish population of any city in the world. The ruling descendants of Alexander's general Ptolemy, who took control of Egypt after the conqueror died, lavished their new capital with palaces, monuments, baths, and temples.

From the first Ptolemy to the twelfth, an unbroken line of Macedonian kings sat on the ancient throne of pharaoh and ruled over Egypt from Alexandria. They issued decrees and collected taxes from the natives, but made no effort to become part of Egyptian civilization. They mixed only with other Greeks, leaving Alexandria on rare occasions for pleasure cruises along the Nile or to wage war abroad. The Alexandrians themselves were an unruly sort who had no love for the extravagant Ptolemies, bestowing on them nicknames such as Fat Boy and the Bastard.

By the time of Cleopatra's father, Ptolemy Auletes, Rome had become an overwhelming presence in the eastern Mediterranean. But through diplomacy, treachery, assassinations, and an endless supply of gold, Auletes managed to maintain Egypt's independence in spite of repeated exile from his capital. In 58 B.C., Caesar as consul had restored Auletes to the throne thanks to an enormous bribe that he and Pompey were to share. To make sure of his cut, Pompey sent Aulus Gabinus, the Roman governor of Syria, to collect the payment while Caesar was still in Gaul. In Alexandria that year, a young cavalry commander on Gabinus's staff named Mark Antony probably met Auletes' fourteen-year-old daughter Cleopatra.

The money Gabinus squeezed from the land was not enough to cover debts owed to Rome or pay his army. Soon many of his soldiers went native and married the local Egyptian women, abandoning any thought of returning home. They were joined by ruffians, exiles, and runaways from every land to form a mercenary band that alternately protected and plundered Egypt. It's likely that these former Roman legionaries were the very men Pompey had hoped to recruit for his new army.

In 51 B.C., Auletes died and left the throne to the teenaged Cleopatra and his even younger son, Ptolemy XIII, as joint rulers. By

Egyptian custom, sister and brother ruled together not only as monarchs but as husband and wife. Sometimes in Ptolemaic history the sibling king and queen worked well together, but in Cleopatra's case there was bad blood from the start as her brother was controlled by powerful advisors who resented her interference. The new queen of Egypt had firm ideas on the proper way to rule her father's kingdom that did not include the eunuch Pothinus or general Achillas. From the start she surprised everyone by working to integrate herself with the native Egyptians and their priests. She was the first Ptolemy to actually learn the Egyptian language (along with Hebrew, Ethiopian, and several other tongues). A stone monument carved with hieroglyphs, now in Copenhagen, records that she even participated in a sacred bull ceremony near Thebes at the start of her reign, escorting the divine animal to the temple by boat. Such concessions to native sentiments must have impressed Egyptians accustomed to neglect, at best, from their Ptolemaic rulers for the last two centuries.

But support from native Egyptians was not enough to rescue Cleopatra from the eternally disgruntled Alexandrians. While Caesar's old nemesis Bibulus was still alive and governing Syria, he sent his two sons to collect the renegade Gabinian legionaries for a planned attack on the Parthians—but the soldiers murdered them both rather than leave the delights of Egypt. Young Cleopatra boldly arrested the assailants and sent them to Bibulus for punishment, much to the displeasure of the Alexandrians, who felt she was succumbing to Roman pressure. This affair, along with crop failures and the scheming of her brother's advisors, soon forced Cleopatra to flee her capital and recruit her own army. The adolescent Ptolemy XIII now ruled from Alexandria alone, watched over diligently by Pothinus and Achillas.

Caesar arrived in Alexandria at the beginning of October 48 B.C. accompanied only by one undersized legion and eight hundred cavalry.

When Pompey's head was brought to him, he recoiled in horror and bitter disappointment. This was not the end he had wished for his most gifted enemy. Caesar had hoped to pardon Pompey and perhaps reestablish their partnership—though with Pompey in a decidedly secondary role—but now all he could do was weep as he received his former son-in-law's signet ring with the image of a lion bearing a sword. He asked about Pompey's body, only to discover that it had been thrown into the harbor after his decapitation. A servant of Pompey's named Philip had managed to rescue the corpse and cremate it on shore using wood from an old fishing boat. Caesar then found the rest of Pompey's party that were still alive and made sure they were treated well. The head of Pompey was eventually presented to his widow with all honors and taken back to Rome for burial at their villa.

The Egyptians had sought to win Caesar's favor by the murder of Pompey, but Pothinus and Achillas had achieved just the opposite. Caesar now scorned the rulers of Alexandria who had robbed him of his magnanimous victory over Pompey. He might have returned to Rome immediately, but there was the matter of money. To help finance his war against the remaining Pompeians, Caesar demanded the rest of the funds promised by Auletes years before—ten million denarii, the equivalent of a generous annual salary for almost fifty thousand soldiers. Pothinus was indignant, but swore he would send the money to him in Italy. Caesar, instead, decided to stay put in Egypt until he had the cash in hand, claiming the winds were unfavorable for a voyage to Italy. Extortion was foremost on Caesar's mind, but he had legitimate political reasons to remain in Alexandria. The ongoing civil war in Egypt meant dangerous instability that his remaining enemies might use to their own advantage. It was imperative that he not leave a country as important as Egypt in chaos, no matter how pressing his affairs in Rome.

The Alexandrians had nothing but contempt for Caesar and his soldiers, showering them with abuse from the moment they set foot on the docks. The citizens of the city were proud of their independence from Rome and saw Caesar's presence as an imminent threat to their sovereignty. When he landed on shore, they erupted in violent protests as the fasces—the symbol of Roman power—were carried before him. Several of Caesar's men were killed in the riots that followed throughout the city. But much to the consternation of the Alexandrians, Caesar settled inside the protected walls of the royal palace to await the promised money and bring peace to the warring factions of the land.

Unlike Rome with its narrow alleys and crooked backstreets, Alexandria was laid out in a neat grid pattern of wide thoroughfares and checkerboard neighborhoods. The city stretched for several miles between the Mediterranean coast to the north and brackish Lake Mareotis to the south, while a canal over twenty miles long brought fresh water from the Nile inside the city walls. The royal precinct housing Caesar faced the harbor along the eastern side of the city next to the Jewish quarter with its magnificent synagogue. In the royal quarter were the Ptolemaic palace as well as the celebrated tomb of Alexander the Great, along with the fabulous Alexandrian museum and library. The library had declined in recent years, but once had held almost half a million precious scrolls. The museum, however, was still home to the greatest scholars of the age. It was not a museum in the modern sense of the word, but a research and study center for scientists and writers. Lectures were held for students and visitors during the day in an impressive lecture hall, while the evenings were filled with dinners and drinking parties brimming with learned conversation and biting wit.

Most of the million or so residents of Alexandria lived to the west of the royal quarter along the many residential and commercial streets between the Serapeum and the harbor. The hilltop Serapeum was an international center of pilgrimage dedicated to the native

Egyptian god Osiris, though with a large measure of Greek influence. Those seeking healing or advice from the god made their way
to the immense temple complex, well-financed by the Ptolemies.
Pharos Island lay off the coast almost a mile north of the city but was
connected to Alexandria by a causeway that divided the harbor into
two parts. The fabled Pharos lighthouse—one of the seven wonders
of the ancient world—stood over 300 feet tall just beyond the eastern
edge of the island, its beacon fire beckoning ships from the whole
Mediterranean world.

From his window in the royal palace, Caesar could look out on the
lighthouse and the sea beyond. He could also see the streets of
Alexandria teeming with angry Greeks eager to kill any Roman soldier they could find. The eunuch Pothinus did everything he could
to stir the anger of the Alexandrian mob. He also plotted to murder
Caesar before the Roman ruler could force an accord between the
royal siblings, thereby ending his own role as the power behind the
throne.

Caesar, as guarantor of their father's will, decided to put a quick
end to the Egyptian civil war by ordering both young Ptolemy and
his sister Cleopatra immediately to disband their armies and attend
him at the palace to settle their differences. Pothinus fumed, but sent
Ptolemy to Caesar, all the while plotting with the general Achillas to
secretly move the royal army from the Nile delta to Alexandria.

Cleopatra meanwhile was prevented by her brother's army and
ships from reaching Caesar at the palace—so she devised a plan to
gain entry that has become legend. As Plutarch tells the story,
Cleopatra journeyed to the royal quarter of Alexandria by night in a
small boat easily overlooked among the many trade vessels in the
harbor. She traveled alone except for a single attendant, a Sicilian
merchant named Apollodorus. When they arrived at the dock,
Cleopatra knew she would quickly attract unwanted attention so she

stretched herself out in an old linen sack used by slaves to carry bed-clothes. Apollodorus then rolled her up, tied the ends of the sack, and carried the queen of Egypt into the royal palace disguised as dirty laundry.

Caesar could not believe his eyes when Cleopatra emerged from the sack before him. She had quite cleverly chosen a method of entry that would not only get her past hostile guards and enemy agents, but make a profound impression on Caesar. The boy from the slums of Rome who had fought his way to the top of the political ladder through boldness and cunning was immediately taken by the daring young queen. Like most Romans, he believed the Alexandrian roy-alty to be cowardly prima donnas who maintained their rule only through intrigue, backstabbing, and bribery. But in Cleopatra, with her obvious courage and intelligence, he saw a resourceful monarch with whom he might work to secure Egypt for himself and bring an end to civil war on the Nile.

Caesar was also personally captivated by the twenty-one-year-old queen. Later sources would have us believe their famous affair began that very night, but it is impossible to know just when Caesar first shared Cleopatra's bed. Caesar himself never mentions a physical re-lationship with the young monarch, implying that their contacts were purely professional. Contemporary sources loyal to Caesar fol-low his lead and speak of Cleopatra only as a factional leader in the Egyptian civil war. But enough ancient authors mention the ro-mance to make us sure that it did indeed happen. Modern readers must wonder why a fifty-two-year-old general from the Roman aris-tocracy would involve himself with a foreign queen half his age when Rome traditionally looked at eastern women as treacherous partners in love. Some would say the question answers itself. Al-though now middle-aged, Caesar was a notorious womanizer who saw young Cleopatra as another in a long line of conquests. But oth-ers would point out that Caesar was anything but a fool. If he were simply looking for an exotic fling, there were ample women, slave and free, available to him. No matter how active Caesar's libido might be, he would never have been so imprudent as to involve himself with Cleopatra unless it suited his overriding political aims. In this case, his goal would have been to cement the loyalty of the Ptolemaic kingdom to himself and thereby secure control of Egypt's resources. With Cleopatra on his side he could be sure that the fertile lands of the Nile would maintain their fealty to Rome—and to him personally.

But what did Cleopatra have to gain by making Caesar her lover? In this case the answer is simpler—absolutely everything. Her brother and his advisors controlled a more powerful army as well as the loyalty, for the moment at least, of the Roman-hating Alexandrians. Without powerful support from outside her realm, Cleopatra was doomed to failure in her bid to regain the throne. The best she could hope for without Caesar was a futile war, perhaps ending her life as a pathetic exile in some foreign court. But with Caesar's support she gained the military might of the whole Roman empire. We don't know if Cleopatra's feelings for Caesar were genuine or feigned—she probably would have found the question irrelevant—but Caesar's affection guaranteed the throne. If by some chance she were to bear Caesar a son, she might even hope the boy could join together Egypt and Rome just as Alexander had united Greece and the ancient lands of the East.

Whatever the history and motives of their love affair, Caesar was so taken by Cleopatra that he immediately sent for her brother in an attempt to reconcile them that same night. Ptolemy was stunned to see Cleopatra in his own palace seated beside Caesar. He was even more amazed when he realized that Caesar had taken Cleopatra's side in the dispute. Screaming betrayal at the hands of Rome, the young man rushed outside into the crowd gathering early that morning, threw his crown from his head, and collapsed in tears. The Alexandrians knew Ptolemy was a spoiled child and puppet of his advisors, but they resented one of their own being humiliated by a

Roman consul. The crowd rose in anger and soon threatened to take the palace by force. Caesar quickly appeared before them and assured them his intentions were honorable—he merely wanted to carry out the wishes of their previous king Ptolemy Auletes and bring peace to their troubled land. He called together the Alexandrian assembly and urged them to restore young Ptolemy and Cleopatra to joint rule. As leader of Rome, he even sweetened the deal by promising to restore Egyptian rule to the island of Cyprus, annexed to Rome by Cato years earlier.

Several days passed as Caesar worked to calm the Alexandrians and reconcile the factions at court. Just when he thought he might be making progress he received word that Achillas had suddenly arrived on the edge of the city with 20,000 veteran soldiers, more than five times the size of Caesar's forces. The Egyptian navy was threatening his ships in the harbor, while the people of Alexandria were attacking his troops on all sides. Caesar sent messengers, including an adopted son of Mithridates on his staff, to Syria and Asia Minor calling for more troops, but any relief force was weeks away at best. Caesar seized young Ptolemy before he could flee from the palace and detained him. He seized and executed the eunuch Pothinus, mastermind of the anti-Roman movement. But Caesar and his vastly outnumbered troops were now trapped inside a hostile city of a million raging Greeks out for Roman blood. One of the most vicious campaigns of urban warfare in the history of the ancient world was about to begin.

Caesar occupied the palace grounds and a marshy area to the south with several thousand infantry troops as well a few hundred cavalry. He also controlled the docks of the royal quarter and a small fleet of ships in the harbor nearby. But Achillas now threw his army against Caesar's stronghold with all his might, while the Alexandrians outside the combat zone flocked in to attack the Romans as well. Caesar beat back the initial assault on the palace, but soon realized he was in a kind of war very different than he had ever faced before. He had besieged and conquered many cities during his career, but he had never been on the defensive in an urban environment. Alexandria was so tightly packed that there was no room for traditional battle-field movements and certainly not enough space to deploy his cavalry in any useful fashion. The fighting was waged house by house, day and night, with ground gained or lost measured in feet rather than miles. To add to his troubles, Caesar was fast running out of supplies and had only limited access to fresh water.

Caesar ordered his troops to build fortifications, covered en-trenchments, and towers around the palace quarter. To gain ground along the heavily defended city blocks, the Roman troops employed a surprisingly modern technique of urban warfare. Instead of assault-ing a house through the well-guarded doors, they used battering rams to break through the walls from connecting homes. Roman troops would then pour into the gap, kill the defenders, and repeat the procedure to take the next house. Caesar also demolished count-less buildings to create a deadly no-man's-land around his perimeter. He could only be thankful that, unlike the cities of Gaul built with wood and thatch, the Alexandrian homes he occupied were virtually fireproof with their mud brick walls and tile roofs.

None of Caesar's actions intimidated the Alexandrians in the least. Messengers went out to all the towns of Egypt to come and join in the war against the hated Romans. Thousands flocked into the city carrying armloads of weapons and dragging artillery pieces be-hind them. Workshops for making spears, swords, and other arma-ments sprang up overnight throughout Alexandria. Wealthy masters even armed trusted slaves and donated their services to guard strate-gic points in the city, freeing the professional soldiers to move along the lines as needed. The townspeople built stone barricades up to forty feet high across streets, adding lofty towers to rain down mis-siles on the Romans when the nearby buildings were too low. The citizens also constructed mobile towers drawn by oxen to reinforce any neighborhood the legionaries threatened.

The Alexandrians relentlessly attacked the Roman lines at the same time they defended their own fortifications. Being quite clever, as even the Romans grudgingly acknowledged, they expertly reproduced any weapon or technique used successfully by their adversaries. But even while the battle was raging, the citizens of the city continued to argue techniques and strategy in public meetings. One thing they all agreed on, however, was the absolute necessity of defeating the enemy:

> *The Romans have been nibbling away at our sovereignty for years. First Aulus Gabinius came with his legions, then Pompey arrived followed by Caesar and his army—but he hasn't left even though Pompey is dead. If we fail to drive him out, Egypt will become just another Roman province.*

The Alexandrians also knew they had to strike a fatal blow against Caesar before his reinforcements could arrive from across the sea.

At the same time he was assailing the Romans relentlessly on land, Achillas ordered his forces to attack the Roman ships in the harbor. He knew that if he could eliminate the Roman fleet Caesar would be totally cut off from the outside world. With the stakes so high, both sides fought ferociously to gain the advantage. The Romans finally pushed the Alexandrians back, after destroying many of their ships. But realizing he could not defend so many of his own vessels with so few men, Caesar put most of his fleet to the torch to prevent the enemy from capturing them. Burning his transport home was an understandable though drastic step, but his troops apparently acted with such haste that the fire soon spread beyond the ships to the docks, warehouses, and uphill to the great library. Scholars still argue whether or not the fire completely destroyed this treasury of ancient literature, but even if the flames consumed only a fraction of the scrolls, the loss to scholarship remains immeasurable.

Almost immediately after burning the ships, Caesar moved to secure his still-threatened access to the sea by launching an assault on the island of Pharos at the mouth of the harbor. The Romans landed on the eastern end of the island and seized the nearby residential neighborhoods as well as the lighthouse itself. With a garrison on the island controlling the harbor entrance, Roman ships were assured safe passage to and from the royal quarter of the city. Although Caesar doesn't mention it in his concise narrative, he must have climbed the many steps to the top of the lighthouse to enjoy the magnificent view.

▨

Inside the palace, Caesar was facing more than just military problems. Cleopatra's young but precocious sister, Arsinoe, escaped confinement along with her capable tutor, a eunuch named Ganymedes, and fled to Achillas. Caesar had intended to make Arsinoe the puppet ruler of Cyprus along with her brother Ptolemy XIV, the youngest of the four siblings, but now she was enthusiastically hailed as queen of Egypt by the Alexandrians. Achillas soon resented the interference of Arsinoe, who, like her sister, was much more intelligent and assertive than her brothers. She quarreled repeatedly with Achillas over the leadership of the Egyptian army. Then, after buying the loyalty of his troops, she had him murdered. After his death, Ganymedes took command of the troops in Arsinoe's name.

The new leader of the Egyptian army struck at Caesar in a very clever fashion. Alexandria had a sophisticated subterranean conduit system that brought water from the distant Nile directly into the homes of private citizens. The main canal carrying the water from the river passed through the southern part of the city with pipes branching off into every neighborhood. Ganymedes realized that since his forces held the parts of the town near the main canal, he could control the water to Caesar's entire army. But cutting off the water supply entirely as Caesar had done to Pompey at Dyrrachium was impossible given the complex nature of the conduit system, so Ganymedes instead began pumping seawater into the pipes heading to the palace. At first the legionaries couldn't understand why their water was suddenly tasting so brackish. Then they realized they were the victims of enemy sabotage.

Caesar's men could stand weeks of endless battle on little food, but the prospect of dying of thirst threw them into a panic. They rose up and begged Caesar to abandon Egypt at once. Caesar did not respond in anger as he had when mutiny threatened in years past, but instead explained to his men that retreat was both impossible and unnecessary. They could not abandon their defensive positions in the city even for a moment without the Alexandrians seeing what was happening. This was not Gaul with hills and forests to hide an army behind, but a city where the enemy was practically on top of them. The instant they began to pull back the Egyptians would break through the barricades and overwhelm them as they tried to reach the ships. In any event, they were not dependent on Ganymedes for water. The Alexandrians piped in all their water from the Nile because the population was too large to rely on wells—but there was always fresh water for those willing to do a little digging. The Roman soldiers took heart from Caesar's words and dug enthusiastically through the night. By morning they had struck an abundant vein of sweet water.

The spirits of the Romans were lifted again when a messenger arrived from Caesar's lieutenant Domitius Calvinus announcing that he was anchored just down the African coast with fresh supplies in a fleet of merchant ships. A strong east wind was all that was holding them back from Alexandria as they had only sails to power them. Caesar was desperate for the supplies Calvinus brought, so he decided to mount a risky rescue operation. He set off from the docks of the royal quarter, but as he could spare no troops from the barricades to serve as marines, his small fleet was manned only by rowers. Caesar sailed west along the coast for a few miles until he found Calvinus, tied the supply ships to his own, and began to tow them back to the city. However, several of Caesar's men who had gone ashore nearby were captured and revealed to the Egyptians that the Romans had no soldiers on board the ships. When this news was relayed to the Alexandrians, the experienced sailors of the city rushed to pounce on Caesar as he returned.

Caesar had expected just such a trap and held his ships in tight formation when the Alexandrians drew near. One of the remaining Roman ships from the island of Rhodes brazenly steered too close to shore and was set upon by the Egyptians smelling easy prey. Caesar was tempted to leave the Rhodians to the fate they deserved, but seeing how they fought with uncommon bravery, he ordered his fleet into action. Even without soldiers on board, the Romans soon captured one Egyptian ship, sank another, and killed many of the enemy. Towing the relief ships behind, that evening Caesar's flotilla rowed back into the harbor of Alexandria in triumph.

The Alexandrians were deeply distressed by Caesar's naval victory. They had lost only a few ships in the battle, but over the course of the last few weeks Caesar's forces had slowly destroyed most of their fleet. Since they had long prided themselves on their renowned skill as sailors, they began to have serious doubts about the war. If we can't even beat this Roman at sea, they asked themselves, how can we overcome him on land? Will he use his ships to attack parts of the city we had thought safe? Is Alexandria doomed?

Ganymedes knew that such uncertainty was far more dangerous to the Egyptian cause than any Roman military threat, so he declared to the people that they would build an even bigger and better navy than they had before. We are Alexandrians, he reminded them, trained from childhood to sail the seas. We can construct and outfit a mighty fleet that will cut Caesar off from the world once and for all.

The Alexandrians shouted their approval and threw themselves into the task of building ships. Since the Romans controlled the eastern harbor, they worked in the western part of the city beyond the causeway to Pharos Island. Lacking enough wood, the Alexandrians tore the rafters from public buildings to make oars. They also sent for the customs ships patrolling the Nile and resurrected ancient vessels rotting in the shipyards. The whole town worked with such spirit and energy that in just a few days they had outfitted twenty-seven warships as well as a number of smaller craft. The ships weren't sturdy enough to survive a distant ocean voyage, but close to shore they were an awesome force.

Caesar watched the construction of the Egyptian fleet and knew a great battle was inevitable. Rather than wait for the Alexandrians to choose the time and place, Caesar gathered ships from Rhodes and Asia Minor, manned them with Roman soldiers, and sailed out of the harbor and westward to the far side of Pharos Island. There his outnumbered ships drew up facing the Egyptian fleet and dared them to attack. The Alexandrians also prepared for battle, putting most of their warships in the front line armed with marines and artillery to launch flaming arrows.

A hush fell over both sides as the Romans and Egyptians waited to see who would move first into the narrow channel. At last, a Rhodian captain named Euphranor shouted: "Leave it to us, Caesar! We'll begin the battle and won't let you down. The rest can follow behind." Caesar applauded the Rhodians and gave the signal to advance. Euphranor and his four warships headed for the Egyptian fleet. It was a tight squeeze, but with practiced skill the Rhodians rammed the first enemy vessels and sheared off their oars without suffering any damage themselves. The remaining Roman ships followed and the battle was under way.

All along the rooftops of the city, thousands of Alexandrians watched, cheering when their side seemed to gain the upper hand and howling when the Romans pulled ahead. If the Egyptian fleet could win, the citizens knew they would sail triumphantly into the eastern harbor and attack the palace itself. The Roman soldiers in the city also watched, knowing that everything depended on the success of their fleet. If the Alexandrians won, they would at last be trapped without supplies or hope of reinforcement. But fortune continued to smile on the Romans as Caesar's fleet gained the upper hand and drove the enemy fleet back to shore, sinking three warships and capturing two. For the time being at least, the Romans maintained control of the eastern harbor.

⬚

Caesar was elated at the performance of his crews, but he knew the Alexandrians would strike again unless he gained mastery of the sea by seizing all of Pharos and the causeway connecting it to the city. He already controlled the area around the lighthouse, but he now launched a naval assault on the main part of the island with a fleet of small ships packed with several thousand troops. At first it was a replay of the disastrous invasion of Britain. The beach was heavily guarded by islanders, who knew the lay of the land and prevented the Romans from gaining a foothold. The defenders fought on shore and from fast ships while launching spears and arrows at the Romans from the roofs of nearby buildings. Finally, a few of the legionaries struggled onto land and held a beachhead while the rest of the troops came ashore. The islanders fell back to defend their homes, but soon panicked and fled down the causeway or began swimming for the mainland. Caesar's troops killed many on the run and captured 6,000 prisoners for the slave markets. The Romans were granted permission to plunder the island, then ordered to demolish all the buildings. Caesar wanted to make a vivid impression on the people of Alexandria that this was the fate awaiting the mainland unless they came to terms.

But the Alexandrians were among the most tenacious foes Caesar had encountered in his many years at war. They were fighting to preserve not only their lives but their freedom and independence from Rome. Accordingly, they refused to surrender even an inch of their city to Caesar without bloodshed. The Romans satisfied themselves that evening with seizing the northern end of the mile-long causeway to Pharos and fortifying it with a barricade and garrison. The Alexandrians held the end closer to the city with hundreds of their own soldiers.

The next morning the Roman troops with Caesar in the lead attacked the southern end of the causeway. It was an awkward battlefield, long and narrow, so that there was no room for most of the Roman troops to advance by foot toward the city. The majority stayed on the ships on the eastern side of the causeway and launched artillery at the Alexandrian positions. The defenders countered with a rain of spears and arrows from ships on the western side and from buildings on shore. The battle raged for hours with the Romans slowly gaining ground until Egyptian ships began landing behind the legionaries and attacking them from the rear. The thousand or so Roman troops on the causeway were now facing the enemy on both sides with no room to maneuver. Alarm gripped even the veteran troops, who began to dive into the water in full battle armor and swim for their nearby ships. The commanders of the Roman fleet, however, fearing the Alexandrians would capture their vessels, had pulled away from the causeway to open water.

Caesar tried to restore order to his soldiers but the panic spread like wildfire. Those soldiers who made it to the fleet began pulling themselves into the overloaded ships until they started to capsize, throwing even more troops into the water. The frantic legionaries even forced their way onto Caesar's small ship until it began to sink. Realizing what was about to happen, Caesar jumped into the harbor fully clothed and began to swim toward Pharos. He had mastered swimming in the Tiber as a boy, but as a man of fifty-two years in heavy armor hundreds of yards from shore, he was in serious danger of drowning. Nonetheless, he was determined not to damage some important papers in his possession and held them in his left hand above the water as the arrows poured down on him. Some sources say he gripped his purple general's cloak in his teeth as he swam to the beach, but others record that the Alexandrians seized the cloak as a trophy and hung it up for all to see. Whatever the truth, Caesar finally struggled to shore but had lost an astonishing 400 soldiers and even more sailors in the bungled attempt to take the causeway. The Romans continued to hold Pharos, but the Alexandrians had won a crucial military and moral victory.

Far from being demoralized by their defeat, Caesar's troops were energized to fight even harder against the Alexandrians. The Romans hated to think that Egyptians could get the better of them. All along the lines the legionaries pushed the Alexandrians back in fierce street battles that raged around the clock. The citizens of the city were amazed to see that the Roman soldiers took heart from a setback that would have left any other army in despair.

Whether out of genuine weariness of the war or—as is more likely—because of a nefarious plot by the anti-Arsinoe faction at the Egyptian court, the Alexandrians sent an embassy to ask Caesar if he might release their young king. They claimed they were weary of Arsinoe and the tyrannical Ganymedes. If only they had Ptolemy to guide them, they might come to terms with Caesar. The king's inspired leadership could persuade those recalcitrant citizens among them to reach some mutually acceptable accord with the Romans.

Caesar was highly suspicious of this proposition, but he carefully weighed the pros and cons of handing over young Ptolemy to the Alexandrians. The boy clearly had no military skills or leadership abilities to inspire his people, so he was no direct threat to the Romans. Inside the palace he was a constant irritation to his sister Cleopatra, who would undoubtedly be thrilled to see him go. And there was always the slim chance, Caesar considered, that at least some of the Alexandrians sincerely wanted peace. In that case, releasing the king to their custody might smooth the way to a graceful victory.

However, Caesar placed little hope in the good intentions of the Egyptians. Whatever their reasons for wanting the king back, he believed he could use Ptolemy's departure to serve his own goals. If the king turned against him, as was almost certain, Caesar would look better defeating an army led by a legitimate monarch than one commanded by a devious queen and her eunuch general. More crucially, Ptolemy would be a source of division within the Alexandrian leadership. Some would champion him while others backed his more cunning sister, so that dissension would spread throughout the enemy camp like a virus. And, of course, once the Alexandrians had been defeated, Caesar could dismiss Ptolemy as a rebel and retain the cooperative Cleopatra on the throne.

Young Ptolemy shed crocodile tears as he took his leave of Caesar, claiming he would much rather stay with the Romans than return to his own people. But as Caesar suspected, as soon as Ptolemy was back with the Alexandrians he declared Caesar his mortal enemy. Some of the Romans thought their general had been duped, but Caesar had known all along exactly what he was doing. The Alexandrians quickly began to weaken themselves with factional fighting. Arsinoe was forced to yield leadership to her brother, while the capable general Ganymedes was pushed into the background to make room for Ptolemy's less talented advisers.

The new Alexandrian leadership was notably unsuccessful in waging war over the next few weeks. When they heard a convoy of supplies for the besieged Romans was on the way along the coast, they sent their navy to lie in wait near the mouth of the Nile. But Caesar received word of their plan and sent Tiberius Nero—father of the future emperor Tiberius—to intercept them. The Romans routed the Egyptian fleet, but lost the daring Rhodian captain Euphranor and his ship when he pursued the enemy with too much vigor.

In early March, news arrived at the Roman camp that Mithridates of Pergamum, the man Caesar had sent away weeks earlier to raise a relief force, was fast approaching the eastern end of the Nile delta near Pelusium. Mithridates brought Caesar a fresh army gathered from Arabia, Syria, and Palestine, including a contingent of three thousand Jewish troops. These had been sent by the Judean ruler and high priest Hyrcanus, but the force behind the throne was his gifted minister Antipater, father of Herod the Great. The Jews of Palestine were natural allies of Caesar since they had suffered greatly at the hands of Pompey, who had defiled the great temple in Jerusalem and stripped Judea of much of its territory during his eastern campaign. A new alliance with Caesar at this crucial moment, Antipater hoped, would strengthen the Jewish state. Hyrcanus and Antipater could also provide crucial help in swaying Alexandria's large Jewish population to Caesar's side.

The army of Mithridates took Pelusium after a fierce battle and headed southwest around the Nile delta, rather than cross the many waterways and marshes along the more direct path to Alexandria. Near modern Cairo Mithridates turned to follow the western branch of the Nile toward Alexandria. Ptolemy's army quickly left the city and sailed up the river to confront the outnumbered Mithridates. As soon as he saw the enemy soldiers leaving town, Caesar gathered every man he could spare and sailed east out of the harbor in pursuit. But to avoid a naval battle with the king, the Romans secretly backtracked that night and landed west of Alexandria. From there they marched double-time around Lake Mareotis and joined Mithridates before the Egyptian army arrived.

Ptolemy's soldiers disembarked from the ships and set up camp on a high point just west of the river. Caesar pushed close to the enemy camp by using his German cavalry to scatter the Egyptians, then made his own camp near the king's army to await the dawn. On the next day, March 27, 47 B.C., the Romans attacked the Alexandrian forces. It was a tough uphill struggle that lasted hours beneath the

Egyptian sun until finally, Caesar's men drove the enemy toward the Nile and slaughtered them. Young king Ptolemy himself fled the battle, but drowned in the river when his boat overturned. Caesar was so elated with the victory after three months of bitter struggle that he rode with his cavalry all the way back to Alexandria that very night. The citizens of the city rightly feared for their lives and met Caesar at the gates dressed as suppliants, begging him to spare their city the accustomed fate of conquered people. Caesar must have been tempted to sell the whole lot into slavery for the trouble they had caused him, but he was realistic enough to know that the commercial benefits of a flourishing Alexandria far outweighed any satisfaction from revenge. He pardoned the Alexandrians and made his way back to the palace and Cleopatra.

The next day Caesar began to reorganize the government of Egypt. The will of Ptolemy Auletes designated Cleopatra as joint ruler with her brother, the now deceased Ptolemy XIII, so Caesar fulfilled at least the spirit of the bequest by appointing the twelve-year-old Ptolemy XIV as the new coregent with Cleopatra. The two monarchs were also granted sovereignty over Cyprus—an arrangement that must have been particularly galling to Cato, who had worked so hard years before to organize direct Roman rule of the island. Although Ptolemy XIV officially held equal sway with Cleopatra, he lacked any real power, just as Caesar had planned. The rebellious sister Arsinoe was put in chains and sent to Rome to march in Caesar's future triumphal parade along with Vercingetorix. To make sure everyone behaved, Caesar ordered three of his legions to remain in Egypt.

Why didn't Caesar now annex Egypt as he had planned to do so many years before? He had conquered the Alexandrians in war and could have easily pacified any resistance in the south with the troops he had available. All the resources of Egypt were now open to Rome, so all he had to do was appoint a governor to manage the new province. The explanation for Egypt's continued independence lies in Caesar's very astute deduction that any Roman governor of Egypt could become a powerful threat to him. If Roman senators were led astray by greed in poor provinces, the vast riches of the Nile valley would be too much temptation even for a ruler with the integrity of Cato. A rebellious governor could use Egypt as a power base to launch a rebellion or squeeze Rome with an embargo of essential grain. Caesar was wise enough to realize that Cleopatra, bound to him by ties of necessity even more than love, was the ideal lord of Egypt. Cleopatra needed Caesar's support to maintain her rule over the resentful Alexandrians. Without his legions behind her, the citizens of the city would rise up as they had so often against rulers in the past and drive her from her throne. But to make sure even the commander of Roman troops in Egypt would prove no threat, Caesar took the unprecedented step of appointing a trusted subordinate named Rufio, son of a former slave.

Caesar had now been in Egypt for almost eight months and away from Rome for over a year. It seemed certain that he would now hurry home to settle pressing affairs of state and organize strikes against the remaining Pompeian forces in Africa and Spain. Instead, what occurs next is one of the most puzzling interludes of Caesar's life. Rather than sailing for Rome, Caesar went on a monthlong luxury cruise up the Nile with Cleopatra. Ancient sources favoring Caesar as well as some perplexed modern scholars either omit or downplay this episode, but there can be little doubt that it did occur.

Why would the most ambitious man in Roman history pause in the middle of a civil war for a vacation? If Caesar was true to his character—and not merely suffering from an astonishing midlife crisis—we can be certain that he had a very good reason for the trip. Like Cleopatra, Caesar knew that the wealth of Egypt did not derive ultimately from Alexandria. Along the fertile Nile valley to the south was the true heart of the Mediterranean's oldest civilization. It was the rich, black soil of tens of thousands of farms from the pyramids to the first cataract of the Nile that fed much of the Roman world and filled the treasuries of Alexandria with gold. If Caesar wanted to hold Egypt for Rome, he had to secure the Nile valley. It is important to note that Caesar did not voyage up the Nile with just Cleopatra, but took along 400 ships full of Roman troops. If the natives of the south had any thoughts of rebellion, Caesar wanted to impress upon them that Rome was willing and able to crush them. Certainly the cruise was a well-deserved respite for Caesar after years of war, but it was more business than pleasure.

The final act of Caesar's visit to Egypt came later that spring when Cleopatra gave birth to their son. Cleopatra called him Ptolemy XV, but the Alexandrians mockingly gave him the Greek name Caesarion, "Little Caesar." Ancient historians struggled with the birth of this child, some omitting any reference to Caesarion or claiming Caesar was not the father. But again, there is little reason to doubt the truth of the matter as even friends of Caesar grudgingly acknowledged his paternity. In any case, Caesar would never have considered a son by the Egyptian queen as a threat to Rome, merely the product of a foreign liaison that might prove useful in assuring Cleopatra's continued loyalty. How Caesar's long-suffering wife Calpurnia reacted when she heard the news, we have no record.

XIII

AFRICA

> "I am not willing to be grateful to the tyrant Caesar
> for his criminal acts," said Cato. "And he most cer-
> tainly is a criminal who, like a master, grants mercy
> to those who are not slaves, but free men."
>
> —Plutarch

When Caesar finally left Alexandria in early June of 47 B.C.,
he began to receive detailed reports of just how badly things
had been going elsewhere in the Mediterranean during his months
in Egypt. In Africa, Cato, Scipio, Labienus, and many others had
joined forces with Caesar's old enemy King Juba of Numidia to form
a huge army just across the straits from Sicily. Led by Scipio and inspired by Cato, they controlled fourteen legions, thousands of Numidian cavalry, and several dozen war elephants. They were
threatening to invade Italy and had already launched raids on both
Sicily and Sardinia.

In Spain, Caesar squandered whatever popularity he had gained
after his recent victory by choosing Quintus Cassius Longinus as
governor in the further province. A land that had once been sympathetic to Caesar revolted against his appointee, who surpassed even
the most rapacious optimates in his greed and abuse of the natives.

After Longinus was driven out, Caesar's enemies found a warm welcome among the Spaniards.

But one of the worst blows to Caesar came from Pharnaces, a son of Mithridates the Great, who sailed from his kingdom in the Crimea to reclaim his father's empire in Asia Minor. Caesar's lieutenant Domitius Calvinus met Pharnaces with the help of Galatian troops led by King Deiotarus. Domitius was anxious to reach Caesar in Egypt as soon as possible and so engaged the enemy in haste. Most of his army was thereby lost, though he managed to flee to safety in the Roman province of Asia. Pharnaces enthusiastically seized his father's old domain of Pontus on the north coast and promptly castrated all the Roman citizens he could find.

Even in Rome, chaos was threatening to destroy Caesar's vision for a new world order. He had been woefully out of touch with events in the capital—Cicero says that no one in Rome had received a message from Caesar in over six months. In his absence Caesar had again been elected dictator, but Mark Antony served as his surrogate while he was in the East. Left to his own devices, Antony ruled Rome with casual brutality and unrestrained violence. Among a multitude of problems, murderous riots soon broke out anew between advocates of debtors and creditors. Instead of bringing order to Rome, Antony abandoned the city to quell the beginnings of rebellion among troops quartered near Naples. Rome soon degenerated into a madhouse of gang warfare and street battles. When Antony returned from Campania, the terrified Senate issued its ultimate decree authorizing him to bring peace to the capital by any means necessary. To Antony's mind, this meant sending troops into the city and killing hundreds of Roman citizens, throwing the worst offenders from the Tarpeian Rock on the Capitoline Hill. But even before the blood was dry, factional fighting was again sweeping Rome, leaving the citizens to wonder if the violence would ever end.

Caesar was deeply troubled by the news from Rome, but he believed it was vital to secure the eastern provinces before he headed west. Affairs in Egypt had been settled, yet internal dissention and external incursions still threatened Palestine, Syria, and Asia Minor. The success of Pharnaces demonstrated all too clearly that instability in Roman and allied territories was an invitation to foreign intervention, especially from the aggressive Parthian Empire. Caesar therefore decided to take the long way to Rome along the Mediterranean coast, rewarding those who had served him well, settling long-standing disputes, and strengthening the provinces and kingdoms of the east against Rome's enemies.

In Palestine, Caesar showed his gratitude to Hyrcanus for his help in Egypt by confirming him as king and high priest, as well as allowing the Jews to rebuild the walls of Jerusalem. Antipater was given Roman citizenship, a benefit he passed on to his son Herod. Caesar must have met this young man who would one day rebuild the great temple in Jerusalem and, according to the New Testament, kill all the young children around Bethlehem in an attempt to murder the infant Jesus.

Caesar's journey was also a major fund-raising expedition. He continued north into Lebanon, stopping at the city of Tyre to empty the temple of Hercules of its treasure. All along the coast he demanded for himself any money the provincials had earlier promised to Pompey, plus a little extra. He also encouraged the Oriental custom of granting golden crowns to traveling conquerors. Caesar did all this, the Roman biographer Dio Cassius records, not out of base greed but simply because his expenses were so vast. Machiavelli himself would have approved of Caesar's straightforward explanation of his actions:

> *There are two things that create, protect, and increase a sovereign's rule—soldiers and money—both being dependent on each other. Armies need money and money is acquired by the strength of arms. If you lose one, you lose the other.*

Caesar spent extra time in Syria settling disputes among local officials. This province was the front line of defense against the Parthians and had to be absolutely secure before he returned to Rome.
When he had finished, he moved on to the city of Tarsus in Asia Minor, calling together local officials and repentant Pompeians. Among
the latter was Gaius Cassius, a noted military commander under
Crassus and former admiral for Pompey who was destined to play a
central role in Caesar's assassination. Caesar was most gracious and
forgiving in his reception, especially as Cassius was warmly recommended by his brother-in-law Brutus. Cicero, however, claims that
even at this point Cassius was planning to murder Caesar.

Traveling north through the center of Asia Minor, Caesar next
came to the borders of Galatia and there met Deiotarus. The Galatian
leader appeared before Caesar without his royal insignia, dressed as a
humble suppliant to beg forgiveness for his earlier support of Pompey.
Deiotarus explained that he had been forced to support Caesar's foe
under threat of arms. In any case, he had felt it was no business of his to
judge the internal disputes of the Roman people. He was merely a
loyal ally of Rome doing his best in a dangerous corner of the world.

Caesar was not impressed by the arguments of this slippery old
monarch. He reminded Deiotarus that as consul twelve years earlier
he had personally confirmed his rule over Galatia before the Senate.
If gratitude for that action wasn't enough to win his loyalty, then the
fact that he was the lawfully elected consul of Rome when Deiotarus
took up arms against him nullified any excuses the king might offer.
However, since the king had long-standing ties to Rome, he was
willing to tolerate him for the moment—but he reserved the right to
judge him at a later date and demanded the use of his army in the
upcoming battle he was planning.

Pharnaces was just settling in as the new king of Pontus, in north-
eastern Asia Minor, when Caesar arrived at the border with his army

at the beginning of August in 47 B.C. The son of Mithridates could not believe how swiftly Caesar had crossed the mountains of Galatia to suddenly appear near the town of Zela in the hills of western Pontus, near the Black Sea. Pharnaces had sent embassies to Caesar bearing golden crowns as gifts and explaining he did not want a conflict with Rome, merely sovereignty over his ancestral lands. He was, so he claimed, more worthy of Caesar's friendship than Deiotarus as he himself had never provided any aid to Pompey. Caesar responded kindly enough at first so that he could gain time to move deep into Pontus, but he sent back the final messengers declaring there could be no peace with a man who mutilated Roman citizens.

Pharnaces occupied the hilltop fortress at Zela while Caesar made camp five miles away. But in the middle of the night, Caesar ordered his troops to build to a new camp only a mile away from Pharnaces on the opposite side of the precipitous valley. At dawn the legions were still digging trenches when they saw Pharnaces move his army into attack position outside his fortress. Caesar assumed this was just posturing and laughed when the Pontic forces began running down their hill toward the Roman camp. He knew that no general in his right mind would send troops down into a valley, then up a steep slope to attack an enemy. But whether very foolish or very brave, Pharnaces and his army kept coming.

Caesar shouted to his soldiers to throw down their shovels and grab their weapons just as the first war chariots burst into the Roman camp. Caesar was caught totally off guard by this unexpected attack, and the legionaries panicked at the sight of enemy chariots with scythed wheels tearing toward them. But the Romans quickly pulled themselves together and turned to face the enemy charging their unfinished walls. It was bitter hand-to-hand fighting at first, but soon the Romans began to push the Pontic forces back down the hill. The enemy began to fall on top of their comrades as they fled while the Roman troops mercilessly cut them down.

Caesar was so pleased with the speedy and successful outcome of the war that he allowed his men to plunder the royal fortress and keep all the booty for themselves. He then summed up the campaign for his friends in Rome with words of immortal brevity:

Veni. Vidi. Vici.
(I came. I saw. I conquered.)

From Pontus, Caesar traveled west to the coast of Asia Minor collecting money and rendering judgments along the way. To Mithridates of Pergamum, who had provided crucial assistance to him in Egypt, he granted portions of Pontus and Galatia as a reward. Deiotarus lost part of his kingdom and paid a hefty fine, but Brutus, because of previous financial connections to the king, persuaded Caesar to spare the ruler any further punishment for his previous alliance with Pompey.

From the coast of Roman Asia, Caesar sailed for Italy as quickly as possible. Waiting for him in Brundisium was a very nervous Cicero, who, though he was terrified of Caesar's reaction to his support for Pompey, nevertheless felt it was best to face the dictator as soon as possible. When Caesar saw Cicero on the road he jumped down from his horse, rushed up to the orator, and embraced him with genuine affection. The two continued down the Appian Way in conversation for several miles, walking side by side as the rest of Caesar's party followed behind.

The first thing Caesar did when he reached Rome was to punish Mark Antony for his profligate living and gross misuse of power. Caesar could forgive Antony a great deal because of his loyalty, but his infamous drunkenness, greed, robbery, violence, and shameful neglect of the city's affairs had put Caesar in an untenable situation with the Roman public. Cicero later accused Antony, among other scandals, of making every dining room in his house a tavern and every bedroom a brothel. Accordingly, he was removed from office and languished in political limbo for the next two years. Caesar did not want to permanently alienate Antony as he might prove useful in the future, but his headstrong assistant needed the firmest of reproaches for the sake of Caesar's image.

The advocates of loan forgiveness hoped Caesar would at last issue a general cancellation of debts, especially as he owed more money to creditors than any man in Rome. Instead, Caesar again sided with Rome's powerful financial community and demanded full repayment. He appeared to be the model of justice, claiming that it would be unfair to issue a decree that would benefit himself more than any other. But in fact he forced everyone else to repay their loans while he neglected to settle his own debts. To curry the favor of the lower classes, however, he greatly reduced rents for a full year and increased free food distribution.

During his short stay in Rome, Caesar also raised money for his African campaign by auctioning the property of his deceased enemies to the highest bidders. Mark Antony hoped that his old commander might let him pick up Pompey's estate as a bargain, but Caesar demanded full price. Only Caesar's former mistress Servilia was allowed to buy choice properties at a below-market rate. Some claimed that this was because she was now prostituting her own daughter, Tertia, to Caesar. Cicero wittily remarked that Servilia's purchases were discounted by a third (Latin *tertia*).

Finally, Caesar reorganized the government to function more smoothly during his upcoming absence. As his dictatorship was coming to an end, he had himself selected as consul for the next year with his trustworthy but undistinguished follower Marcus Lepidus as co-consul. He also increased the number of praetors and priests to reward those who had supported him at Rome or on the battlefield. Most shockingly to the conservative nobility, he appointed lowly centurions and other loyal soldiers from his army to fill many of the empty seats in the Senate.

Caesar's plans for a speedy departure for Africa were put on hold when he received alarming news that his legions in southern Italy were on the march toward Rome. Trouble had been brewing in the legionary camps for months. Many of Caesar's men had been serving him for years without their promised discharge, bonuses, or gift of land. Gaul, Italy, Spain, Greece, Egypt, Asia—the wars seemed to stretch on with no end in sight. The men loved Caesar and had served him faithfully, but they were tired. Many who had joined the legions as teenagers were now nearing thirty and ready to settle down. All they wanted was a nice bit of farmland, a pretty girl to marry, and a bagful of silver coins to spend at the local tavern. They had waited patiently, but enough was enough. A few days later when the troops arrived in Rome, they camped outside the walls north of the city and refused to move until they received their due.

Although his friends could not believe it, Caesar rode out to the riotous legionary camp alone. Before anyone knew how he had gotten there, Caesar suddenly appeared on a platform at the center of the camp. When all the troops had gathered around him, Caesar calmly asked what they wanted. The soldiers were so stunned by the presence of their commander that they couldn't bring themselves to mention money or land, but only asked that they be discharged as he had promised long ago. Like children expecting a scolding, they waited for Caesar to yell at them, berate them as cowards, and scorn them as unworthy to wear the uniforms of Roman soldiers, but instead he looked down at them with profound disappointment and said—"*I discharge you.*"

The soldiers who had fought side by side with him against the ferocious Germans and Gauls, sailed with him across the unknown sea to Britain, and stood by him against enemies from the shores of the Atlantic to the streets of Alexandria were speechless. In the silence that followed, Caesar curtly told them that they would receive everything he had promised them when he returned in triumph from Africa with other soldiers marching behind him. But the greatest blow came when he concluded his address by calling them "citizens" rather than "my fellow soldiers" as he had done for so many years.

At these words they all collapsed into tears and begged Caesar to disregard their foolish request. They would gladly follow him to Africa or anywhere he might lead for as long as he wished. They could not bear the shame of waiting in Italy while he defeated the last of his enemies with fresh recruits. But Caesar sadly turned away from them and walked off the platform. The troops called on him to stop, to please reconsider. The tenth legion, long Caesar's favorite, begged him to execute soldiers chosen from among them by lot as punishment for their betrayal of his trust. He paused at the edge of the stairs and seemed to hesitate, then returned to the stage. He reluctantly forgave the troops, then vowed that on their return from Africa they would obtain everything they had been waiting for all these years. Every soldier would receive his discharge, money, and a donation of land from the public domain or his own estates if necessary. The troops shouted themselves hoarse with thanks and praise, reveling in the fact that they were once again in the good graces of their commander.

Caesar was finally ready to sail for Africa to face the remaining optimates. He left Rome even before his troops were ready and arrived at Lilybaeum (modern Marsala), in westernmost Sicily by the middle of December. The only soldiers he had at first were one small legion of fresh recruits and a few hundred cavalry, but he was impatient to begin the war. The troops were terrified that Caesar was planning to take them across the stormy Mediterranean in midwinter. To calm the nervous legionaries, he planned a public sacrifice to the gods to ensure a safe voyage, but the intended animal bolted and ran away from the altar as soon as he raised the knife—a horrible omen. Still, Caesar pitched his tent on the beach facing Africa as a sign he was eager to leave as soon as the weather allowed. He ordered his army to be ready to depart at a moment's notice.

Some of the troops had whispered that the expedition was doomed to failure unless they were accompanied by a member of the famous Scipio family, an heir to the great Scipio Africanus, who had defeated Hannibal on his native soil two centuries earlier. The optimates were led on the battlefield by their own Scipio, a proven general of the same lineage, who had commanded the center legions for Pompey at Pharsalus. To counter these fears Caesar brought along a ridiculous character named Scipio Salvito, a distant relative of the illustrious family. Although he was nothing more than a professional mime by trade, Caesar planned to put the poor man on the front lines to inspire the troops.

For a week Caesar sat on the beach and watched the storms rage. More legions arrived from Italy, but his forces were still greatly outnumbered by the immense army across the sea. At last Caesar could wait no longer and ordered his troops to board the ships. The captains asked which harbor they should steer for, but Caesar knew there was no safe landing site in Africa. He therefore trusted to fortune that they would find a secure port once they arrived.

The expedition was plagued with disasters from the start. The ships were scattered by storms as they crossed to Africa, leaving Caesar only one legion and a few dozen cavalry when he finally arrived near the coastal settlement of Hadrumetum, in modern Tunisia. Caesar landed near the town and jumped out of his ship, but in his haste he stumbled and fell on his face. The sight of their commander crashing to the ground with his first step on enemy soil sent a gasp through the superstitious troops. But Caesar was nothing if not quick-witted. He quickly grabbed a handful of sand and turned the omen to his favor shouting—"*I hold you now, Africa!*"

Caesar made camp in front of Hadrumetum and rode around the town looking for weaknesses. Unfortunately for him, the walls were strongly defended by an optimate garrison led by Gaius Considius. Caesar realized he couldn't take the well-fortified town with his small army, so he turned to diplomacy in hopes that he could persuade Considius to surrender. He sent a prisoner into the town bearing a message for the commander, but when the man arrived Considius first asked him who wrote the letter. "Caesar," the prisoner responded, "the commander-in-chief." Considius sneered at the man and declared, "There is presently only one commander of the Roman people—our leader Scipio." He then had the messenger executed.

Since there was no point in remaining at Hadrumetum, Caesar struck camp and headed southwest toward the city of Leptis Magna to await the ships bearing the rest of his army. This retreat was an ignominious beginning to the war, especially as Caesar's troops were harried, as they withdrew, by emboldened townsfolk from Hadrumetum and some Numidian horsemen, who happened to be passing through the area. Caesar's Gallic cavalry and veterans held back the Africans as the rest of the troops moved out, but it was a slow and discouraging march south along the coast.

Caesar's men had never faced an enemy like the Numidian cavalry of King Juba. The Africans had no trouble finding forage in the desert, while the Romans were reduced to feeding their horses seaweed. The Numidians would appear like ghosts out of the hills and strike when least expected, then disappear. It didn't help that Caesar's Gaulish cavalry were easily distracted. One night when some of his horsemen were off duty they were enchanted by an African musician who could dance and play the flute at the same time. They were sitting around a fire applauding the performer when a band of Numidians suddenly appeared from the shadows and began to cut them down. Only Caesar's chance arrival saved them all from slaughter.

A few more of the scattered ships caught up with Caesar at Leptis Magna, but he was still woefully short of men and supplies. Numidian cavalry repeatedly attacked any foraging parties venturing into the nearby hills, prompting Caesar to dispatch messengers back across the sea to order more men and all the food the ships could carry. In the meantime, the army was becoming ever more worried. What was their commander planning to do next? How could he feed them? How could they fight such a treacherous enemy? It was only Caesar's inexhaustible energy and good cheer that kept the men going during those first dark days of the campaign.

They would soon need every bit of courage they could muster. Caesar decided the only way he could feed his army was to lead a major raiding expedition into the surrounding countryside. He set off with his men at a fast march into the interior and had proceeded a few miles when he saw a dust cloud approaching. Caesar knew these were thousands of Numidian cavalry who would overtake his foot soldiers if he tried to flee, so he told his men to put on their armor and prepare for the fight of their lives.

The cavalry was led by none other than Labienus, the most talented of Caesar's enemies in the art of war. Labienus had served as Caesar's loyal lieutenant in Gaul, but by the time his commander had crossed the Rubicon, Labienus had become his bitter enemy. Pompey fought to preserve his honor, Cato to save his beloved Republic, but Labienus fought out of a burning hatred for Caesar. In any other period of Roman history, Labienus would have been the greatest general of his age, but he had the misfortune of living under the shadow of Caesar. Doomed for so many years to second-rank status, Labienus yearned for nothing more than to grind Caesar into the dust. Now at last, it seemed his chance had come.

Labienus ordered his Numidian horsemen into a tightly packed line that some of the Romans mistook at first for infantry. But as they approached, the men realized what Caesar had known from the start—they were facing an enormous force of cavalry that would very likely cut them to pieces. In response, Caesar drew up his men in a single line to face the enemy. Positioning his soldiers with no reserves behind them was unusual but necessary since his numbers were so small, though it left Caesar's legions particularly vulnerable to being flanked by Labienus's cavalry. The Romans were so terrified that one standard-bearer bolted and tried to run back to camp, only to have Caesar grab him by the neck and shout, "The enemy is *that* way!"

Labienus ordered his cavalry to strike at the two ends of Caesar's forces. Just as the Romans had feared, the Numidians poured around their line and encircled them. Caesar was now in the worst situation any general could imagine—completely surrounded by a superior enemy. He ordered his men to quickly reform in two lines back-to-back facing outward against the enemy, but even the bravest legionaries knew they stood little chance of surviving.

Labienus knew it too. He rode up and down the lines taunting his former comrades:

> *How's it going, recruit?*
> *My, you look ferocious.*
> *Looks like Caesar's led you all astray.*
> *You're up to your necks in it now, boys.*
> *Sure wish I could help.*

One of Caesar's veterans tore off his helmet so Labienus could recognize him and shouted back that he was no raw recruit, but a veteran of the famous Tenth legion. The soldier then threw his javelin at Labienus with all his might, missing the general, but skewering his horse and sending Labienus tumbling into the dust.

Caesar had no time to savor the moment as the Numidians dragged Labienus off the field. He knew their only hope was to reach a nearby hill, so he ordered his men to begin a slow retreat while they maintained their double-sided formation. It was slow and awkward with many men falling to enemy spears and arrows as they inched along, but somehow in the hours before dusk Caesar and his troops reached the high ground. Here where infantry had the advantage over cavalry, the legionaries were finally able to hold their own and drive back Labienus's men. The enemy at last withdrew and the Roman survivors made their way back to camp, but Caesar knew it was only by the grace of the gods that his army had escaped destruction that day.

In spite of the fact that he had lost the battle, Labienus was greatly encouraged. He had bloodied Caesar and shown his men that the legendary Roman leader was vulnerable. Caesar and his troops were ill prepared to fight in the desert, said Labienus, especially against thousands of Numidian cavalry so skilled on horseback that they rode without bridles. In addition, the optimates had thousands of Roman soldiers battle-hardened by life in Africa, along with countless archers, slingers, Gallic and German mercenaries, and more than a hundred elephants. Labienus assured his men they had nothing to fear from Caesar, who could barely escape alive from a little foray into the countryside.

News of Caesar's troubles spread quickly throughout the Mediterranean, encouraging his enemies. In Syria, a former Pompeian named Caecilius Bassus killed Caesar's kinsman Sextus Caesar and seized the province. In Rome, Cicero gleefully shared the latest rumors of Caesar's demise. But the reports of doom and gloom did not reflect reality. Caesar's men were tired and hungry, but they never lost faith in their commander, even when an unnaturally ferocious thunderstorm charged the air with such electricity that the spear points of the fifth legion danced with St. Elmo's fire.

More legions and supplies trickled in as the weeks passed, not to mention a number of deserters from the optimate army who were growing increasingly disgruntled about fighting against their fellow Romans. Caesar skillfully played on this discontent with a propaganda campaign aimed at national pride. He portrayed Scipio and the optimates as cowardly servants of the barbarian king Juba and promised any man who would come over to his side an equal share of the spoils with his own troops. Scipio circulated his own pamphlets in response but promised no rewards, only tepid exhortations to save the Roman state. Caesar even managed to win over the crucial backing of the Gaetulian natives in the interior since he was the nephew of Gaius Marius, a man still revered by many Africans for his patronage sixty years earlier. The Mauritanians also joined Caesar's war effort with coordinated attacks on Numidia's western border that drew Juba and his army away from the Romans, at least temporarily.

The African war dragged on through the first months of 46 B.C. with neither side able to gain a clear advantage. Scipio and Labienus struck repeatedly at Caesar's smaller force, but resisted the temptation to face him in a major battle. They knew if they could deny Caesar any clear victory in Africa, his men would grow weary of the fight while his political support throughout the empire would begin to waver. Caesar himself knew that he could not win the respect of the Roman world with an endless war of attrition or even a victory that cost the lives of countless soldiers. He needed a stunning triumph over the optimates in Africa to silence his critics once and for all. Though he hated delay, he knew he had to await more reinforcements to strike decisively at the optimates.

The ships did come, but slowly and not always without incident. One warship from Sicily carrying a squadron of veterans became separated from the rest of its fleet and was captured by Scipio's men. The legionaries on board were imprisoned, but treated well by the optimates. They were brought before Scipio, who decided to win them over to his cause through mercy. He commended their bravery in service to Caesar and assured them that he held no grudge against them for fighting against their fellow Romans. They were but pawns in a political game beyond their control. If they would join his army and become true patriots, he would grant them their lives and richly reward them.

Scipio was certain the prisoners would jump at the chance to save their own lives, but a centurion of the Fourteenth legion arose and spoke for them all:

> We thank you for your benevolence, Scipio—please forgive me for not addressing you as commander in chief. We are most grateful that you promise us our lives as is due lawful prisoners of war. We would choose life, but the conditions you attach to your offer are unacceptable. We will never fight against Caesar.

The centurion suggested instead that Scipio choose a few thousand of his best men to fight against ten of them that they might demonstrate the true worth of Caesar's men. Scipio was livid at the insolence of these veterans and ordered them to be tortured to death outside the walls of the camp.

By the beginning of April, Caesar was at last ready to risk a great battle. More legions had arrived from Italy, but he was still outnumbered by Scipio's forces and those of King Juba, who had returned from the western marches of his kingdom. Caesar needed to force Scipio into a fight on a battlefield that would limit the advantage of his numbers. So on April 4, Caesar and his legions arrived before the coastal town of Thapsus and began to lay siege.

Thapsus was held by an optimate garrison that immediately sent to Scipio for help. He might have ignored the request and left the soldiers to hold out as best they could, but Scipio realized that this was his golden opportunity. Like Alexandria, Thapsus lay on a narrow isthmus with the sea on one side and a wide salt marsh on the other. If the optimates could block both ends, Caesar would have no means of escape. They could then squeeze him in a vise and overwhelm his army. He ordered Juba and Afranius to bar the southern escape route while he took his legions, cavalry, and elephants in from the west.

Caesar was now trapped—but it was exactly what he had intended. By luring Scipio into open battle Caesar was taking a terrible risk, but he was gambling that he could win. The neck of land across which Scipio would have to approach was narrow, reducing the number of men he could place on his front lines. It was a classic maneuver that had been used by the Spartans at Thermopylae and the Athenians at Salamis, but could easily turn into a massacre if the enemy broke through.

On the morning of April 6, Caesar and Scipio faced one another at last. Caesar saw that his adversary had deployed his elephants on his right and left wings to break through his lines. Elephants were terrifying in battle, but they were almost impossible to control and were vulnerable to a steady rain of spears and arrows. Caesar therefore placed his most experienced veterans on each of his own wings to face the beasts.

Caesar noticed that the enemy lines seemed unusually disorganized. There was always some confusion before a battle, but Scipio's men were running in all directions in a most undisciplined fashion. Caesar's officers noticed this as well and urged Caesar to attack at once. Their commander snapped at them that they would move only when he was ready and not a moment before. Suddenly on Caesar's right wing, a trumpeter sounded the charge. The men began to rush forward even though the centurions tried to force them back, but there was no stopping the eager soldiers. Caesar knew it was too late, so he gave the command to advance and joined in the charge.

Although Caesar's men began before their commander was ready, they attacked Scipio's army with tremendous success. The slingers and archers on each wing launched a barrage against the elephants that caused the animals to suddenly turn and run the other way. One wounded elephant was so crazed that it pinned down a camp follower from Caesar's army who had somehow wandered onto the battlefield and began crushing him. A veteran from the lines rushed up to save the man only to have the elephant grab him with its trunk and lift him into the air. The soldier then hacked at the elephant with all his might until it finally dropped him and ran away.

Scipio's men collapsed in panic at the ferocity of Caesar's veterans. After years of fighting, the men who had followed him across the Roman world were determined to end the war once and for all. They killed over ten thousand of Scipio's troops—Roman and African alike—paying no heed to cries for mercy. The men ignored Caesar's direct orders to disengage and even cut down some of their own officers who tried to stop the slaughter.

The optimate army was utterly destroyed that day at Thapsus. Scipio fled by sea but drowned on the way to Spain. Other leaders such as Considius perished soon afterward. King Juba was banished by his own people and died in a joint suicide pact with his friend Petreius after a fine dinner and sword fight to the death. Among the few to escape from Africa was Labienus.

Caesar spared the lives of almost everyone who surrendered to him. This included the noted scholar Varro, whom Caesar uncharacteristically forgave even though he had been pardoned once before. Afranius, another general he had faced in Spain, was not so lucky as Caesar had him put to death without trial.

The one man who refused to flee or surrender was Cato. The intractable republican had spent most of the war guarding the town of Utica, just to the north of ancient Carthage. Even though the inhabitants favored Caesar, Cato had treated them fairly and labored diligently to ensure their safety. When word arrived of Caesar's victory at Thapsus, the townspeople rejoiced—but Cato faced a difficult decision. He was not afraid for his life as he knew Caesar would be only too willing to spare him, but he could not bring himself to abandon his ideal of Rome as a free state. As for clemency, he regarded Caesar's pity as far more hateful than death.

Cato showed no bitterness against those who wished to surrender to Caesar, even advising his own son to submit. Still as meticulous in his financial dealings as he had been during his service as Rome's treasury quaestor years before, Cato then presented the citizens of Utica with a careful accounting of civic funds and bade them farewell. His son and friends were suspicious that the feisty leader was suddenly so calm; they suspected that he might be planning suicide—an honorable end for a defeated Roman nobleman. They kept a constant watch on him that night and removed any weapons from his quarters.

After dinner with his companions, Cato retired for the evening with a copy of Plato's *Phaedo* as bedtime reading. Apparently his friends missed an obvious clue to his plans. This dialogue features the condemned Socrates discoursing on the nature of the soul just before he drank hemlock. When he had read the book through, Cato set it aside and drew out a knife he had hidden in his robes. He then plunged the blade into his belly and ripped out his bowels. He would not have been discovered until the morning except that he fell off his bed and hit the floor, alerting the guard who stood outside his door. His son and friends rushed in to find him unconscious and bleeding to death. A doctor quickly arrived and placed his intestines back inside his body, then sutured the wound and left him to recover. Cato, however, had no intention of remaining in this world. When he awoke to find he was still alive, he furiously ripped out his stitches and died at last.

Caesar arrived in Utica the next day and heard the news. As he stood by the body of his old enemy, a man he had fought against most of his life but still greatly respected, he mourned for them both: "Cato, I begrudge you your death, just as you begrudged me the chance to pardon you."

There was little left for Caesar to do in Africa after Cato's death. He made the rounds to the important cities of the province, rewarding those who had served him well and levying hefty fines on those towns that had sided with the optimates—2 million silver coins from Thapsus, 3 million from Hadrumentum, and 3 million pounds of olive oil annually from Leptis Magna. On June 13, he left Africa to return to Rome via Sardinia—"the only one of his properties he had not yet visited," Cicero wrote disdainfully to Varro. Battling storms all the way to Italy, Caesar at last returned home in late July, just a few days after his fifty-fourth birthday.

XIV

TRIUMPH

> To conquer one's spirit, abandon anger, and be mod-
> est in victory . . . whoever can do this I compare not
> to the greatest of men but to a god.
>
> —Cicero

On a bright summer morning in the year 46 B.C., the gates of
Rome's *porta triumphalis* swung open at last. This city gate was
used only to admit a conquering hero beginning his triumphal parade, the greatest honor Rome could grant one of her citizens. Fourteen years earlier Caesar had forfeited the triumph for his Spanish
victories so that he might stand for consul. But now Rome was about
to witness a victory celebration unlike any before.

Over the next few weeks Caesar staged no fewer than four triumphs—one for each of his victories in Gaul, Egypt, Asia Minor,
and Africa. The commemoration of the Gallic war was by far the
grandest. Caesar rode in a chariot drawn by white horses and surrounded by dozens of lictors bearing the fasces before them. Carts
bearing countless pounds of silver and gold treasures moved into the
city, followed by high-ranking captives and slaves. Caesar's soldiers
sang provocative and obscene songs mocking their commander, as
was the ancient custom:

Men of Rome, lock up your wives—
we bring you the bald adulterer!
The gold you loaned him here in Rome,
he wasted on the whores of Gaul.

The crowd finally glimpsed the featured attraction of the Gaulish triumph—Vercingetorix. Caesar had kept his famous adversary in prison for the last six years awaiting this moment. The man who had once led all of Gaul in rebellion spent the last few hours of his life in a cage rolling through the Roman Forum. The crowd felt no pity for the Gaulish king when Caesar gave the signal for his execution.

But the day had its difficulties. Opposite the temple of Fortune, the axle of Caesar's chariot snapped cleanly in half nearly spilling him onto the street. He quickly jumped into another chariot and finished the procession, but atoned for this disastrous omen by climbing the steps to the temple of Jupiter on his knees.

The Egyptian triumph a few days later went well until Caesar brought forth Cleopatra's sister, Arsinoe, wrapped in chains. Barbarian kings were one thing, but the Roman spectators were moved to pity by the broken queen. Caesar had misjudged the mood of the crowd and wisely decided to grant Arsinoe her life and freedom.

Caesar intended the triumph honoring his victory in Africa to be a glorious finale to the monthlong festivities. After Caesar had passed, giant displays portraying his defeated enemies moved slowly through the Forum. These floats had been a big success in the Egyptian and Asian triumphs when the crowd had laughed at the Alexandrian general Achillas and eunuch Pothinus. They also loved King Pharnaces fleeing from the battle of Zela, but the mood changed when they saw the Roman nobles. Scipio was there before them, stabbing himself in the chest and jumping into the sea, while Petreius was slain by his loyal servant after killing Juba in their duel. What they witnessed next disturbed the crowd even more—a huge picture of Cato on his bed at Utica with his guts ripped open for all the world to see. Although most in the crowd were ardent fans of Caesar, this tasteless mockery of a renowned Roman senator was too much for them to bear. They had no love for Cato, but they admired the man for holding to his principles and dying for what he believed in. That day through his own foolish pride, Caesar turned Cato into a martyr.

After the triumphal parades were complete, Caesar at long last distributed the war booty to his soldiers and the people of Rome. Every citizen received as much silver as he might earn during four months of hard labor, together with allotments of grain and olive oil. All his veterans received the equivalent of almost fifteen years of wages for the average worker. This was in addition to their regular pay and previous bonuses. Centurions were rewarded with twice the amount given to legionaries, while officers were granted double that of centurions. Each soldier also received a generous grant of land to retire on and raise a new generation of sons for the Roman army. These farms were scattered widely throughout Roman territory so as not to dispossess previous owners and, quite wisely, to hinder any organized actions by disgruntled veterans in the future.

The soldiers and people of Rome were also treated to banquets and entertainment on an unprecedented scale. One dinner featured 22,000 tables spread with every kind of food and drink. Animal shows at the Circus Maximus were also a favorite part of the celebration. Among the many exotic creatures he brought back from Africa for the occasion was one never before seen in the city. Onlookers thought it was some kind of cross between a camel and a leopard since it had a high back and spotted skin, but the neck was amazingly long. They called it a *camelopardalis*—today known as a giraffe.

In addition, music, dance, and drama were available throughout the city. Significantly, the plays were performed in a great variety of languages for the huge foreign population of the capital as well as for

native Latin speakers. Caesar forced the popular comedy writer Decimus Laberius to appear in one of his own plays as a Syrian slave.
The elderly Laberius, however, had his revenge for this humiliation
by pointedly emphasizing a few of his lines with a wink to the audience: "Come, citizens, for we have lost our freedom!" And more
ominously:

He whom many fear must fear many.

Caesar sponsored gladiatorial combats at the same time in memory of his daughter, Julia. In the Forum there were traditional contests pitting one man against the other, often criminals or prisoners of
war, and occasionally knights and even an ex-senator. But in the
larger venues whole armies made up of hundreds of condemned
men fought for their lives on foot or horseback. There were also battles with twenty elephants and their riders on each side. Caesar even
dug an enormous lake so spectators could watch warships complete
with marines fighting their way onto enemy vessels. All these shows
were so popular that visitors flocking into Rome slept on the streets
and trampled to death many of their fellow citizens vying for a better
view.

Some among Caesar's opponents began to grumble that the
bloodshed was getting out of hand, but even more—especially
among Caesar's veterans—complained that the money spent on such
extravagances should have been distributed among his soldiers instead. At one event at which Caesar had erected a costly silk covering
to keep the sun off the crowd, some of his legionaries began to decry
this waste of money so loudly that Caesar himself grabbed the ring-
leader and hauled him off for execution. Two other troublemakers
from the legions met a more disturbing end. Since time immemorial,
a horse had been sacrificed to the god Mars every October 15 just outside of the city. Its head and tail would then be rushed to the Regia in
the Forum for pubic display. This year Caesar decided to supple-

ment the horse sacrifice with a positively druidic ceremony, in which the priest of Mars ritually killed the two soldiers and hung their heads near the Regia. Human sacrifice had been a rare event in Roman history, practiced only during the gravest threats to the state. For Caesar to use his powers as chief priest to revive such an outdated ritual simply as a warning to those who might complain about his conduct must have sent a chill through the city.

So many Romans had died during the previous three years of civil war that the people were now willing to grant Caesar anything he wanted as long as he would promise peace. Because of this desperate longing for stability as well as a very real fear of what he might do next, the senators now outdid themselves in bestowing upon Caesar honors and privileges unknown to any previous leader.

Caesar was first installed as dictator for an unprecedented ten years. He had held the office before for short periods, but for the next decade he could act with absolute power and legal impunity throughout the Roman world. The Senate also made him *praefectus morum*—master of morality—an office derived from the traditional role of the censor. With this power he could reprove high-ranking scoundrels and remove senators from office if they offended public standards. The irony of granting this role to a man who was the subject of scandalous songs in every tavern in the city was lost on no one.

The senators also voted Caesar a thanksgiving celebration of forty days, a statue of himself straddling the globe, and the coveted right to give the signal starting the chariot races at the Circus Maximus. In the Senate chamber he was to sit in front with the two consuls, speak first on all issues, and appoint whomever he might desire to serve as magistrates. Caesar graciously accepted all these honors and many more.

In public at least he proclaimed that his only desire was to restore order and prosperity to his beloved country:

Let none of you suppose, my dear senators, that I shall issue any harsh decrees or perform any cruel deeds now that I have won the war and may act freely.

Even cynical politicians such as Cicero believed that Caesar would indeed return Rome to its republican glory and lay down his extraordinary powers once he had achieved this goal. The signs of this new beginning were promising, such as the favorable treatment of former enemies. Brutus had been appointed governor of Italian Gaul, Cassius was an important official, and Marcus Marcellus—once one of Caesar's most venomous opponents—was granted a full pardon through Cicero's intervention. But those who hoped for a quick return to the days of senatorial rule apparently missed some of Caesar's other proclamations:

The Republic is nothing, just a name without substance or form.

And: "Sulla was an ignorant child to ever lay down his dictatorship." Finally:

Men ought to speak to me more courteously and treat my word as law.

Soon after Caesar's triumphs, Cleopatra and her royal court arrived in Rome. There was nothing unusual about a foreign monarch visiting the capital, but Cleopatra was far from typical. With her thirteen-year-old husband/brother in tow, the queen of Egypt held in her arms the infant Caesarion, son of Julius Caesar. This must have caused a tremendous scandal throughout Rome, not because of any infidelity—such behavior was expected of generals abroad—but because of the intimate ties that now existed between Caesar and the ruling family of Egypt. Rome was just getting used to Caesar as de facto ruler of its empire. Did his relationship with Cleopatra mean he would preside over Egypt as well? Would he establish a dynasty? Would he try to join East and West like Alexander the Great?

Caesar only encouraged such speculations when he dedicated the new temple to his ancestor Venus that he had vowed after the battle of Pharsalus. This dedication to the goddess was perfectly acceptable and admirable according to Roman tradition, but next to the statue of Venus Caesar placed a beautiful image of Cleopatra herself. Perhaps Caesar saw this only as a representation of Cleopatra as an incarnation of Isis, the Egyptian equivalent of Venus, but traditional Romans were deeply troubled by this unprecedented honor.

The Senate formally recognized Cleopatra and her puppet husband as friends and allies of the Roman people. The security of this political relationship was at the top of Cleopatra's wish list, but even more vital to the queen was the chance to reestablish her personal ties with Caesar. He obliged handsomely by housing Cleopatra and her companions just across the Tiber in one of his own homes. There the queen held court, receiving Roman officials and senators who flocked to her in spite of themselves because of her influence with Caesar. Endless duties kept Caesar busy much of the time, but he must have been able occasionally to visit his mistress and young son on the far side of the river.

Cicero, in spite of his efforts to warm to Caesar in his new role, was never able to come to terms with the incarnate goddess from Egypt:

> I detest Cleopatra . . . I cannot even describe the insolence of this queen in her gardens across the Tiber without bursting into anger. I want nothing to do with her since she clearly doesn't appreciate my feelings.

Cicero had apparently tried to impress Cleopatra with his gifts of learning only to be rebuffed. Once while waiting for a summons to attend the queen, he was mortified to find her servant had arrived at his house seeking his cultured friend Atticus instead.

We don't know how long Cleopatra stayed in Rome, but her visit was a great success. She received official Roman support for her crown while strengthening her personal ties with Caesar. Before she left, Caesar honored her with many gifts for her and their son. Under Roman law, Caesarion could never follow in his father's footsteps along the Path of Honors, but it undoubtedly pleased Caesar to know that his only son would one day rule Egypt.

Caesar spent the next few months enacting a series of groundbreaking civic and social reforms. He had begun some of his initiatives even before crossing the Rubicon, but now that absolute power was in his hands he was at last free to shape the future of Rome to his liking. Some in the upper classes, such as Cicero, found cause to complain for no other reason than that Caesar was altering Roman tradition, even though the benefits to everyone were obvious. Caesar spared neither the wealthy ruling classes nor his populist backers in his sweeping campaign to transform Rome from an inward-looking oligarchy into a international empire. He was not creating a modern democracy by any stretch of the imagination, but in the year 46 B.C. Caesar began a revolution that would change Rome forever.

Caesar's first act was to conduct a proper census of the city. This was in part motivated by the massive fraud that for years had enabled many thousands of ineligible residents to obtain free grain meant only for the poorest citizens. But Caesar was also curious to learn how many people were resident in the city after years of civil war. Rejecting previous surveys of population that had yielded wildly inaccurate figures, Caesar commissioned auditors to go door to door through all of Rome's neighborhoods to obtain an accurate count. When the process was complete, it was found that the true number of eligible food recipients in the city was 150,000 rather than the previous estimate of 320,000. Caesar was pleased to cut the grain dole by half and save the state a great deal of money, but he was troubled by the marked decline in population. Urban workers, like their counterparts in the countryside, were a mainstay of the army. He therefore offered grain supplements and prizes to encourage large families.

To keep citizens at home producing children, Caesar forbade all Roman men between the ages of twenty and forty to travel abroad for more than three years unless they were serving in the army. The sons of senators were forbidden to leave Italy for any length of time unless they were on duty as military or government officials. Caesar knew he could not manage the affairs of a great empire on his own, so he took steps to increase the numbers in the Senate to almost a thousand members, even if it meant the traditional ruling families became a minority in Rome's most distinguished body. Soldiers, sons of former slaves, and even foreigners who had served him well were enrolled as senators of Rome. When conservatives complained of the quality of the new appointees, Caesar shot back: "If thieves and murderers had stood beside me to defend my honor, I would be granting them the same rewards."

Even though the population of Rome had declined, city workers still posed a serious danger to public order if they were allowed to organize. Caesar accordingly banned all clubs and guilds unless specifically sanctioned by his government. This sweeping curtailment of civil liberties was tempered by the announcement that organizations of ancient standing would be allowed to continue their meetings. These groups were usually made up of men from a particular trade or profession. They were often dominated by freedmen, although even slaves could join certain clubs. Whatever their official charter, most groups were primarily social in purpose. Caesar had no objections to peaceful gatherings, but like most Romans he was deeply suspicious of foreign religious organizations. Under his decree, however, Caesar was careful to exclude Jews from any ban. As long as they restricted themselves to religious worship and community welfare, the synagogues of Rome were allowed to remain open.

Caesar promoted an increase in the number of middle-class professionals in Rome by granting citizenship to physicians and teachers who settled in the city. On the other hand, he was selective concerning the type of citizens he wanted in Roman government. Auctioneers, grave diggers, fencing teachers, pimps, and actors were all banned from serving as magistrates.

Perhaps inspired by his stay in Egypt—or by guilt at having burned down the great Alexandrian library—Caesar planned a huge public library in Rome full of the best Greek and Latin works. The twice-pardoned optimate and noted scholar Marcus Varro was given charge of collecting and cataloging these works. Caesar also planned to codify for the first time the immense body of Roman law, a project that would not be completed until the early Byzantine era.

Caesar took seriously his role as director of public morals. He was determined to enforce a measure of moderation on a nobility better known for extravagant dinner parties than old-fashioned Roman virtues. Of course, Caesar was famous for his own exquisite tastes—especially in married women—but he did not allow his personal indulgences to stand in the way of making rules for others. When one ex-praetor married a woman just one day after her divorce, Caesar annulled the union even though there was no evidence of previous adultery. He imposed heavy duties on foreign luxury items and placed guards throughout the city markets to seize imported goods he deemed too extravagant. Sometimes his agents even made raids on private homes, confiscating ornate tableware in the middle of dinner. He forbade the use of litters to carry wealthy citizens through the streets, while the wearing of scarlet robes and pearls was restricted to special occasions.

Caesar was harsh on senators and wealthy citizens who broke the law. Previously nobleman were able literally to get away with murder, facing exile at worst if they were unable to bribe their way out of a conviction. For most, this meant only the inconvenience of relocating to one of their estates abroad. Caesar changed the rules to hit the nobility where it hurt the most, so that if convicted they lost at least half of their personal property. In addition, governors found guilty of extortion while managing their provinces were dismissed from the Senate. But Caesar did not follow a strict populist line in all legal matters. He revised the composition of juries to exclude members of the lower classes, who had been admitted in recent years. Under Caesar's new legislation only senators and knights could decide cases as these groups were considered better able to understand the complexities of the law.

Caesar was equally active in affairs beyond the gates of Rome. He drew up plans for a new harbor at nearby Ostia to provide a proper port for the city of Rome. He also planned large-scale public improvement projects, such as draining the malaria-ridden swamps of Italy and digging a canal across the isthmus of Corinth in Greece. He encouraged owners of large farms to hire more free laborers by laws mandating a reduction in slave labor by a third. Caesar remembered well the revolt of Spartacus thirty years earlier and was determined to reduce Roman dependency on slaves, for security reasons as well as economic stimulation.

Caesar also made unprecedented strides in expanding Roman citizenship. He had already granted full citizen rights to northern Italy three years earlier. Now he extended the franchise to leading citizens from the provinces, especially Spain and Gaul. Many of these began making their way to Rome to seek their fortune or even serve in government. Cicero complained that Rome was becoming overrun by barbarians wearing pants. It would be several centuries before Rome extended citizenship to all free males in the empire, but Caesar was the first to bestow this most precious of Roman rights on large numbers beyond Italy. It was a crucial step in creating a truly international state.

Equally important in spreading Roman civilization was Caesar's establishment of citizen colonies. Such settlements were not entirely new, but Caesar was the first to send Romans abroad by the tens of thousands. Farmers, skilled craftsmen, and professionals were welcomed into Italy, but the idle poor from slums of Rome were given incentives to move to the new colonies. This served both to expand Roman influence in foreign lands and to rid the capital of its expensive and potentially troublesome underclass. Eighty thousand Roman citizens from the lowest strata of society were enticed onto ships with promises of a new life in Spain, Gaul, Africa, or Greece.

But of all of the reforms Caesar initiated during his months in Rome, his creation of a new calendar stands above the rest for its lasting impact. Before Caesar the Romans used a calendar based on the movement of the moon across the sky. This worked well for most purposes, but since there are only 355 days in a lunar year, the Roman calendar was forever out of alignment with the solar year. This meant that the priests had to add extra days to each year to keep the calendar from creeping ahead of the seasons. Most years they did just that, but it was an awkward ad hoc system that was forever in need of adjustment. Some years harvest festivals were celebrated weeks before the crops were ripe. By Caesar's day, the disruptions of civil war had caused the seasons to fall behind the civic calendar by over two months.

Caesar used his office as chief priest to fix the problem once and for all by converting Rome to a solar calendar. Relying on an Alexandrian astronomer named Sosigenes for expert advice, he added extra days to 46 B.C., so that by the end of December the year was 445 days long. This was a one-time adjustment to synchronize the days and seasons, but to make sure the calendar functioned properly in the future he lengthened the months to yield an annual total of 365 days. Since the actual solar year is 365 1/4 days long, he also invented leap year by adding an extra day every fourth February to make up the difference.

This revolutionary transformation of the calendar was such an obvious improvement over previous practice that even traditionalists like Cicero had to concede its advantages. Still, when he was told by a companion that the constellation Lyra would be appearing the next day, Cicero could only grumble that it was rising by decree. Caesar's system worked so well, however, that it survives largely unchanged to this day.

▣

Ever since his victory in Africa Caesar had been receiving regular reports concerning the surviving Pompeian rebels in Spain. At first he considered them no more than a nuisance, the last remnant of beaten force. But by the autumn of 46 B.C. Pompey's son Gnaeus had raised an impressive army thirteen legions strong consisting of both native troops and disaffected Roman veterans. With the arrival of Labienus from Africa, Gnaeus now threatened to revive a war Caesar thought he had already won.

By November, the Pompeians dominated the southern part of the peninsula, trapping Caesar's few Spanish forces near Cordova. He therefore appointed Marcus Lepidus to manage affairs in Rome while he marched to Spain with the fifth and tenth legions. Caesar's legendary speed was once again in evidence as he covered the 1,500 miles to Cordova in less than a month, composing a now-lost poem called *The Journey* along the way.

It might be expected that the conservative senators of Rome would be thrilled for Caesar to face death once again at the hands of the Pompeians. But as much as they despised the dictator in their hearts, they did not prefer a victory by Gnaeus Pompey. As Cassius wrote to Cicero:

> *Let me know how things are going in Spain. I'm deeply worried. I'd rather have our old kind master in charge than this young cruel one. You know what a fool Gnaeus is. He thinks that cruelty is courage—and he thinks that we're always laughing at him. I'm afraid he'll act like the peasant he is and run us all through with his sword.*

By the middle of winter Caesar was advancing on Cordova to lure the Pompeians into open battle, but Labienus urged a strategy of attrition rather than confronting Caesar directly. At first the plan worked well, with Caesar's legions in a constant struggle to find enough food in enemy territory, but after a few weeks the Pompeians began to suffer regular setbacks. Caesar began to win over Spanish towns to his cause, while more enemy soldiers deserted to him every day. Gnaeus Pompey knew by early March that he would have to face Caesar in battle soon or face losing the support of his army.

On March 17, 45 B.C., Caesar and the Pompeians faced one another across a level valley at Munda, southwest of Cordova. Between their hilltop camps was level ground perfect for maneuvering large numbers of infantry and cavalry. When Caesar saw the enemy troops line up for battle that morning, he quickly readied his own forces and prepared to move them to the plain. Caesar waited for the Pompeians to move down the hill, but Gnaeus Pompey and Labienus stood their ground, daring Caesar to attack uphill. Even though it was a risky move to attack a superior force by charging high ground, Caesar gave the signal to his eager troops and began the attack.

What followed was the bloodiest and most vicious battle of Caesar's life. His men engaged the Pompeians hand-to-hand for hours, but were slowly pushed back down the hill. Caesar knew everything he had struggled for his whole life would end that day if his troops faltered. As the enemy overcame his soldiers he even considered falling on his own sword to spare himself the humiliation of capture. Instead, the ruler of the Roman world jumped off his horse and charged the Pompeian lines on foot, shouting back to his own troops that they should be ashamed to see him facing the enemy alone.

Caesar's good fortune and daring once more carried the day as his legions followed him up the hill. By evening 30,000 Pompeian soldiers were dead, though Caesar himself had lost an unprecedented number of men. Gnaeus Pompey fled, only to be slain a few days later. Among the enemy dead was Labienus. Caesar buried his former lieutenant and relentless enemy with honor there on the plains of Munda.

❖

Caesar spent the next few months settling affairs and raising money in Spain, followed by a leisurely journey back across southern Gaul to Rome. His great-nephew Octavius—the future emperor Augustus—joined him in Spain for the return trip, as did Mark Antony in Gaul, at last forgiven for his previous indiscretions and soon to be consul. Antony rode in Caesar's private carriage and shared with the dictator all the latest gossip from Rome—but neglected to mention that their old friend Gaius Trebonius had come to him whispering that it was time to do something about Caesar.

THE IDES OF MARCH

> And so every kind of person conspired against him—
> great and small, friend and enemy, soldier and civil-
> ian. Each had his own reasons for doing so and
> gladly heard the complaints of others.
> — Nicolaus of Damascus

In February of 44 B.C., Cicero's daughter Tullia died. Although the death of a child was all too common in ancient Rome, Cicero was inconsolable. One of his friends, Servius Sulpicius Rufus, wrote to him from Greece as soon as he heard the news. Servius was a former consul and one of the leading lawyers of the day. He had reluctantly joined Pompey when the civil war began, but Caesar had gladly pardoned him and even appointed him governor of Greece. The letter of Servius begins with heartfelt sympathy for Cicero's loss, but quickly turns into mourning not for a daughter, but for Rome itself:

> *Look at what fortune has done to us. Everything that a man should hold no less dear than his children—country, reputation, dignity, honors—all have been lost. Could this misfortune of yours really make matters any worse?*

The opposition of implacable enemies like Cato or Labienus had been one thing, but with the victory now won, moderates like Servius and even old friends of Caesar like Gaius Trebonius felt only frustration and despair at the new Rome he had created. How could a man who had gained the whole world lose the support of those who had served him loyally?

Caesar had not begun to understand the depths of the enmity against him until Cicero published a eulogy entitled *Cato* in praise of the slain optimate soon after the African campaign. In this work Cato was held up as the ideal of Roman virtue, a martyr to the ancient Republic. Caesar was furious with Cicero, but greater than his anger was his bafflement at the warm reception of the book among the public. As always, Caesar was unable to understand how others could not see what was so obvious to him—*the Republic was dead*. Moreover, it was a death well deserved as it had served only to perpetuate the rule and enrichment of a few powerful families at the expense of everyone else. To make Cato the shining hero of a failed and corrupt system was unforgivable.

Caesar resisted the urge to separate Cicero's head from his shoulders and instead sent a warm letter to the orator praising his marvelous writing style. But as soon as the war in Spain was finished Caesar wrote a virulent response called the *Anti-Cato*. This work, now lost except for fragments, was one of Caesar's greatest mistakes. Instead of ignoring the praise heaped on Cato, Caesar vented his spleen against his deceased enemy in the crudest manner. He accused Cato of being a miser, a drunkard, and a heartless schemer who gave his wife, Marcia, to his wealthy friend Hortensius only so that he could later remarry her:

> *Why did Cato give up a wife he loved? Or if he didn't love her, why did he take her back? He must have used her as bait for Hortensius so that he could reclaim her later as a rich widow.*

As Plutarch says, calling Cato greedy was like calling Hercules a coward. Even Caesar's closest friends were embarrassed by this baseless tirade against a dead man. Cicero was so delighted at Caesar's overreaction that he urged everyone to read the *Anti-Cato* because its vindictiveness served to make Cato look even more noble compared to Caesar.

Brutus joined in the fray soon after by publishing his own pamphlet in praise of Cato. Caesar had never believed he would gain Cicero's sincere support, but had always tried to win Brutus to his cause. Caesar had praised his service as governor of Italian Gaul and announced that as a reward he was nominating Brutus to serve as praetor, followed by a consulship. Caesar kept his faith in the younger man even when Brutus married Cato's daughter, Portia, the widow of his old enemy Bibulus. The dictator would never have trusted anyone else who made such obvious declarations of optimate values, but Caesar's affection for Brutus was undiminished.

❖

Caesar seemed to have learned nothing from the mistakes during his triumphal parades the previous year. The Roman people loved a good show, but when Caesar decided to celebrate his victory over the Pompeians in Spain by staging a grand triumph through the streets of the capital, it turned into a public relations disaster. Gaul and Egypt had been foreign wars and even in Africa Caesar could argue that a significant portion of the defeated army were Juba's Numidians, but Romans saw the war in Spain as a slaughter of their own sons and brothers. They understood that it had been necessary for Caesar to defeat the last of the rebels, but to hold a public celebration as if he had conquered the blue-skinned Picts of Caledonia was in horrible taste.

No one in power had the courage to object to Caesar's behavior except a young tribune of the people named Pontus Aquila. As Caesar rode past in his triumphal cart all the magistrates rose to honor him—except Aquila. Caesar was so enraged at the man for this public disrespect that he lost his customary control and shouted out: "Tribune Aquila, why don't you take back the government from me?" For days afterward, whenever he promised anything to anyone, he added with pointed sarcasm: "That is, if Pontus Aquila will permit me!"

However, the rest of the senators vied with each other in flattering the dictator with ever greater honors. He was allowed to wear his triumphal garments at all future games along with a laurel crown. His victory at Munda was to be celebrated annually with races at the Circus. The Senate bestowed upon him the titles *liberator* and *imperator,* the latter of which, previously restricted to conquering generals, would pass automatically to his sons and grandsons regardless of military victories. A golden chair was built for his pleasure in the Senate chamber, while the state was to construct a temple to the goddess of liberty in his honor as well as a private palace for his residence on the Quirinal Hill. Caesar's birthday was declared a public holiday in perpetuity. Moreover, the month of his birth, which had previously been known simply as *Quinctilus* (the fifth month, from when the Roman year began in March) was renamed *Julius* in his honor—hence our modern July. He was allowed to wear the purple regalia of the ancient Roman kings and to be buried, contrary to all tradition, within the walls of the city. He was proclaimed Father of his Country and declared consul for ten years. More significantly, he was named dictator for life.

But as unprecedented as these honors were, it was the astonishing transformation of Caesar from conquering hero to divine figure that most troubled the ancient Romans, as it does modern students of history. The Egyptians and much of the eastern Mediterranean had long been accustomed to revering their leaders as demigods, but such veneration of rulers was contrary to the very core of Roman beliefs. How could the Senate permit such apparent blasphemy—and why did Caesar allow it? Perhaps the answer lies in the huge foreign population of Rome that was not troubled by the thought of a divine ruler. Perhaps the Romans so yearned for stability after decades of civil war that they were willing to give up cherished traditions in exchange for anyone who would bring peace to their world. Perhaps the senators granted divine honors to Caesar merely to curry favor or feared that he would yet become a bloodthirsty tyrant unless appeased. Caesar may have accepted such honors to humor the common people or to guarantee the success of his reforms for the good of the empire—or perhaps he fell victim to the very human vice of pride. Caesar surely knew that hubris, the arrogance of the king who thinks himself equal to the gods, was a favorite subject of Greek drama. But as a supposed descendant of the goddess Venus through her son Aeneas, Caesar may have genuinely come to believe he deserved divine honors.

When the Senate decreed his ivory statue would be carried in procession with the gods of Rome, Caesar did not object. When it voted to establish a new cult to Caesar with Mark Antony as chief priest, the dictator graciously concurred. When an image of Caesar with the inscription *to the unconquered god* was to be erected at the temple of Quirinus—the deified Romulus, first king of Rome—there was scarcely a whisper of discontent, least of all from Caesar. But beneath the public calm a storm was brewing among the surviving aristocracy. As Cicero quietly commented to his friend Atticus: "I'd prefer Caesar share a temple with Quirinus than Salus." Salus was the goddess who guarded the health of the state, while Romulus had been torn to pieces by Rome's first senators when they believed he was becoming a tyrant.

Caesar had long planned a war against the Parthians, in part to avenge the death of his former partner Crassus nine years earlier. But Caesar had other reasons for a grand campaign to the east. The Parthian king had already sent his son Pancorus to successfully aid rebel troops in the province of Syria. If the Romans did not respond quickly and forcefully, the Parthians could threaten Asia Minor, Egypt, and the rest of the eastern Mediterranean. Fortunately for Caesar, the Roman people enthusiastically backed the war. Caesar also undoubtedly wanted to get out of Rome to escape scheming senators and the fickle mob. Although he was a master politician, he had spent most of the previous twenty years as a general on the battlefield, where life was so much simpler. It was at war that Caesar felt most in control of his world. But the greatest reason for an eastern campaign was Caesar's unquenchable ambition—or as Plutarch puts it, the rivalry between what he had done and what he hoped to do. Caesar, now in his mid-fifties, still dreamed of conquering new worlds.

Caesar realized he had to settle affairs in Rome before leaving and so worked furiously to enact laws, appoint magistrates, and deal with a thousand problems that might come up while he was on a campaign that could take him away from the capital for at least three years. He had already sent sixteen legions and ten thousand cavalry across the Adriatic to prepare for war. He himself had decided to leave Rome at the beginning of spring, three days after the Ides of March.

Rumors flew through Rome that Caesar would not be coming back from the East, but would move the capital of the empire to Egypt or his supposed ancestral home at Troy. In fact, he had every intention of returning to Rome once the long campaign was finished. He planned to strike first against the troublesome Dacians on the lower Danube to secure the northern Balkans. Then he would march across Asia Minor to Armenia and invade the Parthian empire from the north. How far east he planned to go is unknown— whether he would be content with the conquest of Mesopotamia or press on to the Indus River like Alexander before him. However far he might go, reports were that he would return by way of the Caucasus Mountains and Caspian Sea, crushing the wild Scythian tribes of the steppes along the way. From there he would follow the Danube west to the Alps and overwhelm the Germans before returning to Italy through Gaul. If such stories were told of any other general they could safely be dismissed as fantasy, but Caesar may very well have planned to conquer the Near East and all of Europe to the North Sea.

But before setting out on this expedition, he had to face his own mortality. Caesar had no legitimate Roman son, so he chose his great-nephew Octavius as his chief heir. This exceptionally bright young man was barely eighteen years old, but he had greatly impressed Caesar. Octavius was to receive three-quarters of Caesar's immense wealth, while two other great-nephews were to divide the remainder of his estate. But before filing his will, Caesar added one last line, adopting Octavius as his son upon his death. Such an adoption by last will and testament was common enough in ancient Rome, but given Caesar's position, the choice of Octavius as his next of kin marked the teenager as his intended political heir as well. In case anyone doubted Caesar's faith in Octavius, the dictator declared his grand-nephew would become Master of the Horse, the post previously held by Mark Antony, as soon as he departed for the Parthian War.

On December 18 of 45 B.C., Caesar visited Campania for a few days of relaxation amid the planning for his eastern campaign. Even at leisure, Caesar was always a frenetic worker. While attending races at the Circus Maximus, he had repeatedly annoyed the crowd by answering letters and hearing petitions rather than watching the show. But at Puteoli on the Bay of Naples, Caesar did manage to find a few moments of peace as he gazed across the water at Mount Vesuvius.

Cicero gives us a remarkable glimpse of Caesar during his visit as he owned a home nearby and was the dictator's dinner guest. As he wrote to his friend Atticus, Caesar arrived with two thousand attendants—scribes, slaves, and soldiers—at the house of his neighbor

Philippus, the stepfather of Octavius. The estate was overflowing with Caesar's retinue so that most camped in a nearby field. The next day Caesar worked undisturbed until early afternoon with his comrade Balbus, then went for a walk on the beach. At midafternoon he bathed and heard a report concerning his follower Mamurra, whom Catullus had years before accused of being Caesar's lover.

As evening fell, Caesar was anointed with perfume and joined his guests for dinner. As was common at the time, Caesar's doctor had prescribed a course of emetics to clean out his patient's digestive system, so the dictator felt free to indulge himself that night rather than follow his customary restraint at meals. Cicero says the dinner was splendid, the entertainment lively, and the conversation warm. Aside from the inner circle of diners, of which Cicero was a part, Caesar had tables laid out for freedmen and even slaves. Talk among Caesar and his guests revolved around literature, not politics. In spite of the good time had by all, Caesar and his entourage, as Cicero says, were so overwhelming that one would scarce invite them back again.

Once Caesar returned to Rome, he began to act more like a king than the leader of a republic. One day when he was sitting in front of the temple of his ancestor Venus transacting business, a large group of senators approached him to announce new honors they had voted for him. Caesar started to rise to greet them, but his confidant Balbus whispered in his ear that if he wanted to be treated like a ruler he should start acting like one. Therefore, contrary to all custom, Caesar remained seated like a king while the most respected body in ancient Rome stood and addressed him. Not only were the senators deeply offended by this haughty behavior, but the crowd that had followed them was stunned that Caesar would show such disrespect to the venerated body. Once they had left and Caesar realized just how insulting his actions had been, he cried out to his friends in a fit of melodrama that he was ready to offer his throat to the knife of anyone who felt slighted. Instead of suicide, however, he spread the story that he had suddenly felt ill and was unable to rise for the senators.

Although Caesar was king of Rome in all but name, he still lacked the actual title of *rex*. Ever since Tarquin the Proud, the last king of Rome, had been overthrown five centuries earlier, *rex* had been a cursed word among Romans. As dictator for life, commander of the armies, and chief priest of Rome, he held power over millions that a title of royalty would not augment. Yet there was something about being king of Rome that must have appealed to Caesar. His Julian ancestors, after all, had been kings of nearby Alba Longa when Rome was still just a village of refugee cowherds. Moreover he governed a mighty empire in a world where all other rulers, whether in Egypt, India, Parthia, or even Britain, were kings over their people. It must have been very tempting for Caesar to add this one last title to his name—if only the Senate and people would allow it.

The stories that survive from the first few weeks of 44 B.C. show Caesar toying with the idea of kingship—publicly rejecting the title, but in a half-hearted way as if he were testing the waters. A rumor arose (spread by Caesar?) that the sacred Sibylline books predicted that only a king could conquer the Parthians. Caesar's cousin Cotta, one of the priests in charge of interpreting these texts, was to propose that Caesar be named *rex*, but only outside of Italy.

In another incident, one of Caesar's statues in the Forum was found adorned with a ribbon on its head, an eastern symbol of kingship. Two tribunes named Marullus and Flavius immediately ordered it removed, declaring that Caesar had no need of such offensive devices. In one account, Caesar was perturbed at the pair for removing the ribbon, in another for not allowing him to reject it himself. Still other sources believed that Caesar thought Marullus and Flavius had set up the whole thing to rouse the people against his bid for kingship.

Soon afterward, Caesar was riding home when someone in the

crowd hailed him as king. The dictator laughed and shouted: "My name is Caesar, not Rex." But Marullus and Flavius grabbed the offending spectator and hauled him off to court. This time Caesar believed the presence of the two tribunes was too convenient and decided they were trying to provoke the crowd. He brought them before the Senate and declared they were worthy of death for their insidious manipulation of the mob. They were, he asserted, trying to lay the odious title of king upon him against his wishes. The two cried out that Caesar was preventing them from exercising their sacred rights as tribunes of the people. In the end, both Marullus and Flavius were removed from the Senate rolls, though they kept their lives. It is difficult to know whether they had interrupted a staged attempt by Caesar to have himself declared king by popular acclaim or if they had in fact instigated the entire affair to make him look as if he were grasping for a royal title.

The matter of kingship finally came to a head at the festival of the Lupercalia on February 15. The Lupercalia was so ancient a ceremony that no one had any clear idea of its origins or the meanings of its rituals. It was conducted by a brotherhood of the Luperci, who apparently took their name from the she-wolf (*lupa*) who had suckled the infants Romulus and Remus. A dog and several goats were first sacrificed at a cave on the Palatine Hill, where the wolf had raised the boys. The blood from the sacrificial knife was daubed on the foreheads of two boys, who for some reason were expected to laugh, then they were wiped clean by wool dipped in milk. After this the members of the brotherhood—naked except for the skin of the sacrificed goats around their waists—ran around the center of Rome striking eager women with goatskin thongs for purification (*februare,* thus our month February). This was also thought to promote fertility and ease the pains of childbirth.

This year Mark Antony was consul and also one of the Lupercalia brotherhood selected to dash through the streets. When he came to the Forum, he found Caesar sitting on his golden throne and wearing a purple robe. Suddenly he pulled a diadem wreathed in laurel from somewhere under his goatskin and held it out to Caesar proclaiming: "The people ask me to give you this crown."

There was a notable silence from the crowd at this supposedly popular gesture as Caesar sat staring at the gift in Antony's hands. Antony offered it to him again, but Caesar pushed it away and declared: "Jupiter alone is king of the Romans!" At which point the crowd erupted in wild applause.

Some ancient commentators say Caesar had staged this spectacle to put to rest once and for all any rumors that he desired the kingship. By refusing the crown in the most public of settings he was making it abundantly clear that he had no desire to be king. But most sources take the opposite view, that Caesar had arranged for Antony to offer him the kingship so that he might gauge the reaction of the Roman populace and accept the monarchy if they approved. Since it turned out they did not, he made a great show of rejecting Antony's offer. In any case, most of the Roman nobility certainly believed that Caesar would have become king of Rome that day if the crowd had been on his side and so began to lay their plans in earnest. Cicero, who witnessed the entire scene, later wrote that the Lupercalia marked the beginning of the end of Caesar.

There were three kinds of men who wanted Caesar dead. The first were old enemies who had sided with Pompey but had been granted pardon. These men, such as Cassius, had joined Caesar's cause due to expediency, not conviction. When they realized the optimates would lose the war, they chose to cut their losses and transfer their loyalty. They followed Caesar out of desire for profit and high office, which he had gladly given them. But as one ancient historian said:

> *They hated him precisely because he had forgiven them and treated them so kindly. They could not stand the thought of receiving as a*

gift from Caesar that which they might have gained on their own through victory.

The second group to plot Caesar's downfall was his friends. Many of these men, like Trebonius, had followed Caesar faithfully since the Gallic war and now found themselves in positions of great favor in Caesar's government. They respected Caesar greatly as a military leader, but deeply resented his policy of reconciliation with his former enemies. They had sided with Caesar because they had seen in him the genius to overthrow the entrenched optimates. However, instead of purging the ruling families as they had hoped, he had brought them into his new government on an equal footing. His disgruntled friends had no interest in Caesar's vision for a harmonious new Rome; they simply wanted the fruits of victory for themselves.

The final conspirators were idealists who truly believed in the Republic. These few, like Brutus, had other motives as well, but their dedication to the ancient Roman tradition of shared power was genuine. The very thought of their beloved Rome ruled by a single man was unbearable. For generations their ancestors had fought and died to preserve their constitutional freedoms, but now they served the uncrowned king of Rome. What did it matter if he named them as consuls or made them governors of some wealthy province? When they returned home at night they still had to face the wax masks of their forefathers, who looked down on them and silently asked how they could have allowed this to happen.

The four leading figures of the conspiracy came from Caesar's longtime companions as well as those who had fought against him. Gaius Trebonius had worked with Caesar since the days of the triumvirate, performing especially valuable service during his last years in Gaul. He had organized the siege of Massalia during the early months of the civil war and had fought for Caesar in Spain as well. Through Caesar, he had become praetor and served briefly as consul in 45 B.C. Decimus Brutus, from the same family as the more famous Brutus, had masterminded the naval victory against the Gaulish Veneti twelve years earlier and had also been one of Caesar's most reliable commanders in Gaul. He had worked with Trebonius to subdue Massalia for Caesar and had been appointed governor of Gaul, where he had distinguished himself by suppressing a rebellion of the fierce Bellovaci. Caesar had honored Decimus repeatedly and had designated him as consul for 42 B.C. Both Trebonius and Decimus owed everything they had to Caesar, but neither felt it was enough.

Cassius was violent and ruthless, but Caesar respected him as a man who could get things done. He had served brilliantly under Caesar's old triumvirate partner Crassus, then joined Pompey as a naval commander in the civil war. When he heard of the optimate defeat at Pharsalus, however, he quickly appealed to Caesar for pardon. He was made a praetor in 44 B.C. under Caesar's sponsorship, but the dictator never fully trusted him and in fact suspected that he might be planning treachery. More than once Caesar said to friends that Cassius looked much too pale in his presence.

Brutus had long been Caesar's favorite among the younger generation of Roman nobles. Caesar knew Brutus could be greedy and arrogant, but perhaps because he was the son of his long-time mistress, Caesar lavished him with honors. His brief service with Pompey was easily forgiven, after which he was made a pontifex and governor of Italian Gaul. He was chosen as praetor for the city of Rome in 44 B.C. and marked for the consulship three years later. Caesar would not hear a word against Brutus, even when a friend warned he was involved in a plot against his life. "Brutus will wait for this shriveled skin," Caesar replied as he sent the man away. But Brutus was under increasing pressure from Cassius and other disgruntled senators to end Caesar's tyranny, just as his illustrious ancestor, also named Brutus, had overthrown the last Roman king

centuries before. Every night new graffiti would appear on the statues dedicated to this hero of Rome's past with provocative messages:

> *Oh that you were still alive!*
> *Your seed has failed you.*
> *We need a Brutus!*

In the end the pressure was too much for Brutus to resist. He decided
to lead the plot to assassinate Caesar in spite of the forgiveness and favor the older man had gladly granted him.

There was no time to spare if they were to eliminate Caesar since
he would leave for the Parthian campaign on March 18. Absent from
Rome and surrounded by his faithful soldiers, he would be untouch-
able. Although it might be possible to waylay him on the streets, the
conspirators were determined to slay Caesar in a public place. This
was not to be a tawdry back-alley murder as if they were thugs steal-
ing a rich man's purse. This was a political statement, the restoration
of power to the Senate and people of Rome—it had to be done in the
open, yet in a setting they could control. They finally decided on the
Senate meeting scheduled for the Ides of March. The Ides were on
the thirteenth day of most months, but in March they would fall on
the fifteenth. There was no opportunity to get to Caesar before that
date and there would be no second chance if something went wrong.

Caesar had little use for signs and wonders, but if he had been paying
attention in those days before the Ides he might have noticed some
ominous warnings of approaching doom. According to ancient authors, who delighted in reporting such events, strange lights lit the
sky, crashing sounds echoed through the night, and birds of ill omen
flocked to the Forum. As in a story told of Caesar's ancestor Julus
fleeing with his father, Aeneas, from Troy (and the New Testament
episode of Pentecost), fire shot from the bodies of men but left them

unharmed. Caesar himself, while conducting a sacrifice, found that one of the animals he had just killed had no heart. Beyond Rome, settlers in one of Caesar's colonies in southern Italy demolishing an ancient tomb found a tablet warning that whenever the bones therein were disturbed a son of Troy would be slain. If this were not clear enough, Caesar was confronted on the streets by an old soothsayer named Spurinna who warned him plainly that grave danger awaited him on the Ides of March.

But Caesar scoffed at such omens and had little fear of death. He had already dismissed his bodyguard, trusting in an oath by the senators to protect his life with their own. On the night of March 14, as he dined with his friend Lepidus, conversation turned to the best kind of death. Caesar mentioned that he had read of the Persian emperor Cyrus, who at death's door had enough time to carefully plan his own funeral. Caesar shuddered at the thought of a lingering demise and said that by far the best kind of death was one that was sudden and unexpected.

On the morning of March 15, Caesar awoke to find his wife, Calpurnia, in a panic beside him. She had been visited that night with horrible dreams that she was holding Caesar's lifeless body in her arms. Calpurnia was not a woman given to premonitions, but she begged Caesar to cancel the meeting of the Senate that day. At first he dismissed her fears as groundless, but she was so insistent that he began to have second thoughts. Just then Decimus arrived to escort him to the meeting. Hearing that Caesar was considering not attending the Senate that morning, he took him aside and urged him to reconsider. How would it look, he asked, if word got out that Caesar was afraid to leave his home because of a woman's dreams? Caesar agreed and bade his wife farewell, urging her not to worry.

On the way Caesar was accompanied by the usual crowd of well-wishers and suppliants seeking a moment of his time. Among these was a Greek philosophy teacher named Artemidorus who was a frequent visitor to the homes of Brutus and his friends. He had overheard that an attempt was to be made on Caesar's life that very day and was anxious to warn the dictator. Knowing he could scarcely reveal the details to Caesar in public, he quickly prepared a scroll giving Caesar the details of the conspirators' plans. He fought his way through the crowd and thrust the scroll into Caesar's hands saying he must read it, privately, and right away. Caesar agreed, but pressed for time he put the message aside to look at after the meeting.

Passing the soothsayer Spurinna along the way, Caesar cheerfully called out that the Ides of March had arrived and he was still alive. Spurinna replied: "Yes, the Ides have come, but not yet passed."

The Senate meeting that day was to take place in the hall adjoining Pompey's theater to the west of the Forum. Pompey had completed this building, first stone theater in Rome, in 55 B.C. in celebration of his eastern victories. Not a modest man, Pompey had placed a statue of himself in the hall to look down on all who gathered there.

Antony accompanied Caesar to the entrance of the hall but was called aside by Trebonius on supposedly pressing business. Many of the conspirators had wanted to kill Antony as well, but Brutus had insisted that they strike down Caesar alone. If we slay any of Caesar's friends, Brutus argued, it will look like factional fighting rather than the justified killing of a tyrant.

When Caesar entered the meeting, all the senators rose to greet him. He was anxious to finish the proceedings as quickly as possible and so took his seat at the front. A senator named Tullius Cimber, whose brother Caesar had exiled, then approached the dictator with a petition to have his sibling pardoned. Caesar dismissed the man, but Cimber grabbed his toga and beseeched him for mercy. This was the signal. Another senator named Casca rushed at Caesar with his dagger drawn and stabbed him in the neck. Casca was so nervous, however, that he barely scratched Caesar, who in response sprang from his chair, plunged his stylus (his writing implement) through Casca's arm, and threw him off the podium.

The other conspirators now joined in and began stabbing Caesar with their knives as he fought them off furiously. From the front, side, and back they struck him over twenty times until the pain and loss of blood made him falter. It was then that he saw Brutus approaching, with his dagger raised to strike. Until that point Caesar had been ready to fight for his life against the senators, but as the younger man drew near he could only stare at him in shocked disbelief. Contrary to Shakespeare's immortal question—*Et tu, Brute?*— the last words of Caesar were in fact whispered to Brutus in Greek:

> *Kai su, teknon?*
> *(Even you, my child?)*

With that, Caesar wrapped his toga about his face and died at the foot of Pompey's statue.

Epilogue

CAESAR AND CATO AT VALLEY FORGE

Oh, could my dying hand but lodge a sword
In Caesar's bosom, and revenge my country,
By heavens, I could enjoy the pangs of death,
And smile in agony.

—Joseph Addison
Cato

General George Washington left the crowded, makeshift theater at his camp in the snowy hills of Pennsylvania and walked slowly back to his quarters. It had been a miserable winter for his men. The British army had outmaneuvered Washington during the autumn of 1777 and captured Philadelphia in spite of his best efforts. It seemed that nearly everything he had done since assuming command of the continental army two years earlier had ended in disaster. The invasion of Quebec had failed, New York had been abandoned to the British, and now the capital of the fledgling republic was in enemy hands.

Washington's only hope was to retreat to the settlement of Valley

Forge, eighteen miles northwest of Philadelphia, and wait for spring. But the situation was perilous. Primitive huts were the only shelter for his 12,000 men, there was little food aside from flat cakes made of flour and water, and most lacked clothing to keep out the bitter winds that blew constantly from the north. Disease—typhus, dysentery, typhoid, pneumonia—swept through the camp, killing as many as 2,000 of his soldiers that winter.

Faced with imminent defeat, Washington decided to put on a play. The drama he chose was *Cato* by the English writer Joseph Addison, one of the most popular productions in eighteenth-century America. The play, set in the final days of Cato's life, was one of Washington's favorites. In it Cato is the embodiment of republican and patriotic values for all ages, the noble foe of tyranny fighting against all odds to free his country from the oppression of Caesar. Washington saw the ancient Roman Republic as the embodiment of all he held most dear. Although Cato dies at the end of the play, Washington hoped his sacrifice would inspire his beleaguered soldiers in their own war against the tyranny of King George III. If, like Cato at Utica, the Continental army was defeated at Valley Forge, the new American republic would vanish forever.

The battle for Caesar's legacy began with his assassination on the Ides of March. Brutus and Cassius had assumed that the Roman people would welcome the death of Caesar and that the Republic would rise again. They failed to realize that the army had become the deciding factor in Roman politics. Whoever could control the most troops controlled the empire.

At Caesar's funeral, Mark Antony, holding the dictator's blood-stained toga aloft, evoked the legacy of the slain leader before the crowd, many of whom were Caesar's angry veterans. In time the conspirators were forced to flee east to rally their forces. Octavius adopted Caesar's name as his own while he kept an uneasy truce with

Antony and steadily increased his own power. The clemency of Caesar was forgotten as Antony and Octavius began a massacre of their political enemies at home, including Cicero, and attacked the Republican armies abroad. With the defeat of Antony and Caesar's old love, Cleopatra, at Actium in 31 B.C., Octavius emerged as sole ruler of Rome. As Caesar's heir, Octavius, now Caesar Augustus, lauded his great-uncle as a visionary leader and downplayed any hint of tyranny. After the fall of Rome, the courts of medieval Europe held Caesar up as the model of the ideal king—the Germans even borrowed his name for the title *Kaiser,* as did the Russians with *czar.* Beginning with Shakespeare the modern world became more ambivalent about Caesar. When Thomas Jefferson showed Alexander Hamilton his portraits of Francis Bacon, Isaac Newton, and John Locke as the three greatest men in world history, Hamilton, a republican to the core, spoke for many when he shook his head and reluctantly proclaimed:

The greatest man who ever lived was Julius Caesar.

SOURCE NOTES

PREFACE

Page

2 Mark Twain: *The Mysterious Stranger,* Chapter 8.

PROLOGUE: ON THE BANKS OF THE RUBICON

Page

7 *when the rains were scarce:* Lucan 1.214.

9 *"Let the dice fly high:"* Plutarch, *Caesar* 32, *Pompey* 60. Caesar quoted the line in Greek from the fourth century B.C. writer Menander.

I: THE EARLY YEARS

Page

13 Epigraph: Plutarch, *Caesar* 2.

15 *caesarean section:* Pliny, *Natural History* 7.7; Servius, *Commentary on the Aeneid* 1.286.

16 *Roman law considered women incompetent:* See Lefkowitz and Fant, *Women's Life in Greece and Rome,* esp. pp. 94–128.

18 *the Belly and the Limbs:* Livy 2.32; Dionysius of Halicarnassus 6.86.

18 *the Subura neighborhood:* Suetonius, *Caesar* 46.

22 *Metellus Macedonius:* The speech is from Aulus Gellius, *Attic Nights* 1.6.2.

23 *the law required:* Dionysius of Halicarnassus 2.15.1.

24 *a skilled tutor named Marcus Antonius Gnipho:* Suetonius, *Rhetoric* 7.

25 *Caesar's own youthful compositions:* Suetonius, *Caesar* 56.7.

25 *The one surviving fragment of Caesar's poetry:* From Suetonius, *Life of Terence* 7 in Morel, Büchner, and Blänsdorf, *Fragmenta Poetarum Latinorum,* 3rd ed., 189–91; Spaeth, "Caesar's Poetic Interests," 600–601.

25 *holding his hands behind his back:* Plutarch, *Caesar* 17.4.

28 *"They tossed headless bodies into the streets:"* Plutarch, *Marius* 44.6.

28 *Cornelius Merula:* Velleius Paterculus 2.22.

28 *flamen dialis:* The restrictions and responsibilities of the office are discussed in Aulus Gellius 10.15. See also Dumézil, *Archaic Roman Religion,* 151–53 and Puhvel, *Comparative Mythology,* 156–57.

29 *Cossutia:* Suetonius, *Caesar* 1.

30 *Sulla landed unopposed:* For the life of Sulla, see Plutarch, *Sulla.*

32 *"I see many a Marius":* Suetonius, *Caesar* 1; Plutarch, *Caesar* 1.

33 *the lover of Nicomedes:* Suetonius, *Caesar* 2; Dio Cassius 43.20.

33 *bawdy songs:* Suetonius, *Caesar* 49.

34 *corona civica:* Suetonius, *Caesar* 2; Polybius 6.39; Pliny, *Natural History* 16.11–14; Aulus Gellius 5.6.13.

34 *eaten from the inside by worms:* Plutarch, *Sulla* 36; *Acts of the Apostles* 12.23.

35 *the plot of Lepidus:* Suetonius, *Caesar* 3–4.

35 *Gnaeus Cornelius Dolabella:* Cicero, *Brutus* 261–62; Suetonius, *Caesar* 4; Plutarch, *Caesar* 4.

38 *Cilician pirates:* Suetonius, *Caesar* 4; Plutarch, *Caesar* 2; Velleius Paterculus 42; see also de Souza, "Greek Piracy."

40 *Crucifixion:* See Hengel, *Crucifixion.*

40 *Caesar mercifully cut the throats:* Suetonius, *Caesar* 74.

41 *another campaign against the pirates:* Gelzer, *Caesar,* 24–25.

41 *passage at night:* Velleius Paterculus 42.

II: THE PATH TO POWER

Page

42 Epigraph: Plutarch, *Caesar* 4.

42 *Spartacus:* The best sources for the war against Spartacus are Plutarch, *Crassus* 8–11 and Appian, *Civil War* 1.14.116–21. See also Shaw, *Spartacus and the Slave Wars.*

43 *an inscription from the first century A.D.:* Corpus Inscriptionum Latinarum 4.1189 (Shaw, *Spartacus and the Slave Wars,* 43).

49 *the patrician Cincinnatus:* Livy 3.26; Cicero, *On Old Age* 56 (16).

50 *to restore power to the tribunes of the plebs:* Suetonius, *Caesar* 5.

51 *the death of the family matriarch, Julia:* Suetonius, *Caesar* 6; Plutarch, *Caesar* 5.1–2.

52 *Tragedy struck Caesar again:* Suetonius, *Caesar* 6; Plutarch, *Caesar* 5.

53 *epitaph later written by a Roman man in Egypt:* Cagnat, Merlin, and Chatelain, *Inscriptions Latines d'Afrique* # 175L; Lefkowitz and Fant, *Women's Life in Greece and Rome,* 206–7.

53 *quaestor under the governor Antistius Vetus:* Suetonius, *Caesar* 7; Plutarch, *Caesar* 5; Dio Cassius 37.52.1–2; Velleius Paterculus 2.43.4; *Spanish War* 42. Plutarch, *Caesar* 32.6, places Caesar's dream of having sex with his mother just before his crossing of the Rubicon.

55 *the disgruntled Italians north of the Po:* Suetonius, *Caesar* 8.

55 *a young woman named Pompeia:* Suetonius, *Caesar* 6; Plutarch, *Caesar* 5. Plutarch calls Pompeia his third wife, including Cossutia to whom he had been engaged before his marriage to Cornelia.

56 *curator of the Appian Way:* Plutarch, *Caesar* 5.

57 *to destroy the pirates once and for all:* Plutarch, *Pompey* 25–29.

58 *to settle affairs in the eastern Mediterranean:* Plutarch, *Pompey* 30; Dio Cassius 36.43.

59 *the feuding Maccabees of Judea:* Josephus, *Antiquities of the Jews* 14.1–5.

60 *he was elected as an aedile:* Suetonius, *Caesar* 10; Plutarch, *Caesar* 6.5; Dio Cassius 37.8; Velleius Paterculus 2.43.4; Pliny, *Natural History* 33.53 (33.16).

61 *a taste for the finer things in life:* Suetonius, *Caesar* 46–48.

61 *the dazzling trophies of Marius's victories:* Plutarch, *Caesar* 6; Suetonius, *Caesar* 11; Velleius Paterculus 2.43.4.

61 *"This Caesar is no longer trying to undermine the Republic secretly":* Plutarch, *Caesar* 6.4.

62 *The biographer Suetonius mentions a plot:* Suetonius, *Caesar* 9; Sallust, *Catiline* 18; See Gelzer, *Caesar,* 38–40. Gelzer details several of the reasons for rejecting Caesar's involvement in any plot.

62 *the plodding anti-Caesarian historian Tanusius Geminus:* Seneca, *Letters* 93.11.

63 *the ancient kingdom of Egypt:* Suetonius, *Caesar* 11; Plutarch, *Crassus* 13.

64 *Cato's assignment was to manage the treasury in Rome:* Plutarch, *Cato the Younger* 16–18.

65 *among ex-aediles, including Caesar:* Suetonius, *Caesar* 11.

III: CONSPIRACY

Page

66 Epigraph: Plutarch, *Caesar* 7.

67 *Caesar declared himself a candidate for the office of pontifex maximus:* Plutarch, *Caesar* 7; Suetonius, *Caesar* 13; Dio Cassius 37.37; Velleius Paterculus 2.43; Sallust, *Catiline* 49.

68 *"Mother, today you will see your son":* Plutarch, *Caesar* 7.2; Suetonius, *Caesar* 13.

69 *Cicero's stinging oratory:* See Cicero, *On the Agrarian Law.*

69 *Gaius Rabirius:* Suetonius, *Caesar* 12; Cicero *For Rabirius Postumus*; Dio Cassius 37.26–28.

70 *"Because of my friendship with King Nicomedes":* Aulus Gellius 5.13.6.

71 *prosecutor of the optimate Gaius Calpurnius Piso:* Sallust, *Catiline* 49.2; Cicero *For Flaccus* 98 (39).

71 *his speech in favor of Masintha:* Suetonius, *Caesar* 71.

71 *a nobleman named Catiline:* the primary sources for the Catilinian conspiracy are Cicero *Catiline,* and Sallust, *Catiline.* Key texts for Caesar's relationship to Catiline also include Suetonius, *Caesar* 14, and Plutarch, *Caesar* 7–8.

73 *"O Catiline":* Cicero, *Against Catiline* 1.33 (1.13).

73 *the Celtic Allobroges tribe in Gaul:* Sallust, *Catiline* 40–41.

75 *the harshest possible penalty:* Plutarch, *Cicero* 21.3; *Cato the Younger* 22.5. Although Plutarch wrote in Greek, the original Latin of the Senate proceedings must have been *ultima poena.*

75 *it was at last Caesar's turn:* Sallust, *Catiline* 51; Cicero, *Against Catiline* 4.7–10 (4.4–5); Suetonius, *Caesar* 14; Plutarch, *Cato the Younger* 22.5, *Caesar* 7.4–5; Dio Cassius 37.36.1–2.

76 *"As I see it, Senators . . . The problem is that people will remember":* Sallust, *Catiline* 51.15.

77 *Cato rose to speak:* Sallust, *Catiline* 52; Plutarch, *Cato the Younger* 23; *Caesar* 8.1–2; Suetonius, *Caesar* 14; Dio Cassius 37.36.

77 *"The more harsh the punishment":* Sallust, *Catiline* 52.18.

77 *a love letter to Caesar from Servilia:* Plutarch, *Brutus* 5; *Cato the Younger* 24.1–2.

78 *Cicero rescued Caesar from this debacle:* Plutarch, *Caesar* 8.1–2, *Cicero* 21; Sallust, *Catiline* 49.4.

78 *their place of execution in the Forum:* Sallust, *Catiline* 55; Plutarch, *Cicero* 22.1–2.

78 *"They have lived":* Plutarch, *Cicero* 22.2.

78 *In the aftermath of the executions:* Sallust, *Catiline* 56–61.

79 *forbade Cicero to say another word:* Dio Cassius 37.38.

79 *Caesar called an assembly of the people:* Suetonius, *Caesar* 15.

81 *Cato marched to the Forum:* Plutarch, *Cato the Younger* 26–28; Dio Cassius 43.

81 *Caesar and Nepos had overplayed their hand:* Dio Cassius 43.3–44; Suetonius, *Caesar* 16.

82 *letters in Caesar's own handwriting linking him to Catiline:* Suetonius, *Caesar* 17.

83 *The juicy scandal that hit Caesar next:* Plutarch, *Caesar* 9–10, *Cicero* 28–29; Brouwer, *Bona Dea,* 363–370; Tatum, *The Patrician Tribune,* 62–86.

84 *Caesar's wife must be above suspicion:* Plutarch, *Caesar* 10.6; *Cicero* 29.7.

85 *Pompey finally returned triumphantly to Italy:* Plutarch, *Pompey* 43.

86 *Caesar had set off at breakneck speed for his province in Spain:* Plutarch, *Caesar* 11.

86 *"I would rather be first man here than second in Rome":* Plutarch, *Caesar* 11.2. In Milton, *Paradise Lost* 2.163, Satan declares, "Better to reign in Hell than serve in Heaven!"

86 *Caesar's exploits in Spain:* Plutarch, *Caesar* 11–12; Suetonius, *Caesar* 18, 54; Dio Cassius 57.52–53; Catullus 29.19–20.

89 *But Caesar faced a conundrum:* Suetonius, *Caesar* 18; Plutarch, *Caesar* 13; *Cato the Younger* 31. 2–3; Dio Cassius 37.54.

90 *One of the consular candidates for 59 B.C.:* Suetonius, *Caesar* 19.1.

90 *woods and pastures:* Suetonius, *Caesar* 19.2.

91 *Caesar's only hope for a productive magistracy:* Suetonius, *Caesar* 19.2; Dio Cassius 37.55–58.

IV: CONSUL

Page

93 Epigraph: Dio Cassius 38.11.3.

93 *Caesar was unusually tall:* Suetonius, *Caesar* 45.

93 *He was a notorious ladies' man:* Suetonius, *Caesar* 50; Plutarch, *Brutus* 5.
94 *the falling sickness:* Suetonius, *Caesar* 45; Plutarch, *Caesar* 17.2–3. See also Temkin, *The Falling Sickness,* 3–81.
94 *Even in the gospels: Matthew* 17.14–20; *Mark* 9.14–29.
94 *But as Plutarch says:* Plutarch, *Caesar* 17.2–3.
94 *"Vatinius the tribune did nothing for free":* Cicero, *Against Vatinius* 38 (16).
95 *Caesar borrowed a trick:* Suetonius, *Caesar* 20.1.
95 *Caesar, however, ordered his lictors to march behind him:* Suetonius, *Caesar* 20.1.
95 *Caesar's first significant action as consul:* Dio Cassius 38.1; Suetonius, *Caesar* 20; Plutarch, *Caesar* 14.
96 *Caesar urged all the senators:* Dio Cassius 38.2.
97 *"I would rather be in jail with Cato":* Dio Cassius 38.2–3.
97 *When Caesar presented his new land proposal to the popular assembly:* Dio Cassius 38.4–6; Plutarch, *Caesar* 14; *Pompey* 47–48; Suetonius, *Caesar* 20.
97 *"The law will pass," Caesar cried:* Dio Cassius 38.4.3.
98 *Bibulus, meanwhile:* Dio Cassius 38. 6.1–2; Suetonius, *Caesar* 20.1.
98 *Caesar fixed a day for the assembly:* Dio Cassius 38.6.2–6; Plutarch, *Pompey* 48.1–2; Suetonius, *Caesar* 20.1.
99 *Bibulus withdrew to his own house:* Suetonius, *Caesar* 20.2; Dio Cassius 38.6.4–6.
99 *"Done in the consulship of Julius and Caesar":* Suetonius, *Caesar* 20.2.
99 *"There was a deed just now done by Caesar, not by Bibulus":* Suetonius, *Caesar* 20.2.
99 *As a result, he introduced a new bill to the people:* Cicero, *Letters to Atticus* 36 (2.16.1–2), 37 (2.17.1), 38 (2.18.2); Velleius Paterculus 2.44.4.
100 *Most of the Senate saw that there was little point in resisting:* Dio Cassius 38.7.5; Suetonius, *Caesar* 20.4.
101 *the gift of the Nile:* Herodotus 2.5.
102 *Caesar now pushed through legislation ratifying Ptolemy's rule:* Caesar, *Civil War* 3.107; Suetonius, *Caesar* 64.3.
102 *Caesar completed his eastern legislation:* Suetonius, *Caesar* 20.3; Dio Cassius 38.7.4; Cicero, *Letters to Atticus* 17 (1.17.9), 18 (1.18.7), 21 (2.1.8); *Against Vatinius* 29 (12).
103 *We should all be very afraid:* Cicero, *Letters to Atticus* 37 (2.17.1).
103 *Caesar offered his daughter, Julia:* Plutarch, *Caesar* 14.4–5; *Pompey* 47.6; Suetonius, *Caesar* 21.
103 *Cato proclaimed that it was disgusting:* Plutarch, *Caesar* 14.5.
104 *the ex-consul Gaius Antonius:* Dio Cassius 38.10.
104 *Everyone acknowledged that Caesar had a mild and forgiving nature:* Dio Cassius 38.11.2–3.
104 *Publius Clodius:* Suetonius, *Caesar* 20.4; Dio Cassius 38.12.1–2; Cicero, *Letters to Atticus* 18 (1.18.4); *On his own Household* 41 (16); Tatum, *The Patrician Tribune,* 87–113.
106 *Caesar's monumental* lex Julia de repetundis: Cicero, *For Rabirius Postumus* 4.8; *Letters to his Friends* 8.8; Johnson, Coleman-Norton; and Bourne, *Ancient Roman Statutes,* 78.

106 Cicero called it *justissima atque optima:* Cicero, *Against Piso* 37 (16).

106 *This infuriated Cato so much:* Dio Cassius 38.7.6.

108 *"He desperately wanted great power":* Sallust, *Catiline* 54.4.

109 *In the late spring of 59 B.C.:* Suetonius, *Caesar* 22; Plutarch, *Caesar* 14.6–7; Dio Cassius 38.8.5; Cicero, *Letters to Atticus* 153.3 (8.3).

109 *The vast tribal lands of Gaul:* Caesar, *Gallic War* 1.31.

110 *a prince and trained druid named Diviciacus:* Cicero, *On Divination* 1.90 (1.41).

110 *But the agents of Ariovistus reached the senators first:* Caesar, *Gallic War* 1.35.

111 *"jump on their heads":* Suetonius, *Caesar* 22.2.

111 *A murder plot against Pompey:* Suetonius, *Caesar* 20.5.

111 *Clodius finally began his long-awaited term as tribune:* Dio Cassius 38.13, 17; Cicero, *Letters to Atticus* 46 (3.1).

111 *Bibulus rose to deliver his own address:* Dio Cassius 38.12.3.

111 *news had reached Rome that the Helvetii were about to move:* Caesar, *Gallic War* 1.6–7.

V: GAUL

Page

112 Epigraph: Caesar, *Gallic War* 1.1.

112 *a people known as the Celts:* The best modern sources for the study of the ancient Celts are Mac Cana, *Celtic Mythology,* Rankin *Celts and the Classical World,* Megaw and Megaw, *Celtic Art,* Kruta, *The Celts,* Cunliffe *The Ancient Celts,* Green, *The World of the Druids,* and Haywood, *Atlas of the Celtic World.* I also discuss many aspects of the early Celts in my book *The Philosopher and the Druids.*

115 *The Gauls were polytheists:* Caesar discusses Gaulish gods, religion, and the Druids in his *Gallic War* (6.13–14, 16–19).

116 *Orgetorix urged the Helvetian leaders:* Caesar, *Gallic War* 1.2–4.

117 *Dumnorix is, after all, Gaulish for "king of the world":* See Evans, *Gaulish Personal Names,* 196–97.

121 *Caesar received word:* Caesar's struggles with the Helvetii are best told in the *Gallic War* (1.7–29), but also by Dio Cassius (38.31.1–34.2) and Plutarch, *Caesar* 18.

129 *Caesar's horse was a unique animal:* Suetonius, *Caesar* 61.

132 *tablets written in the Gaulish language:* For the ancient Gaulish language, see Eska and Evans, "Continental Celtic."

135 *The Germans:* Caesar describes the Germans in his *Gallic War* (4.1–4), as does Tacitus throughout his *Germania.*

135 *Those who betrayed their people:* Tacitus, *Germania* 12.

135 *especially devoted to divination:* Tacitus, *Germania* 10.

135 *He invited Ariovistus to a meeting:* For the discussion between Caesar and Ariovistus as well as the subsequent war, see the *Gallic War* (1.34–54), Dio Cassius (38.34–50), and Plutarch, *Caesar* 19.

VI: THE BELGAE

Page

143 Epigraph: Caesar, *Gallic War* 2.27.

143 *There were always cases to be heard:* Caesar, *Gallic War* 1.54.

143 *he would keep a scribe at hand:* Plutarch, *Caesar* 17.3.

144 *he used a code based on switching letters of the alphabet:* Suetonius, *Caesar* 56.6.

144 *a constant stream of high-level visitors from Rome:* Plutarch, *Caesar* 20.2.

144 *Clodius had already passed an unprecedented free-grain bill:* Dio Cassius 38.13. For the actions of Clodius during his term as tribune, see Gelzer, *Caesar* (112–113) and especially Tatum, *The Patrician Tribune* (114–75).

144 *He managed to have Cicero exiled:* Cicero, *Letters to Atticus* 46 (3.1); Plutarch, *Cicero* 31–33; Dio Cassius 38.17.4–7.

144 *Many years earlier, Clodius:* Dio Cassius 38.30.5.

145 *But Pompey rejected this ploy:* Plutarch, *Pompey* 49.1–3.

145 *the fearsome Belgic tribes in northern France:* For Caesar's campaigns against the Belgae in 57 B.C., see the second book of his *Gallic War,* along with Dio Cassius (39.1–5) and Plutarch, *Caesar* 20.3–5.

146 *the nickname* alauda *(Gaulish for "lark"):* Suetonius, *Caesar* 24.2; Pliny, *Natural History* 11.121 (11.44); Delamarre, *Dictionnaire de la langue gauloise,* 36.

149 *Some slingers used smooth stones:* See Goldsworthy, *The Complete Roman Army,* 180–81, 188–192.

152 *No Roman general ever pressed his troops harder than Caesar:* Suetonius, *Caesar* 45–48.

156 *He rushed to the front lines:* Caesar, *Gallic War* 2.25.

157 *Later events show the Nervii:* Caesar states (*Gallic War* 7.75) that they contributed five thousand men to the rebellion in 52 B.C.

159 *the Great St. Bernard Pass into Italy:* Caesar, *Gallic War* 3.1–6.

161 *The consensus among the more moderate senators:* Cicero, *Against Vatinius* 15 (6).

161 *He began to mutter against Caesar:* Dio Cassius 39.25–26.

162 *to give Pompey extraordinary powers:* Cicero, *Letters to Atticus* 73 (4.1); Dio Cassius 39.9.

162 *Pompey took this rebuff with ill humor:* Dio Cassius 39.12–16; Plutarch, *Pompey* 39.

162 *Caesar was, of course, keeping a close watch:* Suetonius, *Caesar* 24; Plutarch, *Caesar* 21; Cicero, *On the Consular Provinces* 29–35 (12–14); *Letters to Atticus* 80.1 (4.5.1). Gelzer, *Caesar* (116–25), has an excellent discussion of the politics at Rome during the winter of 57–56 B.C.

164 *he traveled to nearby Illyricum:* Caesar, *Gallic War* 3.7.

164 *as Caesar says was typical among the Gauls:* Caesar, *Gallic War* 3.8.

164 *the Veneti and their allies had now started a war with Rome:* Caesar discusses the campaign against the maritime tribes and Aquitania in the third book (7–28) of his *Gallic War.* See also Dio Cassius (39.40–45).

165 *Caesar inserts an amazing statement in his* Gallic War: Caesar, *Gallic War* 3.10.

170 *The Gauls are by nature:* Caesar, *Gallic War* 3.19.

VII: BRITAIN

Page

172   Epigraph: Cicero, *Letters to Quintus* 2.16.4.

172   *Cato brought charges against Caesar's trusted counselor Balbus:* See Cicero, *In Defense of Balbus.*

173   *Marcellinus, one of the two consuls for the current year:* Dio Cassius 39.27; Plutarch, *Pompey* 51.5–6.

173   *As Domitius and Cato worked to secure last-minute votes:* Plutarch, *Pompey* 52.1–2.

174   *Pompey declared that he had heard thunder:* Plutarch, *Cato the Younger* 42.3–4.

174   *Pompey and Crassus spent the next few weeks:* Dio Cassius 39.33–34; Plutarch, *Pompey* 52.3–4; *Cato the Younger* 43.

174   *the Usipetes and Tencteri:* Caesar, *Gallic War* 4.1–15; Dio Cassius 39.47–48.

175   *Caesar writes that the Suebi:* Caesar, *Gallic War* 4.1–3.

175   *Caesar writes that some Belgic tribes:* Caesar, *Gallic War* 4.6.

175   *"soothe their spirits and encourage them":* Caesar, *Gallic War* 4.6.

177   *Caesar decided to cross the Rhine:* Caesar, *Gallic War* 4.16.

179   *Caesar's bridge across the Rhine:* Caesar, *Gallic War* 4.17; Plutarch, *Caesar* 22.3–4. Caesar's description of the bridge and its construction is not as clear as we might hope. Presumably his Roman audience was much more familiar with the technical aspects and terminology than we are. For a closer look into this remarkable structure, I recommend the notes and diagrams from the relevant section of the Loeb Classical Library volume of Caesar's *Gallic War* and O'Connor, *Roman Bridges* (139–41).

179   *Caesar's intention in crossing the Rhine:* Caesar, *Gallic War* 4.18–19.

180   *the mythic island of Britain:* Caesar discusses his first campaign in Britain in his *Gallic War* (4.20–38). See also Dio Cassius 39.50–53; Plutarch, *Caesar* 23.2.

180   *Some Romans even claimed that the island didn't exist:* Plutarch, *Caesar* 23.2.

180   *He could not discover the size of Britain:* Caesar, *Gallic War* 4.20.

181   *Pytheas of Massalia:* See Cunliffe, *The Extraordinary Voyage of Pytheas the Greek,* and Roseman, *Pytheas of Massalia.*

181   *used to call their island* Albion: Avienus, *Ora maritima* 108–19; Pliny, *Natural History* 4.102. The early classical sources for Britain can be found in Ireland, *Roman Britain: A Sourcebook* (13–18) and my own *War, Women, and Druids* (61–63).

183   *"Soldiers, follow me":* Caesar, *Gallic War* 4.25.

183   *claimed it was only his lack of cavalry:* Caesar, *Gallic War* 4.26.

186   *As Caesar says, fighting in chariots:* Caesar, *Gallic War* 4.33.

186   *The Senate announced twenty days of public thanksgiving:* Caesar, *Gallic War* 4.38.

186   *Cato rose to denounce him on the Senate floor:* Plutarch *Cato the Younger* 51; *Caesar* 22.1–3.

187   *he set about designing an entirely new kind of vessel:* Caesar, *Gallic War* 5.1.

188   *an Alpine tribe called the Pirustae:* Caesar, *Gallic War* 51.

188 *Young Catullus:* Suetonius, *Caesar* 73.

188 *Catullus had also failed to reap any expected profit:* Catullus 10.

189 *Who can look at this:* Catullus 29.1–4.

189 *They're a pretty pair of sodomites:* Catullus 57.1–3. See also Catullus 93.

190 *Cicero even sent samples of his poetry:* Cicero, *Letter to Quintus* 18.2 (2.14.2), 20.5 (2.16.5).

190 *Although Quintus was a literary man:* Cicero, *Letter to Quintus* 20.3 (2.16.3), 25.7–8 (3.5.7–8).

190 *a now-lost work entitled* On Analogy: Suetonius, *Caesar* 56.5; Plutarch, *Caesar* 17.3.

190 *"Avoid strange and unfamiliar words":* Aulus Gellius, *Attic Nights* 1.10.4.

190 *Caesar dedicated the work:* Cicero, *Brutus* 253 (72).

190 *When Caesar arrived back at the Channel:* Caesar, *Gallic War* 5.2.

190 *The one tribe that had refused Caesar's summons:* Caesar, *Gallic War* 5.3–4.

191 *At the top of the list of potential troublemakers was Dumnorix:* Caesar, *Gallic War* 5.5–7.

192 *I am a free man of a free people!:* Caesar, *Gallic War* 5.7.

192 *A gentle southwest breeze:* Caesar, *Gallic War* 5.8–23.

194 *The parts of Britain:* Caesar, *Gallic War* 5.12–14.

194 *The claim that the southern Britons:* Among the many excellent discussions of Britain in the first century B.C. are De la Bédoyère, *Roman Britain: A New History* (10–22), Jones and Mattingly, *An Atlas of Roman Britain* (16–63), and Snyder, *The Britons* (11–28).

194 *the ancient British language:* Tacitus, *Agricola* 11. Tacitus also states that the same ritual and religious beliefs are found in both Gaul and Britain.

194 *The Britons in turn exported:* Strabo 4.5.2.

195 *tales of sacred birds in Celtic mythology:* See Anne Ross, *Pagan Celtic Britain* (302–77).

195 *the rebellous British queen Boudicca released a hare:* Dio Cassius 62.2.

197 *he reports that there was "suddenly trouble in Gaul":* Caesar, *Gallic War* 5.22.

197 *The news awaiting Caesar on his return to Gaul:* Caesar, *Gallic War* 5.24–26.

198 *his beloved daughter, Julia:* Plutarch, *Caesar* 23.4; *Pompey* 53; Suetonius, *Caesar* 26.1; Dio Cassius 39.64; Cicero, *Letters to Quintus* 21.17, 25 (3.1.17, 25).

VIII: VERCINGETORIX

Page

199 Epigraph: Caesar, *Gallic War* 7.76.

199 *Their leader, Ambiorix:* Caesar, *Gallic War* 5.26–38; Dio Cassius 40.5–6.

200 *Quintus Cicero:* Caesar, *Gallic War* 5.38–52; Dio Cassius 40.7–10; Plutarch, *Caesar* 24; Cicero, *Letters to Atticus* 93 (4.19).

205 *leaving his hair and beard uncut:* Suetonius, *Caesar* 67.2.

206 *Caesar spent the few remaining weeks of 53 B.C.:* Caesar, *Gallic War* 5.53–58.

206 *Three new legions soon joined him in Gaul:* Caesar, *Gallic War* 6.1; Plutarch, *Caesar* 25.1–2; *Pompey* 52.3.

206   *Caesar trusted only the Aedui in the southeast and the Remi:* Caesar, *Gallic War* 5.54.

206   *He deposed his rival and Caesar's friend Cingetorix:* Caesar, *Gallic War* 5.56.

207   *Caesar's campaign of terror and revenge in Gaul:* Caesar, *Gallic War* 6.1–10, 29–44.

210   *Caesar had been working to endow Rome with magnificent buildings:* Cicero, *Letters to Atticus* 89.8 (4.16.8); Appian, *Civil War* 2.102; Richardson, *A New Topographical Dictionary of Ancient Rome,* 52–53, 165–67.

210   *Marcus Crassus:* Plutarch, *Life of Crassus* 20–25.

211   *two of Rome's most infamous thugs:* Caesar, *Gallic War* 7.1; Cicero, *In Defense of Milo;* Dio Cassius 40.48–49; Suetonius, *Caesar* 26; Tatum, *The Patrician Tribune,* 239–240.

212   *consul without a colleague:* Plutarch, *Cato the Younger* 47.1–3; Cicero, *In Defense of Milo* 61.

212   *Caesar attempted to renew family ties with Pompey:* Suetonius, *Caesar* 27; Plutarch, *Pompey* 55; Dio Cassius 40.51.

213   *did not escape the notice of the Gauls:* Caesar, *Gallic War* 7.1

213   *the sacred center of Gaul:* Caesar, *Gallic War* 6.13.

214   *a tall young warrior named Vercingetorix:* For the rebellion of Vercingetorix, see Caesar, *Gallic War* 7.4–90; Dio Cassius 40.33–41; Plutarch, *Caesar* 25–27.

214   *considered a friend by the Roman general:* Dio Cassius 40.41.1.

216   *The Romans opened up a path through the mountains:* Caesar, *Gallic War* 7.8.

218   *If this plan seems drastic or cruel to you:* Caesar, *Gallic War* 7.14.

219   *two nobles of the tribe both claimed the title of chief magistrate:* Caesar, *Gallic War* 7.32–33.

220   *the fortifications of Gergovia:* Caesar, *Gallic War* 7.34–53.

223   *Caesar could not imagine how things could get much worse:* Caesar, *Gallic War* 7.54–67.

224   *the towering walls of nearby Alesia:* Caesar, *Gallic War* 7.68–89; Plutarch, *Caesar* 27.

225   *Caesar even lost his sword:* Plutarch, *Caesar* 26.4.

227   *only the most ardent Gaulish patriots still pressed for independence:* the final year of the conflict in Gaul is described by Caesar's lieutenant Aulus Hirtius in Book 8 of the *Gallic War.*

IX: RUBICON

Page

228   Epigraph: Suetonius, *Life of Julius Caesar* 4.

228   *the ancient historian Tacitus:* Tacitus *Agricola* 30.

228   *The number of Gaulish dead:* Plutarch, *Caesar* 15.3; Pliny, *Natural History* 7.92.

229   *the Gallic war had enormous benefits:* Suetonius, *Caesar* 25.1.

229   *Caesar's personal wealth:* Suetonius, *Caesar* 28.1, 54.2.

230   *Cato had, in fact, long been threatening:* Suetonius, *Caesar* 30.3.

231   *Those Gauls who had served him well:* Caesar, *Civil War* 3.59.

231   *The Romans could not countenance human sacrifice:* Suetonius, *Claudius* 25; Pliny, *Natural History* 30.13; Lucan, *Pharsalia* 1.450–58.

231   *Cato had tried and failed to gain the consulship:* Dio Cassius 50.58.

232   *while even Cicero praised the work:* Caesar, *Brutus* 262.

232   *Marcellus cleverly countered:* Suetonius, *Caesar* 28.2.

232   *Marcellus also attacked Caesar's power base in Italian Gaul:* Plutarch, *Caesar* 29.2; Suetonius, *Caesar* 28.3; Appian, *Civil War* 2.26.

233   *Now that I am the greatest man in Rome:* Suetonius, *Caesar* 29.1.

233   *"What do you think I would do":* Cicero, *Letters to His Friends* 8.8.9.

234   *a new campaign against the Parthian empire:* Cicero, *Letter to Atticus* 111.1 (5.18.1), 115.14 (6.1.14).

234   *In preparation for any military conflict:* Caesar (Hirtius), *Gallic War* 8.24.

234   *He dismissed no troops:* Suetonius, *Caesar* 26.3.

234   *he continued to stockpile weapons and recruit additional soldiers:* Dio Cassius 40.60.1.

235   *Lucius Aemilius Paullus:* Suetonius, *Caesar* 29.1; Plutarch, *Caesar* 29.3.

235   *Gaius Marcellus:* Suetonius, *Caesar* 27.1.

235   *Gaius Scribonius Curio:* Suetonius, *Caesar* 29.1; Plutarch, *Caesar* 29.3; Velleius Paterculus 2.48.3; Pliny, *Natural History* 36.177; Dio Cassius 40.61–62; Cicero, *Letters to Atticus* 117.4 (6.3.4).

235   *Pompey magnanimously offered:* Caesar, *Civil War* 1.4; Dio Cassius 40.65–66; Plutarch, *Caesar* 29.3.

236   *Cicero was not a military man:* Cicero, *Letters to Atticus* 113 (5.20), 124.7 (7.1.7).

236   *Curio rose from his bench:* Caesar (Hirtius), *Gallic War* 8. 52; Plutarch, *Caesar* 30; Dio Cassius 40.62.

237   *then maneuvered the election of Antony:* Caesar (Hirtius), *Gallic War* 8.50; Plutarch, *Antony* 5; Caesar, *Civil War* 2.

237   *Caesar also returned to northern Italy:* Caesar (Hirtius), *Gallic War* 8.50–51.

238   *Cicero, writing to his friend Atticus:* Cicero, *Letters to Atticus* 123.5 (6.9.5).

238   *Pompey's supporters spread stories:* Plutarch, *Caesar* 29.4–5, *Pompey* 57.

238   *"All I have to do is stamp my foot":* Plutarch, *Pompey* 57.5.

239   *Labienus:* Caesar (Hirtius), *Gallic War* 8.52; Plutarch, *Caesar* 34.1–3; Dio Cassius 41.4.3–4.

239   *The current state of affairs terrifies me:* Cicero, *Letters to Atticus* 129.2 (7.6.2).

240   *Curio finally succeeded in forcing the Senate to vote:* Plutarch, *Pompey* 52.4–6.

240   *Gaius Marcellus marched across the Forum to Pompey:* Plutarch, *Pompey* 58. 5–6, 59.1; Appian, *Civil War* 2.31.

240   *Caesar moved to Ravenna:* Suetonius, *Caesar* 30.1; Caesar (Hirtius), *Gallic War* 8.54–55; Appian, *Civil War* 2.32.

241   *Caesar laid out his ultimatum:* Appian, *Civil War* 2.32–33.

241   *Cicero labored over the next few days:* Plutarch, *Pompey* 59.3, *Caesar* 31; Suetonius, *Caesar* 29.2–30.1.

242   *but at last he plunged forward into civil war:* Caesar does not mention crossing

the Rubicon in his own account, but other ancient writers rightly portray it as a pivotal moment (Suetonius, *Caesar* 31–32; Plutarch, *Caesar* 32; *Pompey* 60; Lucan, *Civil War* 1. 213–222; Appian, *Civil War* 2.35).

X: CIVIL WAR

Page

243 Epigraph: Caesar, *Gallic War* 6.30.

243 *Caesar played up his arrival:* Caesar, *Civil War* 1.7; Suetonius, *Caesar* 33.

244 *Meanwhile in Rome:* Plutarch, *Caesar* 33; *Pompey* 60–61; Appian, *Civil War* 2.36–37.

245 *It wasn't long until Caesar received two visitors:* Caesar, *Civil War* 1.8–11; Dio Cassius 41.5–6.

246 *Cicero, who was in Pompey's camp at the time:* Cicero, *Letters to Atticus* 138.1 (7.14.1).

246 *"It was an unfair offer":* Caesar, *Civil War* 1.11.

246 *"Caesar would be mad not to accept":* Cicero, *Letters to Atticus* 141.2 (7.17.2).

246 *Caesar now sent Mark Antony:* Caesar, *Civil War* 1.11–13.

247 *Pompey was near Naples:* Caesar, *Civil War* 1.14.

247 *Meanwhile Caesar was having much better luck:* Caesar, *Civil War* 1.15.

247 *Lucius Domitius Ahenobarbus:* Caesar, *Civil War* 1.15–23; Plutarch, *Caesar* 34.3–4; Dio Cassius 41.11; Suetonius, *Caesar* 34; Cicero, *Letters to Atticus* 162B–D (8.12B–D).

248 *According to Plutarch:* Plutarch, *Caesar* 34.3–4.

250 *Cicero wrote to Atticus:* Cicero, *Letters to Atticus* 163 (8.13).

250 *Pompey beat him to Brundisium:* Caesar, *Civil War* 1.24–29.

251 *Caesar sent a messenger to Pompey:* Caesar, *Civil War* 1.26.

252 *He therefore decided to strike his enemy first:* Caesar, *Civil War* 1.29–31.

253 *Caesar had written to Cicero:* Cicero, *Letters to Atticus* 172A (9.6A).

253 *When Caesar heard of this he wrote:* Cicero, *Letters to Atticus* 185 (9.16).

253 *the two men settled down to business:* Cicero, *Letters to Atticus* 187, 189 (9.18–19).

254 *He did call together the Senate:* Caesar, *Civil War* 1.32–33; Dio Cassius 41.15–17.

254 *Lucius Metellus:* Caesar, *Civil War* 1.33; Dio Cassius 41.17; Cicero, *Letters to Atticus* 195.8 (10.4.8); Appian, *Civil Wars* 2.41; Lucan *Civil War* 3.141–68.

255 *15,000 bars of gold:* Pliny, *Natural History* 33.56.

255 *Massalia:* Caesar, *Civil War* 1.34–36.

256 *Caesar optimistically claimed:* Suetonius, *Caesar* 34.2.

256 *Caesar crossed the Pyrenees:* Caesar, *Civil War* 1.37–87; Appian, *Roman History* 2.42–43; Dio Cassius 41.20–24.

257 *When news of Caesar's difficulties reached Rome:* Caesar, *Civil War* 1.53; Dio Cassius 41.21.

258 *Quintus Sertorius:* Plutarch, *Sertorius*.

260 *"We have done our duty":* Caesar, *Civil War* 1.84.

260 *The town of Gades:* Dio Cassius 41.24; Caesar, *Civil War* 2.21.

261 *Back in Massalia:* Caesar, *Civil War* 1.56–58, 2.1–22; Dio Cassius 41.25.

261 *"Human nature is such":* Caesar, *Gallic War* 2.4.

261 *At the town of Placentia:* Suetonius, *Caesar* 69; Dio Cassius 41.26–35; Appian, *Civil War* 2.47.

263 *Dolabella:* Dio Cassius 41.40.

263 *the loss of his army in north Africa:* Caesar, *Civil War* 2.23–44; Dio Cassius 41.41–42; Appian, *Civil War* 2.44–46.

264 *When Caesar arrived in Rome on the way to Brindusium:* Caesar, *Civil War* 3.1–2; Dio Cassius 2.48; Plutarch, *Caesar* 37.1; Lucan, *Civil War* 381–402.

XI: POMPEY

Page

267 Epigraph: Caesar, *Civil War* 3.73.

267 *an enormous international force in Greece:* Caesar, *Civil War* 3.3–4; Appian, *Civil War* 2.49, 71.

268 *Caesar, on the other hand:* Caesar, *Civil War* 3.2, 6–7; Appian, *Civil War* 2.52–54; Plutarch, *Caesar* 37; Dio Cassius 41.44.

269 *By some miracle of fate or fortune:* Caesar, *Civil War* 3.8; Appian, *Civil War* 2.54–56.

270 *Bibulus:* Caesar, *Civil War* 3.14.

270 *Caesar decided to try diplomacy once again:* Caesar, *Civil War* 3.10–18; Plutarch, *Pompey* 65.

270 *"What is the point":* Caesar, *Civil War* 3.18.

271 *"Don't bring us any more of your proposals":* Caesar, *Civil War* 3.19.

271 *There was also news of dissension:* Caesar, *Civil War* 3.20–22.

272 *"Come now, my friend":* Plutarch, *Caesar* 38. Caesar omits this episode from his own narrative, but the story is found in Dio Cassius (41.46) and Appian (*Civil War* 2.57–58).

272 *sails on the western horizon:* Caesar, *Civil War* 3.25–28; Appian, *Civil War* 2.59; Dio Cassius 41.48.

273 *why not build a wall around Pompey?:* Caesar, *Civil War* 3.43–45.

274 *"It was a totally new type of warfare":* Caesar, *Civil War* 3.50.

274 *Caesar's men suffered most:* Caesar, *Civil War* 3.47–48.

274 *he exclaimed that if Caesar's army could eat such food:* Appian, *Civil War* 2.61; Plutarch, *Caesar* 39.

275 *a letter to Cicero:* Cicero, *Letters to his Friends* 9.9. The letter was written by Cicero's son-in-law Dolabella.

275 *Two brothers of the Gaulish nobility named Raucillus and Egus:* Caesar, *Civil War* 59–61.

275 *Pompey used this information to attack Caesar:* Caesar, *Civil War* 3.52–53.

275 *About a week later, Pompey struck again:* Caesar, *Civil War* 3.62–73.

276 *"Today the enemy would have won the war":* Plutarch, *Caesar* 39.39; Suetonius, *Caesar* 36.

277 *Gomphi:* Caesar, *Civil War* 3.80; Dio Cassius 41.51; Appian, *Civil War* 2.64.

277 *Pharsalus:* Caesar, *Civil War* 3.81–99; Plutarch, *Pompey* 67–72, *Caesar,* 40–46; Dio Cassius 41.53–63; Appian, *Civil War* 2.65–82.

278 *Pompey was already fighting his own battle:* Plutarch, *Pompey* 67; *Caesar,* 61; Caesar, *Civil War* 3.82.

278 *"He was a man who craved glory":* Plutarch, *Pompey* 67.4.

278 *"They fought over honors":* Caesar, *Civil War* 3.83.

281 *This was their doing, not mine:* Suetonius, *Caesar* 30.4.

282 *Marcus Brutus:* Plutarch, *Brutus* 6.

282 *the outrageous abuses of Caesar's appointed governor:* Alexandrian War 51–64.

282 *the capture of Pompey himself:* Caesar, *Civil War* 3.102–6.

282 *Caesar quickly hurried after him in a small passenger boat:* Suetonius, *Caesar* 63; Dio Cassius 42.6.

282 *the ancient city of Troy:* Strabo 13.1.26–27.

283 *Most uncharacteristically at this point:* Caesar, *Civil War* 3.105.

283 *The cities, people, and tribes of Asia:* Dittenberger, *Sylloge Inscriptionum Graecarum* #760.

284 *Pompey arrived at the grand city of Alexandria:* Plutarch, *Pompey* 77–79; Caesar, *Civil War* 3.104.

XII: CLEOPATRA

Page

285 *Epigraph:* Plutarch, *Antony* 27.

286 *Soon many of his soldiers went native:* Caesar, *Civil War* 110.

287 *She was the first Ptolemy to actually learn the Egyptian language:* Plutarch, *Antony* 27.

287 *a sacred bull ceremony near Thebes:* See Jones 2006, 34–38.

287 *Bibulus:* Valerius Maximus 4.1.

287 *Caesar arrived in Alexandria:* Caesar, *Civil War* 3.106; Plutarch, *Caesar* 48, *Pompey* 80; Dio Cassius 42.7–8. Appian (2.90) says that Caesar buried Pompey's head near Alexandria in a small plot of ground dedicated to the goddess Nemesis.

288 *ten million denarii:* Plutarch, *Caesar* 48.3–5.

288 *claiming the winds were unfavorable:* Caesar, *Civil War* 3.107.

289 *When he landed on shore, they erupted in violent protests:* Caesar, *Civil War* 3.106.

290 *He also plotted to murder Caesar:* Plutarch, *Caesar* 48.3.

290 *Caesar, as guarantor of their father's will:* Caesar, *Civil War* 107.

290 *As Plutarch tells the story:* Plutarch, *Caesar* 49.1–2. Dio Cassius (42.34–35) says only that she arrived at night and appeared before Caesar without her brother's knowledge.

292 *he immediately sent for her brother [Ptolemy] . . . that same night:* Dio Cassius 42.35.

293 *Achillas had suddenly arrived on the edge of the city:* Caesar, *Civil War* 3.110.

293 *an adopted son of Mithridates:* Alexandrian War 26.

293 *Achillas now threw his army against Caesar's stronghold:* Caesar, *Civil War* 3.111; *Alexandrian War* 1–3; Dio Cassius 42.38.

295 *The Romans have been nibbling away:* Caesar, *Alexandrian War* 3.

295 *Achillas ordered his forces to attack the Roman ships:* Caesar, *Civil War* 3.111.

295 *the great library:* Plutarch, *Caesar* 49; Dio Cassius 42.38. See Fraser, *Ptolemaic Alexandria,* vol. 1, 334–35.

296 *the island of Pharos:* Caesar, *Civil War* 3.111–12.

296 *Arsinoe:* Caesar, *Civil War* 3.112; *Alexandrian War* 4; Dio Cassius 42.39–40.

296 *Alexandria had a sophisticated conduit system:* Alexandrian War 5–7; Dio Cassius (42.38.4) says Achillas cut off the water supply.

297 *Caesar did not respond in anger:* Alexandrian War 8–9.

297 *He set off from the docks of the royal quarter:* Alexandrian War 10–11.

298 *The Alexandrians were deeply distressed:* Alexandrian War 12–16.

299 *"Leave it to us, Caesar":* Alexandrian War 15.

300 *seizing all of Pharos:* Alexandrian War 17–22; Dio Cassius 42.40; Plutarch, *Caesar* 49.4; Suetonius, *Caesar* 64; Appian, *Civil War* 2.90.

302 *Caesar's troops were energized to fight:* Alexandrian War 22–23.

302 *to ask Caesar if he might release their young king:* Alexandrian War 23–24; Dio Cassius 42.42.

303 *Tiberius Nero:* Alexandrian War 25; Dio Cassius 42.40.6.

304 *Mithridates of Pergamum:* Alexandrian War 26–32; Josephus, *Jewish War* 1.187–92, *Jewish Antiquities* 14.127–36; Dio Cassius 42.41.

305 *The next day Caesar began to reorganize the government of Egypt:* Alexandrian War 33; Suetonius, *Caesar* 35; Dio Cassius 42.44.

306 *Rufio, son of a former slave:* Suetonius, *Caesar* 76.3.

306 *a monthlong luxury cruise up the Nile:* Appian, *Civil War* 2.90; Suetonius, *Caesar* 52.

307 *Caesarion:* Plutarch, *Caesar* 49, *Antony* 54; Suetonius, *Caesar* 52.

XIII: AFRICA

Page

308 Epigraph: Plutarch, *Cato* 66.

308 *Cato:* Plutarch *Cato the Younger* 55–57; Appian, *Civil War* 2.96.

308 *Cassius Longinus:* Dio Cassius 42.15–16; *Alexandrian War* 48–65.

309 *Pharnaces:* Alexandrian War 34–41, 70; Dio Cassius 42.45–46.

309 *Cicero says:* Cicero, *Letters to Atticus* 229 (11.17a).

309 *Mark Antony:* Dio Cassius 42.21–33; *Alexandrian War* 65.

310 *Caesar was deeply troubled:* Alexandrian War 65.

310 *allowing the Jews:* Josephus, *Jewish War* 1.194–200, *Jewish Antiquities* 14.137–44, 190–95.

310 *according to the New Testament:* Matthew 2.16–18.

310 *There are two things:* Dio Cassius 42.49.

311 *the city of Tarsus:* Alexandrian War 66.

311 *Gaius Cassius:* Cicero, *Philippic* 2.11 (2.26).

311 *Deiotarus: Alexandrian War* 67; Cicero, *Deiotarus* 13–14.

311 *Pharnaces: Alexandrian War* 69–77; Dio Cassius 42.47–48; Plutarch, *Caesar* 50; Suetonius, *Caesar* 35.

313 *Veni. Vidi. Vici:* Suetonius, *Caesar* 37. Plutarch, *Caesar* 50.2 records the same phrase but admits it doesn't work as well in Greek.

313 *From Pontus, Caesar traveled to the coast of Asia Minor: Alexandrian War* 78; Dio Cassius 42.48–49.

313 *Deiotarus lost part of his kingdom: Alexandrian War* 78; Dio Cassius 42.48; Cicero, *Letters to Atticus* 14.1, *On Divination* 1.27.

313 *a very nervous Cicero:* Plutarch, *Cicero* 39; Cicero, *Letters to Atticus* 234 (11.24), 235 (11.20).

313 *to punish Mark Antony:* Plutarch, *Antony* 10, *Caesar* 51; Cicero, *Philippic* 2.29 (2.71).

313 *Cicero later accused Antony:* Cicero, *Philippic* 2.28 (2.69).

314 *He appeared to be the model of justice:* Dio Cassius 42.50–51; Suetonius, *Caesar* 38; Cicero, *Philippic* 2.29 (2.71).

314 *Cicero wittily remarked:* Suetonius, *Caesar* 50; Macrobius, *Saturnalia* 2.2.5.

314 *Finally, Caesar reorganized the government:* Plutarch, *Caesar* 51; Dio Cassius 42.51, 43.1.

315 *Trouble had been brewing in the legionary camps:* Appian, *Civil War* 2.92–94; Dio Cassius 42.52–55; Plutarch, *Caesar* 51; Suetonius, *Caesar* 38.

315 *"I discharge you":* Appian, *Civil War* 2.93.

316 *Caesar was finally ready to sail for Africa: African War* 1–2; Plutarch, *Caesar* 52.

316 *he planned a public sacrifice to the gods:* Suetonius, *Caesar* 59.

317 *Scipio Salvito:* Suetonius, *Caesar* 59; Dio Cassius 52.58; Plutarch, *Caesar* 52; Pliny, *Natural History* 7.10, 35.2.

317 *which harbor they should steer for . . . in Africa: African War* 4.

317 *"I hold you now, Africa!":* Suetonius, *Caesar* 59; Dio Cassius 42.58.3.

318 *"Caesar, . . . the commander-in-chief": African War* 4.

318 *the Numidian cavalry of King Juba:* Plutarch, *Caesar* 52.

319 *He set off with his men: African War* 11–18.

320 *"The enemy is that way":* Plutarch, *Caesar* 52.

320 *"How's it going, recruit?" African War* 16.

321 *Labienus was greatly encouraged: African War* 19.

321 *Caecilius Bassus:* Josephus, *Jewish War* 1.10.10 (1.216), *Jewish Antiquities* 14.11.1 (14.268).

321 *Cicero gleefully shared the latest rumors:* Cicero, *Letters to Atticus* 238 (12.2); *Deiotarus* 25.

321 *St. Elmo's fire: African War* 47.

321 *Caesar skillfully played on this discontent: African War* 8, 57; Dio Cassius 43.5.

322 *Gaetulian natives:* Dio Cassius 43.4.

322 *The Mauritanians also joined Caesar's war effort:* Dio Cassius 41.42, 43.3; *African War* 25.

322 *Caesar himself knew: African War* 31.

323 *We thank you for your benevolence, Scipio: African War* 45.

323 *Thapsus: African War* 80–86; Dio Cassius 43.7–9; Plutarch, *Caesar* 53.

325 *Scipio fled by sea: African War* 96.

325 *King Juba: African War* 94.

325 *Caesar spared the lives:* Dio Cassius 43.12; *African War* 89; Suetonius, *Caesar* 75.

325 *Cato:* Dio Cassius 43.10–11; Plutarch, *Cato the Younger* 59–72, *Caesar* 54; *African War* 87–88.

326 *"Cato, I begrudge you your death":* Plutarch, *Caesar* 54.

326 *He made the rounds to the important cities: African War* 97–98.

327 *"the only one of his properties he had not yet visited": African War* 98; Cicero, *Letters to His Friends* 9.7.2.

XIV: TRIUMPH

Page

328 Epigraph: Cicero *On Behalf of Marcellus* 3.

328 *Caesar staged no fewer than four triumphs:* Dio Cassius 43.19–24; Appian, *Civil War* 2.101; Plutarch, *Caesar* 65; Suetonius, *Caesar* 37.

329 *"Men of Rome, lock up your wives":* Suetonius, *Caesar* 51.

330 *Caesar at long last distributed the war booty:* Suetonius, *Caesar* 38–39; Dio Cassius 43.21–22; Appian, *Civil War* 2.102; Plutarch, *Caesar* 55.

330 camelopardalis: Dio Cassius 43.23; Pliny, *Natural History* 8.69.

331 *Decimus Laberius:* Macrobius, *Saturnalia* 2.7.2–5; Suetonius, *Caesar* 39; Cicero, *Letters to His Friends* 12.18.

331 *"Come, citizens, for we have lost our freedom":* Macrobius *Saturnalia* 2.7.4.

331 *Some among Caesar's opponents began to grumble:* Dio Cassius 43.24.

331 *a horse had been sacrificed to the god Mars:* Polybius 12.4b; Plutarch, *Roman Questions* 97; Dumézil 1996, 154–55, 215–18.

332 *honors and privileges:* Dio Cassius 43.14; Suetonius, *Caesar* 76.

332 praefectus morum: Cicero, *Letters to His Friends* 196.5 (9.15.5).

333 *"Let none of you suppose":* Dio Cassius 43.15–18.

333 *Even cynical politicians such as Cicero:* Cicero, *Letters to His Friends* 190 (9.16), 191 (18.1); Cicero, *Marcellus*.

333 *The Republic is nothing:* Suetonius, *Caesar* 77.

333 *Cleopatra and her royal court arrived in Rome:* Suetonius, *Caesar* 52; Appian, *Civil War* 2.102. Dio Cassius 43.27. See also Grant 1972, 83–94.

334 *"I detest Cleopatra":* Cicero, *Letters to Atticus* 15.15.

335 *a proper census of the city:* Suetonius, *Caesar* 41; Plutarch, *Caesar* 55; Dio Cassius 42.21, 25.

336 *Caesar forbade all Roman men:* Suetonius, *Caesar* 42.

336 *he took steps to increase the numbers in the Senate:* Dio Cassius 43.47.

336 *"If thieves and murderers":* Suetonius, *Caesar* 72.

336 *Caesar accordingly banned all clubs and guilds:* Suetonius, *Caesar* 42; Josephus, *Jewish Antiquities* 14.8 (14.215).

337   *granting citizenship to physicians:* Suetonius, *Caesar* 42.

337   *Auctioneers, grave diggers, fencing teachers:* Cicero, *Letters to His Friends* 218
      (6.18); *Tabulae Heracleenses* 94, 104, 113, 123; See Gelzer, 291, and Hardy, *Six
      Roman Laws,* 149ff.

337   *Caesar planned a huge public library:* Suetonius, *Caesar* 44.

337   *Caesar took seriously his role as director of public morals:* Suetonius, *Caesar* 43.

337   *Caesar was harsh on senators:* Suetonius, *Caesar* 41, 43; Dio Cassius 43.25.

338   *Caesar was equally active in affairs beyond the gates of Rome:* Pliny, *Natural
      History* 4.10; Suetonius, *Caesar* 44; Plutarch, *Caesar* 58.

338   *He encouraged owners of large farms:* Suetonius, *Caesar* 42.

338   *Cicero complained:* Cicero, *Letters to His Friends* 196 (9.15).

338   *Caesar's establishment of citizen colonies:* Suetonius, *Caesar* 42; Dio Cassius
      43.50. See also Gelzer 1968, 297–99.

339   *his creation of a new calendar:* Suetonius, *Caesar* 40; Plutarch, *Caesar* 59; Dio
      Cassius 43.26; Censorinus, *Birthday Book* 20.8–11; Macrobius, *Saturnalia*
      1.14.6–12; Pliny, *Natural History* 18.211.

340   *Cicero could only grumble:* Plutarch, *Caesar* 59.

340   *it survives largely unchanged to this day:* Pope Gregory XIII made adjustments
      to Caesar's system in 1582 that were adopted as the Gregorian calendar, but
      the Julian calendar of Caesar is still used by Orthodox churches.

340   *the surviving Pompeian rebels in Spain:* Dio Cassius 43.28–40; *Spanish War.*

340   *a now-lost poem called* The Journey: Suetonius, *Caesar* 56.

340   *"Let me know how things are going in Spain":* Cicero, *Letters to His Friends* 216
      (15.19).

341   *he even considered falling on his own sword:* Suetonius, *Caesar* 36; Plutarch,
      Caesar 56.

341   *Antony rode in Caesar's private carriage:* Plutarch, *Antony* 11; Cicero, *Philippics*
      2.14; Nicolaus of Damascus, *Life of Augustus* (*Fragmente der griechischen His-
      toriker* F127.11–12).

XV: THE IDES OF MARCH

Page

343   Epigraph: Nicolaus of Damascus, *Life of Augustus* (*Fragmente der griechis-
      chen Historiker* F130.19).

343   *Look at what fortune has done to us:* Cicero, *Letters to His Friends* 248 (4.5).

344   *Cicero published a eulogy entitled* Cato: Suetonius, *Caesar* 56; Cicero, *Orator*
      35, *Philippic* 13.30; *Letters to Atticus* 12.40, 41, 44, 45, 48, 13.46; Plutarch, *Ci-
      cero* 39; *Caesar* 54; *Cato the Younger* 36, 52; Dio Cassius 43.13.

344   *"Why did Cato give up a wife he loved":* Plutarch, *Cato the Younger* 52.

345   *Brutus:* Plutarch, *Brutus* 6–7, 13; Cicero, *Letter to Atticus* 13.46.

345   *Caesar decided to celebrate his victory over the Pompeians in Spain:* Plutarch,
      Caesar 56; Dio Cassius 43.42; Suetonius, *Caesar* 38, 78.

346   *"Tribune Aquila":* Suetonius, *Caesar* 78.

346   *ever greater honors:* Dio Cassius 43.43–45, 44.6–7; Appian, *Civil War* 2.106.

347   *"I'd prefer Caesar share a temple with Quirinus":* Cicero, *Letters to Atticus* 12.45.
347   *Caesar had long planned a war against the Parthians:* Appian, *Civil War*
2.110–11; Dio Cassius 43.51; Plutarch, *Caesar* 58; Suetonius, *Caesar* 44; Cicero, *Letters to Atticus* 13.27, 31, 14.9.
348   *as Plutarch puts it:* Plutarch, *Caesar* 58.
348   *Rumors flew through Rome:* Suetonius, *Caesar* 79.
349   *he chose his great-nephew Octavius as his chief heir:* Suetonius, *Caesar* 83; Dio Cassius 43.51.
349   *While attending races at the Circus Maximus:* Suetonius, *Augustus* 45.
349   *Cicero gives us a remarkable glimpse of Caesar:* Cicero, *Letters to Atticus* 13.52.
350   *One day when he was sitting:* Plutarch, *Caesar* 60; Dio Cassius 44.8; Appian, *Civil War* 2.107; Suetonius, *Caesar* 78.
351   *A rumor arose:* Suetonius, *Caesar* 79; Plutarch, *Caesar* 60; Appian, *Civil War* 2.110; Dio Cassius 44.15; Cicero, *On Divination* 2.110.
351   *one of Caesar's statues in the Forum:* Appian, *Civil War* 2.108; Dio Cassius 44.9–10; Suetonius, *Caesar* 79.
352   *"My name is Caesar, not Rex":* Suetonius, *Caesar* 79. Caesar is making a pun on the Roman family name *Rex* (a cognomen as *Caesar* was among the Julii), found among the Marcii clan.
352   *the festival of the Lupercalia:* Plutarch, *Caesar* 61; Suetonius, *Caesar* 79; Dio Cassius 44.11; Appian, *Civil War* 2.109; Nicolaus of Damascus, *Life of Augustus* (*Fragmente der griechischen Historiker* F130.21); Censorinus, *Birthday Book* 22; Cicero *Philippics* 2.85, 13.41.
353   *"The people ask me to give you this crown":* Dio Cassius 44.11.
353   *They hated him precisely because he had forgiven them:* Nicolaus of Damascus, *Life of Augustus,* (*Fragmente der griechischen Historiker* F130.19).
355   *Caesar said to friends that Cassius looked much too pale:* Plutarch, *Caesar* 42; *Brutus,* 7–9.
355   *"Brutus will wait for this shriveled skin":* Plutarch, *Caesar* 42.
356   *new graffiti would appear on the statues:* Suetonius, *Caesar* 80; Appian, *Civil War* 2.112; Dio Cassius 44.12.
356   *signs and wonders:* Plutarch, *Caesar* 53; Suetonius, *Caesar* 81; Dio Cassius 44.18.
356   *Caesar's ancestor Julus . . . (and the New Testament episode of Pentecost):* Virgil, *Aeneid* 2.679–91; *Acts of the Apostles* 2.1–4.
357   *He had already dismissed his bodyguard:* Dio Cassius 44.7.
357   *conversation turned to the best kind of death:* Suetonius, *Caesar* 87; Plutarch, *Caesar* 63; Appian, *Civil War* 115.
357   *Calpurnia:* Plutarch, *Caesar* 63; Appian, *Civil War* 2.115; Dio Cassius 44.17; Suetonius, *Caesar* 81.
358   *Artemidorus:* Plutarch, *Caesar* 65; Appian, *Civil War* 116.
358   *"Yes, the Ides have come, but not yet passed":* Plutarch, *Caesar* 63; Dio Cassius 44.18.
358   *Antony:* Appian, *Civil War* 2.114; Dio Cassius 44.19.
358   *When Caesar entered the meeting:* Suetonius, *Caesar* 82; Plutarch, *Caesar* 66;

Appian, *Civil War* 2.117; Dio Cassius 44.19; Nicolaus of Damascus, *Life of Augustus* (*Fragmente der griechischen Historiker* F130.24).

359 *Kai su, teknon?:* Suetonius, *Caesar* 82; Dio Cassius 64.19.

EPILOGUE: CAESAR AND CATO AT VALLEY FORGE

Page

360 Epigraph: Joseph Addison, *Cato* 2.3.

360 *George Washington:* For the legacy of Caesar, I highly recommend *Julius Caesar in Western Culture,* edited by Maria Wyke, especially the essay by Margaret Malamud on "Manifest Destiny and the Eclipse of Julius Caesar" (pages 148–69) for Caesar's reputation in early America. For Joseph Addison's play *Cato,* I recommend *Cato: A Tragedy and Selected Essays,* edited by Christine Dunn Henderson and Mark E. Yellin.

362 *"The greatest man who ever lived was Julius Caesar":* Letter of Thomas Jefferson to Dr. Benjamin Rush, Monticello (January 16, 1811). See Chernow 2004, 398.

BIBLIOGRAPHY

A□□□□□ S□□□□□□

Considering that most of Greek and Roman literature has been lost to fire, flood, vermin, and neglect over the last two thousand years, we are fortunate to possess as much information about Caesar's life as we do. Still, the challenge for any biographer is to sift through the scattered and often incomplete ancient accounts—all written by authors with their own prejudices—to piece together a coherent picture of Caesar's life and times.

We are immensely fortunate to have two surviving texts written by Caesar himself, the *Gallic War* and the *Civil War*. The *Gallic War* is Caesar's year-by-year record of events in Gaul originally composed as annual dispatches to the Senate. Even Caesar's enemies admired the clear prose of his Gaulish war narrative in seven books, with an eighth added soon after by Caesar's faithful friend Hirtius. Since the *Gallic War* is the only complete, contemporary source we possess on this formative event in Caesar's life, we largely depend on the author's view of his own actions. There is, of course, a great danger in this, but objective readers cannot help but be impressed by the accuracy of his account. The *Civil War,* detailing Caesar's own victory over Pompey and the senatorial forces, must also be read with care as Caesar is ever anxious to justify his overthrow of the Republic, but other sources from the period do allow us to judge his narrative. The accounts of the Alexandrian, African, and Spanish campaigns appended to the *Civil War,* though not composed by Caesar, are important contemporary sources for his campaigns. Caesar's other genuine works, including letters, a grammatical treatise, poetry, and his venomous *Anti-Cato,* survive only in fragments or not at all.

Cicero, Caesar's prolific and highly opinionated contemporary, is a treasury of firsthand information on Roman life and politics at the end of the Republic. Especially valuable are hundreds of his letters to family members and friends, including the correspondence with his comrade Atticus. Several of Caesar's replies to Cicero's letters are preserved in Cicero's collected works. Cicero's many public speeches and philosophical writings, while more formal than the letters, nevertheless shed important light on the events of Caesar's life.

The Roman historian Sallust commanded a legion under Caesar in the civil war, then—after extorting vast amounts of money as governor of Numidia—he retired to his estate to write. His *Conspiracy of Catiline, War of Jugurtha,* and fragmentary *Histories* display a marked bias against the entrenched nobility, but show Cato in as favorable a light as Caesar. His style is terse, skeptical, and often gloomy, while his grasp of geography and chronology can be frustratingly vague.

The Latin poet Catullus insults Caesar briefly but viciously in his verse, providing an important contemporary look at Caesar's reputation among the avant-garde of Rome's literary community.

The versatile Greek historian Nicolaus of Damascus wrote a highly flattering life of the emperor Augustus in the late first century B.C. that preserves an invaluable description of Caesar's final days. Nicolaus was a friend to Herod the Great of biblical fame and a tutor to the children of Anthony and Cleopatra. The work of Nicolaus is, unfortunately, preserved only in part through quotations in a Byzantine encyclopedia.

The Greek biographer Plutarch, born in the mid-first century

A.D., is one of the most readable authors from antiquity. His *Lives of Noble Greeks and Romans,* a major source for Shakespeare, contains parallel biographies of famous Greeks and Romans, including Caesar paired with Alexander the Great. Plutarch draws widely on many earlier sources in his stated goal of teaching moral lessons from the lives of great men. Aside from Caesar, he features biographies of Marius, Sulla, Pompey, Cato, and Brutus, among Caesar's contemporaries.

The famed Roman biographer of emperors, Suetonius, lived at roughly the same time as Plutarch, but was much more interested in scandal than morality. Suetonius was fortunate to be appointed a secretary at the imperial palace, which gave him unprecedented access to official archives. He was later dismissed for an alleged scandal involving the wife of the emperor Hadrian.

Appian of Alexandria wrote a history of Rome almost two hundred years after Caesar's death, but he is especially valuable as he, like Plutarch, preserves material from the firsthand reports of Asinius Pollio, one of Caesar's officers.

Dio Cassius (also known as Cassius Dio) was a Greek historian and Roman senator who lived in the turbulent third century A.D. His *History of Rome* survives only in part, but fortunately includes Caesar's era. He has a notable interest in supernatural events and invents many of his characters' speeches, but his descriptions are valuable as they draw on many earlier authors now lost.

Modern Sources

I highly recommend *Caesar: Life of a Colossus* by the military historian Adrian Goldsworthy to anyone who desires a richly detailed look at Caesar's life, especially his generalship. In writing my biography, I have been especially indebted to Matthias Gelzer's abundantly annotated *Caesar: Politician and Statesman* as an indispensable guide to the ancient Greek and Latin sources on Caesar's life. The first part of Ronald Syme's *The Roman Revolution* puts Caesar's actions within the political context of the first century B.C., as does Erich Gruen's *The Last Generation of the Roman Republic.* H. H. Scullard's *From the Gracchi to Nero* is an eminently readable and authoritative study of Roman society before, during, and after Caesar's day. Among more recent works on the period, I recommend Christian Meier's *Caesar: A Biography,* Tom Holland's highly accessible *Rubicon: The Last Years of the Roman Republic,* and Anthony Everitt's *Cicero* and *Augustus.*

Batstone, William, and Cynthia Damon. *Caesar's Civil War.* Oxford: Oxford University Press, 2006.

Boatwright, Mary, Daniel Gargola, and Richard Talbert. *The Romans: From Village to Empire.* New York: Oxford University Press, 2004.

Bonfante, Larissa. *Etruscan.* Berkeley: University of California Press, 1990.

Brouwer, H. H. J. *Bona Dea: The Sources and Description of the Cult.* Leiden: E.J. Brill, 1989.

Burns, Thomas S. *Rome and the Barbarians, 100 B.C.—A.D. 400.* Baltimore: Johns Hopkins University Press, 2003.

Cagnat, R., A. Merlin, and L. Chatelain. *Inscriptions Latines d'Afrique.* Paris: E. Leroux, 1923.

Cary, M., and H. H. Scullard. *A History of Rome.* New York: St. Martin's Press, 1975.

Chauveau, Michel. *Cleopatra: Beyond the Myth.* Ithaca, New York: Cornell University Press, 2002.

Crawford, Michael H. *Roman Republican Coinage.* London: Cambridge University Press, 1974.

Cunliffe, Barry. *The Ancient Celts.* Oxford: Oxford University Press, 1997.

————. *The Extraordinary Voyage of Pytheas the Greek.* New York: Penguin, 2003.

Dando-Collins, Stephen. *Caesar's Legion.* Hoboken, New Jersey: John Wiley & Sons, 2002.

De la Bédoyère, Guy. *Roman Britain: A New History.* London: Thames and Hudson, 2006.

Delamarre, Xavier. *Dictionnaire de la langue gauloise.* Paris: Editions Errance, 2003.

De Souza, Philip. "Greek Piracy." In *The Greek World,* edited Anton Powell. London: Routledge, 1995. Pp. 179–198.

Dittenberger, Wilheim. *Sylloge Inscriptionum Graecarum.* Hildesheim: Georg Olms Verlag, 1982.

Dumézil, Georges. *Archaic Roman Religion.* Translated Philip Krapp. 2 vols. Baltimore: The Johns Hopkins University Press, 1996.

Duncan, David Ewing. *Calendar: Humanity's Epic Struggle to Determine a True and Accurate Year.* New York: Avon Books, 1998.

Eska, Joseph, and D. Ellis Evans. "Continental Celtic." In *The Celtic Languages,* edited by Martin Ball. London: Routledge, 1993. Pp. 26–63.

Evans, D. Ellis. *Gaulish Personal Names.* Oxford: Clarendon Press, 1967.

Everitt, Anthony. *Cicero: The Life and Times of Rome's Greatest Politician.* New York: Random House, 2001.

Fraser, P. M. *Ptolemaic Alexandria.* Oxford: Clarendon Press, 1972.

Freeman, Philip. *War, Women, and Druids: Eyewitness Reports and Early Accounts of the Ancient Celts.* Austin: University of Texas Press, 2002.

————. *The Philosopher and the Druids: A Journey Among the Ancient Celts.* New York: Simon & Schuster, 2006.

Fuller, J. F. C. *Julius Caesar: Man, Soldier, and Tyrant.* New Brunswick, New Jersey: De Capo Press, 1965.

Gardner, Jane. *Roman Myths.* Austin: University of Texas Press, 1998.

Gelzer, Matthias. *Caesar: Politician and Statesman.* Cambridge, Massachusetts: Harvard University Press, 1968.

Goldsworthy, Adrian. *Caesar's Civil War.* Oxford: Osprey Publishing, 2002.

————. *The Complete Roman Army.* London: Thames and Hudson, 2003.

————. *Caesar: Life of a Colossus.* New Haven: Yale University Press, 2006.

Gordon, Arthur. *Illustrated Introduction to Latin Epigraphy.* Berkeley: University of California Press, 1983.

Grant, Michael. *Julius Caesar.* London: Chancellor Press, 1969.

————. *Cleopatra.* Edison, New Jersey: Castle Books, 2004.

Green, Miranda. *The World of the Druids.* London: Thames & Hudson, 1997.

Gruen, Erich S. *The Last Generation of the Roman Republic.* Berkeley: University of California Press, 1974.

Gulliver, Kate. *Caesar's Gallic Wars.* Oxford: Osprey Publishing, 2002.

Hannah, Robert. *Greek and Roman Calendars: Constructions of Time in the Ancient World.* London: Duckworth, 2005.

Haywood, John. *Atlas of the Celtic World.* London: Thames and Hudson, 2001.

Hengel, Martin. *Crucifixion.* Minneapolis: Augsburg Fortress Publishers, 1977.

Holland, Tom. *Rubicon: The Last Years of the Roman Republic.* New York: Doubleday, 2003.

Ireland, S. *Roman Britain: A Sourcebook.* London: Routledge, 1986.

Johnson, Allan, Coleman-Norton, Paul, and Frank Bourne. *Ancient Roman Statutes.* Austin: University of Texas Press, 1961.

Jones, Barri, and David Mattingly. *An Atlas of Roman Britain.* Oxford: Blackwell, 1990.

Jones, Prudence. *Cleopatra: A Sourcebook.* Norman, OK: University of Oklahoma Press, 2006.

Kagan, Donald. *The Peloponnesian War.* New York: Penguin, 2004.

Kagan, Kimberly. *The Eye of Command.* Ann Arbor: University of Michigan Press, 2006.

Kahn, Arthur. *The Education of Julius Caesar.* Lincoln, NE: Authors Guild, 2000.

Kamm, Anthony. *Julius Caesar: A Life.* London: Routledge, 2006.

Kleiner, Diana E. E. *Cleopatra and Rome.* Cambridge, MA: Harvard University Press, 2005.

Kruta, Venceslas, ed. *The Celts*. London: Hachette Illustrated, 2004.

Lefkowitz, Mary R., and Maureen B. Fant. *Women's Life in Greece and Rome*. Baltimore, MD: The Johns Hopkins University Press, 1992.

Le Glay, Marcel, Jean-Louis Voisin, and Yann Le Bohec. *A History of Rome*. Oxford: Blackwell, 1996.

Lendon, J. E. *Soldiers and Ghosts: A History of Battle in Classical Antiquity*. New Haven, CT: Yale University Press, 2005.

Mac Cana, Proinsias. *Celtic Mythology*. New York: Peter Bedrick Books, 1983.

Mallory, J. P. *In Search of the Indo-Europeans*. London: Thames and Hudson, 1989.

Malamud, Margaret. "Manifest Destiny and the Eclipse of Julius Caesar" in Maria Wyke, ed. *Julius Caesar in Western Culture*. Malden, MA: Blackwell, 2006.

Matyszak, Philip. *Chronicle of the Roman Republic*. London: Thames & Hudson, 2003.

Megaw, Ruth, and Vincent Megaw. *Celtic Art*. London: Thames & Hudson, 1989.

Meier, Christian. *Caesar: A Biography*. New York: Basic Books, 1982.

Mitchell, Stephen. *Anatolia: Land, Men, and Gods in Asia Minor*. Vol. 1. Oxford: Clarendon Press, 1993.

Morel W., K. Büchner, and J. Blänsdorf, eds. *Fragmenta Poetarum Latinorum*. 3rd ed. Stuttgart: Teubner, 1995.

Moscoti, Sabatino, ed. *The Celts*. New York: Rizzoli, 1991.

O'Connor, Colin. *Roman Bridges*. Cambridge: Cambridge University Press, 1994.

Oikonomides, Al. N., and M. C. J. Miller. *Hanno the Carthaginian: Periplus or Circumnavigation*. Chicago: Ares Publishers, 1995.

Osgood, Josiah. *Caesar's Legacy: Civil War and the Emergence of the Roman Empire*. Cambridge: Cambridge University Press, 2006.

Pallottino, Massimo. *A History of Earliest Italy*. Ann Arbor: University of Michigan Press, 1991, 2006.

Parenti, Michael. *The Assassination of Julius Caesar: A People's History of Ancient Rome*. New York: The New Press, 2003.

Peddie, John. *Conquest: The Roman Invasion of Britain*. New York: St. Martin's Press, 1987.

Puhvel, Jaan. *Comparative Mythology*. Baltimore, MD: Johns Hopkins University Press, 1987.

Rankin, H. D. *Celts and the Classical World*. London: Areopagitica Press, 1987.

Richardson, L., Jr. *A New Topographical Dictionary of Ancient Rome*. Baltimore, MD: Johns Hopkins University Press, 1992.

Riggsby, Andrew M. *Caesar in Gaul and Rome: War in Words*. Austin: University of Texas Press, 2006.

Roseman, Christina. *Pytheas of Massalia: On the Ocean*. Chicago: Ares Publishers, 1994.

Ross, Anne. *Pagan Celtic Britain*. London: Constable, 1993.

Scarre, Chris. *The Penguin Historical Atlas of Ancient Rome*. New York: Penguin, 1995.

Scullard, H. H. *From The Gracchi to Nero: A History of Rome from 133 B.C. to AD 68*. New York: Routledge, 1982.

Shaw, Brent D. *Spartacus and the Slave Wars: A Brief History with Documents.* Boston: Bedford / St. Martin's, 2001.

Snyder, Christopher. *The Britons.* Oxford: Blackwell, 2003.

Spaeth, John. "Caesar's Poetic Interests." *The Classical Journal* 26.8 (1931): 598–604.

Syme, Ronald. *The Roman Revolution.* Oxford: Oxford University Press, 1939.

Tatum, W. Jeffery. *The Patrician Tribune: Publius Clodius Pulcher.* Chapel Hill: University of North Carolina Press, 1999.

Temkin, Owsei. *The Falling Sickness.* Baltimore, MD: Johns Hopkins University Press, 1994.

Wills, Garry. *Cincinnatus: George Washington and the Enlightenment.* Garden City, NY: Doubleday, 1984.

Wistrand, Erik. *Caesar in Contemporary Society.* Göteborg, Swed.: Kungl. Vetenskaps-och Vitterhets-Samhället, 1978.

INDEX